The National Co-ordination of EU Policy

The National Co-ordination of EU Policy

The European Level

edited by

HUSSEIN KASSIM

ANAND MENON

B. GUY PETERS

and

VINCENT WRIGHT

OXFORD

UNIVERSITY PRESS

OXFORD
UNIVERSITY PRESS

Great Clarendon Street, Oxford OX2 6DP

Oxford University Press is a department of the University of Oxford.
It furthers the University's objective of excellence in research, scholarship,
and education by publishing worldwide in

Oxford New York

Athens Auckland Bangkok Bogotá Buenos Aires Cape Town
Chennai Dar es Salaam Delhi Florence Hong Kong Istanbul Karachi
Kolkata Kuala Lumpur Madrid Melbourne Mexico City Mumbai Nairobi
Paris São Paulo Shanghai Singapore Taipei Tokyo Toronto Warsaw

and associated companies in Berlin Ibadan

Oxford is a registered trade mark of Oxford University Press
in the UK and certain other countries

Published in the United States
by Oxford University Press Inc., New York

British Library Cataloguing in Publication Data

Data available

Library of Congress Cataloging in Publication Data
The national co-ordination of EU policy : the European level / edited by Hussein Kassim . . . [et al.].
p. cm.
Includes index.
1. Political planning—European Union countries. 2. European Union. I. Kassim, Hussein, 1965–
JN32 .N38 2001 320′.6′094—dc21 2001036029
ISBN 0-19-924805-2

1 3 5 7 9 10 8 6 4 2

Typeset by Best-set Typesetter Ltd., Hong Kong
Print in Great Britain
on acid-free paper by
T.J. International Ltd., Padstow, Cornwall

PREFACE

All chapters, except the conclusion, are based on extensively revised versions of papers presented at a workshop, held at Nuffield College, Oxford, on 13–14 May 1999. We should like once again to express our gratitude to the Warden and Fellows for their generous hospitality and to Stephanie Wright for her efficient organization of the event.

We should like to extend our particular thanks to the participants for making the occasion so intellectually stimulating and enjoyable. It has been a pleasure to work with them. We do, however, regret the sad circumstances that prevented the inclusion of Ignacio Molina's planned contribution to this volume.

Our co-editor, Vincent Wright, was unfortunately unable to attend the workshop. The project on the national co-ordination of European policy had been conceived and designed by the four of us, but by the time of the meeting Vincent was too ill to be present. He died the following month. At a conference earlier in the year, Sidney Tarrow commented that had Vincent been present—he had had to withdraw due to ill health—'we would have been ruthlessly teased, mocked and provoked, but we would have learned a great deal'. The same was true of the May event. We continue to miss him as a colleague and friend.

H. K., A. M., B. G. P.

CONTENTS

LIST OF CONTRIBUTORS

RUDY B. ANDEWEG is Professor of Political Science at Leiden University. Having published on elections, legitimacy, government formation, and legislative behaviour, his current research interests focus on the comparative study of governmental decision-making and executive-legislative relations. He co-authored *Dutch Government and Politics*, (Macmillan, 1993).

JAN BEYERS, currently post-doctoral Research Fellow at the Katholieke Universiteit Leuven, conducts research on the social basis of European policy and recently completed his Ph.D. dissertation on this subject. He has published articles in the *Journal of Common Market Studies*, the *European Journal of International Relations*, and *West European Politics*.

GIACINTO DELLA CANANEA is Professor of Administrative Law at the Faculty of Political Sciences, University of Urbino. He is the author of *Inirizzo e controllo della finanza pubblica* (1996) and co-edited with Giulio Napolitano *Per una nuova constitzione economica* (1998) and with Jean Paul Costa *Public Administration and Human Rights* (1997).

HUSSEIN KASSIM is Senior Lecturer in Politics at Birkbeck College, University of London. He writes on EU policy and institutions, and the relationship between the EU and the member states. He is the co-editor of *The European Union and National Industrial Policy* (1996) and co-author of *The European Union and Air Transport: The Limits of Europeanisation* (forthcoming).

BART KERREMANS, currently Associate Professor of International Relations at the Katholieke Universiteit Leuven, conducts research on EU-decision-making and on the external economic relations of the European Union. He has published books and articles on EU decision-making in foreign trade and EU decision-making in general. Articles have been published in *Governance*, *Regional and Federal Studies*, and the *Journal of World Trade*.

BRIGID LAFFAN is Jean Monnet Professor of European Politics and Director of the Dublin European Institute, University College Dublin.

JOSÉ MAGONE is Lecturer in European Politics in the Department of Politics and Asian Studies, University of Hull. He has published extensively on

Southern European politics and the European Union. He is author of *The Changing Architecture of Iberian Politics* (1996) and *European Portugal* (1997).

ANDREAS MAURER is Jean Monnet Chair of Political Science, University of Cologne, and Deputy General Secretary of the Trans- European Policy Studies Association, Brussels. Recent publications include *What Next for the European Parliament?* (London 1999) and *Le pouvoir renforcé du Parlement européen après Amsterdam* (Bruxelles/New York 2000).

SONIA MAZEY is Faculty Lecturer in Politics and a Tutorial Fellow at Hertford College, Oxford University. She has researched and published widely on the EU policy-making process and European integration.

ANAND MENON is Professor of European Politics and Director of the European Research Institute, University of Birmingham. He is editor with Vincent Wright of *From the Nation State to Europe? Essays in Honour of Jack Hayward* (OUP, 2000) and with Jack Hayward of *Governing Europe* (forthcoming OUP, 2002).

WOLFGANG C. MÜLLER is Professor of Government at the University of Vienna. He specializes in West European politics. His most recent publications include *Coalition Governments in Western Europe*, co-edited with Kaare Strøm (OUP, 2000).

B. GUY PETERS is Maurice Falk Professor of American Government at the University of Pittsburgh. He is author of *Comparative Politics: Theory and Method* (1998) and *The Future of Governing* (1996).

BEN SOETENDORP is Associate Professor in International Relations at Leiden University. He writes on (foreign) policy making in Western Europe in a comparative perspective, focusing on the interaction between the European Union and its Member States. He has recently published *Foreign Policy in the European Union*, (London and New York: Longman, 1999) and edited with Kenneth Hanf *Adapting to European Integration: Small States and the European Union*, (London / NewYork: Longman, 1998).

CALLIOPE SPANOU is Associate Professor of Administrative Science in the Department of Political Science and Public Administration, University of Athens. She has published extensively on public administration. She is the author of *Fonctionnaires et Militants* (1991), *Administration, Citizens & Democracy* (2000, in Greek).

WOLFGANG WESSELS is Jean Monnet Professor at the University of Cologne, Professor at the College of Europe, Bruges/Natolin, and President of the Trans

European Policy Studies Association, Brussels. Recent publications include *Die Öffnung des Staates. Modelle und Wirklichkeit grenzüberschreitender Verwaltungspraxis* 1960–1995 (Opladen, 2000).

VINCENT WRIGHT was Fellow of Nuffield College, Oxford University. As well as writing important books on French government and politics, most notably on French prefects and on the Conseil d'État, he edited and co-edited many volumes on government and administration in Western Europe.

LIST OF FIGURES

LIST OF TABLES

Introduction: Co-ordinating National Action in Brussels

Hussein Kassim

Achieving successful coordination in any area of governmental activity is extremely problematic (Jennings and Crane 1994; Pressman and Wildavsky 1984; Peters 1998: 295; Hayward and Wright 1998; Hayward and Wright forthcoming), but membership of the European Union confronts governments with a set of particularly testing organizational and managerial challenges. Not only are member states locked into a 'continuous policy making process of both an active and reactive nature' (Wright 1996: 149) across a broad and expanding terrain where they interact with multiple partners in a complex institutional environment, but their action must be must be coordinated at and between at least two levels: the domestic and the European.[1] Each dimension imposes its own requirements, and has its own dynamics, and feedback between the two levels is continuous. Different constituencies put forward their demands, different sets of actors jostle for attention, and different rules must be followed. As a result, governments find themselves subject to varying, often contradictory, imperatives.

The institutions, structures, and procedures developed by governments to manage domestic coordination form the subject of a first companion volume (Kassim *et al.* 2000).[2] This second book offers a comprehensive, comparative analysis of national coordination at the European level. It investigates the way in which eleven member states—Austria, Belgium, France, Germany,

I should like to thank my co-editors for their useful suggestions, Guy Peters, for his thought-provoking introduction on the day of the workshop, and Anand Menon for reading an earlier draft. Any errors are my own.

[1] Though, as Wright observes, 'the various levels of co-ordination may be usefully distinguished for analytical purposes, but, in practice, they intertwine in constant fashion' (1996: 149).

[2] Ten case studies were undertaken in all: Austria, Belgium, Denmark, France, Germany, Greece, Italy, Portugal, Spain, and the United Kingdom.

Greece, Ireland, Italy, the Netherlands, Portugal, Sweden, and the United Kingdom—coordinate their European policy in Brussels.[3] It examines their coordination ambitions, the value attached to coordination and their conception of it, and the strategies adopted by the member states for defining and defending a national position in EU policy-making. It looks in detail at the organization and operation of the permanent representations—the principal institution charged by governments with safeguarding the 'national interest' in Brussels[4]—and at how, to what extent (indeed, whether) they succeed in reconciling their responsibilities as both agencies of the national government and part of the EU decision-making system (see e.g. Wallace 1973: 56; Ziller 1992; de Zwann 1995: 26). The book assesses the effectiveness of the various national arrangements in achieving their intended goals, and identifies the factors that influence or determine performance at the European level. The institutions, structures, and processes utilized by the member states in Brussels are compared with a view to discovering whether there is evidence of convergence around a common model or whether national differences persist.

With few notable exceptions,[5] national coordination at the European level has attracted little attention. Such oversight is surprising for several reasons. First, as European integration has become an extremely salient domestic political issue—not only among sceptical latecomers, such as Denmark and the UK, but among founder members, including France, Germany, and the Netherlands—the question of how effectively governments defend 'the national interest' in Brussels might have expected to have aroused greater concern. The treatments that have been attempted have typically been limited to individual policy sectors, issues, events, or proposals. Second, knowing about national processes is essential for understanding the dynamics of European integration and the functioning of the EU. Discussing the Council, Spence (1995a: 354) reasons that '[I]f these negotiations [between member states] are ultimately about how governments put their point across and defend the "national" interest in the search for acceptable compromise, clearly the way in which governments arrive at a definition of the national interest is an important part of the process'. European integration is not only about the transfer of tasks, powers, and responsibilities between levels of government, but also about changing relations and balance between governmental

---

[3] The benefit of exploring how governments have responded to the challenges presented at each of level outweighs in our opinion the danger of repetition.

[4] The concept of the 'national interest' is of course a useful fiction rather than a real entity.

[5] Notable exceptions include Salmon (1971), Hayes-Renshaw *et al.* (1989), Westlake (1995), de Zwann (1995), and Hayes-Renshaw and Wallace (1997). The role of permanent representations is also examined in broader discussions of the national co-ordination of European policy. See e.g. Wallace (1973), Lequesne (1993), Rometsch and Wessels (1996), and Mény *et al.* (1996).

institutions (Olsen 1997: 158) and administrative interaction or 'fusion' between national administrations (Wessels 1997).

The dependence of the Union on the administrations of the member states provides further grounds for surprise at the relative neglect of national coordination. The transaction of business within the Council, for example, relies to a considerable extent on the speed and quality of national institutions, structures, and processes (Lequesne 1993: 215; Wright 1996), a dependence that has long been recognized.[6] More recently, with enlargement pending, the European Council has underlined the importance of effective national coordination to the efficient operation of the Council.[7] At the Helsinki summit on 10–11 December 1999, the Heads of State and Government declared that:

The Council must have an overview of all Union policies. For it to do so, there has to be at the heart of the system a single chain of coordination capable of ensuring that Union action is consistent with the will of its political leaders. This chain of command starts in the Member States themselves with effective interdepartmental coordination and arbitration, and extends through COREPER, the General Affairs Council to the European Council. The Council's ability to meet the challenges ahead largely depends on strengthening the effectiveness of this channel—the backbone of the system. Action to preserve the Council's ability to act decisively therefore needs to be taken at all levels. (1999: 6)

The effects of national processes on EU institutions are not only felt within the Council. Despite its independence and vocation as the champion of the general European interest, the Commission is subject to varying degrees of pressure from the member states (Donnelly and Ritchie 1997; Kassim and Wright 1991). Nor is the dependence on national coordination systems limited to the decision-making phases of the policy cycle. From a public management perspective, Metcalfe (1994) has argued that the administrative capacity of the Union, its ability to implement common policies, crucially depends on national administrations. More broadly, Spence notes that 'all levels of government are now involved in or concerned by EU affairs' and

---

[6] See de Zwann (1995: 34–5). The author cites instances, as early as 1974 or 1980, where Heads of State and Government called for improvements to be made in national coordination to make decision-making at the European level more effective.

[7] Co-ordination between the various formations of the Council has been a longstanding matter of concern that grown even more pressing in the 1990s (*European Voice* unions). The ability of the General Affairs Council to co-ordinate the work of the technical Councils—a role traditionally entrusted to it—has been severely tested by the expansion of EU competencies, the multiplication of Council formations, and, in particular, the increasing prominence of ECOFIN. COREPER has been considering the broader question of Council reform, based largely on the 'Trumpf–Piris' report of March 1999. This provided the grounds for the guidelines and recommendations approved by the European Council in Helsinki in December 1999 (Dinan 2000: 36).

underlines 'the indispensability of appropriate new arrangements for national policy-making and adequate co-ordination of these levels of government in order to guarantee effective performance not only of individual Member States, but of the system of European governance itself' (1995*a*: 353). In other words, 'Europeanization requires more rather than less of national governments' (Spence 1995*a*: 354).

The relevance of the interaction between national and European levels to debates about how the EU is best conceptualized also makes the neglect of member state organization and action in Brussels surprising. The nature of the processes by which national preferences are formed, delivered, and defended in Brussels, and the character of state interaction, as well as between states and other actors, are viewed very differently in the literature. Authors writing from a intergovernmentalist perspective conceive the EU as a forum for inter-state bargaining that differs from other international or regional organizations only due to the extreme degree to which cooperation has been institutionalized (see e.g. Hoffmann 1966, 1982; Moravscik 1993, 1998). Initial and continued cooperation between states is explained in terms of the pursuit of national self-interest, choices accounted for by strategic rationality, and policy outcomes determined by relative power. In older forms that are closer to its realist antecedents (cf. Hoffmann 1966), intergovernmentalists take the view that the interests pursued by a state are given by its position in the international order. In its more sophisticated 'liberal' version (Moravscik 1993, 1998), governments act upon preferences that are shaped by domestic societal groups. 'The result[ing image] is a unidirectional causal chain beginning with the preferences of societal actors and powerful constituencies and translated through the state to the national interests and positions which are then represented in Brussels negotiations' (Lewis 1999: 8–9). EU policies are thus conceived as the outcome of 'hard bargaining' between states in the Council.

The intergovernmentalist perspective has been subject to a series of challenges.[8] Criticisms are directed particularly at its accounts of preference formation and its understanding of decision-making in the Council. With respect to the first, authors have argued that the account offered by intergovernmentalism neglects an important organizational dimension by downplaying the role that governments play in defining policy (Metcalfe 1994) and precluding the possibility that 'bureaucratic politics' are a feature of EU policy-making at the national level (Kassim *et al.* 1999). The position ('preference') that is presented and defended by a member state in Brussels may not be the result simply of consultation by government of societal interests,

---

[8] A representative cross-section of literature hostile to intergovernmentalism would include Marks *et al.* (1996), Sandholtz (1996), Pierson (1996), Pollack (1998), Sandholtz and Stone Sweet (1998), Schmidt (1996) and Wincott (1995).

but rather the outcome of negotiation, bargaining, or conflict between ministries, ministers, and/or officials, each with their own constituencies and clienteles.[9] The intergovernmentalist view that the policy positions defended by national governments in Brussels are the product of a strictly endogenous process has also been contested. Critics argue that the stances adopted by state executives in EU negotiations are influenced by the policy initiatives launched by the European Commission, affected by the anticipated reactions of other actors, and shaped by considerations of what objectives are negotiable in the light of the position taken by other member states (Sandholtz 1996). Preference formation does not take place in splendid domestic isolation, but is a process that is subject to exogenous pressures.

The intergovernmentalist view of the Council is opposed by an alternative image that arises from the testimony of officials with direct experience of EU decision-making, as well as academic research.[10] This alternative perspective, which draws on the work of early neofunctionalists, sociological treatments, and Wessels's 'fusion' theory, emphasizes the impact of the shared norms and collective identity that develop in Council forums as a result of repeated interaction and serial exchange (Wallace 1991), and are internalized by national officials negotiating at the European level. Haas (1958) used the term 'engagement' to refer to circumstances under which: 'if parties to a conference enjoy a specific and well-articulated sense of participation, if they identify themselves completely with the procedures and codes within which their decisions are made, they consider themselves completely "engaged" by the results by the even if they do not fully concur with them' (Haas 1958: 522, cited in Edwards 1996: 127).[11] The result is a 'cumulative pattern of accommodation in which the participants refrain from unconditionally vetoing proposals and instead seek to attain agreement by means of compromises upgrading common interests' (Haas 1958, cited in Edwards 1996: 128). Recent studies of the Council dispense with the teleological conception of integration advanced in early neofunctionalist writings, but confirm the importance of values that arise from negotiating in the Council. Fiona Hayes-Renshaw and Helen Wallace, for instance, observe that: 'decision-makers in the Council . . . become locked

---

[9] See e.g. the analysis of the UK in the negotiation of the Maastricht Treaty carried out by Anthony Forster (1998).

[10] e.g. Peter Pooley, formerly the Ministry of Agriculture, Fisheries and Food's most senior official at the UK permanent representation, recalled that: 'You are pulled in these two directions. First, all of us want to do the very best we can for our governments and negotiate as hard as we can . . . But you want the committee to win as well, in that you want the committee to reach agreement, put up the dossier, the file, in good form for ministers to negotiate upon' (Young and Sloman 1982: 82).

[11] Leon Lindberg also commented on the way in which national interests are refined during the decision-making process as actors 'learn new rules, develop new identifications and new patterns of mutual trust and regard' (1970: 98).

into the collective process . . . this does not mean that the participants have transferred loyalties to the EU system, but is does mean that they acknowledge themselves in certain crucial ways as being part of a collective system of decision-making' (cited in Lewis 1999: 10).

COREPER, in particular, has developed a strong collective identity and ethos (see below and Wallace 1973; de Zwann 1995; Barber 1995; Edwards 1996 and especially Lewis 1998, 1999). The development of these norms, and the fact that participants in the Council recognize that they are involved in an iterated game—a 'marathon' rather than a 'dash' (Derlien 2000)—has led authors to reject the rather stark intergovernmentalist image of Council proceedings in favour of a conception that emphasizes cooperation. In the late 1970s, for example, Sasse wrote that '[i]ts institutions are, for all the inadequacies, something more than mere forums for intergovernmental coordination exercises' (1977: 86), while fourteen years later. Wessels commented (1991: 137) that 'the Council is not an "interstate body" . . . but a body at the supranational level' (see Lequesne 1993; Spence 1995*a*; Edwards 1996; Hayes-Renshaw and Wallace 1997; Beyess and Dierickx 1998; Lewis 1998, 1999; and Kerremans 1996). Wessels contends that increased administrative interaction between officials from national administrations has brought about a 'fusion' of member state bureaucracies (1997). As a consequence, civil servants no longer consider EU policy-making as foreign affairs in which they act as 'guard dogs' (Maurer and Wessels, this volume) of national interests, but regard Brussels as an arena in which routine decisions are taken and the officials of other member states as partners. A process of 'post-national socialization' (Maurrer and Wessels, this volume) has transformed the nature of interaction between national officials from negotiation and interpretation of legal texts to effective transnational collegiality. An examination of how member states coordinate at the European level, how EU policy is made, and what strategies and tactics are deployed in Brussels, should assist in deciding which image should assist in deciding which image is to be preferred.

Finally, it is surprising that concerns about the accountability of national negotiators in international negotiations, and how competing demands of domestic policy and international bargaining are resolved, have not generated greater interest in national processes. The former relates to a version of the democratic deficit that portrays Brussels as a 'mandarins' paradise', where unelected officials take decisions free from ministerial control and beyond public scrutiny—a view given apparent support by the finding that up to 70 per cent of Council decisions are taken at the working-group level or in COREPER (Van Schendelen 1996).[12] Examining the basis on which national representatives negotiate at the EU level, the systems of control in place, and

[12] For diagnoses of, and prescriptions for, the democratic deficit, see Weiler *et al.* (1995), Chryssochoou (1998), Williams (1991), and Bogdanor and Woodcock (1991).

the mechanisms that exist to monitor the action of officials would seem to provide a necessary first step in seeking to resolve this issue (see discussions in Edwards 1996; Derlien 2000). The latter concerns the extent to which the 'two-level game' (Putnam 1988; see also Hayes-Renshaw and Wallace 1997: 270–3) works in favour of the international arena, whether their participation in international bargaining strengthens the hand of state executives *vis-à-vis* domestic constituencies (Moravscik 1994; Hoffmann 1982), or whether governments or societal interests most benefit from the 'nested games' (Tsebelis 1990) played by state executives. An investigation of the role of Brussels-based officials in national EU policy-making processes, and the control from the national capital to which they are subject, should contribute towards extending knowledge of the precise dynamics of this relationship.

This volume contributes towards remedying the neglect of this important subject. The purpose of this introduction is to provide a point of reference and context for the country studies that follow.[13] It begins with a brief discussion of coordination and why it matters to governments at the European level. It then outlines the tasks that face national coordinators in Brussels, looking in particular at the Council of the Union—the 'decision-making centre' (Wessels 1991) of the Union—where the attention of the member states is principally focused, and considers the formidable obstacles that confront them. The third section identifies key points of comparison at the national level, and discusses the question of effectiveness. The emergence of an overall pattern—of convergence or divergence—is considered in the fourth. The eleven case studies are introduced in the concluding section.

Coordination, Domestic and European, and Why it Matters

In the public sector, coordination refers to the action of, and interaction between, the individual departments, agencies, politicians, and officials, involved in a particular policy area or with respect to an activity or task. It 'implies the bringing into a relationship otherwise disparate activities or events' (Frances *et al.* 1991: 3). Coordination carries strongly positive connotations. Effective coordination on the part of government, it is believed, delivers greater efficiency, because it ensures that scarce resources are used rationally in the pursuit of policy goals, that the waste that results from the

---

[13] The assumption is that readers will not have read the introduction to the first volume, where pressures on governments to co-ordinate and the specific challenges presented by the EU are also discussed. The intention is that this second volume should be free-standing.

duplication of effort or persistence of redundant programmes is avoided, and that, by reconciling the competing demands of actors inside and outside government or facilitating concerted action, objectives which otherwise may not be realized can be achieved. Poor coordination, by contrast, is likely to result in chaos, delay, and inefficiency. Without effective mechanisms, different parts of government may pursue their own interests to the detriment of the whole, efforts to achieve general goals are likely to be jeopardized, and resources may be used inefficiently.

Findings of a recent study suggest that in Western Europe the pressures on governments to coordinate have, if anything, become more urgent (Hayward and Wright 1998).[14] Resources are increasingly scarce, calls to reduce public expenditure more strident, and public mistrust of government widespread. At the same time, the apparatus of the state has grown more complex, governments must manage a wider range of activities inside and beyond their borders, and old certainties (the post-war social democratic consensus, agreed territorial hierarchies, and an established policy agenda) eroded. Governments draw on a wide repertoire of techniques—internal self-government by agencies, the devolution of coordination, improving pre-cooking arrangements at political level, reducing the size of arenas to be coordinated, improving information flows among bureau officials, mobilizing vertical and horizontal networks of politically sympathetic, constructing a consensus of policy frames around a set of central ideas—but have not generally been successful in their efforts to meet the growing demands for strong central coordination. Partly, this is because coordination has been traded off against other important values, such as organizational harmony, transparency, flexibility, and accountability. However, it also reflects the fact that governments do not often enjoy a free hand in selecting their coordination strategy. Their choices are constrained by existing structures, institutions, and cultures.

Governments choose between the available options. Coordination takes different forms, each of which imposes different requirements. Positive coordination involves a sustained effort usually from the centre aimed at ensuring that all parts of government actively engage with each other, while negative coordination envisages a situation where 'compartmentalised units pursue mutual avoidance strategies to reduce tensions' (Hayward and Wright 1998: 1). Coordination can be strategic, directed towards the common pursuit of an overarching objective, or selective: issue-oriented, reactive, or concerned only with certain stages of the policy cycle. It can be directive, designed to achieve a particular policy goal, or it may be procedural, concerned to ensure that

---

[14] I am extremely grateful to Jack Hayward and Vincent Wright for allowing me to view the end-of-award report to the ESRC on their project on co-ordination in Western Europe. This section of the chapter draws heavily on that report.

issues are dealt with by the appropriate machinery—or even more modestly that relevant information is circulated to the interested parties.

These conceptions carry different organizational implications. Positive coordination, for example, is an active conception that requires strong central authority. It implies that decisions are arrived at though negotiation or imposition which reconcile potentially competing societal interests and departmental views. Stringent demands are made of all actors within the system, well-established procedures are required that are strictly observed, and a strong degree of vertical and horizontal integration is necessary. The operation of this conception depends to a large degree on the existence of political and administrative cultures that value coherence. Other conceptions are far less demanding in terms of institutional infrastructure and pre-existing system of values. In practice, governments may not have much latitude in choosing which conception, if any, to adopt. The available options are a function of broader features of the domestic polity, including institutional structure, form of party government, party coherence, and administrative tradition.

If the pressure on governments to coordinate in areas of domestic policy is strong, it is even more intense with respect to EU policy-making. In many policy sectors, the Union is an important, if not the most important, policy-maker or decision-making venue, and governments play for high stakes. Decisions taken in Brussels can have far-reaching consequences for the member states. The adoption by the EU of legislation that is consistent with existing domestic policy and practices can produce positive benefits for a member state: it may eliminate or minimize the costs—political or economic—of policy adjustment (Héritier *et al.* 1996; Kohler-Koch and Eising 1999); companies that are accustomed to a national regulatory regime may win a competitive advantage if that regime is extended across the Union; or a government may succeed in Europeanizing a policy objective that could otherwise have been achieved only through complex and painstaking bilateral efforts (Kassim 1996; Kassim and Stevens forthcoming). Conversely, the adjustment costs to governments, firms, and other domestic constituencies imposed by legislation that is out of step with traditional domestic policy orientations can be extremely heavy (Héritier *et al.* 1996; Hayes-Renshaw and Wallace 1997: 212–13).

It is not only EU legislation that can have far-reaching effects. Decisions taken by the Commission when it acts in a quasi-judicial capacity, as in the area of competition policy, may have serious domestic consequences. State aid or merger cases often assume a high profile in the home country of the firms involved, and governments can be damaged if a ruling goes against its 'national champion' or other major companies. In addition, as the EU has become an increasingly salient political issue at home, governments are often under pressure to demonstrate to sceptical publics that they have been suitably vigilant in their defence of the 'national interest'. This applies especially to policy sectors that have a particular domestic resonance, such as agriculture in France, or fisheries in Spain and the UK. Moreover, the EU disposes of substantial resources, particularly in the area of agriculture and regional development policy. Governments and domestic groups, subnational authorities, or businesses have an interest in securing a share of the funds available, and organization will be necessary to ensure effective campaigning or lobbying in these areas. Countries that have been eligible for funding under the EU's cohesion policy, including Greece, Portugal, Spain, and Ireland, have reaped substantial rewards, when they have demonstrated their adeptness at 'grantsmanship'.[15]

If the importance of ensuring that national interests are effectively represented in Brussels creates general incentives on the part of the member states to establish effective coordination procedures, the institutions of the EU and the obligations that they impose also encourage these efforts. Participation in the Council of the Union calls for coordination on the part of governments. Meetings must be prepared, and positions defended at different levels and across different sectors (see below). Heads of state and government have been compelled by the enhancement of the European Council's leadership role and the broadening of its agenda to develop the institutional resources available to the chief executive to handle the increased flow of business. Similarly, intergovernmental conferences call for careful organization, strategic action, and tactical thinking across a wide territory, particularly now that governments have been alerted to the fact that seemingly innocuous institutional reforms can have far-reaching consequences on policy outcomes, as well the balance of power between actors at the European level. In addition, effective coordination on the part of national governments is necessary to carry out the duties of the Council Presidency, which is held in rotation by member states for six months.[16] The responsibilities of the office have grown increasingly onerous as the competencies of the Union have expanded (Hayes-Renshaw and Wallace 1997: 134–57). The Presidency is responsible for formulating its programme seven months in advance of taking up office, organizing meetings at all levels of the Council (with the assistance of the Council secretariat), representing the Council in its relations with external delegations, as well as with other EU institutions, responding to any crises that arise, and generally overseeing and managing the work of the Council in internal and external affairs. The official Council guidebook warns ominously that '[m]ajor deployment of

---

[15] To my knowledge, this term was first coined by Brigid Laffan.
[16] For discussion of the tasks and challenges confronting the Council Presidency, see de Bassompierre (1988), O'Nuallain and Hocheit (1985), Westlake (1995: 37–54), and Hayes-Renshaw and Wallace (1997: 134–57).

the entire national administrative apparatus is required to get the Presidency up and running' (General Secretariat 1996: 6).[17]

These pressures create powerful incentives for governments to ensure that they have the institutions, structures, and processes necessary to defend national interests at the European level and to meet the demands of EU membership. This is not to assume, however, that they have responded fully or effectively to these pressures, still less that their responses have been identical. The extent to which member states have developed a coordination ambition, and the strategies that they pursue, at the European level, and whether the general pattern that emerges is one of convergence or divergence, are questions that require empirical investigation of national arrangements. However, where they do respond, member states are likely to develop systems of coordination that are designed to achieve at least some of the following objectives:

- 'foreseeing opportunities to promote national interests' (Spence 1995*b*: 368)
- 'anticipat[ing] new EU legislation and its impact at the national level' (Wright 1996: 162)
- collecting and circulating information to interested parties at home (Wallace 1973: 57)
- 'elaborating negotiating strategy' (Spence 1995*a*: 368) aimed at lobbying for action or inaction or for the abandonment, dilution, or strengthening of a Commission proposal (Spence 1995*a*: 354, 356–7)
- ensuring that national negotiators are well-briefed and have a clear idea of the issues at stake
- 'assessing trade-offs which may serve national interests in other areas' (Spence 1995*a*: 368)
- 'monitoring deadlines for implementation of legislation by lead ministries' (Spence 1995*a*: 368)
- 'foreseeing legal implications of proceedings in the European Court of Justice' (Spence 1995*a*: 368).

Of course, the nature of the EU makes it far more difficult to achieve these goals than it is to describe them. The challenges confronting national coordinators are considerable. In the next section, a discussion of the general problems posed by the structures and procedures of the EU is followed by a more detailed description of the difficulties encountered in the legislative cycle— the principal focus of member state action in Union processes. For reasons of space, the account is greatly simplified.

---

[17] It adds, somewhat ominously, 'The size of this extra workload for national administrations . . . even for the larger Member States, should not be underestimated' (General Secretariat 1996: 6).

The EU as a Political System: The Difficulties Facing National Coordinators

The European Union is an extremely complex political system, in which individual governments lack the kind of resources—authority, agenda control, party discipline, established networks, administrative traditions—that can be mobilized in domestic policy-making. It presents national coordinators with a distinctive set of problems and difficulties. First, the EU is 'fluid, ambiguous and hybrid' (Olsen 1997: 165; see also Wright 1996). It is 'not based on a single treaty, a unitary structure, or a single dominating center of authority and power. Rather, the Union is built on several treaties and a complex three-pillar structure . . . [where] the pillars are organized on different principles and supranational/intergovernmental mixes' (Olsen 1997: 165). The official portrayal of the EU as a unified system—three pillars within a single institutional framework—is somewhat misleading in view of differences in the way that powers and responsibilities are distributed between the main institutions in each of the pillars, and between their procedures and structures. The framework remains disjointed, despite efforts to integrate the various intergovernmental bodies that had serviced ministers in EPC and Justice and Home Affairs before the Treaty of European Union came into effect (Noël 1992; Hayes-Renshaw and Wallace 1997: 90–7; Monar 2000). More broadly, 'There is no shared vision or project, or common understanding of the legitimate basis of a future Europe' (Olsen 1997: 165). Its membership, its rules, the relationships between, and authority of, its institutions are constantly evolving (Wright 1996; Olsen 1997).

Second, the EU policy process is unusually open (Peters 1994; Wright 1996: 151). Although the European Commission has a formal monopoly over the initiation of legislation, items on the EU's policy agenda come from a variety of sources, there are a number of influential policy advocates and the policy menu is long, ever-changing, and more varied than at the national level. In addition, decision-making involves a multiplicity of actors, including, besides the fifteen member governments, the EU institutions, and other European bodies and agencies, representatives of regional and local authorities, and a host of lobbyists of varying size and importance (Mazey and Richardson 1993; Greenwood 1997; Aspinwall and Greenwood 1997; Pedlar and Van Schendelen 1993). Each is at once an actor with its own interests, an institution with its own rules, code of conduct, and operating style, and an arena in which individuals, groups, and associations compete for influence. Decisions are rarely the result of action on the part of a single actor or institution. Interested parties must search for allies and create coalitions, despite the precariousness of the exercise: 'alliance-building is unpredictable and time-consuming . . . [and] the cleavages which shape the coalitions are often cross-cutting' (Wright 1996: 152).

The task of coordination is further complicated by the absence of a constitutionally defined separation of powers or a tidy division of responsibilities (Lenaerts 1991; Hix 1999; Kohler-Koch and Eising 1999). Legislative power is shared by two institutions, the Council and the European Parliament, that form 'a classic two-chamber legislature' (Hix 1999: 56), and executive authority is spread between the member states (collectively in the Council and individually) and the Commission.[18] Moreover, legislative procedures are long and complex, and, combined with the different decision rules that apply to the Council in different policy sectors and subsectors, present those involved with a bewildering array of formal processes with which they must grapple.[19] Each distributes the power between institutions in different ways, thereby establishing variations in the inter-institutional balance according to which procedure is used (Garrett 1995; Scully 1997), encouraging different strategies and imposing different 'bargaining requirements' (Pollack 1994), and privileging certain outcomes over others (Tsebelis 1990). The most intricate of these procedures—co-decision—retains its essential complexity even after the simplifications introduced at the Amsterdam IGC and has been extended to a wider range of policies (Falkner and Nentwich 2000).

Furthermore, as a political system, the EU is characterized by a high degree of institutional fragmentation. Whichever image of the Union is preferred—the 'governance model' (Kohler-Koch 1998; Kohler-Koch and Eisnig 1999; Jachtenfuchs 1995; Scharpf 1999), which presents the EU as uniquely polycentric and non-hierarchical or the more ordered vision of the EU projected by Simon Hix (1998, 1999)—there is no disagreement that the main institutions are internally differentiated and segmented or that it is distinguished by a high level of organizational density. Formations of the Council have proliferated, its tripartite structure complicated by the addition of new bodies and

---

[18] I follow Hix's definitions where executive power has two elements: '*political*, the leadership of society through the proposal of policy and legislation; and *administrative*, the implementation of law, the distribution of public revenues, and the passing of secondary and tertiary rules and regulations' (1999: 21). The member states' executive responsibilities involve setting the long-term policy goals of the EU (Council), setting the medium-term policy agenda (European Council), implementing EU legislation through their own bureaucracies, and managing the day-to-day administration of EU policies with the Commission through comitology (Hix 1999: 25); the Commission's responsibilities include developing medium-term strategies for the development of the EU, drafting legislation and arbitrating in the legislature process, making rules and regulations, managing the EU budget, and scrutinizing the implementation of the Treaty of secondary legislation (Hix 1999: 32).

[19] The Commission in its review of the operation of the Treaty of European Union found twenty-four combinations in use (CEC 1995).

tiers after Maastricht and later Amsterdam to handle the Common Foreign and Security Polity and Justice and Home Affairs, and coordination has become increasingly difficult. The Commission is segmented into twenty-four directorates general, each with its own operating style (Abélès *et al.* 1993; Page 1997; Cini 1997), and there is permanent tension in relations between the political Commission (Commissioners and their *cabinets*) and the services. The European Parliament is a multiparty chamber, where partisan affiliations cut across the functional allocation of legislative scrutiny between its twenty committees. Moreover, intra-and inter-institutional interactions take place in a universe of permanent and *ad hoc* committees and subcommittees that has only recently begun to be charted (Buitendijk and Van Schendelen 1995; Van Schendelen 1998; Dogan 1997). As Wright (1996: 151–2) has noted, '[t]hese committees are largely responsible for the mass of micro-level sectoral decisions . . . and . . . are interwoven with a set of overlapping bargaining networks'. Systematic control over these committees and subcommittees has yet to be exercised, and their relative functions and status have fluctuated considerably over time.

Finally, sectoralization is a strongly pronounced characteristic of the EU (Mazey and Richardson 1993; Menon and Hayward 1996). Although a feature of domestic policy-making, 'the extent and nature of these problems in Brussels is of a different order' (Wright 1996: 130). The main distinction is between polity issues, such as treaty reform, the power of institutions, external relations, and enlargement, and more technical areas (Derlien 2000; Maurer and Wessels, this volume), which can be divided into regulatory, redistributive and distributive (Lowi 1964). Each policy type has a different logic and conflict potential, and demands a particular type of expertise. In addition, EU competence varies from sector to sector, different legislative procedures and decision rules apply, and distinct constellations of actors are engaged. The scope and pace of policy development varies accordingly (Wright 1996; Menon and Hayward 1996).

If the general characteristics of the EU make it difficult for national coordinators to negotiate, a further difficulty for the member states is the need simultaneously to ensure that action taken in Brussels is acceptable at home. What may be desirable for domestic policy purposes may be infeasible as an objective at the European level. One prominent view is that the constraints at one level may be transformed into opportunities at the other: 'National bargaining positions in Brussels may be reinforced by invoking "problems back home" whilst essential but unpalatable politics . . . are imposed on domestic constituencies which readily finger Brussels as the real culprit' (Wright 1996: 149; see also Hoffmann 1982; Putnam 1988; Moravscik 1993, 1994; and Smith 1995). Examples of both are to be found in the literature, but the coverage is decidedly in favour of the latter. Cases of compromise or humiliating climb-down may in reality outnumber instances of successful strategic action on the part of individual member states, but are less dramatic. Governments no longer enjoy, if in fact they ever did, the far-reaching autonomy in European policy with respect to domestic constituencies that is implied by earlier versions of intergovernmentalism. 'Europe's salience as a domestic political issue ensures that government are kept under the glare of the national press. In addition, governments are no longer the gatekeepers of the "national interest"' (Marks *et al.* 1996). Domestic interests, including not only private actors, such as businesses and pressure groups, but public-sector bodies, such as bankers, regions, and local authorities, have an independent presence in Brussels, making direct contact with the EU institutions and their counterparts from other member states (Mazey and Richardson 1993; Greenwood 1997; Aspinwall and Greenwood 1997; Pedlar and Van Schendelen 1993). Although they continue to lobby their national governments, they are also ready to exploit the possibilities that Brussels presents to challenge domestic policies to which they are opposed and to take advantage of the altered political opportunity structure that European integration has brought about (Marks and McAdam 1996).

Routine Policy-Making

The tasks that national co-ordinators are called on to perform in routine policy-making can be identified by differentiating different stages of the policy cycle.[20] Four phases can be usefully distinguished: policy initiation; policy formulation; deliberation and decision; and implementation and enforcement.

Policy Initiation

The policy process begins at the pre-proposal stage. The Commission has a formal monopoly over the introduction of policy proposals in the first pillar, but shares this prerogative with the member states in the second and third. Officials in the Commission services, where drafts are drawn up, are open to suggestions from national officials. Member states that are able to intervene to set the agenda at this stage can be well rewarded, since as much as 80 per cent of the original proposal may survive in the text that is finally adopted by the Council (Hull 1993). The benefits may be even greater where a member state proposes action before the Commission has considered it or before it has

---

[20] This concept of the policy cycle is a useful fiction, but in practice the stages of the policy process are not discrete.

drafted a text. This may also be the best time for a member state to lobby for inaction by the Commission. There are strong incentives, therefore, for governments to monitor the Commission services so that when the early signs of action are detected the interested departments at home can be alerted and begin to take steps to decide a policy line. This requires the assiduous cultivation of contacts by national officials in the permanent representation and domestic ministries with their opposite numbers in the Commission, as well as an effective system of reporting from Brussels, and procedures for ensuring that information is conveyed to the appropriate destination at home.

Formulation

Extensive consultations are undertaken by Commission officials when a draft proposal is being formulated, since the Commission is concerned to maximize the chances that it will be accepted by other policy actors, particularly, national governments (Edwards 1996; Mazey and Richardson 1993). The consultation process may be more or less formal. In some policy areas, there are standing consultative committees.[21] In others, where consultation is more informal, national officials may have to act on their own initiative to ensure that their government's position is registered.

Once the consultation process has been completed, the draft proposal passes to the College. Consideration at the political level begins with a meeting of the 'special chefs'—a meeting of the Commissioners' *cabinet* member responsible for the area under discussion. It is then examined at the weekly *chefs de cabinet* meeting, before it is discussed by the College and a final decision taken.[22] Where the stakes are high, and sometimes even when they are not, member states may attempt to influence the College through one of 'their' Commissioners or their *cabinets*. Although the Commission embodies the general interest of the European Union and, on taking office, its members swear an oath of independence, it is accepted—indeed, expected—that Commissioners will report on the reservations about proposed legislation held in the country that he or she 'knows best'.[23] Maintaining good relations with 'its' Commissioner(s) and *cabinets* can, therefore, be extremely valuable, in terms of gaining access to information, or influencing policy-making.

---

[21] There are two main types—expert committees, which are composed of national experts, and consultative committees, where private interests are represented—but hybrid committees also exist (Nugent 1999: 121).

[22] The College is, in addition, involved at crucial stages when the Commission investigates planned mergers or state aid operations, and makes appointments to senior positions in the Commission services.

[23] All Commissioners have in their *cabinet* a member whose job is to maintain contact with the national capital.

Deliberation and Decision

Deliberation begins when the proposal is submitted to the Council and the European Parliament.[24] As the arena of intergovernmental bargaining and the main legislative body of the Union, the Council is the central focus for national action. Its structure and processes are extremely important for understanding the tasks of national co-ordinators in Brussels.[25] The Council is a complex institution, reproducing internally the institutional fragmentation and sectoralization that characterizes the Union in general. Council formations have expanded considerably over time (see Table 0.1), the number of meetings grown substantially, placing considerable strain on human resources in the member states (see Table 0.2), and co-ordination is poor (Edwards 1996: 134, *European Voice* various). Two further characteristics of the Council are relevant. First, negotiations within the Council take the form of joint problem-solving (Spence 1995*b*: 374). Member states recognize that they cannot secure favoured outcomes by unilateral action, and that, whatever their policy preferences, some form of co-operation or collaboration with partners in the Council will be necessary, either to form a qualified majority or a blocking minority.[26] The veto is a last resort (Edwards 1996: 130–4).[27] Second, formal vote taking rarely takes place. Deliberations continue until the Presidency knows where the delegations stand and considers that the relevant majority or minority has been achieved.

Discussion begins in Council working parties composed of national experts, either from the permanent representation or the national capital.[28] Working groups exist in all areas where the Union has policy responsibilities, and new ones are created by COREPER. Estimates of the number of active working groups vary, but as of 1 September 1996 the Council Guide (1996) lists nearly 300. Meetings of the working group are convened by the Council Presidency to discuss new legislative proposals. At the first meeting, the usual practice is for the Commission to introduce its proposal. National delegations run through the text and express their initial thoughts on the basis of briefs

[24] It is also sent to the Economic and Social Committee (ECOSOC) and in certain cases to the Committee of the Regions (COR).

[25] For detailed discussion of the Council, see Westlake (1995) and Hayes-Renshaw and Wallace (1997). For informative overviews, see Wessels (1991) and Edwards (1996).

[26] See Hix (1999: 366–75) for a list of the areas where, following the Amsterdam Treaty, QMV is the decision rule in Council. The number of areas has increased after Nice and the conclusion of the IGC 2000.

[27] Sixty-two out of a total eighty-seven votes are required for a qualified majority. Twenty-six votes constitute a blocking minority. The weighting of votes and these thresholds are set to change after the next enlargement.

[28] See Gonzáles Sánchez (1992) for an insider's account of how Council working groups operate. See also Council Guide (1996), vol. i.

TABLE 0.1. *Development of Council formations*

	1974	1975	1976	1977	1978	1979	1980	1981	1982	1983	1984	1985	1986	1987	1988	1989	1990	1991	1992	1993	1994	1995
Agriculture	14	15	13	12	13	12	14	11	15	14	16	14	11	16	12	12	16	13	13	12	11	10
External Relations/General Affairs (since 1988)[a]	13	16	14	15	15	12	13	12	13	12	20	14	11	12	12	14	13	13	15	20	14	14
Economic and Financial	7	8	7	12	10	6	2	3	3	3	2	3	3	2	2	2	10	13	11	11	11	9
Development Co-operation	5	3	—	3	2	1	1	3	2	2	2	2	2	3	2	2	4	3	2	2	2	2
Education	1	1	1	—	—	—	1	1	1	1	1	1	2	1	2	3	2	1	2	2	2	2
Energy	1	—	—	4	3	6	2	3	3	3	2	3	3	2	2	2	3	3	2	3	2	2
Environment	1	1	1	2	2	3	2	2	2	4	3	3	3	4	3	5	5	5	4	6	5[b]	2
Justice/JHA	1	—	—	—	—	—	—	2	—	—	—	—	—	—	—	1	—	1	3	4[c]	4	4
Taxation	—	1	2	1	—	1	1	1	3	—	4	2	4	3	4	5	4	—	3	4	4	3
Research	—	—	—	2	2	2	1	2	3	4	4	3	4	4	4	4	4	6	4	5	5[d]	4
Transport	—	—	—	3	2	2	2	2	2	4	4	3	4	4	4	4	2	2	2	2	2	2
Budget	—	—	—	3	4	4	3	3	4	4	4	5	5	6	5	2	3	2	2	2	2	2
Fisheries	—	—	—	5	7	4	7	8	7	9	5	3	3	3	2	4	4	4	5	5	5	4
Public Health/Health	—	—	—	1	1	—	—	—	—	—	—	1	—	—	2	2	2	—	2	3	3	2

Post & Telecom's[e]	—	—	1	—	—	—	—	—	—	—	—	—	—	1	3	2	3	3	3	3[f]	2
Social Affairs[g]	—	—	—	—	2	2	4	3	2	3	3	2	2	2	5	3	3	4	4	4	4
Industry & Iron and Steel	2	—	2	4[h]	2	—	6[i]	3	2	6[j]	2	—	—	—	—	—	—	—	—	—	—
Industry	—	—	—	—	—	2	—	2	1	—	—	2	6	2	4	4	2	5	5	5[k]	3
Internal Market	—	—	—	—	—	—	—	6	6	2	5[l]	8	8	8	10[m]	7	5	7	6	3	2
Consumer Affairs	—	—	—	—	—	1	—	1	1	—	1	2	2	1[n]	2	2	1	2	2	2	2
Cultural Affairs	—	—	—	—	—	—	—	2	2	—	1	1	—	1	1	2	2	—	2	2	3
Civil Protection	—	—	—	—	—	—	—	—	—	—	—	1	—	1	—	1	—	1	—	—	1
Tourism	—	—	—	—	—	—	—	1	—	—	2	2	2	1	1	1	1	—	1	—	—
Other	3	2	1	1	3	3	3	3	1	1	—	2	2	2	1	1	—	1	1	4	1
TOTAL	44	53	61	63	56	60	63	63	84	83	73	79	80	77	89	90	83	87	94	92	76

Source: General Secretariat of the Council of the European Union, (various issues), *Review of the Council's Work in 19.* (Luxembourg: Office for Publications of the European Communities).

a Includes General Affairs and Political Co-operation, and Foreign Affairs (1984).
b Includes 1 joint with Transport.
c Justice and Home Affairs, and 3 Immigration.
d Includes 1 joint with Environment.
e Telecommunications from 1988.
f Includes 1 joint Industry and Telecommunications.
g Includes Labour and Social Affairs.
h Iron and Steel only.
i Iron and Steel only.
j Include Telecommunications.
k Includes 1 joint with Telecommunications.
l Internal market and consumer protection.
m Includes 1 joint with consumer protection.
n Joint with Internal Market.

Hussein Kassim

TABLE 0.2. *Number of days spent in meetings in the Council of the European Union*

	Council	COREPER	Working Groups
1958	21	39	302
1959	21	71	325
1960	44	97	505
1961	46	108	655
1962	80	128	783
1963	63.5	146.5	744.5
1964	102.5	229.5	1,002.5
1965	35	105.5	760.5
1966	70.5	112.5	952.5
1967	75.5	134	1,233
1968	61	132	1,253
1969	69	129	1,412.5
1970	81	154	1,403
1971	75.5	127.5	1,439
1972	73	159	2,135
1973	79.5	148	1,820
1974	66	114.5	1,999.5
1975	67.5	118	2,079.5
1976	65.5	108.5	2,130
1977	71	122	2,108.5
1978	76.5	104.5	2,090
1979	59	107.5	2,000
1980	83	106.5	2,078.5
1981	83	110	1,976
1982	86	107	1,885
1983	121.5	105.5	1,912.5
1984	133	86	1,868.5
1985	118	117	1,892
1986	107	118.5	1,842.5
1987	123	120.5	1,828
1988	177.5	104	2,000.5
1989	119.5	100	1,932
1990	138	107	2,021.5
1991	115.5	145.5	2,239
1992	126	133.5	2,147
1993	119	115.5	1,105.5
1994	98	127	2,662
1995	98	112	2,364.5
1996	106	100	2,596

Source: General Secretariat of the Council of the European Union, *Review of the Council's Work in 1996* (Luxembourg: Office of Publications of the European Communities 1999).

prepared in the national capital and, where they have consulted their counterparts, in the light of calculations taken about what negotiating objectives are realizable. Negotiations begin at meetings thereafter. Officials at the permanent representation and in the lead ministry at home are conscious of the need to find allies and sound out other member states about their ultimate intentions, fallback positions, and bottom lines. At successive meetings, the text is amended and revised on issues where all parties approve. Deliberations continue until agreement is reached or there are obstacles that can only be removed at a political level. At this stage, the dossier is passed to COREPER.[29]

COREPER, the Committee of Permanent Representatives,[30] is universally recognized as 'one of the most powerful organs within the EU's institutional structure' (Westlake 1995: 285), though not an institution of the European Union nor of the European Communities (de Zwann 1995: 301). It plays a key role within the Council apparatus and in the Union more broadly (see de Zwann 1995: 25–70; Westlake 1997: 285–307; Hayes-Renshaw and Wallace 1997: 72–84; Barber 1995; Lewis 1998, 1999).[31] Despite its importance, COREPER was not provided for directly in the Treaty of Rome (Salmon 1971; de Zwann 1995), although it was agreed that a preparatory committee composed of national officials should be created to prepare the work of ministers. Following an initial disagreement among the member states about the status of their representatives, the foreign ministers decided at their inaugural session on 6–7 January 1958 that the members of the committee would be permanent (unlike COCOR, its corresponding body within the ECSC) and that they would be high-ranking diplomats of ambassadorial status (Houben 1964: 142 n. 85; de Zwann 1995: 7–11). The body met for the first time on the following day with each member state appointing a representative. The development of diplomatic staffs to support the permanent representative followed,[32] and technical specialists began also to be appointed from the early 1960s.[33] The tasks to be performed by COREPER were set out in Article 16 of

[29] The most detailed discussion of COREPER is to be found in de Zwann (1995). See also Westlake (1995: 285–352) and Hayes-Renshaw and Wallace (1997: 72–84).

[30] COREPER is an acronym of the French title of this Committee, namely, the Comité des Représentants Permanents.

[31] 'Wide areas of the *acquis* owe their very existence to the political commitment, the extraordinarily high technical and specialist efficiency and the sense of responsibility of most of the committee's members . . . the day to day life of the Community would be unthinkable without . . . [its] presence', (Sasse *et al.* 1977: 101, quoted in Edwards 1996: 136).

[32] Foreign ministries were keen to reassert themselves in European affairs after the creation of the ECSC, where they felt peripheralized. The establishment of permanent representatives as diplomatic posts was an indication of their resurgence.

[33] The permanent representations of member states other than the original Six grew out of the permanent delegations that these countries established in Brussels once they

the Council Rules of Procedure, and following the Merger Treaty, COREPER assumed COCOR's responsibilities, but the permanent representations remained 'diplomatic missions created by unilateral appointment of the relevant government' (Hayes-Renshaw *et al.* 1989), without needing to secure accreditation from the Community itself.

COREPER has a unique dual function, acting both as 'a bridge to national capitals' and 'a clearing house for the Council' (Barber 1995).[34] The fact that its members are charged with representing national interests, but also can 'easily become interpreters and defenders of the points of view of the Commission before their own governments and administrations' (Spinelli 1996: 76, quoted in Edwards 1996: 137), has attracted considerable attention (see, for example, Lewis 1998, 1999; Barber 1995; Hayes-Renshaw and Wallace 1997; important earlier appraisals include Noël 1967 and Noël and Etienne 1971). Though COREPER is usually referred to in the singular, there are in fact two bodies, both of which are responsible for preparing dossiers for discussion by ministerial Councils, reaching agreement on outstanding issues where possible, and clarifying what is at stake with respect to the remainder. COREPER II, the more senior body, is composed of the permanent representatives of each member state. Its remit includes institutional matters, the preparation of the General Affairs, ECOFIN, Development, Justice and Home Affairs, and Budget Council meetings. COREPER I, (deputy permanent representatives), manages the 'technical' Councils.[35] The non-veterinary and plant-health aspects of agriculture are not dealt with by COREPER, but by a dedicated equivalent, the Special Committee on Agriculture. It is also worth noting that, although COREPER's purview was extended by the Treaty of the European Union to cover the Common Foreign and Security Policy and Justice and Home Affairs, the integration of the committees that previously supported the work of ministers in this area—the Political Committee and K4—proved problematic. The situation has been further complicated by the new arrangements introduced after the Amsterdam Treaty, which came into effect in May 1999. With respect to the second pillar, a Policy Planning and Early Warning Unit was created, and the first meeting of EU foreign and defence ministers took place in November 1999. Moreover, agreement at the

---

acceded to the Communities, though the transition from delegation to permanent representation involved a radical transformation. Whereas delegations were essentially diplomatic outposts, permanent representations are involved in day-to-day decision-making within the Council.

[34] Or, as Helen Wallace puts it: 'Not only do the Representations represent and bargain on behalf of their governments but they have also become part of the Community system itself' (1973: 56).

[35] Internal Market, Energy, Research, Industry, Telelcommunications, Fisheries, Transport, Environment, Consumders, Labour and Social Affairs, Health, Education, Cutlure, Tourism and Agriculture (veterinary and plant-health questions).

Helsinki European Council in December 1999 to implement the common European security and defence policy (CESDP) agreed at the 1996 IGC produced, as well as a commitment to 'a militarily self-sustaining' force of fifteen brigades before 2003, a series of institutional reforms. These included the creation of a standing Political and Security Committee (PSC) in Brussels, composed of national representatives of senior and/or ambassadorial level, a Military Committee (MC) composed of the Chiefs of Defence, and the Military Staff (MS) within Council structures to provide military expertise and support to the CESDP (Forster and Wallace 2000: 490). With respect to Justice and Home Affairs, the Amsterdam Treaty bifurcated the Council structure put in place after Maastricht, as some policy areas moved to the first pillar, but others were left within the third. The K4 Committee, renamed the Article 36 Committee, remained in place as a co-ordinating body in the third pillar, while a new Strategic Committee was created to co-ordinate matters of asylum, immigration and external border control. Both committees are interposed between technical working parties and COREPER, reflecting the unwillingness of some member states to transfer powers to the permanent representatives (Monar 2000: 136).[36]

COREPER I and II—and the SCA—usually meet once a week, the former on a Wednesday, but sometimes also on a Friday, and the latter on a Thursday, except for weeks preceding meeting of the General Affairs Council or ECOFIN, when it meets on a Wednesday.[37] COREPER agendas are divided into two sections: Part I, where items require no further debate and are passed up to ministers as A points (i.e. agreed, but requiring ministerial approval) and Part II, where outstanding issues need to be discussed. Meetings of COREPER II are prepared by the Antici Group, composed of officials from each of the permanent representations, who are given a briefing on the day before by the Council Presidency on how it intends to conduct business the following day.[38] Antici Group meetings are useful in highlighting key issues or problems. The 'Anticis' typically report back to the permanent representation, will alert colleagues where difficulties look likely, and may call home to check and verify positions, making last-minute adjustments or calculations as necessary. The Mertens Group plays a similar, though less developed, role for COREPER II. Unlike the working groups or the ministerial formations of the

---

[36] See Monar (2000) for a discussion of Council arrangements in JHA after Amsterdam.

[37] As well as heading the permanent representation, attending meetings of COREPER, and participating in national decision-making, permanent representatives attend at least one ministerial Council each week. They are always on duty, even on informal occasions.

[38] 'Occasionally, the Secretary-General of the Commission may brief the Anticis on the outcome of the weekly Commission meeting where particularly important matters have been discussed. This allows them to pose questions of national concern' (Spence 1995*a*: 371).

Council, COREPER's composition remains constant and its members tend to remain in post for relatively long periods (see Westlake 1995: 305–7). The stability of its membership, close and regular contact, combined with a common background in the diplomatic service, has turned COREPER into a club (Barber 1995).

COPERER's responsibility for horizontal co-ordination of the various Council formations and vertical co-ordination of the working groups (de Zwann 1995: 298; Edwards 1996), its location at the intersection between the, and where the political meets the technical, and its function as the filter through which virtually all items of Union business must pass, make it an important venue for promoting and defending national interests. For these reasons, at the domestic level, the point at which issues appear on COREPER's agenda is a crucial one, and often the moment at which formal interdepartmental co-ordination processes are initiated. The centrality of COREPER, moreover, makes permanent representatives and the deputy permanent representatives key figures.[39] They are extremely busy (de Swann 1995; Westlake 1995), and never 'off-duty', having to defend national interests on informal, as well as formal, occasions (Barber 1995).

Files that have been prepared by COREPER move to the ministerial level for decision. It is estimated that up to 90 per cent of Council business has been agreed before it reaches this level—70 per cent at working group level and an additional 15–20 per cent is in COREPER—but only ministers can take decisions formally.[40] Ministerial agendas are divided into A points—agreed without need for further discussion, though any government can decide to reopen a dossier—and B points, where agreement still needs to be sought. Ministers are usually briefed at home and in Brussels, and are accompanied to the Council by the permanent representative. As is the case with COREPER, it may be necessary to communicate with the national capital as negotiations progress.

States that decide that their interests are best served by the careful crafting and coherent presentation of positions will, at each stage, ensure that a policy stance is agreed and that the necessary alliances are assured against the background of information about the preferences of the Commission and the other member states. Close, constant contact between officials in the

---

[39] De Zwann (1995: 25) identifies five functions: intermediary between the national government and the Community institutions; participant in the preparation and co-ordination of national positions; participant in the activities and decision-making of Community institutions; participant in intergovernmental co-operation between the member states; and participant in decision-making within the framework of the Community's external relations.

[40] It was agreed by the Six that only ministers should have the power to take decisions and that this power could not be delegated to lower levels of the Council.

permanent representation and their interlocutors at home can be expected. At the domestic level, co-ordination processes may mirror the EU process (Kassim *et al.* 2000; Spence 1995: 357; Metcalfe 1994b).

At the same time that it navigates its way through the Council, a proposal is examined by the European Parliament. With its evolution from consultative committee to co-legislator, national governments have a greater interest in monitoring the Parliament's treatment of a dossier as it makes its way through the legislature. The incentive to do so is especially strong in areas where co-decision applies.[41] While co-operation strengthened the Parliament's hand in the legislative process, co-decision has enhanced its role and, where conciliation is necessary, brings the Council and the EP into direct contact for the first time. Both procedures make possible the construction of trans-institutional coalition-building (Fitzmaurice 1988; Corbett 1989; Hix 1999: 84–96). Member states may endeavour not only to ensure that its nationals in the Parliament are kept informed of the government's position, but also to maintain links with committee chairs, committee members, and *rapporteurs* with a view to influencing the direction of discussion and to assessing what stance the Parliament is likely to adopt. The national capital may be involved in these efforts, but it is more likely that officials in the permanent representation will be made responsible.

Implementation and Enforcement

The final stage of the policy cycle covers several somewhat disparate activities. National administrations are responsible for the implementation of policy, since the Commission has no field services. This is a phase of the process which co-ordinators may not anticipate and may be inclined to overlook. National officials are also involved in comitology, where they exercise varying degrees of influence over the Commission's exercise of its executive function. This can be important, because under certain conditions member states can 'fine-tune legislative outcomes' (Dogan 1997: 38). There may be advantages to individual member states that monitor advisory, management, and regulatory committees or that act strategically when they meet. Finally, concerning enforcement, member states may have an interest where the Commission is conducting an investigation into suspected infringement of Community rules or in legal proceedings before the European Court of Justice. With respect to the former, the ability to lobby effectively may be extremely effective. In regard to the latter, being able to foresee the likely outcome of a referral may prove beneficial. In both cases, monitoring, the circulation of information, and adroit action, could be very useful.

[41] See Hix (1999: 366–75) for a list of the policy areas where the co-decision procedure applies.

'Heroic' Decision-Making

The demands on national governments are not restricted to day-to-day policy-making, but extend also to 'heroic' decision-making. The latter encompasses two main forums, the European Council and intergovernmental conferences. The European Council usually meets twice a year. The Paris Communiqué in 1974 made the foreign ministers responsible for preparing European Council meetings, 'and through them . . . COREPER, the Political Directors, and subsidiary preparatory groups, particularly the "Anticis" ' (Westlake 1995: 28). The General Affairs Council discusses the European Council a week before the latter is due to meet and the Antici Group is briefed by the Council Presidency in the week before. The permanent representation and domestic ministries, including the Prime Minister or President's office, are likely to be deeply involved in the process of national co-ordination.

Intergovernmental conferences are not formal instances of the Council, but 'a stylized form of Conference of Representatives of the Member States' (Westlake 1995: 55).[42] The work of IGCs lies is not prepared by Council bodies, therefore, but by committees of representatives appointed by the member states (Westlake 1997: 56). Given the high stakes and the range of issues involved, as well as the pressure to secure a 'good deal', member states have a strong incentive to ensure that positions are well co-ordinated and that negotiating strategies and tactics are clearly defined. Responsibility for co-ordination is likely to be vested with the foreign ministry or the Prime Minister's office, but the permanent representation, and the permanent representative, typically play a major part.

National Co-ordination in Brussels: Towards Convergence or the Persistence of Diversity?

Discovering how the member states have responded to the pressures to 'get it right' in Brussels and finding how they have attempted to overcome the difficulties discussed above are the principal concerns of this volume. The degree to which national arrangements have converged is a further theme. This section discusses competing perspectives on whether convergence or divergence should be expected. It also describes the main characteristics of national

---

[42] The Treaties reserve certain acts to the member states, for example, the appointment of the European Commission, rather than to the Council. 'Where the Member States have to act in this way, they do so through a Conference of the Representatives of the Member States' (Westlake 1997: 55).

co-ordination systems that contributors were asked to identify in their country studies. These features—the overall co-ordination ambition and the organization of, and functions performed by, the permanent representation— serve as the main points of comparison between the member states. The effectiveness of national systems in Brussels is a further concern discussed in this section.

Convergence or Divergence?

The discovery of overriding similarity or persisting differences is an interest whenever national arrangements are compared. Existing theoretical perspectives suggest that there are good reasons for expecting both in terms of the way that national co-ordination in Brussels is organized.

Convergence

The 'convergence hypothesis' draws from two versions of the new institutionalism: the rational choice school and the sociological school (Hall and Taylor 1998). The rational choice strand would expect to find increased similarity on the grounds that permanent representations, as organizations in a shared institutional environment and subject to common pressures, are likely to adopt those arrangements that demonstrate themselves to be most efficient. A process of 'optimization' (Harmsen 1999: 84) is predicted as member states copy from their counterparts the structures or procedures that have proved successful. The anticipated result is 'a gradual convergence of national practices around the most effective solutions to . . . common problems' (Harmsen 1999: 84). '[D]riven by a logic of optimization to adopt increasingly similar processes and structures' (Harmsen 1999: 84), representations would be expected to converge around a single model.

  The sociological version anticipates convergence on the grounds that 'institutions that frequently interact or are exposed to each other over time develop similarities in organizational structures, processes, recruitment patterns, structures of meaning, principles of resource allocation, and reform patterns' (Olsen 1997: 161),[43] The mechanisms that bring this about include coercion— in an EU context, the obligations and duties imposed by Union-level rules and regulations (DiMaggio and Powell 1991), and mimicry—the copying by some organizations of the mechanisms or features of other organizations without necessarily improving efficiency (March and Olsen 1989). In addition, frequent contact and interaction between national representatives may lead to the development of common norms, as officials are 'gradually socialized into

---

[43] Olsen cites the work of Meyer and Rowan (1977); Thomas *et al.* (1987); DiMaggio and Powell (1991); Brunsson and Olsen (1993); Scott and Meyer (1994).

the shared values and practices of the EU system' (Harmsen 1999: 84; see also Haas 1958; Derlien 2000; Kerremans 1996; Lewis 1998). The result may be a 'gradual diffusion of those shared values within national administrative systems', producing a culture over time that leads eventually to the 'emergence of increasingly similar national structures and processes' (Harmsen 1999: 84).

Divergence

The 'continuing divergence hypothesis' also builds on new institutionalist theorizing. From this perspective, variation between national arrangements at the European level is to be expected. The differences that this approach anticipates are likely to be rooted in domestic structures and national idiosyncracies (Wallace and Hayes-Renshaw 1997; Edwards 1996; Harmsen 1999).[44] Applying the insights of March and Olsen (1989) to national co-ordination systems, Harmsen (1999) argues that the responses of the member states to the demands of EU membership are likely to be interpreted in terms of pre-existing institutional structures and values. The differences that exist between domestic polities can be expected to be reproduced in structures in Brussels. Sophisticating this view, cross-national differences in co-ordination in Brussels may be expected on the grounds that there are significant differences between the member states in terms of European policy, domestic political and administrative opportunity structures, and national policy style. Countries that are strong supporters of integration ('locomotives'), such as Germany, as well as those that might be characterized as 'spectator states', such as Greece, Portugal, and Spain, may have smaller missions that take a special interest in particular areas of EU policy-making and which are not tightly integrated into the domestic policy-making system. More sceptical states ('brakes') that prefer intergovernmental over supranational solutions, such as Denmark, France, and the UK, may be expected to have larger permanent representations that are capable of surveying the full range of EU activity and are closely integrated in national policy processes.

The political opportunity structure of the member state is also likely to affect the mission and the functioning of the permanent representation. The basic structure of the state—whether it is unitary (Denmark, France, Greece, Ireland), federal (Austria, Belgium, Germany) or somewhere in between (the UK)—the structure of the executive—whether it is unified, as in the UK, bicephalous as in France, or collegial, as in Italy or the Netherlands—and the nature of the party system—whether it is dominated by a small number of large, relatively coherent, ideologically moderate parties, or composed of

[44] This is not an original observation. Hayes-Renshaw *et al.* note that: 'It cannot be denied that national traditions and idiosyncrasies have repercussions on both the formal attributes and the behaviour of these missions' (1989: 135).

a large number of small, weakly disciplined parties, that range across the political spectrum—are perhaps the three most important variables. The administrative opportunity structure of the domestic administration may additionally influence the operation of the permanent representation. The extent to which an administration is unified or fragmented institutionally (for example, by strong departmental traditions, fierce interministerial rivalries, low levels of horizontal mobility, or by the existence of a *corps* or *cuerpos* system) and culturally (whether an official's primary loyalty is to the service as a whole or to the administrative unit in which he or she services, and whether there is a tradition of information-hoarding or interdepartmental information-sharing) are particularly relevant. Finally, national policy styles (Richardson *et al.* 1982) may lead member states to construct very different co-ordinating structures. Countries that incline towards a statist approach, such as France, may be expected to adopt practices that are similarly exclusive in EU policy-making. The permanent representation of such member states may not attach a high priority to consulting private interests in Brussels or representing their concerns in the negotiation of EU decisions. Countries with a more inclusive approach at home, such as Austria or Denmark, by contrast, may regard consulting social partners and other interested parties as similarly routine at the EU level.[45]

Comparing Systems of National Co-ordination in Brussels

In examining the institutions, structures and processes put in place by the member states at the European level, the contributors to the volume were

---

[45] While these reasons suggest that differences are likely to persist between national co-ordination systems in Brussels because of continuing domestic differences between the member states, a more radical approach focuses more narrowly on the permanent representations as individual institutions. Olsen (1997: 161) outlines an autonomy hypothesis, which 'argues that all institutions develop robustness towards changes in their functional and normative environments, as well as towards reform attempts. The argument is not that institutions are immune to environmental changes and reforms. The central idea is that history is "inefficient" in matching practices and structures to environments and reforms. Internal processes of attention, interpretation, decision making and work may slow down, accelerate, reverse or redirect change, as a function of how well external changes and reforms "match" institutional identities, histories and dynamics (March and Olsen 1989, 1995)'. This hypothesis suggests that there may be specific features of an institution that limit the extent to which external factors influence their development, organization, or operation. Extending the point further, it may be that permanent representations enjoy a degree of independence *vis-à-vis* both the wider European and the narrower national environment. Resources such as expertise, experience, access to information, or positional advantage may, for example, provide the leverage that enables permanent representations to develop a distinct identity and escape the total control of the national capital. However, there is not sufficient space to pursue this idea here.

asked to investigate the co-ordination ambition of the member states, the organization, operation, and responsibilities of the permanent representation, and the effectiveness of national arrangements in Brussels. The emphasis on representations reflects the key role that they play in national efforts at the European level, but is not intended to suggest that member state action begins and ends with the activities of officials posted at the mission in Brussels.

National Co-ordination: Ambition and Strategy

A starting-point in each country study is to establish whether there is a co-ordination ambition and, where it exists, the nature of that ambition. As discussed above, there are several different conceptions of co-ordination. 'At a minimum', Wright notes, co-ordination 'may imply an attempt to avoid particular mishaps or fiascos, or a wish "not to impeded, frustrate or negate one another's activities"' (Metcalfe 1987). At the other end of the spectrum, co-ordination involves overall steering and, as such, is persistent, generalised and purposeful' (1996: 148). With respect to EU policy, the concern is with whether the co-ordination ambition is global or selective, to what extent coherent action on the part of national officials is a priority, and whether or not attention is directed across the entire policy cycle or focused on particular phases. Also important is the strategy—institutions, structures, and procedures—devised to deliver co-ordination. How labour and responsibility are divided within the system and the role and status of the permanent representation are especially relevant.

The Permanent Representation

The permanent representation is the centrepiece of national co-ordination efforts in Brussels and, as such, was the principal focus of investigation. Its location on the front line as the representative of national interests and participant in Council processes, as well as its integration into both the national administration and the EU system, make it a fascinating subject of study. Contributors were asked to examine the structure of the permanent representation and the functions that it performs, both 'upstream' in Brussels and 'downstream' *vis-à-vis* the domestic political system.

Organization, composition, and internal operation

In looking at the structure of the permanent representation, a first—if rather basic—feature is size. The size of the permanent representation may be important as an indicator of a member state's desire to co-ordinate national action in Brussels and its capacity to carry out responsibilities, such as ensuring representation in Council working groups or Commission committees.[46] Peters (1999) suggests that size may be a function of the importance assigned to the task of co-ordination by the national government and may also reflect differing conceptions about how the task should be performed. A positive conception of co-ordination, for example, may call for a relatively small number of officials to make authoritative decisions about the appropriate stance to be struck, while a more inclusive approach that prefers the direct participation of interested departments may favour the posting of a larger complement of personnel in Brussels. Alternatively, size may be related to co-ordination ambition or a reflection of the breadth of a state's interests or its personnel resources (Hayes-Renshaw and Wallace 1997: 222). Size might also be correlated with age. It is possible that new member states favour large permanent representations as they undergo a probationary period during which they become familiar with EU business and are keen for civil servants to gain experience that may then be deployed at home in the domestic administration (de Zwann 1995: 22; Hayes-Renshaw and Wallace 1997: 223). However, maintaining a small co-ordinating body in Brussels is increasingly difficult as the scope of EU activity has expanded (see Table 0.2 above; see also Wright 1996; Hayes-Renshaw and Wallace 1997; European Council 1999).

Personnel is a second concern. The background of officials, and the composition of staff at the permanent representation, is important in assessing the assets available to the mission. It also gives an indication of the difficulties involved in internal co-ordination—for example, are domestic rivalries in the national administration reproduced at the European level?—and provides clues about where real influence over European policy is exercised in the national capital. While the incumbent in the top job invariably comes from the diplomatic service, 'it is wrong to view the permanent representations as the extended arm of foreign ministeries' (Spence 1995*a*: 361). Officials from deputy downwards may come from a variety of backgrounds, and the balance between diplomats and officials from other ministries may be revealing. The method of recruitment is of particular interest. The main question concerns where responsibility for appointments lies (whether the permanent representative, central co-ordinators in the national capital, or individual ministries select new officials), who pays the salaries of staff in Brussels, and which bodies or interests in addition to officials from the national administration are represented. Also of interest are the considerations that are relevant in appointing officials, such as whether party affiliation makes a difference. The

---

[46] Hayes-Renshaw *et al.* (1989) suggest that size is one of three factors that explain the differences between permanent representations. The others are length of membership and national political characteristics.

answers to these questions suggest where primary loyalties on the part of officials at the representation are owed. Candidates include the member state, the permanent representative, or the home department.

As well as their backgrounds, it is useful to know at what stage in their career officials are posted to Brussels. Whether they come from the junior ranks of domestic ministries or whether they are relatively senior may be important in terms of the authority and status that the permanent representation commands in the national capital, as well as providing an indication of the importance attributed to cultivating European expertise or developing a cadre of officials with experience of the EU by the national government or individual ministries. Also relevant in this connection is how easy or difficult is it to recruit officials, and whether there is an established career path for officials attracted to working in Brussels. For example, are civil servants encouraged to apply by their home ministries? Is a term in Brussels regarded positively by the departments—or the individuals—concerned? Is the expertise gained by officials who have served in Brussels utilized or neglected? To what extent is there a co-ordinated effort to develop a cadre of officials with European expertise at either civil service level or by individual ministries?

The length of time that officials spend at the permanent representation is also important. At the top, permanent representatives tend to spend a long time in post on account of the experience and skills that are necessary to do the job. At lower levels, however, the length of service may vary. The frequency with which personnel turn over will inevitably affect the ability of officials to develop expertise and to construct networks of personal contacts in the EU institutions and with counterparts from other member states. However, some countries may fear that if their officials remain in Brussels for too long that they will 'go native' and may limit service to a relatively short term.

The age of the permanent representation is a third issue. What matters is less the chronological age and more the degree of institutionalization implied by age (Polsby 1968). As organizations survive, they tend to develop internal patterns of functioning that may be different from the formal patterns, and to develop internal cultures that are functional or perhaps dysfunctional for the performance of their tasks. Longer standing institutions have had a longer time to develop their connections with the other institutions of the European Union and with other national representations, so that they may be more effective at the network-building aspects of their role.

The internal organization of the permanent representation and its *modus operandi* provide further important points of comparison. The division of labour at the top is defined by the structure of the Council and the respective responsibilities of the permanent representative and the deputy. However, the organization of functional units may vary. One possibility is that the permanent representation is organized into sections that reflect Council formations; another, that they follow the lines of demarcation between domestic ministries. Whichever is the case, a problem of 'administrative mismatch' (Wright 1996) is likely to arise, since it would be surprising if the jurisdictions between domestic ministries were to match the division of responsibilities between formations within the Council.

The presence—or absence—of internal co-ordination mechanisms is a very important feature. A degree of segmentation can be assumed, since functional units or officials are involved in different Councils. The extent to which formal or informal practices operate to overcome this fragmentation is an important feature of the permanent representation. Where they do exist, it is useful to know when they are triggered and by whom, at what level they come into play, and if they cover all business or only exceptional cases. Moreover, the level at which decisions are taken is an important concern. It may be the case that technical experts are authorized to make choices about their own policy areas and to confer only where there are disagreements about the direction of policy. Another possibility is that all decisions are referred to senior officials for their approval. Whether organizationally it is collegial or hierarchical contributes significantly to the overall character of the permanent representation.

Collectively, these structural features of the permanent representation are likely to play a large part in determining the permanent representation's capacity to implement national ambitions. More general concerns relate to its status and authority in the national system of EU policy-making, whether it is valued as a front-line source occupying an important strategic position, the servant of the domestic administration, or the mouthpiece of European interests whose staff have 'gone native'.[47] Moreover, permanent representations inevitably accumulate expertise on account of their proximity to, and experience of, EU decision-making. A further question concerns the extent to which domestic authorities are wary of this fact and how they attempt to monitor or control the actions of the mission (Wallace 1973).

Functions

Writers on the subject have typically sought to identify a set of generic functions performed by permanent representations (see e.g. Hayes-Renshaw *et al.* 1989; Hayes-Renshaw and Wallace 1997; Wright 1996; Spence 1995*a*). The approach taken in this volume departs from this approach in two respects. First, it problematizes the idea that there is a fixed list of responsibilities that all permanent representations necessarily carry out. Instead of assuming that all functions are performed by all permanent representations,

---

[47] The remark of Dietrich von Kyaw, a former permanent representative of Germany, that he is known in his native country not as the *ständiger Vertreter* (permanent representative), but as the *ständiger Verräter* (the permanent traitor) is often cited in this context.

contributors to this volume were asked to identify which functions are carried out by the mission that they investigated, how, with what resources, and to what effect. A second assumption treats the performance of a task as a dimension rather than an attribute. In other words, it is presumed that either a permanent representation performs a particular task or that it does not. Contributors to this volume, by contrast, were asked to comment on the level of priority accorded by the permanent representation to the various tasks assigned to it, to describe the resources devoted to each in terms of personnel and time, and to evaluate the level of performance of the organization across the range of its responsibilities. This underlined the aim of this project to compare member states in terms of the mission defined for the permanent representation, its success in fulfilling its remit, and the factors that explain its ability to perform the functions ascribed to it.

An indicative list of functions drawn from the literature provides a useful point of departure, as well as a frame of reference. 'Upstream', the broad mission of the permanent representation is to defend the interests of the member state. More specifically, it is likely that the permanent representation will carry out at least some of the following functions:

- *A postbox* (Spence 1995a)—documents for the attention of the member states, including notice of meetings and their agendas, and policy documents, are sent by the Council Secretariat to the permanent representation for delivery to the national capital, where they are distributed to the relevant departments by the foreign ministry.
- *Providing an official point of contact between government and EU institutions and other member states* (Wallace 1973: 57)—the permanent representation communicates with relevant officers in the Commission or Council on behalf of national delegations in order to obtain information in advance of Council meetings (Spence 1995a).
- *Providing a base for national negotiators* (Spence 1995a; Wright 1996)— 'The permanent representations [may] provide a central point in Brussels for visits, whether at official or ministerial level' (Spence 1995a: 362). They are located relatively close to the EU institutions—at most a fifteen-minute drive away. They 'also keep a suite of rooms in the Council building where most Council working groups take place' (Spence 1995a: 362), from where telephone calls can be made, faxes sent, or where last-minute briefings can take place.
- *Providing the main negotiators at working-group level* (Spence 1995a)— officials from the permanent representations, accompanied by specialists flown out from the national capital, may be responsible for leading negotiations within the Council. Some Councils, however, as noted above, may be run from the capital.

- *A source of information and an antenna* (Wright 1996; Wallace 1973)—staff in the permanent representation may monitor activity in Brussels and collect information from all available sources, including EU institutions, other member states, and private interests. Not only do they use formal channels, but they may be expected to build informal networks of contacts with officials in the EU institutions—particularly, with nationals—and domestic interest groups.
- *A mechanism for sensitizing of EU institutions to national policy stances* (Wright 1996)—officials in the permanent representation may be expected to maintain good relations with their opposite numbers in the Commission services and to ensure that national concerns, objectives, and anxieties are effectively communicated, as necessary. The permanent representation may also keep in close contact with 'their' member(s) of the Commission and 'their' *cabinet* with a view to influencing votes in the College when necessary. Officials may also maintain contact with nationals in the Parliament, as well as other MEPs that may be sympathetic, and let them know about the government's thinking on particular issues.
- *Interacting directly with representations of other member states* (Spence 1995)—officials in Brussels may establish close relations with their counterparts in other permanent representations. They may 'lunch together in the Council building or in the many restaurants seemingly existing precisely for the purpose of providing a social venue for the furtherance of Community business' (Spence 1995*a*: 363). These contacts are important for information-gathering and finding allies for Council negotiations.[48]
- *Influencing the EU policy agenda* (Wright 1996)—officials in the permanent representation may monitor Commission services to detect when new initiatives are being contemplated, so that they can alert policy-makers in the national capital. They may arrange meetings with Commission officials or submit draft texts. Efforts may also be made to influence MEPs at critical junctures in committee or before plenary sessions.
- *Conducting negotiations in Council working groups and COREPER* (Wright 1996: 160).

[48] However, officials may not consider contacts with other delegations to be equally valuable. Beyers and Dierickx (1998) suggest that national representatives are more likely to interact with core members, which they identify as institutional actors, such as the Commission, the Secretariat General, and the Presidency of the Council, and the 'big' member states, namely, France, Germany, and the UK. This group is to be distinguished from peripheral members, such as Italy, Greece, Spain, Portugal, Luxembourg, and Ireland, who interact weakly with all actors.

- *Maintaining contact with private interests*—permanent representations may provide information and advice to interest groups or firms about EU policy, Commission proposals, and their likely impact. They may also assist domestic interests who are eligible for EU grants or funding.[49]
- *Maintaining links with the press* (Spence 1995a)—permanent representations are an important source of information for the national and international media. Releasing information to the press can also be an important element of bargaining.

'Downstream', permanent representations may be expected to perform some or all of the following:

- *Reporting back to the appropriate national bodies* (Wright 1996)—the permanent representation may operating a reporting system that covers meetings in Brussels involving national delegations. These are likely to include mainly meetings at various levels within the Council, but may include meetings with senior officials in the Commission. Permanent representations may also relay intelligence about new initiatives, the positions of other member states, and the progress of legislation through the European Parliament.[50]
- *Advising the capital*—the permanent representation may not only provide information about the positions adopted by other actors, but offer advice to the domestic administration on the policy stance it should adopt. It advises them about what objectives are realistic and negotiable, and suggests tactics or alliance partners. Advice is likely to be transmitted by telephone or fax, and may be given directly to the departments concerned or indirectly via the central co-ordinating body.
- *Participating in domestic co-ordination* (Wallace 1973: 57)—there may be regular telephone contact or meetings in person or video-conferencing between the permanent representation and home-based officials. The permanent representative may return regularly to the capital to participate in formal co-ordination meetings in advance of ministerial Councils and to meet the minister for foreign affairs, the Prime Minister, President or their staff, and senior officials involved in European policy. At a more junior level, officials may be more or less involved in domestic processes relating to EU policy.

---

[49] The UK Department of Trade and Industry suggested that 'Ministers and officials should . . . have the confidence to be open about the difficulties they sometimes face in Brussels, and should be prepared to make use of business contacts and networks in reinforcing the UK negotiating position' (quoted in Mazey and Richardson 1996).

[50] Compare e.g. the UK and France (Kassim and Menon, respectively, this volume).

Effectiveness

The effectiveness of national arrangements in Brussels is a third major comparative interest. A question that inevitably arises is whether some member states are systematically more successful than others. There is no shortage of claims about the recipe for success. Spence (1995*a*: 363), for example, argues that: 'If the Council is disorganised or working groups not well prepared, centralised member states will do better' (Spence 1995*a*: 363). Wright (1996: 162), on the other hand, suggests that centralization provides no guarantee of agreement or quality, and that decentralized countries not only have a network of experts that are able to 'reduce the formal density of the policy arena', but may have a cultural advantage over centralized countries, which are less used to meeting the requirements, such as searching for allies, building coalitions, and demonstrating negotiating flexibility, that are imposed by a fragmented policy process.

However, it is far easier to frame the question than to answer it; assessing effectiveness is a task beset with difficulties. In the absence of a commonly accepted conception or an agreed scale, different senses of 'effectiveness' need to be distinguished. First, there is administrative efficiency of the permanent representation in carrying out the functions, both 'upstream' and 'downstream', that have been entrusted to it according to the division of tasks and responsibilities with the national system of co-ordination. This conception provides a relative measure, according to which the performance of a permanent representation is assessed in terms of its delivery within the system established by the member state and the overall national ambition regarding the co-ordination of European policy. It is intended to overcome the difficulty raised by the fact that the member states may have very different objectives or concerns at the European level and that they may pursue varying strategies (Wright 1996).

The administrative efficiency of a permanent representation is likely partly to be determined by its structure, organization, and composition. More specifically, the following factors are likely to be relevant: the calibre of its staff; the reach and quality of the networks cultivated by its officials in Brussels; the expertise and experience at its disposal in Brussels; the efficiency of its internal co-ordination processes; its credibility, the extent to which its officials are perceived to act with the backing of the government at home; the personal reputations of the permanent representative and the deputy permanent representative; and its age—new EU members may underestimate the demands of membership, particularly the speed with which information must be processed and a position decided (see e.g. chapters by Mazey and by Müller, this volume). However, it is also likely to be affected by properties of features of the domestic European policy-making apparatus, such as: the receptiveness of officials and ministers to information and advice relayed from Brussels; the closeness of its relations with central co-ordinators; the quality of domestic co-ordination procedures; and the tendency of the government to strike unrealistic stances and behave dogmatically.

A second conception of effectiveness is more general and uses an ideal-type drawn from the list of functions enumerated in the preceding section. According to this view, effectiveness can be measured in terms of the extent to which the permanent representation is able:

- to ensure coverage of all meetings in Brussels where national interests need to be represented;
- to collect useful information from public and private sources in Brussels and relay it promptly to concerned parties at home;
- to inform domestic actors about the views of other EU actors and offer accurate and timely advice about negotiating tactics and what positions are realistic;
- to lobby participants in the decision-making process with appropriately timed interventions.

This definition is not altogether satisfactory, since it does not relate performance to specific national ambitions and it makes the assumption that co-ordination is an important goal irrespective of national differences. However, unlike the first conception, it does permit comparisons to be made between the member states.

'Policy effectiveness' (Wright 1996: 148) is a third meaning. This conception relates to the overall ability of a member state to influence EU policy-making. By separating this sense from the first, the idea that administrative efficiency necessarily delivers success in the shaping of Union decisions is avoided. Effective co-ordination may assist member states in realizing their goals, but the possibility is open that administrative efficiency is neither necessary nor sufficient for influencing the substance of policy.[51] Policy effectiveness may result from other completely independent factors, such as 'policy congruence' or 'political clout' (see Wright 1996). As Wright has argued, 'effectiveness must be judged not only according to the nature and resources of formal and informal co-ordinating mechanisms' (1996: 162) and that '[m]erely to examine the machinery of co-ordination is to confuse the means and the outcomes' (1996: 165).

---

[51] Indeed, Wright (1996: 163–4) suggests that political clout, constitutional congruence, existing policy congruence, policy climate congruence, and administrative congruence are the factors that determine the ability of a member state to influence the direction of EU policy.

Contributors to this volume were asked to assess the effectiveness of national arrangements in Brussels, and to identify the factors that affect this effectiveness. However, no single approach was prescribed, and it was left open to the individual authors to select whichever conception was most appropriate to their case study.

An Introduction to the Country Studies

The eleven country studies examine the co-ordination of a representative sample of member states—large and small, Euroenthusiasts and Eurosceptics, long-standing and new members. The first chapter looks how the UK, a member state with a reputation for effective co-ordination, but well-known for its Eurocaution, attempts to ensure that its views are developed early, articulated clearly, and represented coherently by UK officials. In contrast Andreas Maurrer and Wolfgang Wessels, in their study of Germany, unravel the complexities of co-ordination in a political system characterized by vertical and horizontal pluralism, administrative fragmentation, and parallel competition from the 'foreign relations systems' of the Länder. Success in high politics at the European level contrasts with the 'diplomacy of improvisation' that is the outcome of 'autonomy', 'polyphony', and 'organized anarchy' in routine policy-making. In Chapter 3, Anand Menon assesses the extent to which French institutions, structures, and processes are able to meet the aspirations of the political centre for uniformity and unity in the representation of national interests.

In his discussion of Italy, Giacinto della Cananea highlights the difficulty of achieving co-ordination at the European level, due to rivalry, competition, and conflict among central authorities at home. Similarly, in her investigation of national action on the part of Greece, Calliope Spanou locates the sources of poor performance in Brussels in the failings of a domestic system, marked by fragmentation, sectorialization, low formalization, and lack of political leadership at the highest levels. Portugal, examined by José Magone, offers a striking contrast, where policy-makers at home, in a unitary state, governed by a single party, defer to the expertise of officials at the permanent representation.

In their discussion of Belgian co-ordination, Bart Kerremans and Jan Beyers question the rationale for a permanent representation to an international organization whose offices are located 'in its [own] drawing room, in its kitchen, and even its bedroom', in amongst the very ministries whose interests it represents. Their answer, which uncovers the 'added value' that a permanent representation creates, has general significance.

Ben Soetendorp and Rudy Andeweg set out to test the claim that national idiosyncracies are the key to understanding the functioning of the permanent representation. They find, contrary to this contention, that the features of the

Dutch political and administrative system—fragmentation, segmentation, and a lack of central authority—do not produce national arrangements at the European level that are similarly fractured. Indeed, in this important area of policy co-ordination, the machinery put in place by the Netherlands is considerably less idiosyncratic than might have been expected.

Wolfgang Müller and Sonia Mazey examine co-ordination on the part of two small member states—Austria and Sweden respectively—that have recently joined the Union. There the similarity ends. Austria has an extremely inclusive approach to European integration, and must reconcile the ambitions of subnational governments and social partners in a lead department-led system, with no central authority with the power to impose solutions where conflicts arise. Sweden, a reluctant European with a strong preference for inter-governmental solutions and a desire to export the social democratic model to its partners through action on the part of the Union, is a unitary state, where a centralized strategy of co-ordination has not so far proved effective.

In the final country study, Brigid Laffan, also investigates a small country, Ireland. She describes how limited material resources impose severe constraints on the coverage of action and the type of activities that can be pursued at the European level, but at the same time shows that co-ordination can be effectively achieved when relations within an administrative élite are close and there is a political consensus in favour of 'Europe'.

References

Abélès, M., Bellier, I., and MacDonald, M. (1993), 'Approche anthropologique de la commission européene', unpublished report.

Aspinuall, M., and Greenwood, J. (1997), *Collective Action in the European Union* (London: Routledge).

Barber, Lionel (1995), 'The Men Who Run Europe', *Financial Times* (11–12 Mar.).

Beyers, Jan, and Dierickx, Guido (1998), 'The Working Groups of the Council of the European Union: Suprnational or Intergovernmental Negotiations?', *Journal of Common Market Studies*, 36/3: 289–318.

Bogdanor, Vernon, and Woodcock, George (1991), 'The European Community and Sovereignty', *Parliamentary Affairs*, 44/4: 481–92.

Brunsson, N., and Olsen, J. P. (1993), *The Reforming Organization* (London: Routledge).

Buitendijk, G., and Van Schendelen, Marinus P. C .M. (1995), 'Brussels Advisory Committees: A Channel of Influence?', *European Law Review*, 20/1: 37–58.

Chryssochoou, D. N. (1998), *Democracy in the European Union: A Journey into Theory* (London: I. B. Tauris).

Cini, M. (1997), 'Administrative Culture in the European Commission: The Cases of Competition and Environment', in N. Nugent (ed.), *At the Heart of the Union: Studies of the European Commission* (Basingstoke: Macmillan), 71–88.

Commission of the European Communities (1995), *Report on the Operation of the Treaty of European Union*, SEC (95) 731 Final, 10.5.95 (Luxembourg: Office for Official Publications of the European Communities).

Corbett, Richard (1989), 'Testing the New Procedures: The European Parliament's First Experience with its New Single Act Power', *Journal of Common Market Studies*, 27/4: 359–72.

de Bassompierre, G. (1988), *Changing the Guard in Brussels: An Insider's View of the Presidency* (New York: Praeger).

de Zwann (1995), *The Permanent Representatives Committee: Its Role in European Union Decision-Making* (Amsterdam: Elsevier).

Derlien, Hans-Ulrich (2000), 'Germany: Failing Successfully?', in H. Kassim, B. G. Peters, and V. Wright (eds.), *The National Co-ordination of EU Policy: The Domestic Level* (Oxford: Oxford University Press), 54–78.

DiMaggio, Paul J., and Powell, Walter W. (1991), 'The Iron Cage Revisited: Institutional Isomorphism and Collective Rationality', in W. W. Walter and P. J. DiMaggio (eds.), *The New Institutionalism in Organizational Analysis* (Chicago: University of Chicago Press), 63–82.

Dinan, D. (2000), 'Governance and Institutions 1999: Resignation, Reform and Renewal', in G. Edwards and G. Wiessala (eds.), *Journal of Common Market Studies: Annual Review 1999/2000*, 25–42.

Dogan, Rhys (1997), 'Comitology: Little Procedures with Big Implications', *WEP* 20/3: 31–60.

Donnelly, M., and Ritchie, D. (1997), 'The College of Commissioners and the Cabinets', in G. Edwards and D. Spence (eds.), *The European Commission* (London: Cartermill).

Edwards, Geoffrey (1996), 'National Sovereignty vs. Integration? The Council of Ministers', in J. Richardson (ed.), *The European Union: Power and Policy Making* (London: Routledge), 127–47.

European Council (1999), *Presidency Conclusions: Helsinki European Council, 10 and 11 December 1999*, Council of the European Union website, ••.

European Voice (various), see 4/28, 4/31, 5/5.

Falkner, G., and Nentwich, M. (2000), 'The Amsterdam Treaty: The Blueprint or the Future Institutional Balance', in K. Neunreither and A. Wiener (eds.), *European Integration after Amsterdam: Institutional Dynamics and Prospects for Democracy* (Oxford: Oxford University Press), 15–35.

Fitzmaurice, John (1988), 'An Analysis of the European Community's Co-operation Procedure', *Journal of Common Market Studies*, 26/4: 389–400.

——(1994), 'The European Commission', in A. Duff, J. Pinder, and R. Pryce (eds.), *Maastricht and Beyond* (London: Routledge), 179–89.

Forster, Anthony (1998), 'Britain and the Negotiation of the Maastricht Treaty: A Critique of Liberal Intergovernmentalism', *Journal of Common Market Studies*, 36/3: 347–68.

Frances, J., Levačić, R., Mitchell, J., and Thompson, G. (1991), 'Introduction', in G. Thompson, J. Frances, R. Levačić, and J. Mitchell (eds.), *Markets, Hierarchies and Networks: The Coordination of Social Life* (London: Sage), 1–19.

General Secretariat, Council of the European Union (1996), *Council Guide*, vol. i. *Presidency Handbook* (Luxembourg: Office for Official Publications of the European Communities).

Gonzáles Sánchez, Enrique (1992), 'La Négociation des décisions communautaires par les fonctionnaires nationaux: Les Groupes de travail du Conseil', *Revue française d'administration publique*, 63: 391–400.

Garrett, G. (1995), 'From the Luxembourg Compromise to Codecision: Decision Making in the European Union', *Electoral Studies*, 14/3: 289–308.

Greenwood, J. (1997), *Representing Interests in the European Union* (London: Routledge).

——and Aspinwall, Mark (eds.) (1997), *Collective Action in the European Union* (London: Routledge).

Haas, E. B. (1958), *The Uniting of Europe* (Stanford, Calif.: Stanford University Press).

Hall, P. A., and Taylor, R. C. R. (1998), 'Political Science and the Three New Institutionalisms', *Political Studies*, 44/4: 936–57.

Harmsen, R. (1999), 'The Europeanization of National Administrations: A Comparative Study of France and the Netherlands', *Governance*, 12/1: 81–113.

Hayes-Renshaw, Fiona, and Wallace, Helen (1997), *The Council of Ministers* (Basingstoke: Macmillan).

——Lequesne, Christian, and Mayor Lopez, Pedro (1989), 'The Permanent Representations of the Member States to the European Communities', *Journal of Common Market Studies*, 28/2: 119–37.

Hayward, J. E. S., and Wright, V. (1998), 'Policy Co-ordination in West European Core D' Executives', End of Award Report, unpublished mimeo.

——(forthcoming), *Governing from the Centre* (Basingstoke: Palgrave).

Héritier, A., Knill, C., and Mingers, S. (1996), *Ringing the Changes in Europe: Regulatory Competition and Redefinition of the State. Britain, France, Germany* (Berlin: Walter de Gruyter).

Hix, S. (1998), 'Study of the European Union II: The "New Governance" Agenda and its Rival', *Journal of European Public Policy*, 5/1: 38–65.

——(1999), *The Political System of the European Union* (Basingstoke: Macmillan).

Hoffmann, S. (1966), 'Obstinate or Obsolete? The Fate of the Nation State and the Case of Western Europe', *Daedalus*, 95/4: 862–915.

——(1982), 'Reflections on the Nation State in Europe Today', *Journal of Common Market Studies*, 21: 21–37.

Houben, P.-H. J. M. (1964), *Les Conseils de Ministres des Communautés Européennes* (Leiden: A.W. Sythoff).

Hull, R. (1993), 'Lobbying Brussels: A View from Within', in S. Mazey and J. Richardson (eds.), *Lobbying in the European Community* (Oxford: Oxford University Press), 82–92

Jachtenfuchs, M. (1995), 'Theoretical Perspectives on European Governance', *European Law Journal*, 1/2: 115–33.

Jennings, E. T., and Crane, D. (1994), 'Co-ordination and Welfare Reform: The Quest for the Philosopher's Stone', *Public Administration Review*, 54: 341–8.

——Menon, A., Peters, B. G., and Wright, V. (1999), National Policy Co-ordination in Brussels', unpublished mimeo.

——Peters, B. Guy, and Wright, Vincent (eds.) (2000), *The National Co-ordination of EU Policy: The domestic level* (Oxford: Oxford University Press).

Kassim, H. (1996). 'Air Transport', in H. Kassim and A. Menon (eds.), The European Union and National Industrial Policy (London: Routledge), 106–31.

——and Stevens, H. (forthcoming), *Civil Aviation and the European Union: Europeanisation and its Limits* (London: Palgrave).

——and Wright, V. (1991), 'The Role of National Administrations in the Decision-Making Processes of the European Community', *Rivista Trimestrade di Diritto Pubblica*, 832–50.

Kerremans, Bart (1996), 'Do Institutions Make a Difference? Non-Institutionalism, Neo-Institutionalism and the Logic of Common Decision Making in the EU', *Governance*, 9/2: 216–40.

Kohler-Koch, B. (1996), 'Catching up with Change: The Transformation of Governance in the European Union', *Journal of European Public Policy*, 3/3: 359–80.

——and Eising, R. (1999). *The Transformation of Governance in the European Union* (London: Routledge).

Lenaerts, K. (1991), 'Some Reflections on the Separation of Powers in the European Community', *Common Market Law Review*, 28/1: 11–35.

Lequesne, Christian (1993), *Paris-Bruxelles: Comment se-fait la politique européenne de la France* (Paris: Presses de la Fondation Nationale des Sciences Politiques).

Lewis, J. (1998), 'Is the "Hard Bargaining" Image of the Council Misleading? The Committee of Permanent Representatives and the Local Elections Directive', *Journal of Common Market Studies*, 36/4: 457–77.

——(1999), 'Administrative Rivalry in the Council's Infrastructure: Diagnosing the Methods of Community in EU Decision-Making', paper delivered at the Sixth Biennial ECSA International Conference, 2–5 June.

Lindberg, L. N., and Scheingold, S. A. (eds.) (1970), *Europe's Would-be Polity*.

Lowi, T. J. (1964), 'American Business, Public Policy, Case Studies, and Political Theory', *World Politics*, 16/4: 677–715.

March, J. G., and Olsen, J. P. (1989), *Rediscovering Institutions: The Organizational Basis of Politics* (New York: Free Press).

————(1995), *Democratic Governance* (New York: Praeger).

Marks, Gary, and McAdam, D. (1996), 'Social Movements and the Changing Structure of Political Opportunity in the European Union', in G. Marks, F. W. Scharpf, P. C. Schmitter, and W. Streeck (eds.), *Governance in the European Union* (London: Sage), 95–120.

Marks, Gary, Hooghe, Liesbet, and Blank, Kermit (1996), 'European Integration from the 1980s', *Journal of Common Market Studies*, 34/3: 341–78.

Mazey, Sonia, and Richardson, Jeremy (eds.) (1993), 'Introduction Transference of Power, Decision Rules and Rules of the Game', in *Lobbying in the European Community* (Oxford: Oxford University Press), 3–26.

————(1996), 'Interest Groups', in J. Richardson (ed.), *European Union: Power and Policy-Making* (London: Routledge).

Menon, A., and Hayward, I. (1996), 'States, Industrial Policies and the European Union', in H. Kassim and A. Menon (eds.), *The European Union and National Industrial Policy* (London: Routledge), 267–90.

Mény, Yves, Muller, Pierre, and Quermonne, Jean-Louis (eds.) (1996), *Adjusting to Europe* (London: Routledge).

Metcalfe, L. (1987), 'Comparing National Policy Coordination: Do the Differences Matter?' paper presented at the Erenstein Colloquium, Maastricht, European Institute of Public Administration.

Metcalfe, L. (1994), 'International Policy Co-ordination and Public Management Reform', *International Review of Administrative Sciences* 60: 271–90.

Meyer, J., and Rowan, B. (1977), 'Institutionalized Organizations: Formal Structure as Myth and Ceremony', *International Review of Administrative Sciences*, 60: 271–90.

Monar, Jörg (2000), 'Justice and Home Affairs', in G. Edwards and G. Wiessala (eds.), *Journal of Common Market Studies, Annual Review 1999/2000*, 125–42.

Moravcsik, Andrew (1993), 'Preferences and Power in the European Community: A Liberal Intergovernmentalist Approach', *Journal of Common Market Studies*, 31/4: 473–524.

—— (1994), 'Why the European Community Strengthens the State: Domestic Politics and International Cooperation', *Center for European Studies, Working Paper Series*, 52.

—— (1998), *The Choice for Europe* (Ithaca, NY: Cornell University Press).

Noël, Emile (1967), 'The Committee of Permanent Representatives', *Journal of Common Market Studies*, 5: 219–51.

—— (1992), 'Reflections on the Maastricht Treaty', *Government and Opposition*, 27/2.

—— and Etienne, Henri (1971), 'The Permanent Representatives Committee and the "Deepening" of the Communities', *Government and Opposition*, 6/4: 422–47.

Nugent, Neill (1999), *The Government and Politics of the European Union*, 4th edn. (Basingstoke: Macmillan).

Olsen, Johan P. (1997), 'European Challenges to the Nation State', in B. Steunenberg and F. van Vught (eds.), *Political Institutions and Public Policy* (Amsterdam: Kluwer Academic Publishers), 157–88.

O'Nuallain, Colm, with Hocheit, Jean-Marc (1985), *The Presidency of the European Council of Ministers* (London: Croom Helm).

Pedlar, J. H., and Van Schendelen, M. P. C. M. (eds.) (1993), *Lobbying the European Union* (Aldershot: Dartmouth).

Peters, B. G. (1994), 'Agenda Setting in the EU', *Journal of European Public Policy*, 1/1: 9–26.

—— (1998), 'Managing Horizontal Government: The Politics of Co-ordination', *Public Administration*, 76: 295–311.

—— (1999), 'Institutional Isomorphism, But which Institution?: The Politics of Policy Coordination', unpublished mimeo.

Pierson, Paul (1996), 'The Path to European Integration: A Historical Institutionalist Analysis', *Comparative Political Analysis*, 29/2: 123–63.

Pollack, M. A. (1994), 'Creeping Competence: The Expanding Agenda of the European Community', *Journal of Public Policy*, 14: 95–145.

—— (1997), 'Delegation, Agency and Agenda Setting in the European Community', *International Organization*, 51/1: 99–134.

—— (1998), 'The Engines of Integration?', in W. Sandholtz and A. Stone Sweet (eds.), *European Integration and Supranational Governance* (Oxford: Oxford University Press), 217–49.

Polsby, N. (1968), 'The Institutionalization of the US House of Representatives', *American Political Science Review*, 62: 144–68.

Pressman, J. L., and Wildavsky, A. (1984), *Implementation*, 2nd edn. (Berkeley, Calif.: University of California Press).

Putnam, Robert D. (1988), 'Diplomacy and Domestic Politics: The Logic of Two-Level Games', *International Organization*, 43/2: 99–110.

Richardson, J., Gustafsson, G., and Jordan, G. (1982), 'The Concept of Policy Style', in Richardson (ed.), *Policy Styles in Western Europe* (London: Allen & Unwin).

Rometsch, Dietrich, and Wessels, Wolfgang (1996), *The European Union and Member States: Towards Institutional Fusion?* (Manchester: Manchester University Press).

Salmon, Jean A. (1971), 'Les représentations et missions permanentes auprès de la CEE et de l'Euratom', in M. Virally, P. Gerbet, and J. Salmon (eds.), *Les Missions permanentes auprès des organisations internationales* (Brussels: Bruylant).

Sandholtz, Wayne A. (1996), 'Membership Matters: Limits of the Functional Approach to European Institutions', *Journal of Common Market Studies*, 34/3: 403–29.

——and Stone Sweet, Alec (1998), *European Integration and Supranational Governance* (Oxford: Oxford University Press).

Sasse, C., Poullet, E., Coombes, D., and Deprez, G. (1977), *Decision-Making in the European Community* (New York: Praeger).

Scharpf, F. W. (1999), *Governing in Europe* (Oxford: Oxford University Press).

Schmidt, Susanne K. (1996), 'Sterile Debates and Dubious Generalisations: European Integration Theory Tested by Telecommunications and Electricity', *Journal of Public Policy*, 16/3: 233–71.

Scott, W. R., and Meyer, J. W. (1994), *Institutional Environments and Organzations* (Thousand Oaks, Calif.: Sage).

Scully, R. (1997), 'The EP and the Co-Decision Procedures: A Reassessment', *Journal of Legislative Studies*, 3/3: 58–73.

Smith, Mitchell P. (1995), 'The Commission Made Me Do it: Policy Preferences and Domestic Political Capacities', paper presented at the 4th Biennial International Conference of the European Community Studies Association, panel on 'The Delors Commission', Charleston, SC, 11–14 May 1995; also published in N. Nugent (ed.), *At the Heart of the Union: Studies of the European Commission* (Basingstoke: Macmillan, 1997), 167–86.

Spence, David (1995*a*), 'The Co-ordination of European Policy by the Member States', in Martin Westlake (ed.), *The Council of the European Union* (London: Cartermill Publishing).

——(1995*b*), 'Negotiations, Coalitions and the Resolution of Inter-State Conflicts', in Martin Westlake (ed.), *The Council of the European Union* (London: Cartermill Publishing).

Spinelli, A. (1996), *The Eurocrats* (Baltimore: Johns Hophins University Press).

Thomas, G. M., Meyer, J., Ramirez, F., and Boli, J. (1987), *Institutional Structure* (Newbury Park, Calif.: Sage).

Tsebelis, G. (1990), *Nested Games* (Berkeley, Calif.: University of California Press).

Van Schendelen, M. P. C. M. (1996), '"The Council Decides": Does the Council Decide?', *Journal of Common Market Studies*, 34/4: 531–48.

——(1998), *EU Committees as Influential Policymakers* (Aldershot: Ashgate).

Wallace, Helen (1973), *National Governments and the European Communities* (London: Chatham House and PEP).

——(1985), 'Negotiations and Coalition Formation in the European Community', *Government and Opposition*, 20/4: 453–72.

Wallace, Helen (1991), 'Making Multilateral Negotiations Work', in W. Wallace (ed.), *The Dynamics of European Integration* (London: Royal Institute of International Affairs and Routledge, Kegan, Paul).

Weiler, Joseph H. H., with Haltern, Ulrich R., and Mayer, Franz C. (1995), 'European Democracy and its Critique', *West European Politics* 18/3: 4–39.

Wessels, Wolfgang (1991), 'The EC Council: The Community's Decisionmaking Center', in R. O. Keohane and S. Hoffmann (eds.), *The New European Community* (New York: Westview).

——(1997), 'An Ever Closer Fusion? A Dynamic Macropolitical View on Integration Processes', *Journal of Common Market Studies*, 35/2: 267–99.

Westlake, Martin (1995), *The Council of the European Union* (London: Cartermill Publishing).

Williams, Shirley (1991), 'Sovereignty and Accountability in the European Community', in R. O. Keohane and S. Hoffman (eds.), *The New European Community: Decisionmaking and Institutional Change* (New York: Westview).

Wincott, Daniel (1995), 'Institutional Interaction and European Integration: Towards an "Everyday" Critique of Liberal Intergovernmentalism', *Journal of Common Market Studies*, 33/4: 597–609.

Wright, Vincent (1996), 'The National Co-ordination of European Policy-Making Negotiating the Quagmire', in J. Richardson (ed.), *European Union: Policy and Policy-Making* (London: Routledge), 148–69.

Young, Hugo, and Sloman, Anne (1982), *No, Minister: An Inquiry into the Civil Service* (London: BBC).

Ziller, Jacques (1992), 'Au cœur du processus de décision européen: Le Comité des représentants permanents. Entretien avec M. Charles Rutten, Ancien Représentant Permanent des Pays Bas auprès des Communautés Européens', *Revue française d'administration publique*, 63: 383–90.

1

Representing the United Kingdom in Brussels: The Fine Art of Positive Co-ordination

Hussein Kassim

UK co-ordination at the European level is characterized foremost by the coherent presentation of the UK position by ministers and officials (Bulmer and Burch 1998; Derlien 2000; Edwards 1992; Menon and Wright 1999). The early formulation of policy, the cultivation of relations with a wide range of European partners, and the systematic attempt to influence the preliminary phases of Union policy-making are further features that have attracted comment (Schmidt 1996; Spence 1995). Moreover, unlike other member states that regard EU policy-making as fundamentally intergovernmental—France is, perhaps, the prime example (see Menon, this volume)—the UK government engages closely with private interests (Hull 1992).

The UK permanent representation (UKREP) is the centrepiece of the UK system in Brussels. Its front-line responsibilities include monitoring the activities of other member states and the EU institutions, and collecting and relaying information to Whitehall. It also supplies the majority of UK representatives in Council negotiations, as well as providing briefings for, and accompanying, ministers and officials that fly out from the UK. Unlike many of its counterparts, moreover, UKREP also has an important voice in

I should like to express my tremendous gratitude to the forty-four practitioners who kindly gave up their time—at least an hour in most cases and in some instances substantially longer—to answer my questions as part of the research for this project. Interviews were conducted on a strictly non-attributable basis between Jan. 1998 and Sept. 1999. The respondents included officials from UKREP and the Scottish Executive EU Office in Brussels, from 10 Downing Street, the Cabinet Office, the Foreign and Commonwealth Office, MAFF, the DTI, the Home Office, the Northern Ireland Office, and the Office of Fair Trading in London, and from the Scottish Office in Edinburgh. Two former foreign secretaries also kindly granted interviews.

the domestic process. The Brussels-based mission forms with the European Secretariat of the Cabinet Office and the Foreign and Commonwealth Office a 'triad' of central co-ordinators (Bender 1996) with overall responsibility for promoting and defending the UK position in European Union decision-making (Bender 1991, 1996; Edwards 1992; Kassim 2000; Spence 1993; Stack 1983).

This chapter examines the co-ordination of UK policy in Brussels. It puts the institutions, procedures, and policies that the UK has put in place at the European level in the context of the UK's strategic or 'positive' co-ordination ambition. It then focuses on UKREP's role in the system. After briefly describing its history, the chapter discusses the internal organization of the mission, its policies relating personnel, composition, and recruitment, and its internal processes and working methods. An assessment is made of the capacity and effectiveness both of UKREP specifically and UK co-ordination arrangements more generally.

Two arguments are advanced. The first is that the factors that account for the UK's exacting co-ordination ambition—principally, the centralized nature of its political system, scepticism towards the European project, and a preference for intergovernmentalism over supranationalism—also largely explain why it has been administratively efficient, but not politically effective, at the European level. The second argument relates to devolution. Although representing the most significant constitutional reform since the Great Reform Act of 1832 (Bogdanor 1998), on the present evidence, the creation of devolved governments in Scotland and Wales does not threaten the co-ordination strategy pursued by the UK since its accession to the European Communities (see Hogwood *et al.* 2000). While responsibility for important EU policy areas—agriculture, environment, fisheries, structural funds—has been transferred from Westminster, under the terms of the constitutional settlement, European policy remains reserved to the UK government and the administrative centrality of Whitehall is preserved. The institutional adjustments made by the devolved authorities—for example, the creation of the Secretariat General External to co-ordinate Scotland's European Policy and the strengthening of the European Affairs Division in Wales—are designed to be compatible with the pathways and machinery that existed prior to devolution. In Brussels, moreover, UKREP retains its primacy, despite the creation of the Scottish Executive Office and the National Assembly for Wales EU Office.

The Co-ordination of European Policy: The UK System

UK action at the European level takes place within the context of a well-defined and exacting national co-ordination ambition, namely:

to ensure that for any EU activity or proposal . . . agreement is reached on a UK policy in good time, taking account of identified UK interests and advancing or at least protecting those consistent with overall Government policy with realistic objectives taking account of the interests of other member of the EU and that policy agreed is followed through consistently during negotiation, and put into effect once decisions have been taken in Brussels.[1]

This is an extremely ambitious objective, especially given the breadth of UK interests. Only France has a similar ambition (see Menon, this volume). Other member states tend either to focus their activities on particular policy areas (see, for example, Laffan, Magone, this volume) or do not place the same emphasis on crafting an interdepartmentally agreed position, instead allowing lead departments to define national policy (see, for example, Maurer and Wessels, Müller, this volume).

Two factors explain the UK's choice of ambition. The first is the UK's historically ambivalent attitude towards Europe (Denman 1996; George 1992; Young 1998; Wallace 1997; Stack 1983). Suspicion about integration, and a preoccupation with the preservation of British sovereignty, allied in more recent times with a concern to achieve 'value for money' for UK taxpayers, has produced a defensive posture that calls for the close scrutiny of EU activities wherever UK interests may be affected. The second is the tradition of centralized government, informed by the principle of collective cabinet responsibility, and supported by well-entrenched administrative routines that emphasize consultation and co-operation.

The positive conception of co-ordination pursued by the UK has important institutional implications (see Introduction, above). It requires, first of all, an effective communications infrastructure, linking officials in Brussels with those based at home. Officials must be present in sufficient numbers to ensure that the activities of European institutions are monitored, contacts cultivated, and information collected and relayed to the concerned parties. Also, although individual departments can exercise considerable autonomy, a strategic co-ordination ambition requires the presence of a central authority possessed of the legitimacy and the appropriate institutional mechanisms to impose solutions when necessary. Overall, such a conception of co-ordination requires a well-disciplined administration, with clearly defined lines of responsibility, where officials have a full understanding of their roles. These conditions are met in the UK case, and UKREP—whose responsibilities are discussed below—the European secretariat of the Cabinet Office, and the Foreign and Commonwealth Office (FCO), are crucial parts of the machinery.

The European secretariat, one of four secretariats in the Cabinet Office, has

---

[1] Quoted from presentation given by a senior official in the European secretariat, December 1994. See also Bender (1991, 1996) and Butler (1986).

overall responsibility for ensuring that a UK position is defined when necessary and for trouble-shooting where interdepartmental problems arise (see
Bender 1991, 1996; Stack 1983; Kassim 2000). Its authority derives from its
expertise, its proximity to Number 10, and with no specific departmental
interest its reputation for neutrality. A small, compact élite unit with a staff of
about twenty-four, the European secretariat monitors the response of UK
departments to European initiatives and their action with respect to Europe
more generally. It keeps in regular contact with the officials in the home
departments involved with EU dossiers, offering advice as and when necessary, and stays in touch with officials at UKREP. The European Secretariat
actively intervenes only when relevant interests have not all been consulted or
where serious interdepartmental differences arise. In the latter case, informal
methods are tried first—telephone calls and gentle encouragement—but if
these prove ineffective, more formal mechanisms come into play. Representatives from the relevant departments may be summoned to meetings of EQ(Q),
the official level of the cabinet committee responsible for EU matters, a subcommittee of the Ministerial Committee for Defence and Overseas Policy (see
Bulmer and Burch 1998; Edwards 1992; Hogwood *et al.* 2000; Kassim 2000;
Menon and Wright 1999; Spence 1993; Stack 1983; for further discussion of
EQ(O); for a broader perspective, see Hennessy 1989; Kaufman 1980). Where
a matter cannot be resolved at this level, it passes up the line to senior officials in EQ(O*), and if necessary to ministers in (E)DOP.

The European secretariat has maintained its centrality after devolution.
Both the Scotland Act (1998) and the Government of Wales Act (1998)
reserved European policy to the UK government. The administrative concor-
dats agreed by the UK governments and the territorial authorities emphasise
the central co-ordinating role of the European secretariat (Cabinet Office
1999), while the institutional arrangements made by the Scottish Executive
and the Welsh Assembly to manage their input into the UK's EU policy have
'been strongly influenced by considerations of compatibility with the pre-
existing Whitehall machinery' (Hogwood *et al.* 2000: 88). Before devolution,
the territorial departments were routinely involved in the meetings called by
the European secretariat. Subsequently, only UK ministers and officials can be
involved in formal Cabinet Office meetings. However, the European secretariat convenes *ad hoc* informal meetings, which can be attended by officials
from the Scottish Executive and the Welsh Assembly. In addition, the minister for Europe chairs a committee, the Ministerial Group for European Co-
ordination (MINICOR), which brings together ministers of the UK, Scotland,
and Wales (see Hogwood *et al.* 2000).[2]

---

[2] A Joint Ministerial Committee (JMC) with its official counterpart, the Joint Official
Committee (JOC), has been created to serve as the final mechanism for resolving intergovernmental conflict.

The Foreign and Commonwealth Office's involvement in the co-ordination of UK policy takes several forms. First, after the Prime Minister, the Foreign Secretary bears overall responsibility for European policy. He—all incumbents have so far been men—also attends meetings of the European Council, and chairs (E)DOP. The foreign secretary is assisted by a junior minister for Europe. The latter, supported by a newly created division for bilateral relations, EUDB, is responsible for relations with the UK's European partners and has an important role in domestic co-ordination.

Other EU-related functions entrusted to the FCO are carried out by divisions responsible for internal (EUDI) and external (EUDE) EU policies respectively. The former operates the communications infrastructure that links the UK to Brussels and other European capitals. Information and documentation supplied by UKREP and the EU institutions to King Charles Street are relayed by the FCO to recipients on the relevant 'net'. EUDE is the lead department in Whitehall for EU's external relations. An additional division, EUDP, is created in the Foreign Office during the UK Presidency as the centre for co-ordinating Presidency business (Edwards 1985; Kassim 2000).

The European divisions report to a director, who in turn is responsible to a director for EU and Economic Affairs at under-secretary level. The latter figure is, moreover, the figure to which the UK permanent representative is formally accountable. The Common Foreign and Security Policy Department, also located in the Foreign Office, is, however, on a different line of command, and answers to the political director.

UKREP is the third partner in the central co-ordinating triangle. Just as the involvement of the European secretariat and the Foreign Office is not confined to domestic processes, so UKREP's role extends beyond its responsibilities on the front line in Brussels. The following sections explore in detail its organization, composition, functions, and *modus operandi*.

Organization

Following devolution, a Scottish Executive EU Office and a National Assembly for Wales EU Office have been established in Brussels, but UKREP remains the centrepiece of UK co-ordination at the European level. UKREP has its origins in the four-person delegation (UKDEL) to the European Coal and

---

[3] For further discussion of the subcommittee dealing with European questions, see Bulmer and Burch 1998; Edwards 1992; Hogwood *et al.* 2000; Kassim 2000; Menon and Wright 1999; Spence 1993; Stack 1983. For a broader perspective see Hennessy 1986 and Kaufman 1997.

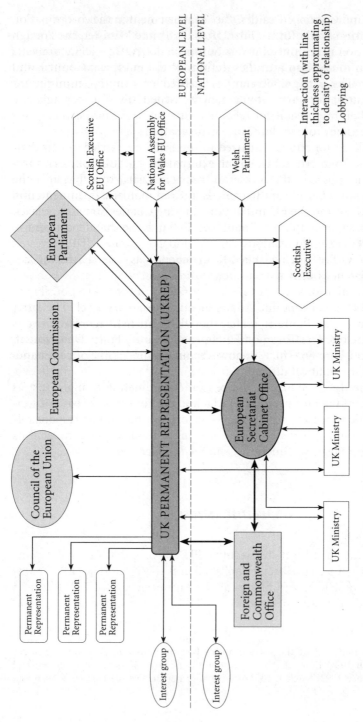

FIG. 1.1. The Co-ordination of UK European Policy (simplified)

Steel Community established under the Treaty of Association in 1955. Following the creation of the EEC and EURATOM in 1958, it became the UK Delegation to the Communities (Wallace and Wallace 1973: 255), and later the UK Mission to the Communities. Its principal function was to monitor policy developments in the Communities likely to have an impact on the UK and act as an official line of communication between the UK government and the European Communities. The Mission steadily grew in size and expertise, and by 1969 employed twenty-nine members of staff, eighteen of whom were diplomats (Wallace 1973: 91). It played an essential role in negotiating the UK's accession to the Communities in the early 1970s, under the FCO's direction and in close liaison with the FCO's European Integration Department. Additional recruitment during this period ensured that by the time of entry the Mission was 'equipped for handling the full range of Community policies, with its staff drawn from the Whitehall departments most directly concerned' (Wallace and Wallace 1973: 255).

The delegation's functions changed fundamentally on the UK's accession. The negotiations for UK entry had been conducted by a team in London, 'composed of senior officials from the key departments (FCO, Treasury, MAFF and DTI)' (Stack 1983: 126) and led by Sir Con O'Neill, deputy undersecretary in the Cabinet Office. However, the Heath government decided that in future UKREP should play the leading role in Brussels (Bulmer and Burch 1998: 615), though it should remain formally accountable to the FCO. Its upgrade was accompanied by a name change—from UKDEL to UKREP—and an increase in its complement of staff, which made it at the time the second largest permanent representation in Brussels with thirty-six officials. It has subsequently remained one of the larger missions in Brussels (see Kassim, Menon, this volume). In December 2000, it had fifty-five officials, the sixth largest after France, Germany, Greece, Portugal, and Spain.

As with other permanent representations, UKREP is headed by two senior figures: a permanent representative of ambassadorial rank, who has overall responsibility for the mission and who takes charge of business destined for COREPER II; and a deputy who is responsible for COREPER I. Also like its counterparts, UKREP has adapted its internal organization to meet the expansion of EU competencies and the increasing demands that issue from Brussels. For example, following the decisions taken by European Council at Helsinki in December 1999 to create standing security and military structures in Brussels, a Representative to the Interim Political and Security Committee (also deputy Political Director) and Military Representative were attached to UKREP for the first time in 2000.

In early 2000 UKREP was organized into eight sections, staffed in most instances by desk officers at first-, second-, and sometimes third- (trainee) secretary level,[4] and headed by a counsellor, adviser, or, in the case of the Agriculture Section, minister. Seven sections have sectoral responsibilities that reflect, to a greater or lesser extent, the organization of the Council. These are: Agriculture; Industry and Internal Market; Social, Environmental, and Regional; Economic Affairs, Finance and Tax; External Relations, Development, and Trade Policy; Justice and Home Affairs, and Security and Defence.

The sections vary in size and internal organization, reflecting the organization of work and the volume of EU business. The Industry and Internal Market Section, for example, covers a relatively large number of technical Councils including industry, Single Market, energy, and high technology, and is responsible for competition and state aid issues. It employs eight staff, six of whom are first secretaries. Although by contrast the Agriculture and Fisheries Section manages the work for only two Councils, agriculture and fisheries, there are frequent meetings at all levels, and six officials are needed to cope. The section is headed by a minister—a grade that denotes ambassador status on par with deputy ambassadors in Washington and Paris, and reflects the responsibilities of its incumbent in representing the UK on the Special Agricultural Committee (SCA). Three first secretaries deal respectively with the Common Agricultural Policy, food and veterinary matters, and fisheries, while one second secretary provides support on the food and veterinary side and takes the lead on state aid issues, and the other answers general enquiries and is responsible for European parliamentary issues. The Justice and Home Affairs Section is small by comparison. As well as the counsellor who heads the unit, it has three desk officers. This reflects the relative newness of the area, and the relatively limited flow of business.

Five specialist departments exist alongside the seven sectoral sections. The responsibilities of the Press and Information Section are self-explanatory. The remit of the Political Affairs Section encompasses the future development of the EU and for horizontal matters, such as institutional reform, and openness and transparency. It also services the Council machinery, and is the home for the Antici Group and the Mertens Group members, and the officials responsible for co-ordinating I/A Points on the Council agenda, and making arrangements for UK ministers attending Council meetings. The section is responsible in addition for the UK's Dependent Territories including Gibraltar, and devolution, and it supervises the Institutions, Press and Information, and Commercial Sections. The Institutions Section manages contact with EU institutions, notably the European Parliament, but also the Economic and Social Committee, the Committee of the Regions, and the European Ombudsman. It is also responsible for trying to ensure that British nationals are adequately represented in the staff of EU institutions. To this end, the EU

---

[4] The UK began to use third secretaryships for training purposes at a very early stage of its history (Wallace 1973).

Staffing Unit aims to help British nationals interested in employment opportunities in the European Institutions. The Commercial Section, finally, is intended to assist British firms to take advantage of the commercial opportunities provided under EU-Funded Programmes. It advises British companies and organisations on various projects that cover development aid, economic co-operation, investment, and export promotion.

Personnel

UKREP, like other permanent representations, recruits staff from the Foreign Office and the line ministries, reflecting the need for both diplomatic and technical expertise.[5] Unlike its counterparts, however, UKREP enforces this balance even in the top two positions: the UK permanent representative is traditionally a career diplomat from the FCO, while the deputy comes from a home department, usually the Department of Trade and Industry (DTI) or the Treasury (see Table 1.1). Although appointment to other posts is in theory open to all on the basis of expertise, qualifications, and overall ability, in

TABLE 1.1. *UK permanent representatives and deputies, 1973–2001*

Permanent Representatives	
Sir Michael Palliser	1973–1975
Sir Donald Maitland	1975–1979
Sir Michael Butler	1979–1985
Sir David Hannay	1985–1990
Sir John Kerr	1990–1995
Sir Stephen Wall	1995–2000
Sir Nigel Sheinwald	2000–
Deputy Permanent Representatives	
Robert Goldsmith	1973–1977
Sir William Nicoll	1977–1982
David Elliot	1982–1991
David Durie	1991–1995
David Bostock	1995–1999
Bill Stow	1999–

Source: Westlake (1995: 307), Vachers (various issues).

[5] An agreement was struck to this effect at the time of accession, but the FCO argued that its leadership role should be maintained in order to prevent the development of sectoral baronies—or 'vertical brotherhoods' (Derlien 2000)—where officials seconded from Whitehall ministries might regard themselves as, and only as, diplomats in the service of their home departments.

practice, the technical knowledge demanded in most positions favours officials from the cognate Whitehall department. Officials in the Agriculture
and Fisheries Section, therefore, typically come from MAFF, and those in
Economic and Financial Affairs from the Treasury.[6] Similarly, officials in the
Political and Institutional Affairs Section are more likely than not to come
from the diplomatic service. In 1995, the ratio stood at about three-to-one in
favour of the home ministries (Hayes-Renshaw and Wallace 1997: 22).

The nature of the job—exceptionally long hours and a high level of responsibility for the grade—demands staff of the highest calibre (Edwards 1992:
72). The fact that there is little support for officials, that no training is provided to new recruits, and that business needs to be transacted at high speed
requires 'people with a higher than usual self-starting ability, tenacity, drive
and organisation' (interview). From the perspective of prospective employees,
on the other hand, a posting at UKREP is an extremely attractive proposition
due to the interesting nature of the work, the impact that can be made, and
the levels of contact that officials enjoy with senior civil servants and ministers. This explains why UKREP is attractive to the most talented officials at
their level. As a former official observed when the Foreign Office's number
two at UKREP:

One of the requirements of a posting here is that people should be of the highest
quality and the Permanent Representative does have the right, which he does very
occasionally exercise, of turning people down because he does not think they're suitable for some reasons. So we can ensure that we get only the very best people here.
(Brian Crowe, quoted in Young and Sloman 1982: 73)

At the top, a succession of high-fliers have passed through UKREP. Sir David
Hannay, ambassador between 1985 and 1990 served as British permanent representative to the UN from 1990 to 1995. Sir John Kerr moved from his position as assistant under-secretary of state at the Foreign Office in 1990 to
become the UK permanent representative, before being appointed British
ambassador to the USA in 1995 and returning to the UK to become the most
senior official in the FCO in 1997. More recently, Sir Stephen Wall became
head of the European Secretariat in the Cabinet Office. David Bostock, meanwhile, moved from a top position in the Treasury to become deputy ambassador at UKREP in 1995, and four years later was appointed to a senior
position in the Cabinet Office. At a junior level, fast streamers and other
talented young officials see UKREP as an important staging post in their
careers (interviews).

At the same time, a stint at UKREP does not provide a guarantee of
rapid promotion for returning officials. Home departments view European

---

[6] There are exceptions. In 1999, the counsellor heading the JHA Section came not from
the Home Office, but from the FCO.

experience quite differently from each other. In general, ministries with a long history of European involvement look favourably on officials that spend time in Brussels. The DTI, for example, sends its best officials to UKREP, and a European career path, or career 'anchor', is well established. MAFF is even more strategic. It aims explicitly to 'recycle' officials through Brussels and to place them in useful and influential positions in UKREP (as well as in the European Commission). Secondment in a department whose involvement with Europe is so intense is not considered to be time spent away at all (interview). Within the Foreign Office too, even if there is not the same level of encouragement or support, the path from the European divisions to UKREP is well-trodden.

Elsewhere, attitudes towards a spell in Brussels can be less positive. Departments where European business is relatively new, such as the Home Office, the Department of Education and Employment, the Department of Health, and the Ministry of Defence, are at an early stage in the development of European expertise, and offer little guidance or encouragement to its officials interested in a secondment at UKREP. Indeed, an official from one of the aforementioned ministries recounted how he had been strongly discouraged by his line manager from seeking such a posting and told that nothing valuable could be learnt from working at UKREP (interview). The official concluded that, despite the increase of work in the department with an EU dimension, it had not even begun to develop a cadre of European experts.

Internal Functioning and Working Methods

The organization and rhythm of the work of the UK permanent representation is dictated to a large extent by outside actors and processes over which it has little or no control. As officials work to different Councils, and have different interlocutors in Brussels and in Whitehall, segmentation is perhaps inevitable. UKREP has adapted to these pressures in three ways: first, its hierarchy is relatively flat; second, officials enjoy considerable autonomy; and third, it has developed a variety of co-ordination mechanisms.

Although the job titles—permanent representative, deputy representative, head of section, first, second, and third secretary—suggest a multi-tiered organization, in practice, officials work more or less directly to the permanent representative or the deputy depending on whether their work falls under COREPER I or COREPER II. Heads of section are not line managers to whom desk officers are expected to report, nor usually do they attend working groups. Their role is to develop a long-term perspective on policy, to ensure that the position defended in negotiations is in line with ministerial guidelines, and to troubleshoot. Heads of section also provide briefings for ministers attending Council meetings, which may take place in London or Brussels, usually on the morning of the meeting or the evening before, and are cleared with home departments beforehand. The permanent representative or the deputy, and the relevant desk officer are also involved. Advice on tactics and nuance forms an essential part of the briefing.

Desk officers, by contrast, are involved with the nuts and bolts of policy on a day-to-day basis. Subject to ministerial guidelines laid down in White-hall and instructions sent via the Foreign Office, they are able to carry out their responsibilities with considerable autonomy. The expectation is that they will keep their section head and the permanent representative or deputy informed of important developments, alerting them if any problems arise or a political dimension emerges that need to be dealt with at a higher level. However, they carry out their work without direct supervision. As one official commented, 'if you get a grip on the job, there is no hierarchy at all' (interview).

Desk officers have four main responsibilities. First, they monitor policy developments in their sector, and keep Whitehall informed, maintaining contact both with the relevant desk officer in the European Secretariat and officials in the appropriate line ministries. As a result of the cross-cutting nature of many EU issues, as well as the 'administrative mismatch' (Wright 1996) between sectoral boundaries at the European level and departmental responsibilities in national administrations, a single desk officer may have to maintain contact with several departments. Environmental issues, for example, involve not only the DETR, but the DTI and the FCO, and agricul-tural and fisheries MAFF, the Scottish Executive, the Northern Ireland Office, and the Welsh Office, while employment matters interest the DEE, the DTI, the HSE, DSS, DH, DETR, HMT, and the MOD. Whatever the case, the desk officer is responsible for keeping the interested parties informed.

Desk officers are also expected to develop ties with their opposite numbers in other member states and in the European Commission, as well as with the members of European Parliament committees—a second responsibility. These contacts are used not only to muster support for the UK position, but to gather information so that Whitehall can make realistic decisions about what is and is not negotiable. Desk officers provide an important input thereby into the process by which the UK negotiating position is formulated.

Participating in working groups and conducting negotiating with repre-sentatives of the other member states and the Commission is a third respon-sibility. The ability of desk officers to cover all the meetings relevant to their section depends on their frequency and the technical knowledge required. In most sectors, officials based in Brussels lead the national delegation, which may also include civil servants who have flown out from the UK. In some areas, however, working groups are effectively operated from London. In agri-culture, for example, the volume of business is such that four desk officers based in UKREP cannot deal with the number of meetings, obliging officials from MAFF to travel to Brussels regularly.

A fourth responsibility is to provide support for senior officials. When the working group closes a file and passes it to COREPER, the desk officer briefs the permanent representative or deputy in advance of the meeting at which the issue is due to be discussed, and reports the outstanding issues to Whitehall. In some cases, unresolved questions will require a further round of co-ordination, in which case it is likely that the desk officer will participate in Cabinet Office co-ordination.

As the work of a desk officers is centred on this other working group, contact with colleagues in different sections of UKREP can be very limited. Indeed, in some sections, such as Social Affairs, Environment, and the Regions, there is little communication even with immediate colleagues. In general, desk officers spend more of their time, and interact more intensively with, their counterparts from other members states and the Commission than they do with colleagues in UKREP.[7] Three mechanisms operate, though do not necessarily overcome the segmentation of work (interviews). The first is the Monday morning meeting, held weekly, which all members of staff attend. The meeting is chaired by the permanent representative who asks officials about current issues in their area of responsibility. Although useful for the transfer of information, the gathering is considered to be somewhat ineffectual and, according to more than one official, 'not a social success' (interviews). A weekly meeting of section heads to discuss issues of particular import—the second mechanism—is considered more helpful. The third is informal, and reflects the Whitehall practice of informing colleagues about issues that may be of interest. Officials copy relevant documentation around and may follow up with with further consultation. However, as officials work very fast, there is a tendency to forget that there may be linkages across or between sectors, making monitoring by the European Secretariat all the more crucial.

Co-ordination of a different order works through the permanent representative and the deputy. Each receives important papers from junior officials relevant to COREPER I or II. The permanent representative receives all documents, though rarely intervenes in matters concerning COREPER I. In addition, the UK Antici Group and Mertens Group members assist the ambassador and deputy in preparing for COREPER meetings. In advance of the weekly Antici Group meeting, the Antici Group member makes a tour of the desk officers in UKREP to canvass opinion on what is likely to happen in COREPER, then passes this information and any advice to the permanent

---

[7] The situation is not improved by the architecture of the Permanent Representation's new home on avenue Cortenberg. Each section is located on a separate floor, and there is no natural meeting place where officials can gather informally.

representative. After the meeting, he or she briefs the UK ambassador about the likely course of business in COREPER II, what the positions of the Council President, the Commissioner and the other member states are likely to be, and to offer advice on what issues are likely to be important with the aim of improving the permanent representative's negotiating position. The Antici Group member also telephones a report to the contact point at the FCO, to be followed later by a written minute (Spence 1993). In the light of the Antici Group discussion, the UK official reflects on the usefulness of the instructions governing points of business. Where there is a problem—if the instructions are wrong or counterproductive—he or she will make immediate contact with the private office of the minister concerned and ask for the instruction to be reviewed and revised in order to prevent the problem from happening. The Mertens Group member performs the same clearing-house function in relation to COREPER I, though the responsibilities of the Mertens Group are not as wide-ranging. While the Antici responsibilities account for 80 per cent of the time of a full-time official, the Mertens Group representative has a much lighter load, equivalent to about 20 per cent (interviews).

A final feature that distinguishes UKREP is its administrative culture. Despite its segmented operation, a number of officials spoke of the sense of a 'common purpose' and the 'co-operative culture' that characterize the mission. The focus on negotiation, many reflected, produces a particular kind of bond between officials. In addition, officials both from the FCO and home departments emphasized that the culture of UKREP was not like that of the Foreign Office, although that was clearly where it had its origins. Some from departments with more egalitarian cultures, such as the Treasury, found UKREP somewhat hierarchical (interviews).

Responsibilities, Roles, and Functions

As the Introduction (above) indicated, the functions performed by, and the relative emphasis placed on them, may vary between permanent representations, reflecting different national strategies, administrative traditions, and styles.[8] In the UK case, the emphasis on teamwork, early intervention, coherent representation, and an awareness of the formidable length and breadth of the national interest, is evident in the work and functioning of UKREP, and informs operation of the system as a whole.

---

[8] It is in this spirit that Edwards (1992: 71) cites Phillippe Moreau Defarges's observation that: 'The attitude of each national administration to the construction of Europe, be it German or Italian, British or Dutch, Irish or French sums up, illustrates—sometimes to the point of caricature—its traditions and its idiosyncrasies.'

In examining the role played by UKREP, it is useful to distinguish between 'upstream' and 'downstream' functions. Collecting intelligence upstream is an extremely important responsibility. The UK is very conscious of the influence that the Commission exercises as the initiator of policy in the EU policy process—it has been estimated that 80 per cent of the original draft survives in the final legislative act (Hull 1993)—and aware of the value of early intervention. For this reason, UKREP desk officers are expected to develop close relations with officials in cognate Commission directorates so that likely initiatives can be detected. Efforts are directed not only towards the services. UKREP is 'plugged into the Commission at all levels' (interview) including the college. The permanent representative and the deputy have open lines of communication to the President's cabinet, and the secretariat general, while close touch is kept with the UK Commissioners and their *cabinets*. The latter relationship is particularly important: it enables the UK to stay informed about Commission intent, the likely fate of policy initiatives, and the attitude of the Commission to particular issues. The relationship is not, however, entirely one-sided. UK Commissioners look to UKREP an alternative as a counter-administration that provides an alternative source of expertise, advice, and information to the Commission services.

UKREP also places an emphasis on monitoring the European Parliament. Designated officials in the Institutions Section have overall responsibility for following legislation as it passes through the various stages of the parliamentary process, and for monitoring 'what the EP is doing in its committees, in plenary and in its corridors' (interview). UKREP supplies information to UK MEPs and informs them about UK concerns on certain issues. Efforts are made to cultivate relations with MEPs—not only those from the UK—in influential positions, such as committee chairs or *rapporteurs* in order to ensure that the UK's interests are well understood.

In addition, desk officers at UKREP are expected to maintain cordial relations with their opposite numbers in the other member states. Officials working in the same sector are likely to get to know each other well as a consequence of attending the same working-group meetings. UK officials are encouraged to cultivate a network of dependable contacts beyond these formal contacts by arranging social events—lunches or drinks—to build up personal relationships and trust with their counterparts. UKREP provides a modest entertainments budget for this purpose. In addition, it is not unusual for a departing official to leave a lists of important contacts for his or her successor.

As well gathering information, UKREP officials act as lobbyists, explaining and finding support for the UK position. Desk officers keep the Commission informed of the UK perspective, and attempt to ensure that proposals take account of UK interests. Officials are encouraged to act early—ideally, before a text has even been drafted—and to aim low, preferably through direct contact with the *chef de file*. To try to push policy initiatives in a favourable direction, UK officials submit written texts to the *chef de file* or the head of unit, hoping that they will find their way into the draft that eventually emerges from the Commission services.

UKREP also keeps the two UK Commissioners informed of UK concerns and the likely reaction at home to Commission proposals. Although Commissioners swear an oath of independence, it is understood that it is part of their function to keep the College informed of opinion in the country that he or she knows best (Donnelly and Ritchie 1994). The relationship between Her Majesty's Government and UK Commissioners has not always been positive. UK Commissioners have found themselves disadvantaged when governments have tended towards Euroscepticism. In the 1970s, for example, Ivor (now Lord) Richards was nominated by a government that was deeply divided over Europe. He lacked the institutional support that other Commissioners enjoyed, and found his status in the College severely diminished. The relationship between government and Commissioners has, by contrast, been good under new Labour.

The closeness of the relationship is particularly important so far as the appointment and promotion of UK officials in EU institutions is concerned. Commissioners and their *cabinets* survey upcoming vacancies in senior positions in the Commission services and lobby on behalf of their nationals for appointment to these posts. UK Commissioners inform UKREP about such opportunities, and UKREP relays the information back to the Cabinet Office in London and assists in the selection of suitable candidates. The UK has been very successful in ensuring that it is well represented in these positions. The decision by the incoming Commission President, Romano Prodi, to relax the informal 'geographical quota', according to which positions were allocated between member states in rough proportion to size, created something of a free market in which UK officials have fared extremely well.

Ensuring that the UK interest is well understood also involves lobbying other member states. UKREP officials meet their counterparts, bilaterally, between or in advance of working-group meetings, to persuade its partners of the merits of the UK position and to find allies to form either a qualified majority or a blocking minority. Constellations of opinion and coalition possibilities vary considerably, not only between, but within, sectors. Desk officers are usually well aware of which countries are likely to be more or less sympathetic to the UK stance, and target their activities accordingly.

The third function performed by UKREP is negotiation. Even where they do not play a leading role UKREP officials form part of the UK delegation in Council negotiations. In working groups, the UK delegation follows negotiating instructions that have been agreed in London, which set down the position to be defended and the tactics to be pursued. Instructions tend frequently to be 'highly elaborate . . . designating preferred and fall-back positions and how to attain them' (Edwards 1992: 74). To that extent, they are flexible. Where necessary, UK negotiators put down reservations. These range 'from the *réserve du fond* which indicates that consultation with the [UK] Government will be required at the highest level through to the *réserve d'attente* which means that time must be allowed for the domestic parliament to be consulted' (Stack 1983: 139). At the political level, UKREP prepares the briefings for UK representatives in COREPER, though they must be approved beforehand in London.

UK negotiators are obliged to follow the instructions that they receive from Whitehall, though of course they are able to influence the content of these to some extent by means of the information that they supply or the advice they offer to officials at home. The ambassador and deputy enjoy greater latitude, depending on contingent factor such as experience, trust, and personal capital in London. UK officials are very conscious that they must follow ministerial guidelines, and are acutely aware of the limits to their authority, as well as the dividing line between their responsibilities and what must be decided by ministers.

The evidence seems to contradict the argument famously made by Tony Benn, a former minister of energy and industry, that Brussels is a 'mandarins' paradise', where civil servants roam free. Asked about this claim, Sir Donald Maitland, a former UK permanent representative responded:

I'm not sure whether mandarins ever actually aspire to a paradise, but I don't really recognise the kind of life that I led in Brussels when I hear that description. To the outside observer, some distance away from the process of taking decisions in Brussels, it may seem that this dividing line is blurred. But I can only say with the greatest emphasis that for those who actually take part in the process there is no blurring of the line. The line is absolutely clear. Even if, say, the Committee of Permanent Representative is dealing with a particularly detailed and complex problem, each one of those Representatives . . . will be acting in accordance with instructions from his government, and those instructions will have been endorsed by a minister. (Young and Sloman 1982: 76–7)

Where Council discussions take an unexpected turn or where there is a danger that the UK will be isolated if it adheres to the agreed position, the practice is to refer back to London, where 'there is a considerable machinery . . . for ensuring the co-ordination of instructions to our representatives in Brussels and ensuring that there is political cover, political authority, for the line which we are going to take' (Maitland, in Young and Sloman 1982: 78). In such cases, ministerial authority is preserved whether or not the relevant minister agrees to amend, alter, or extend the instructions.[9] In addition, a

---

[9] To quote Sir Donald Maitland again, 'I myself used to find in Brussels that there were times in a debate when my instructions left me in an untenable position. In which case I would ask for a period to reflect on this and I would ask the chairman, "Could we come back to this item later in the day?" A lot of telephoning between Brussels and London would

monitoring system ensures that UK officials negotiating in Brussels adhere to the agreed line.

At the ministerial level emerging issues can present a challenge to collective Cabinet responsibility. In theory, ministers are bound by the negotiating objectives laid down by E(Dop). However, when it comes to the actual negotiations, individual ministers may feel less constrained. A former chief secretary to the Treasury, Joel Barnett, writing about a minister for agriculture in a Labour government of the 1970s, who was distrusted by his colleagues, wrote about this anxiety, noting that: 'while we might win the argument in Cabinet Committee, the actual negotiations were in John [Silkin]'s hands' (cited in Stack 1983: 149). In practice, whether or not a minister complies with the line decided in London depends on his or her personal status, government popularity, and Cabinet cohesion. Parliament is also a factor. One former foreign secretary, who served in Conservative governments in the 1980s, commented that uppermost in his mind when negotiating in Brussels was not the response of Prime Minister Thatcher, but the reaction of the House of Commons (interview). UKREP's function is to provide the minister with a briefing in advance of the Council, and to provide back-up and support in the form of the ambassador or the deputy with additional experts where necessary.

Recruitment and ensuring that the UK is sufficiently well represented in EU institutions is a fourth function entrusted to UKREP. This task is carried out by the EU Staffing Unit in association with the Institutions Section. The head of Political Affairs is closely involved and liaises with the office responsible for European Staffing in the Cabinet Office. The unit's primary objective is to promote the overall number and quality of staff in EU institutions, particularly the Commission. Three main functions can be distinguished. First, the unit provides information to UK nationals about permanent and temporary employment opportunities in Brussels. It organizes visits to UKREP, arranges talks, and maintains a website. It operates a vacancy information database, where people who register their details receive information about openings that may suit them. In addition, it circulates information about the fast stream programmes run by the Cabinet Office. Ensuring that the UK is properly represented at all levels of the Commission has proved a

---

then take place, and I would hope to receive a message later in the day saying, 'The minister agrees to amend your instructions in the following respect.' And when we got back to this item, the chairman would say, 'I wonder if you have completed your reflection by telephone? as it is called euphemistically there . . . Now I was in that position from time to time, but so were all my colleagues and there is, as you may know, a considerable machinery at the London end for ensuring the co-ordination of instructions to our representatives in Brussels and ensuring that there is political cover, political authority, for the line which we are going to take' (Young and Sloman 1982: 78). See also ibid. 75–9; Stack 1983: 136–41.

difficult task. Though able to fill its complement of senior positions—at director general and deputy director general level—the UK has historically been under-represented in the lower and middle ranks (Stack 1983). The problem has been long recognized, and efforts, many long-standing, have been made to overcome it. One, the European fast stream, was designed to recruit talented young officials, provide them with European experience, and prepare them for the *concours*. Though increasing UK representation, such initiatives have not so far corrected the imbalance in permanent positions. Whereas its share of the EU population suggests that 13.4 per cent of Commission officials should be recruited from the UK, only 11 per cent are in fact British nationals. Greater success has, though, been achieved with respect to temporary officials. The UK currently contributes about 17 per cent of the total number of detached national experts working in the Commission. This success is partly due to the work of UKREP, which is notified of vacancies, and partly to the willingness of Whitehall ministries to put forward officials for placement in strategically useful positions.

A second role of UKREP's EU Staffing Unit is scruting of EU recruitment policy and practices. In so doing, it has contributed to UK arguments about how these procedures might be improved. The UK has voiced concern that its nationals are disadvantaged by the traditional format of the *concours*. It has campaigned for the introduction of a verbal reasoning element which it argues provides a better method for selecting administrators than a general knowledge quiz. The Cabinet Office has sent observers to Brussels, to the Personnel Directorate General of the Commission, to analyse data from previous *concours*, assess what makes a successful candidate, and to feed this information back to the Cabinet Office in an effort to improve recruitment of UK nationals.

Third, the unit is responsible for liaising with British nationals in EU institutions. It informs them of UK government action, hosts social events, and offers limited pastoral support. Particular attention is paid to the Commission. UKREP has a contact point in all the Commission Directorates-General, whose job it is to forward messages about meetings and other information. Detached national experts are a particularly high priority.

Provision of information is a further upstream function. UKREP officials are expected to be available to explain UK policy on areas of EU action to a host of visitors, including representatives of interest groups and non-governmental organizations from the UK and elsewhere, as well as third countries, notably the USA and countries of Central and Eastern Europe. The openness that UKREP officials shows to private interests is a particularly significant and distinctive feature. The UK government takes the view that the opinions of business and other groups are important and where possible should be channelled by UKREP into the EU policy process.

Although when the UK holds the Council Presidency business is orchestrated from London, UKREP has a special role to play (Edwards 1985; see also

Stack 1983; Ludlow 1998; Henderson 1998; Anderson 1999). In Whitehall, the foreign secretary chairs a ministerial group, a committee at the official level presided over by the head of the European Secretariat, and is supported by EUDP in the FCO, as noted above. UKREP co-ordinates Council business with the Council Secretariat, which provides administrative support, institutional memory, and advice, and manages inter-institutional relations with the Commission, the Parliament, and other institutions on behalf of the Council. Additional staff are drafted into sections of the representation where business is expected to be especially heavy. In addition, the Political Affairs Section has an enhanced role for the duration. An extra official acts as a contact point throughout the period, and the role of officials with responsibilities for liaising with EU institutions is enhanced. Not only must the member state holding the Presidency co-ordinate the policy agenda with the Commission, but it must ensure that proposals move smoothly through the parliamentary phases of the legislative process.

A final and more recently acquired function concerns relations with the Scottish Executive EU Office and the National Assembly for Wales EU Office. The former, which opened on 1 July 1999, is responsible for providing operational support to the Executive, gathering information, assisting influencing EU policy, and raising Scotland's profile in the EU. The latter, reflecting the constitutional asymmetry that underlies devolution, has the more modest aim of raising the Welsh Assembly's profile in Europe and maintaining relations with public institutions and private interests. UKREP keeps in constant touch with both offices, seen as 'part of the UKREP family'. Just as the European Secretariat retained its centrality in Whitehall, so UKREP remains the principal actor in Brussels. As Hogwood *et al.* (2000: 89) note, 'the devolved territories have no direct route in to the Brussels policy-making machinery'.

UKREP also performs important tasks downstream. First, the mission is responsible for relaying the information it collects in Brussels to interested parties on the relevant 'net' in Whitehall and beyond. UKREP desk officers convey intelligence about forthcoming proposals. This information is highly valued in Whitehall, since it enables departments to define negotiating objective in plenty of time, and to make early interventions where this is judged useful. Ministries appreciate that officials at UKREP are much closer and have a better understanding of developments in Brussels than they do. Information about the attitudes of other member states on issues before the Council is also extremely important. UKREP officials are uniquely placed not only to report what positions other national delegations are likely to take, but their experience and personal contacts enable them to identify which of the elements that form part of the initial bargaining position are likely to be dropped as negotiations progress.

A further aspect of UKREP's information-providing responsibility is its reporting function, a unique and invaluable asset, given the importance attached by London to rapid action. UKREP officials are obliged to submit written reports to the FCO (for distribution to the relevant departments) on all meetings that take place in Brussels involving UK representatives. Reports are composed and forwarded subject to a twenty-four-hour 'same day' rule. They provide a record for circulation to all interested parties, and are used to inform further action.

The second function is closely related to the first: informing UK-based actors advice about what negotiating positions are realistic. UKREP delivers advice on negotiability in the routine contact between desk officers in Brussels and Whitehall, and when its officials are involved in meetings in the Cabinet Office. Its close integration in the domestic co-ordination distinguishes it from its peers. To take one example, in the area of agricultural policy, it has long been the practice for the senior official in the Agriculture Section to return every week to participate in MAFF's preparations for forthcoming Council meetings. Little has changed since Peter Pooley described his weekly route in the early 1980s:

Thursday I go to London and there I go to the Ministry of Agriculture to take part in the meeting of officials which winds up what happened on the previous Monday and Tuesday [when the Special Committee on Agriculture meets] . . . It also decides what form of briefing we need for the next Monday or Tuesday Council or special committee; what lines need to be cleared with other departments and with the minister before we put pen to paper on the instructions; and how we shall handle things tactically. (Young and Sloman 1982: 76)

In other cases, particularly where there are inter-departmental differences, the relevant UKREP desk officer returns to London (or uses video-conferencing facilities and remains in Brussels) to participate in the formal co-ordination meetings arranged by the European Secretariat.

The routine involvement of UKREP extends to the permanent representative. The ambassador participates, in person or by video link, in a weekly Friday morning meeting hosted by the Cabinet Office and chaired by the head of the European Secretariat, and attended by teams from the Foreign Office, the Treasury, and other departments with an interest in the agenda items. The purpose is to discuss business in forthcoming Councils and to decide tactics. Instructions on the UK line are settled, and further work arranged in areas judged inadequately prepared. The importance of this meeting—as well as the opportunity it provided to call in on the Prime Minister and foreign secretary before or after—is emphasized by a former UK permanent representative Sir Michael Butler (1986: 115). As Bulmer and Burch have noted, as a major element in fulfilling the 'objective of securing an early, agreed cross-departmental European policy position', the Friday morning meeting is a 'feature which sets the British governmental machinery apart from most of its partners in the EU' (1998: 15).

UKREP's participation in the domestic process is not limited to routine co-ordination. It also contributes to policy formation where issues have become highly politicized, though its influence in these cases is nowhere near as great. Two such cases that arose under the Major government concerned the Common Fisheries Policy and quota-hopping, and BSE. In the first, the relevant desk officer participated in the discussion that took place at Number 10. In the second, the permanent representative attended meetings at Downing Street.

General oversight and co-ordination is the third downstream function performed by UKREP. As well as following the progress of negotiations in Brussels, UKREP plays a troubleshooting role, 'sounding the alarm' when a problem arises. When instructions prove problematic, where a UK official deviates from the agreed position, or when the UK runs a risk of isolation, UKREP officials contact the relevant desk officer in the European Secretariat and the ministry concerned. If the response is not satisfactory, the desk officer at UKREP will go up the line in the home department to ensure that the warning is heeded. The result may be an urgent telephone call to a minister's private office or a meeting in the Cabinet Office with the parties concerned.

Capacity

Like other permanent representations, UKREP's capacity to implement UK ambitions in Brussels is to a large extent determined by two broader systems—the European Union, and the national polity. The complexities of the former are discussed in detail in the first chapter. Briefly, however, the Union is 'fluid, ambiguous and hybrid' (Olsen 1997: 165; see also Wright 1996) with no constitutionally defined separation of powers or tidy division of responsibilities (Lenaerts 1991; Hix 1999; Kohler-Koch and Eising 2000). It is characterized by a high degree of institutional fragmentation, sectoralization, and extreme intricacy in its procedures. Moreover, governments lack the resources—authority, agenda control, party discipline, established networks, administrative traditions—that they mobilize in domestic politics, and must search for allies and build coalitions if they are to have any impact on decision-making.

UKREP's ability to achieve its objectives is inevitably limited by the nature of the EU and the terms that it imposes. The structure of the Council, for example, makes co-ordination between policy areas extremely difficult. The number of formations, the volume of business, and the weak co-ordination between Councils, places a considerable strain on the permanent representation, and is such that it is impossible for the ambassador and the deputy to monitor the work of their officials. More specifically, the rules and conventions that regulate the composition of EU-level bodies—for example, the fact that the Political Committee is staffed from the national capital—seriously limits the ability of the permanent representation to control certain policy areas. Similarly, Commission staffing rules prevent the colonization of particular directorate-generals by the nationals of one member state and limit the possibilities for 'parachutage'.

UKREP must also work within the broader UK political system. On the administrative side, the communications infrastructure operated by the Foreign Office, the information-sharing culture of the home civil service, and domestic co-ordination structures and procedures, tend to support UKREP's efforts in carrying out its responsibilities. The changes following devolution have made arrangements more complex, but have not brought about any radical change in EU policy formation. On the political side, setting a few short-lived periods (1973–4, 1990–1, and 1997–2001), UK governments have veered between caution and outright Euroscepticism. In the most extreme manifestations of the latter, the advice offered by UKREP is generally downgraded, and a siege mentality—such as that that produced the UK campaign of non-co-operation in response to the Commission's decision not to lift restrictions on British beef—has developed around the centre of government.

Although these wider dependencies are important, UKREP's ability to implement the national co-ordination ambition is also related to its own efforts and attributes. Here, UKREP's capacities are impressive. It is one of the larger missions in Brussels, and able to ensure coverage of all meetings of the Council, which is not the case for all permanent representations (see, for example, Spanou, this volume; Hayes-Renshaw and Wallace 1997: 222). It is also able to keep a close eye on the Commission and monitor the European Parliament, ensuring that valuable information is collected and reported to London. The contacts developed by UKREP officers and officials in the Commission and from the other member states are a further asset—a finding confirmed by the study carried out by Beyers and Dierickx (1998), which confirmed the UK's pivotal status in the Council as one of the few member states that the others are most likely to consult. In addition, on the domestic front, UKREP is linked to line ministries and the central co-ordinators, and is a key contact for both. Moreover, UKREP officials enjoy access to senior levels of the civil service. Finally, UKREP attracts highly talented officials, who, despite the lack of prior training, are able to master their briefs and cope well with the demands placed on them.

Effectiveness

Assessing UKREP's effectiveness is an extremely difficult undertaking, not least because the evidence that would be necessary to arrive at a precise judgment is simply not available. Moreover, as Wright (1996: 165) has reminded us, any evaluation must be made 'according to the issue, the policy type, the policy requirements and the polity objectives. Merely to examine the machinery of co-ordination is to confuse the means and the outcomes.'

Despite these qualifications, UKREP has generally performed very effectively in terms of the UK coordination ambition and the functions entrusted to it, as the UK's European partners and Whitehall departments have testified (Spence 1995; interviews). Officials in London may sometimes dislike the recommendations or advice that emanate from UKREP, but nevertheless recognize its expertise and appreciate the flow and quality of information with which they are provided. UKREP's effectiveness can partly be attributed to its success in performing the tasks entrusted to it (see above). However, the organization and operation of the UK's general system for the co-ordination of European policy, as well as broader features of the UK political system, are also important.

With respect to the first, though its co-ordination ambition is extremely demanding, the UK has in place mechanisms and procedures that are able to deliver. At its centre, the division of labour between the European Secretariat, the Foreign and Commonwealth Office, and UKREP works extremely well. In addition, the system for the co-ordination of European policy is similarly to the machinery for managing domestic policy, and is supported by administrative practices that characterize the functioning of Whitehall more generally. The emphasis on teamwork, consultation, and information-sharing has readily been transposed to the co-ordination of EU business, even though the policy chain is longer and more complex.

Administrative efficiency, however, is only one aspect of effectiveness, and perhaps not even the most important. Another crucial measure—and one where the UK does less well—is the ability to influence policy. The UK system in Brussels may ensure that useful information is collected and that meetings are reported on on the same day. The UK position may be defined early, communicated to other policy actors, and defended coherently by ministers and officials who 'sing from the same songsheet'. None of these factors, which are essentially concerned with delivery and presentation, guarantee UK success, however, in shaping EU policy outcomes. More important in this regard is the substance of UK policy and its position relative to other states. The UK's preoccupation with sovereignty and its preference for intergovernmental solutions, as well as its advocacy of policies that reflect the Anglo-Saxon rather than the Rhenish or statist model of capitalism, have tended to make it an outlier in Council negotiations—though there have been very significant exceptions, such as the single market programme. A secondary effect is that, unlike France or Germany, the good faith of the UK, which has tended to take an instrumental rather than a symbolic approach to European integration, is not taken for granted.

Crucially, UKREP is the administrative servant of its political masters, and there are times when the message cannot be distinguished from the messenger. Even if in practice the division of responsibility between elected politicians and appointed bureaucrats contradicts the classic dualist account offered by Max Weber, ministers in the UK ultimately call the political tune. No matter how high the quality of the advice, the reach of its networks, or the assiduousness of its lobbying efforts, UKREP must ultimately deliver a position that has been decided by ministers. The outlook of most UK governments since 1973 has often left it isolated.

Other limits to the effectiveness of UK action at the European level can be located in the co-ordination strategy itself. The system has been designed to enable an early definition of the UK's position, taking into account the opinions of all interested parties. This method has its advantages. Differences are settled before negotiations commence, officials can advance the same position to different parties, and lobbying can begin early. However, there are also serious disadvantages. One is inflexibility: once put together, an interdepartmentally agreed position is hard to unpick, particularly when negotiations are fast-moving. The fact that other national delegations are able to free ride on the UK position without incurring the costs of presenting themselves as anti-*communautaire* is a second problem. A third is that the preference for efficiency and coherence over flexibility may not ultimately serve the long-term interests either of the UK or the EU. As Derlien has argued '[centralization] is counter-productive, for it leaves little room for the recurrent, multi-issue bargaining process at the European level and the informal norm of reciprocity' (cited by Kassim 2000: 255). Furthermore, the 'short-term maximization of benefits or minimization of costs may be detrimental in the long-run when optimization of multiple issues in sequential, recurrent deals eventually counts' (cited by Kassim 2000: 255). Where games are repeated and decision-making is continuous, flexibility and a willingness to compromise may be essential to secure long-term advantages. These problems are well understood within UKREP. One senior official argued, for example, that member states can choose efficiency or flexibility, but not both (interview). Another spoke of the advantages an early response, but saw that being 'trigger happy' (interview) carried potential dangers, particularly with respect to the need to cut a deal in the end-game of negotiations (Hogwood *et al.* 2000).

Conclusion

There are two conclusions to be drawn from the above analysis of the UK's arrangements in Brussels. The first is that the UK's system is unique among EU member states. The ambition it has set itself is extremely exacting, but the machinery it has put in place, and the wider political and administrative structures on which it depends, enable it to be satisfied. What is paradoxical, however, is that the very considerations and mechanisms that account for the definition of the UK's co-ordination strategy also impose severe constraints on what it is able to achieve at the European level.

The second conclusion is that the British approach to devolution—asymmetric arrangements for the devolved territories, the transfer of powers over substantive policy areas, but not their external representation, the complexity of the new system, and its reliance on the goodwill of its participants—may yet bring about a transformation of the system for co-ordinating UK policy. However, if the early signs prove an accurate guide to the future, the centralized approach may well survive.

References

Albert, M. (1991), *Capitalisme contre capitalisme* (Paris: Le Seuil); tr. as *Capitalism against Capitalism* (London Whurr Publishers, 1993).

Anderson, P. J. (1999), 'The British Presidency', in G. Edwards and G. Wiessala (eds.), *The European Union Annual Review 1998/1999* (Oxford: Blackwell/Journal of Common Market Studies), 63–4.

Bender, B. (1991), 'Whitehall, Central Government and 1992', *Public Policy and Administration*, 6/1: 13–20.

—— (1996), 'Co-ordination of European Union Policy in Whitehall', text of a lecture given by Brian Bender, Head of the European Secretariat, at St Antony's College, Oxford, 5 Feb.

Beyers, Jan, and Dierickx, Guido (1998), 'The Working Groups of the Council of the European Union: Supranational or Intergovernmental Negotiations?', *Journal of Common Market Studies*, 36/3: 289–318.

Bogdanor, V. (1998), *Devolution in the United Kingdom* (Oxford: Oxford University Press).

Bulmer, S., and Burch, M. (1998), 'Organising for Europe: Whitehall, the British State and European Union', *Public Administration*, 76: 601–28.

Butler, M. (1986), *Europe: More than a Continent* (London: Heinemann).

Cabinet Office (1999), *Memorandum of Understanding and Supplementary Agreements between the United Kingdom government, Scottish Ministers and the Cabinet of the National Assembly for Wales*, Cm 4444 (London: The Stationery Office).

Campbell, C., and Wilson, G. K. (1995), *The End of Whitehall Death of a Paradigm?* (Oxford: Blackwell).

Christoph, J. B. (1993), 'The Effects of Britons in Brussels the European Community and the Culture of Whitehall', *Governance*, 6/4: 518–37.

Crouch, C., and Streeck, W. (eds.) (1997), *Political Economy of Modern Capitalism* (London: Sage).

Denman, R. (1996), *Missed Chances* (London: Indigo).

Derlien, H-U. (2000), 'Germany', in H. Kassim, G. B. Peters, and V. Wright (eds.), *The National Co-ordination of EU Policy: The Domestic Level* (Oxford: Oxford University Press), 54–78.

Donnelly, M., and Ritchie, E. (1994), 'The Commissioners and their *Cabinets*', in G. Edwards and D. Spence (eds.), *The European Commission* (London: Cartermills).

Edwards, G. (1985), 'The Presidency of the Council of Ministers of the European Communities: The Case of the United Kingdom', in C. O'Nuallain (ed.), *The Presidency of the European Council of Ministers* (London: Croom Helm), 237–59.

——(1992), 'Central Government', in S. George (ed.), *Britain and the European Community: The Politics of Semi-Detachment* (Oxford: Clarendon Press).

George, S. (ed.) (1992), *Britain and the European Community: The Politics of Semi-Detachment* (Oxford: Oxford University Press).

Government of Wales Act (1998), chapter 38 (London: HMSO).

Gregory, F. E. (1983), *Dilemmas of Government: Britain and the European Community* (Oxford: Martin Robertson).

Hayes-Renshaw, F., and Wallace, H. (1997), *The Council of Ministers* (London: Macmillan).

Henderson, D. (1998), 'The UK Presidency: An Insider's View', *Journal of Common Market Studies*, 36/4: 563–72.

Hennessy, P. (1986), *Cabinet* (Oxford: Blackwell).

Hix, S. (1999), *The Political System of the European Union* (Basingstoke: Macmillan).

Hogwood, P. Carter, C., Bulmer, S., Burch, M., and Scott, A. (2000), 'Devolution and EU Policy Making: The Territorial Challenge', *Public Policy and Administration*, 15/2: 81–95.

Hull, R. (1993), 'Lobbying Brussels: A View from Within', in S. Mazey and J. Richardson (eds.), *Lobbying in the European Community* (Oxford: Oxford University Press).

Kassim, H. (2000), 'The United Kingdom', in H. Kassim, B. G. Peters, and V. Wright (eds.), *The National Co-ordination of EU Policy: The Domestic Level* (Oxford: Oxford University Press).

Kaufman, G. (1997), *How to be a Minister* (London: Faber & Faber).

Kohler-Koch, B., and Eising, R. (eds.) (1999), *The Transformation of Governance in the European Union* (London: Routledge).

Lenaerts, K. (1991), 'Some Reflections on the Separation of Powers in the European Community', *Common Market Law Review*, 28: 11–35.

Lord, C. (1992), 'Sovereign or Confused? The "Great Debate" about British Entry to the European Community Twenty Years on', *Journal of Common Market Studies*, 30/4: 419–36.

Ludlow, P. (1998), 'The 1998 UK Presidency: A View from Brussels', *Journal of Common Market Studies*, 36/4: 573–83.

Magone, J. (2000), 'Portugal', in H. Kassim, G. B. Peters, and V. Wright (eds.), *The National Co-ordination of EU Policy: The Domestic Level* (Oxford: Oxford University Press), 141–60.

Menon, A., and Wright, V. (1999), 'The Paradoxes of "Failure": British EU Policy Making in Comparative Perspective', *Public Policy and Administration*, 13/4: 46–66.

Schmidt, V. A. (1996), *From State to Market? The Transformation of French Business and Government* (Cambridge: Cambridge University Press).

Scotland Act (1998), chapter 46 (London: HMSO).

Spence, D. (1992), 'The Role of the National Civil Service in European Lobbying: The British Case', in S. Mazey and J. Richardson (eds.), *Lobbying in the European Community* (Oxford: Oxford University Press), 47–73.

——(1993), 'The Role of the National Civil Service in European Lobbying: The British Case', in S. Mazey and J. Richardson (eds.), *Lobbying in the European Community* (Oxford: Oxford University Press).

——(1995), 'The Co-ordination of European Policy by Member States', in M. Westlake (ed.), *The Council of the European Union* (London: Cartermill).

Stack, F. (1983), 'The Imperatives of Participation', in F. E. Gregory, *Dilemmas of Government: Britain and the European Community* (Oxford: Martin Robertson).

Wallace, H. (1996), 'Relations between the European Union and the British Administration', in Y. Mény, P. Muller, and J.-L. Quermonne (eds.), *Adjusting to Europe* (London: Routledge).

——(1997), 'At Odds with Europe', *Political Studies*, 45: 677–88.

—— and Wallace, W. (1973), 'The Impact of Community Membership on the British Machinery of Government', *Journal of Common Market Studies*, 11/3: 243–62.

Wallace, H. (1973), *National Governments and the European Communities* (European Series, 21; London: Chatham House).

Westlake, M. (1995), *The Council of the European Union* (London: Cartermills).

Wright, V. (1996), 'The National Co-ordination of European Policy-Making Negotiating the Quagmire', in J. Richardson (ed.), *European Union: Policy and Policy-Making* (London: Routledge).

Young, H. (1998), *This Blessed Plot: Britain and Europe from Churchill to Blair* (London: Macmillan).

—— and Sloman, A. (1982), *No, Minister: An Inquiry into the Civil Service* (London: BBC).

2

The French Administration in Brussels

Anand Menon

France has traditionally aspired to play a leading role in shaping the development of European integration. Implicit in this approach has been a vision of integration as a process within which the member states predominate. Debates within the EU are carried out, as far as the traditional French conception has it, on the basis of competing and conflicting national interests. The effectiveness with which individual member states can shape outputs at the EU level is intrinsically related to their success in presenting coherent positions within such debates (Premier Ministre 1994: 3, 6). An emphasis on coherence has led to the creation in Paris of a centralized and institutionalized system of inter-ministerial co-ordination (Menon 2000).

Although often overlooked,[1] the French administration in Brussels also plays a key role in ensuring the coherence of national positions and in defending French interests within the EU. This is most true of the French permanent representation, whose staff represent France in most meetings of the Council of Ministers and which is responsible for keeping Paris appraised of developments in Brussels. Paris has increasingly, however, also come to recognize the need to exert influence over the supranational institutions of the EU, and over the Commission in particular. Hence the French have developed strategies both for ensuring the presence of French officials within these institutions and for maintaining close contact with them.

This chapter is divided into three sections. The first examines the composition, organization, internal workings, and role of the French permanent representation to the European Union. The second investigates French strategies designed to ensure both a sufficient and an effective French 'presence' within the supranational institutions—notably the Commission and, to a lesser extent, the European Parliament. The final section critically evaluates the performance of the French administration in Brussels,

---

[1] A recent textbook on France in the EU, for instance, contains no references to the permanent representation in its index (see Guyomarch *et al.* 1998).

considering first its capacity to carry out its allotted tasks, and second its effectiveness, particularly in terms of its ability to further France's EU policy objectives.

The Permanent Representation

Composition

The Représentation Permanente de la France Auprès de l'Union Européenne was created in 1958 following the signing of the Treaty of Rome. Subsequent years have witnessed a steady growth in its size. The number of 'A' Grade officials has risen steadily—from eighteen in 1965, to twenty-four in 1975, to twenty-eight in 1985 (Lequesne 1993: 192). The figure currently stands at around sixty, and looks set to increase as and when further functions are bestowed on the PR as a function of a steadily expanding EU agenda. FranRep currently has a total staff of some 160 including secretarial staff (for details, see Représentation Permanente de la France Auprès de l'Union Européenne 1999).

Both the permanent representative or ambassador to the EU and his deputy have traditionally hailed from the diplomatic service, not least because of the determination of the Foreign Ministry to ensure that it retained at least one major important role in community affairs (Lequesne 1993: 185–6).[2] The post of permanent representative is a prestigious one within the diplomatic service. Not only is it viewed as an important posting in its own right, but it has also traditionally represented a stepping stone to further career advancement. Former ambassadors have gone on to jobs ranging from the senior Foreign Ministry official (secretary general of the Quai d'Orsay) to high-ranking *cabinet* appointments (Jean Vidal went on to be diplomatic adviser to both President Mitterrand and Prime Minister Jospin). The previous incumbent left his post to become deputy secretary general of the Council of the EU.

The ambassador in Brussels almost invariably has wide-ranging experience of Community affairs (Lequesne 1993: 190). The nomination of candidates with insufficient experience has caused problems for Paris in the past. Philippe Louet was replaced less than a year after his initial nomination, as he was judged to be insufficiently well-versed in the intricacies of the EC successfully

---

[2] The Ministry of Finance has consistently made clear its desire to fill the post of deputy permanent representative with one of its own officials, so far to no avail. However, as the importance of economic issues, and particularly of EMU increases, there is reason to suspect that Bercy's case will become more compelling.

to manage the forthcoming French Presidency (Lequesne 1993: 193). Pierre de Boissieu, ambassador between 1993 and 1999, had long experience of managing EU-related business. He followed a period as first secretary in the French Embassy in Germany with several years as *chef de cabinet* of François-Xavier Ortoli—then vice-president of the European Commission—prior to returning to the foreign ministry to head, first, the Service de la Coopération Économique (charged with handling EC business) and then the Direction des Affaires Économiques et Financières.

The ambassador is selected by the Conseil des Ministres. Because of the perceived importance of the posting, and given the sporadic bifurcation of the French executive during periods of *cohabitation*, the appointment of the EU ambassador can, on occasion, be a politicized process. Luc de la Barre de Nanteuil was recalled to Paris only thirteen months after commencing his second stint in the post, having openly criticized government policy. Given the forthcoming period of *cohabitation*, Mitterrand was keen to ensure that the PR be headed by a Socialist sympathizer (Lequesne 1993: 194). Such politicization stands in sharp contrast to other, outwardly similar, diplomatic postings. Hence, at around the same time, the post of French ambassador to NATO was bestowed on Gabriel Robin, an opponent of the Socialists and one who had previously published an acerbic criticism of Mitterrand's foreign policies (Robin 1985). Moreover, the political affiliation of the ambassador, and a perceived need to maintain political balance within the administration, has repercussions elsewhere in the system. The nomination of Jean Vidal—a Socialist—to the post of ambassador led to his replacement at the head of the European affairs section of the Foreign Ministry by Pascale Andréani, a former member of the *cabinet* (and hence a political supporter) of Jacques Chirac.

TABLE 2.1. *French permanent representatives, 1959–2001*

January 1958–November 1959	Eric de Carbonnel
November 1959–June 1961	Georges Gorse
June 1961–March 1972	Jean-Marc Boegner
March 1972–June 1975	Étienne Burin des Roziers
June 1975–January 1977	Jean-Marie Soutou
January 1977–December 1981	Luc de la Barre de Nanteuil
December 1981–November 1984	Jacques Leprette
November 1984–January1986	Luc de la Barre de Nanteuil
January 1986–September 1988	François Scheer
September 1988–June 1989	Philippe Louet
June 1989–May 1992	Jean Vidal
May 1992–November 1993	François Scheer
November 1993–November 1999	Pierre de Boissieu
November 1999–	Pierre Vimont

Immediately under the ambassador in the formal hierarchy of the PR is the representant permanent adjoint. This position is also much sought after by Foreign Ministry officials. Again, Paris has evinced a desire to have in post people with an intimate knowledge of EU affairs. Deputy permanent representatives have always spent time dealing with EU matters either in the Foreign Ministry or the PR itself prior to their appointment.

Until the mid-1960s, the PR was staffed exclusively with officials from the Foreign Ministry. This situation, however, proved unsustainable for long thereafter. Following the 'empty chair' crisis of the mid-1960s, and as a consequence of the increasingly technical nature of much of the work carried out in Council, the then permanent representative began the practice of introducing officials from other departments into the PR (Lequesne 1993: 187–8). Under the terms of a decree of 1 January 1979, all PR staff— including non-diplomatic staff—are placed under the authority of the ambassador. However, whilst in Brussels, their salaries are still paid by their home ministry, unlike in the Irish case where PR staff are seconded to, and paid by, the Foreign Ministry (Hayes-Renshaw *et al.* 1989: 127). A recent study suggested that 40 per cent of the non-administrative staff of the PR are career diplomats, the other 60 per cent being on secondment from other ministries (de Boisdeffre *et al.* 1996: 751). Length of tenure in the PR varies, but tends to exceed that of normal diplomatic postings (three years). Diplomats are posted to the PR for four years. The current *délégué* for agriculture has been in post for six.

Sectoral ministries who wish to send staff to the PR send their request to the Direction des Personnel in the Foreign Ministry, which then forwards it in a telegram to the ambassador. Foreign Ministry officials, therefore, have ultimate control over the composition of the Embassy.

Moreover, despite the influx of officials from line departments, diplomats may still handle sectoral issues. Lequesne (1993: 197) recounts that in 1992 regional policies, fisheries, and environmental affairs were all dealt with by Foreign Ministry officials. Diplomats still act as *conseiller* in the latter two sectors, though a representative of the Ministry of the Environment has been drafted in as *conseiller-adjoint*. However, regional policy is now handled by two *conseillers* from the Délégation à l'Aménagement du Territoire (DATAR), who work alongside a diplomat. Revealingly, though, the latter deals with the legal and financial aspects of regional policy.

Finally, the staff of the PR is increased during those periods when France holds the Presidency of the Council. One means through which this is accomplished is via increased reliance on *stagiaires* from ENA. There are normally two of these in place within the PR, on six-month postings. During Presidencies, this number is increased to four, who generally remain in Brussels for nine to twelve months. In addition, the ambassador can request extra staff at his discretion.

Organization

The organogram of the PR resembles a short, broad pyramid. At its pinnacle is the permanent representative with his deputy immediately below. Foreign Office officials are entrusted with the key tasks of Mertens and Antici Group representatives. Under the ambassador and his deputy are the numerous sectoral *conseillers* charged with representing France in Council committees and tracking dossiers in their particular area of expertise. Organizationally, these officials are grouped in several cross-sectoral sections.

Changes were carried out in the internal organization of the PR as a consequence of a decision taken in March 1999 by Prime Minster Jospin to confer responsibility for representing France in the K4 committee to the PR. A prefect and a *conseiller* from the Interior Ministry have joined the PR staff to deal with issues relating to this committee.

A further organizational innovation has stemmed from the increased interest manifested by the PR in promoting the interests of French business. In March 1989 a post of *attaché* for relations with business was created, under the authority of the commercial *conseiller*. Subsequently, an increasing awareness of the need to concentrate more resources in this area led to the creation of a Cellule Entreprises et Coopération (CEC) within the PR. This currently comprises fifteen staff, including six *attachés* and two officials with the rank of *conseiller*.

Internal Workings

Given the ever-increasing size of the PR and particularly the varied ministerial provenance of its staff, the need to ensure inter-sectoral coherence has become more pressing. Co-ordination within the permanent representation takes place in several ways. First, through the placing of officials from non-line ministries in posts explicitly designed to foster co-ordination. Many officials justified the occupation of the two senior posts by diplomats in terms of their ability, unlike representatives of line ministries, to achieve coherence between often conflicting sectoral interests (interviews, FRANREP, Quai d'Orsay; cf. also Lequesne 1993: 197). The cross-sectoral nature of COREPER provides a structural boost to the ability of the ambassador and his deputy to play such a role. The day before COREPER meetings, the ambassador chairs a formal meeting to discuss the agenda, which provides an opportunity to ensure the coherence of French positions.

The Antici and Mertens Group members are particularly prominent in the internal co-ordination process. Both have informal discussions with the *conseillers* dealing with issues on the COREPER agenda in order to identify and resolve inter-sectoral conflict. Both are also explicitly charged with co-

TABLE 2.2. *Permanent representation of France: internal organization, staff numbers, and ministry of origin, 2000*

Sector	Officials (conseillers)	Ministry of origin	Support staff (non-secretarial)
French Officials in EU Institutions	1	Foreign Affairs	0
Legal Affairs	1	Conseil d'Etat	0
Press, Information, and EP	3	Foreign Office (2)	4
JHA and Customs	6	Foreign Affairs, Interior, Justice, Finances	3
External Relations	5	Foreign Affairs (2), Engineer, DREE (2)	1
Agriculture*	3	Agriculture	1
Financial Affairs	1	Finances	6**
Commercial Questions	4	DREE	2
Internal Market, Consumer Affairs, Industry, Customs, Environment and Fisheries	6	Foreign Affairs (2), Conseil d'Etat, Industry, Engineer, Fisheries	3
Research, Nuclear Questions	3	Centre d'Études Atomiques	1
Education Culture	2	Foreign Affairs, Industry	1
Employment, Social Affairs, Health	2	Employment	1
Transport	1	Transport	1
Regional policy	3	Foreign Affairs, DATAR (2)	1

* Because of its special status, the agriculture section is headed by a delegate for agricultural affairs. Under him are two deputy delegates and an agricultural *attaché*. The three former officials are listed as *conseillers*, the latter mostly as support staff.
** All *attachés financiers* from the Ministry of Finance.

ordinating specific sectoral policies. The Antici Group representative is also explicitly charged with ensuring the co-ordination of positions on external relations.

One other official plays an explicit co-ordinating role. The *conseiller* for judicial affairs is the major source of expertise on EC legal affairs in the PR. He is, consequently, well placed to identify potential legal problems implied by legislative initiatives in one sector for others not directly involved in the negotiations.

For all the care taken to ensure coherence, officials in certain policy sectors enjoy significantly more autonomy than their counterparts. The sections dealing with Financial Affairs, Commercial Questions, Transport, Employment, Research, and Nuclear Questions are 'enclaves' populated entirely by officials from the relevant ministry. Autonomy is most marked in the case of Agriculture. This is a function of the structure of the EU system as much as of organizational features of the PR itself. As pointed out in the Introduction, agricultural questions are dealt with in the SCA and not in COREPER, an arrangement which bestows considerable autonomy upon the delegate for agricultural affairs—France's sole representative on this committee. Notwithstanding this, however, the delegate must still work closely with colleagues on cross-sectoral issues such as the annual EU budget, trade negotiations such as those in the context of the WTO, and Agenda 2000, which are dealt with in COREPER and can involve explicit trade-offs between agriculture and other sectors.

Role

Representation

The PR is responsible for ensuring that France is represented in meetings at all levels of the Council of Ministers system. At the apex of this system are the ministerial Councils ultimately responsible for approving or rejecting legislative proposals. Under the terms of a prime ministerial circular of 2 June 1986, the permanent representative or his deputy (depending on the sector) accompanies the relevant Minister to Council meetings, along with the relevant *conseiller* from the PR. The latter is responsible for producing a *compte rendu* of the meeting and sending this to Paris (Lequesne 1993: 34–5).

A circular from the Prime Minister of 22 September 1998 insisted that 'France must always be represented by a member of the government in sessions of the Council of Ministers'. However, attendance records of Ministers tend to vary both by sector and as a function of personality (interviews, FRANREP, UKREP, May 1999). When ministerial involvement is not possible, the permanent representative or his deputy acts as the French representative, although the legal position concerning their right to vote is somewhat unclear (Hayes Renshaw *et al.* 1989: 133–4). In 1994, the permanent representative attended ECOFIN five times as head of the French delegation. In contrast, the German Minister was always present (de Boisdeffre *et al.* 1996: 765).

As pointed out in the Introduction, the permanent representative and his deputy are responsible for representing France in COREPER II and COREPER I respectively. Beneath COREPER, the Council functions as a network of sectoral working groups. The PR is responsible for supplying representation for France at all levels, except during French Presidencies, when PR officials hold the chair and officials from Paris carry out the representative function. The proliferation of committees means that it is impossible for the limited staff of the PR alone to ensure adequate representation for France. Hence representation is on occasion provided by Paris-based officials. However, PR staff ensure French representation on the majority of Council committees, sometimes in tandem with a home-based official. The *compte rendu* of such meetings is always sent from the PR, and normally signed by a member of its staff. On those rare occasions when representation is ensured by a Paris-based official, he or she will return to the PR to send the *compte rendu*.

Finally, the PR ensures French representation on the Council–EP conciliation committees introduced under the co-decision procedure at Maastricht. Generally, it is the deputy permanent representative who attends these meetings, though during periods when France holds the Council Presidency, Paris is represented by the relevant Minister.

Informing Paris

The PR also acts as the 'eyes and ears' of the French administration in Brussels. It updates Paris about ongoing negotiations and the positions of other member states on dossiers under discussion. This information is generally contained in the *compte rendu*, although it is also conveyed in phone calls, faxes, e-mails, and via the participation of PR officials in co-ordination meetings in Paris. The permanent representation can also provide useful information to Paris concerning possible breaches of interministerial discipline by individual ministries seeking to pursue their own agendas in Brussels (interviews, FRANREP, 1999).

The Antici member is a particularly valuable source of information. Sectoral *conseillers* turn to him for advice on the positions of other member states. A round of last-minute communications with national capitals usually follows Antici meetings to appraise Paris-based officials of these negotiating stances (Spence 1995: 371). As the Anticis are also briefed by the Commission's Secretary General on College meetings, they are an important source of information on forthcoming Commission initiatives (Spence 1995: 371). Indeed, one of the tasks of the PR is to maintain links with officials within the Commission in order better to be able to anticipate Commission initiatives. Such contacts are particularly close with the *cabinets* of French Commissioners which have, on occasion, provided information about important developments within the Commission prior to them being discussed in the College (interview, European Commission, May 1999).

The PR also acts an information resource for private interests. The CEC in particular maintains links with French businesses with an interest in Commission programmes in third countries. This it carries out via meetings at the PR with representatives of firms, the drafting of *notes de synthèse* on these programmes, and participation by its members in training and information seminars organized by French companies (Representation Permanente de la France Auprès de l'Union Européenne 1999). Cellule members, along with the relevant PR *conseiller* or Paris-based official, attend the Commission management committees that hammer out the fine print of such projects and transmit any information they glean from these to businesses with an interest in bidding for contracts. Firms pay around FF3000 per year, for which they receive: timely information and documents about planned projects; the right to participate in an annual meeting; a brochure produced by the CEC ('Fenêtre sur l'Europe'); and the opportunity to attend seminars run by Cellule staff. In 1998 CEC staff visited ninety French companies, had 250 annual subscribers, ran forty seminars and produced twenty *notes de synthèse* of around 100 pages each. Additionally, the PR undertakes to inform French firms interested in sending employees to work in the EU administration on secondment of forthcoming vacancies (interviews, FRANREP, May and December 1999).

Finally, the press and information service of the PR plays an increasingly important role in providing details about French positions on EU matters. There are some 900 accredited journalists in the EU institutions. The three members of the press and information section of the PR have a heavy workload, involving the need to arrange briefings and press conferences, provide information to those seeking it, and arrange trips for visitors to the Embassy. Again, this workload increases markedly during French Presidencies.

Policy-Making

In its capacity as negotiator and informant, the PR inevitably maintains close contact with Paris, particularly since the introduction of a video-conferencing facility during the French Presidency of 1995. Such contacts precede the issuance of instructions to the PR by the SGCI, and provide PR officials with a role in the formulation of these instructions. As one PR official put it, 'I have been surprised, since my arrival [in Brussels], by the degree to which our work involves formulating policy with Paris as opposed to simply executing policies formulated in Paris' (interview, May 1999).

The permanent representative has always played a role in policy formulation. He travels once a month to the Quai d'Orsay to attend a preparatory meeting for the General Affairs Council. He also participates at the Élysée in preparatory meetings for European Councils. In addition, his staff participate in the formulation of day-to-day policies. They are in frequent telephone contact with Paris and are routinely consulted by Paris-based officials concerning the feasibility of potential negotiating positions, given the attitudes of other member states. During the process of policy formulation, *conseillers* in the PR may discover that the instructions being drafted are not to their liking. Consequently they may intervene personally by phone, or even ask the ambassador to do so on their behalf. Thus an astute *conseiller* can ensure that he or she 'gets the instructions they want' by earning the trust of the relevant *chef de secteur* within the SGCI and suggesting amendments to proposed instructions in such a way as to reflect their own preferences (interview, Paris, 1999).

France in the EU Institutions

The Commission

The 'Union's bureaucratic system is shot through with national officials and influences' (Wright 1997: 161). Consequently, efforts by national administrations to influence developments within the EU are not limited to the Council of Ministers alone. France's attempts to place its nationals within the Commission date back to initiatives taken in the early years of the EC which met with a hostile response from the then Commission President Walter Hallstein (Lequesne 1993: 187). Subsequently, successive French administrations have placed a high premium on maintaining French influence within the higher ranks of the Commission machine. Like its partners, France not only takes care in choosing its Commissioners, but also lobbies hard for them to be appointed to positions of particular influence. Close contact is also maintained with the *cabinets* of French Commissioners, and is facilitated by the fact that a majority of *cabinet* members—particularly *chefs de cabinets*—have tended to be senior officials from the French administration. Pascal Lamy, *chef de cabinet* of Jacques Delors from January 1995, was, between May 1981 and April 1983, *directeur adjoint* of his *cabinet* in Paris, before going on to perform the same function for Prime Minster, Pierre Mauroy (Lequesne 1993: 34). This situation has changed markedly under the Presidency of Romano Prodi. Pascal

Lamy's *chef de cabinet* is a Belgian and his *adjoint* British, whilst the *chef de cabinet adjoint* in Michel Barnier's *cabinet* is Dutch.

Paris pursues a twin-track strategy to maximize the potential benefits to be gained from the presence of French administrators within the EU system. This is intended both to secure the strategic placement of such officials and help maintain contact with them once in post. The PR tracks upcoming vacancies in senior administrative positions—at A1, A2, and A3 level—in order that Paris is informed in good time. The SGCI in Paris also plays a role in considering a broad range of potential candidates for such posts. Final decisions concerning senior appointments are made in Paris, often at the political level.

For candidates at the bottom of the career ladder, there is no French equivalent of the British fast stream to promote the entrance of officials into the Commission via the *concours*. However, the administration is taking steps to encourage officials to take the examination. In particular, officials who have spent time on secondment to the EU institutions are encouraged to sit the *concours*. This is in part a reaction to the changing nature of the examination, in that the last open examination clearly favoured those with experience of working in the Commission (interviews, European Commission, Brussels, 1999).

Once successful candidates are in place, efforts are made to foster amicable relations between them and the national administration. The SGCI has recently provided placements for successful *concours* candidates awaiting job openings within the Commission. During the course of 1996, two such aspirant Eurocrats worked within the SGCI, whilst officials within the organization tried to ensure good postings for them within the Commission. The logic of this is clear: officials who have worked for and formed contacts within the French administrative system are more likely to be well disposed towards it once in Brussels.

The PR also plays a role in maintaining contacts with French nationals who have embarked on a career within the Commission. For the last four years an official has been charged solely with this task. Along with the SGCI, she (sic) monitors their careers, on occasion prompting interventions by the national administration to secure promotions for them. One senior member of the French PR intimated that this is almost expected of them: 'when a French official in the Commission fails to get a job or a promotion, he does not say that the Commissioner concerned is a *salaud*, but rather declares that the staff of the Permanent Representation are *nul*' (interview, FRANREP, May 1999; cf. also Lequesne 1993: 203). The PR has also recently launched a newsletter targeted at French officials in the EU institutions. The intention is explicitly to 'let them know we [the PR] are here', and to try to create a more stable and reliable French network (interviews, FRANREP, Brussels, 1999).

Whilst being increasingly aware of the need to cultivate permanent French officials in the Commission, Paris has also come to recognize the potential importance of short-term secondees, or *experts nationaux détachés* (ENDs), in furthering French influence. This represents something of throwback to French attitudes in the 1950s and 1960s, when Paris made the case for the Commission to be staffed solely by secondees, as a way of undermining the notion of a European public service (Cini 1996: 121). Until relatively recently, prospective French ENDs relied solely on personal contacts with the relevant DG to secure a placement. Since the mid-1990s, both the PR and the SGCI have played far more proactive role in this process. Both have made a conscious effort to identify those areas of the Commission where France finds itself under-represented. The PR official responsible for links with French EC officials tries to ascertain whether individual ministries are satisfied that France is adequately represented in their sectors. Once lacunae are identified, attempts are made to send French candidates to the relevant unit on secondment. It has even been known for this to occur in anticipation of a significant policy initiative over which France is keen to wield influence. On occasion the PR acts on 'tip-offs' about forthcoming vacancies from *cabinets* of French Commissioners.

All those appointed to short-term contracts in the Commission are invited to the SGCI for a briefing by the *secrétaire-général adjoint*. They are given advice on practical matters such as finding housing in Brussels, and are introduced to the staff working in their sector. Once in Brussels, their point of contact with the administration is the official in the PR charged with maintaining links with French nationals. As they come to the end of their stay in Brussels, secondees are again contacted by the SGCI, which provides assistance in their search for postings back in Paris. SGCI staff sometimes contact individual *Directions* within ministries to press the case of candidates. In this way, an effort is made not only to gain influence via French officials within the Commission, but also to make use of the expertise they gain whilst there. In order to facilitate the best use of this expertise, the SGCI has circulated an *annuaire* of present and former ENDs amongst all ministries.

French attitudes towards the Brussels bureaucracy are profoundly schizophrenic. On the one hand, the tradition of the impartial *fonctionnaire* acting in the public interest, so well entrenched at least in the minds of the French administration, engenders a (grudging) respect for the independence of the Commission. On the other, a growing awareness of the importance of the Commission has spawned a desire to exert influence within it. Consequently, policies can appear paradoxical. Strategies exist (in at least nascent form) to ensure the recruitment of adequate numbers of French officials into the Commission, and France fights as hard, if not harder, than most of its partners to make sure these people are placed in strategically important positions. On the other, staffs in both the PR and the SGCI reject the idea of producing a formal list of French officials within the Commission on the grounds that to do so would be to undermine the formal autonomy of the Commission from the member states. French policy self-consciously stops short of the organization of the kind of explicit *filière nationale* which officials routinely accuse the British of having created (interviews, European Commission, FRANREP, May 1999).

The European Parliament

As the brevity of this section implies, the national administration has not made major efforts to develop and maintain links with French MEPs. Yet as the influence of the Parliament within the EC decision-making process has increased, so Paris has also attempted to improve links with French European parliamentarians. Prior to the SEA, the SGCI sent out 'Notes d'Information' to French MEPs via the European Affairs Ministry, which spelt out the government position on major EC legislative initiatives. Following the SEA, the relevant *conseiller* from the PR has routinely attended EP meetings, sometimes accompanied by a member of the SGCI and of the *cabinet* of the Minister of European Affairs, in an attempt to increase direct contact with French MEPs (Lequesne 1993: 119–21). In addition, the European Affairs Minister meets a delegation of French MEPs representing the various French groups in the EP every month. The Maastricht Treaty increased the prerogatives of the EP still further. Subsequently, *fiches* outlining French positions in the Council of Ministers are now routinely sent to French MEPs. A prime ministerial circular of 21 March 1994 made provision for the appointment of delegates for relations with the EP in all ministries, co-ordinated by the relevant official in the SGCI.

On those occasions when the European Parliament discusses issues of major significance, such as occurred recently with the debate over the possible censure of the Santer Commission, French political leaders may become directly involved in attempts to lobby French MEPs. Jospin and other members of the Socialist Party hierarchy are said to have lobbied leading members of the French left in Strasbourg, in an attempt to persuade them to vote against censure; Chirac and his entourage did much the same thing on the right (interviews, Paris and Brussels 1999).

Critical Evaluation

Capacity to Implement Ambitions

As the European Union has developed, so the French administration in Brussels has been reorganized and reinforced to deal with the increasing burdens placed upon it by the need to manage integration. The growth of the permanent representation bears eloquent testimony to the strains being put upon national representations by an ever-expanding workload. The creation of the CEC indicates the recognition of the need for adaptation and has increased the capacity of the PR to deal with and assist French private interests, marking an improvement over the days when their access to the PR was severely limited (Lequesne 1993: 210; Schmidt 1996: 234). One wonders, however, whether the focus of the Cellule on Commission programmes designed to help third countries (a task performed in the British case by DFID in London) is optimal, given the obvious gains to be made from fostering partnerships with private interests over all aspects of EU policy-making.

In addition, reformed structures have provided an increased capacity to ensure an effective French 'presence' in the supranational institutions, though there is reason to wonder whether one official in the PR is sufficient for this task (interviews, Franrep, May 1999). Whilst contacts between the national administration—in both Paris and Brussels—with MEPs have increased, the latter contrast their relations with the French administration unfavourably with those enjoyed by MEPs from other member states with their home administrations (de Boisdeffre *et al.* 1996: 764). Germany, Spain, Italy, and Britain, claims one member of a French Commissioner's *cabinet*, are 'mille fois plus organisés' when it comes to having links with and influence over MEPs (interview, European Commission, May 1999).

The increasing density and scope of EU business poses severe challenges for the capacity of the French system to cope effectively with the perceived need to present co-ordinated, coherent positions in the Council. One solution has been to resort to the palliative of allowing France to be represented in committees by Paris-based officials. Yet this raises the danger of individual ministries sending representatives Brussels to negotiate on the basis of sectoral preferences, thereby undermining the co-ordination system, with possibly negative consequences in terms of the coherence of France's negotiating positions (see Clamen 1996: 80).

The alternative to the increasing involvement of Paris-based officials is to increase the capacity of the PR to deal with an increasing workload. Interview-based evidence suggests that PR officials are generally successful in presenting coherent, co-ordinated positions, although some complaints were voiced (by diplomats) about sectoral staff in the PR who considered themselves as 'l'Ambassadeur de son Ministère' (interviews, Quai d'Orsay, SGCI, Ministry of Finance, Paris, FRANREP, UKREP, Brussels). Lequesne argues that PR staff are generally 'less tempted than their colleagues from [Paris] to adopt sectorally biased positions'. Indeed, PR officials can on occasion even reverse the positions adopted in the Council of Ministers by Paris-based colleagues, by 'sorting things out' with the Presidency after the formal meeting (Lequesne 1993: 212–13).

However, numerous interviewees, among them the then ambassador himself, argued that expanding the size of the PR to deal with an expanded workload would increase the danger of the development of specialized *filières*, prone to pursue their own sectoral interests. Certainly, such *filières* have always existed in sectors such as agriculture or finance where powerful ministries with a long history of involvement in Community affairs enjoy significant autonomy. Increasing the size of contingents from other ministries, however, raises the spectre of this spreading to other sectors. Indeed, some have argued that reducing the workload of PR officials might itself reduce their commitment to working interministerially. One diplomat interviewed by Lequesne argued that the relative efficiency with which the PR staff observed the need for co-ordination was due in part to the very fact that they tend to be overworked:

the permanent representation is one of the only diplomatic postings where one does not hesitate to share *dossiers* out between colleagues, because there is work to be done and sometimes too much. Whilst in a bilateral embassy, there is effectively a race to see who can get hold of a *dossier*, which leads to problems. (Cited in Lequesne 1993: 198)

A similar tension between dealing efficiently with the EU and the capacity effectively to co-ordinate national positions exists in relation to French links with the Commission. On the one hand, the greater the scope and density of such links, the greater the probable ability of a national administration to maintain close contact with officials and consequently to influence Commission decisions and anticipate its actions. On the other, to allow sectoral ministries to carry out their own 'diplomacy' in dealing individually with the Commission is to risk them using this strategy as a means of advancing their own sectoral interests at the expense of others. The French reaction has been to emphasize the need for coherence. A prime ministerial circular of 21 March 1994 stated that correspondence with Commission should be 'carried out by our Permanent Representation on the basis of instructions from the SGCI'. In practice, of course, this has proved impossible to implement. The increasing impact of the Community on domestic politics, and the ease of telephone and fax contact mean that communications between the French administration and the Commission simply cannot be controlled and centralized in this way. Such prime ministerial commandments, however, hardly serve to facilitate the development of effective links between Paris and the Commission.

The capacity of the French administration in Brussels to achieve its objectives is also crucially contingent on a number of factors often largely outside their control. For one thing, the efficiency with which the PR operates—both internally and in its representative function—is linked to the personality of the incumbents of the senior posts, and of the ambassador in particular. Ambassador Pierre de Boissieu was a talented and highly respected figure, known to have direct links with the Matignon and the Élysée (interviews, Brussels, Paris, 1997, 1999). Because of his experience, reputation, and political flair, he was able on occasion to take liberties with instructions from Paris as well as enjoying the authority to run a relatively cohesive PR.

It is difficult to distinguish contingency based on personality from that associated with politics. The capacity of the PR to function effectively can be seriously affected by political circumstances. Thus, if one of the indicators of adequate PR capacity is its ability to run an effective and efficient Presidency, the largely nondescript French Presidency of 1995 illustrates the degree to which *cohabitation* undermines this. Even the ability of the PR to cope with routine policy is hampered in periods of *cohabitation*. Ambassador Scheer, appointed, as noted above, with a view to the forthcoming period of *cohabitation*, suffered as a result of this. He and SGCI secretary general, Elizabeth Guigou, were regularly not informed of informal interministerial meetings held to co-ordinate EU policy, as both were clearly identified as political allies of the President (Guyomarch *et al.* 1998: 52). Similarly, Edouard Balladur, finance minister between 1986 and 1988, was more prone to listen to the advice of his *directeur de cabinet* and *chargé de mission* than to Scheer in the Council of Ministers (Lequesne 1993: 218).

Political factors—structural and otherwise—also limit the capacity of the administration to exercise any leverage over French MEPs. The relative lack of discipline within parties and the presence in the EP of several prominent, high-profile, and independently minded French MEPs meant that Chirac and Jospin were unable effectively to enforce loyalty on French MEPs in the Santer censure vote. Moreover, the French contingent in the EP contains several parties opposed to both the administration of the day and to its policies towards the EU. Indeed, one senior Paris-based official claimed wryly that 'the most effective way to get our MEPs do what we want would be to tell them that we want the opposite' (interview, SGCI, Paris, 1999).

A third area of contingency concerns the EU system itself. Certain modes of decision-making employed within the Council prevent the PR from performing its representative role. In matters pertaining to the CFSP, the ability of the PR to assure effective representation for France is limited because of the role of the Political Committee, staffed by political directors from Paris. Political Committee meetings can lead to problems when decisions have interministerial implications and COREPER is not effectively informed prior to meetings of the General Affairs Council. Several declarations on Kosovo raised the hackles of the Finance Ministry in particular (interviews, FRANREP, Brussels, Quai d'Orsay, SGCI, Paris). Often it is left to the Direction de la Coopération Européenne in the Quai d'Orsay to spot problems in the material contained in the Coreu telegrams which detail CFSP discussions.

Moreover, changes in the rules governing the operation of the Community bureaucracy impact on the effectiveness of national strategies. Thus the *para-*

chutage of Paris-based officials into senior administrative positions is becoming more and more difficult as a consequence of the increased priority being accorded to internal promotion. Moreover, the original six member states are struggling to gain appointments at all, as priority is been given to filling vacancies with candidates from the new entrants (interview, Quai d'Orsay, Paris, FRANREP, Brussels, May 1999).

Finally the capacity of the French administration in Brussels is also highly contingent on the effective working of other parts of the French co-ordinating system. However talented the staff in Brussels, they cannot effectively represent France if they receive no instructions from Paris (which occurs on occasion, though not as often as in the German and Italian cases) or if the instructions they do receive are unhelpful. PR staff commented that instructions sometimes take the form simply of a list of the positions of different ministries, rather than a clear statement of French priorities for the forthcoming negotiations (interviews, FRANREP, Brussels, 1999). A report commissioned in 1993 by the then secretary general of the SGCI, Yves Thibault de Silguy, criticized the instructions sent to the PR for being too concerned with technical details and not sufficiently focused on the overall aims and objectives of French policy. Moreover, instructions also do not always systematically underline the *points durs* of French negotiating positions and those for which there is a margin of manœuvre, (de Richemont *et al.* 1994). In all these cases, French negotiators find their ability effectively to defend French positions and to arrive at compromises with their partners restricted.

Second, given the increased prevalence of resort to Qualified Majority Voting in the Council of Ministers, it no longer suffices for member states to ensure the presence in the Council of talented officials with clear instructions. Alliance-building has become a central element of Council negotiations. Certainly, the PR staff can form partnerships on particular dossiers when the opportunity presents itself, but alliances generally need to be negotiated in advance from Paris on the basis of a thorough discussion of objectives with the partner state concerned. Senior officials pointed to the lack of foresight shown by Paris over important dossiers such as Agenda 2000, where political leaders failed to anticipate the need for effective alliance-building as part of a strategy of achieving specific objectives (interviews, FRANREP, European Commission, Brussels, 1999). The necessity of possessing detailed and accurate information on the preferences of partner states also requires the involvement of bilateral embassies in the process of EU negotiations. This, however, is a channel that was seriously underused by the French administration (de Boisdeffre *et al.* 1996: 765). A former official in the French London Embassy made the point that the UK performs the task of collecting information on its partners' preferences far more effectively than does France (Carnelutti 1992: 479). Nowadays, however, there is a *conseiller* in all fifteen bilateral embassies charged with sending information on developments in other member states directly to the PR.

Against this, it should be noted that the so-called Franco-German axis has provided Paris with the support not only of a large member state, but also one which has shown itself on occasion willing to sacrifice its own apparent interests when French interests have been threatened (Menon 1996). For example, during negotiations in 1999 over the future of the CAP, French annoyance at proposed reforms led Germany to back away from its original position in favour of greater liberalization (*Financial Times*, 10 March 1999). Given the existence of this partnership, it is perhaps understandable that Paris has been slow to improve its relations with, and information about, other member states.

Effectiveness

Evidently, it is difficult accurately to assess the effectiveness of administrative structures. The task is made all the more complex by the fact that: 'the effectiveness of a country's domestic EU co-ordinating capacity must be judged according to the issue, the policy type, the policy requirements and the policy objectives. Merely to examine the machinery of co-ordination is to confuse the means and the outcomes' (Wright 1997: 165).

French objectives have fluctuated over time, altering policy requirements and the relative importance accorded to different issues and policy types. For many years, France's political leaders assumed that exercising leadership in the EC entailed an ability to influence set-piece interstate bargaining rather than perfecting techniques of alliance- and consensus-building in routine negotiations with the Commission or in the Council of Ministers. France's domestic co-ordination system, centring round the SGCI for routine matters and the Presidency and Foreign Ministry for intergovernmental negotiations, reflected these priorities, and the belief that these elements of EU policy-making could be easily and neatly separated (Menon 2000).

For many years, French policies allowed it successfully to shape—along with Germany—the nature of European integration (Menon 1996). In the wake of the Single Market programme, however, a qualitative shift altered the nature of European integration and the ability of member states to shape developments within it. An increased reliance on QMV implied the need to build alliances within the Council in order to secure desirable outcomes in the Council. Moreover, the SEA conferred new and significant powers on both the Commission and the Parliament, with the former in particular exhibiting a new dynamism in its willingness to police the single market in areas such as competition policy. Perhaps most importantly, the Single Market heralded an increase in the stakes involved for member states in the integration process.

EC legislation now touched on issues at the heart of national socio-economic management. As a consequence, the member states, along with increasing numbers of private actors, came to focus their attention on the need to shape legislation emanating from Brussels.

The traditional French approach to managing integration was increasingly ill-adapted to the EC of the late 1980s and early 1990s. Academic assessments of the effectiveness of French EU policy contrasted relative success in shaping history-making decisions with a more limited ability to influence routine policy-making. They pointed to the difficulties experienced by Paris in effective alliance-building in the Council of Ministers (Lequesne 1993: 29), its failure to concentrate enough resources on building up a presence within the EC bureaucracy or to understand its culture (Lamy 1991: 70), and its inability to work effectively in tandem with French private interests (Schmidt 1996: 230–4; De Richemont *et al.* n.d.).

A detailed assessment of the French administration in Brussels in the 1990s provides a more nuanced picture. Comments from both French officials and their counterparts in other member states stress the relative efficacy of the French EU policy-co-ordination system as a whole (interviews, FRANREP, UKREP, German representation to the EU, European Commission, Brussels, July 1997, May 1999). The permanent representation succeeds in keeping Paris informed of developments in ongoing negotiations in Brussels, using its networks in the other institutions to keep abreast of these. Within the PR, sectoral conflict and the development of sectoral fiefdoms have, for the moment at least, been avoided. Paris-based officials expressed the sentiment that the instructions sent to Brussels are general faithfully adhered to and that the PR provides effective representation for the country (interviews, Paris and Brussels, 1997 and 1999, though for a contrasting view, see Hayes-Renshaw *et al.* 1989: 128). In representing France in the Council, the fact that PR officials participate in policy co-ordination is functional in that it ensures that Brussels-based officials are relatively happy with the instructions they receive.

However, two criticisms can be levelled at the PR. First, its officials are prone to delay sending a *compte rendu* of meetings to Paris. Whilst telegrams are always sent from UKREP on the evening of the meetings, in the French case, this process can take as long as three days. One official in Paris sardonically commented that: 'on est souvent mieux informé en lisant Agence Europe qu'en attendant le télégram' (interviews, FRANREP 1999). Such delays matter in that they can hamper attempts to adjust French positions in line with the shifting nature of ongoing negotiating in Brussels.[3] The style of telegrams has also been a target of criticism, not least the flowery, verb-intensive style which

---

[3] During periods when France holds Presidency, however, telegrams are sent the same evening (Lequesne 1993: 223).

line ministries officials attribute to the Quai d'Orsay. In 1993, Foreign Minister Alain Juppé initiated a series of reforms intended to address this problem by insisting on shorter telegrams, including both a brief résumé and a commentary on the major issues of interest. Foreign Minster Hubert Vedrine is currently building on these reforms, encouraging all French embassies to send shorter and more factual telegrams. A direct intranet link has also been set up between the PR and the Foreign Ministry, which, along with frequent fax and telephone communication, means that Paris can at least be provided with a summary of events in Council meetings.

Second, since the early 1990s, the ambassador has ceased to travel to Paris for the Friday morning meetings at which French negotiating positions on important issues were discussed, limiting his attendance to the monthly meetings preparing the General Affairs Council. Some have argued that this reduces the ambassador's grasp not only of the details of a dossier, but also of the state of interministerial disputes, and hence of his possible margin for manœuvre in the Council (de Boisdeffre *et al.* 1996: 778; Menon and Wright 1999). It is easy to see the logic of such criticisms, though harder to assess their validity. PR staff were unanimous in affirming that links with Paris by telephone, fax, and video-conference link were so regular that a weekly trip by the ambassador to Paris was unnecessary (interviews, FRANREP). Against this, however, should be weighed two facts. First, that the *délégué* for agricultural policy—perhaps the sector with the most effective co-ordination procedures—returns to Paris every week to discuss forthcoming SCA meetings. This inevitably raises the question as to why procedures felt to be effective in this highly successful sector are believed not to be generally more appropriate. Second, one of the failings of the French system is the relative lack of strategic planning concerning aims and objectives in substantive as opposed to institutional policy matters, as clearly revealed by discussion in the Council of Ministers over Agenda 2000 (interviews, UKREP, European Commission, FRANREP, Brussels, May 1999). A number of Paris-based officials argued that the presence of the permanent representative at regular, perhaps weekly, meetings would enhance this capacity for strategic leadership, with beneficial results for French EU policy as a whole (interviews Paris 1999).

That the PR generally performs particularly its representative function relatively efficiently is perhaps not surprising, given its role in the kind of intergovernmental negotiating with which France has long felt comfortable. Reforms to other aspects of the French administration also seem to have produced beneficial results in terms of effectiveness. A case in point is the increased attention paid to influencing the Commission from within. Again it is hard to measure the effectiveness of initiatives undertaken in this sphere, though there is evidence of particular instances when having the right people in the right places has been of direct benefit (Spence 1997: 85–6). However, the crude assumption prevalent in the literature, that Commission officials are motivated largely by a desire to increase the power of that organization, is misleading (cf. Hix 1999: 52–3; Menon 2000). This is not to say that they act simply as representatives of their home state. However, ties of nationality are an important factor conditioning the behaviour of officials in Brussels. Added to that, the shared cultural background of many of the French posted in Brussels reinforces such feelings of solidarity and the ability of such officials— notably in the PR and the Commission—to work together closely (interviews, FRANREP, European Commission, Brussels). In some cases, shared beliefs mean that there is no need for Paris to exert direct influence. Delors did not have to be instructed by Paris to pursue the ambition of a social market. Similarly, France's partners were not enamoured by the suggestion that a French Commissioner hold the competition policy portfolio in the Prodi Commission. Having nationals in key positions does not always necessarily imply the triumph of national policy preferences.[4] However, it can undoubtedly help. 'Surely', one French *cabinet* member observed, 'it can be no coincidence that a Frenchman has been Director General of DG6 [Agriculture] since 1958 and that this is a policy area that has served France so well?' (interview, Brussels 1999).

Whilst the administration has adapted its structures and procedures, however, this has not been accompanied by a concomitant shift in the attitudes of French officials. Several areas serve as illustrations of this. French officials have traditionally been wary of forging excessively close relations with private interests. Consequently, and in stark contrast to the attitude of officials in the British permanent representation (interviews, Brussels, 1997, 1999), FranRep staff display a degree of ambivalence about their relationship with French interest groups. As one member of the PR stated, 'nous ne sommes pas là exclusivement pour prendre en compte l'intérêt des grandes entreprises. Ici on represente la France.' Such an approach hardly serves to enhance the effectiveness with which the administration manages either to defend French private interests, or to work in tandem with these to achieve outcomes congruent with the interests of both in the Council of Ministers. It is also illuminating to note that French companies have to pay for the services of the Cellule.

The 'stickiness' of traditional attitudes is most marked when it comes to French relations with the supranational institutions. Certainly, the Commission's 1991 ruling in the *de Havilland* case provided food for thought for an administration which had previously 'tended to view [the institution] as . . . a vehicle through which it would obtain a perfunctory legal blessing for

---

[4] During the recent Agenda 2000 negotiations, Guy Legras, long-time (French) director general of DG VI proposed agricultural reforms that were in fact opposed by Paris. Yet many of France's partners simply assumed, until explicitly told otherwise, that the positions adopted by Legras were those of Paris (interviews, European Commission, May 1999).

the ... ventures in which it was engaged' (Jones 1996: 92). Similarly, the incremental increases in the power of the EP brought about by the SEA, Maastricht, and Amsterdam alerted officials to its increasing influence within the EU policy process. Yet habits persist. Senior French officials within the Commission speak of a *méconnaissance dramatique* in France concerning the role of the Commission. Similarly, a PR official spoke of France having, at least until recently, a 'niveau de connaissance presque basic du fonctionnement des institutions' (interviews, European Commission, FRANREP, Brussels). A tradition of ignoring the Commission, and of not taking parliaments—wherever they are based—too seriously, still hampers the effectiveness with which the administration manages to exert influence over the European institutions.

Moreover, when dealing with the Commission, France has traditionally tended to concentrate resources on maintaining links primarily with senior officials. Partly this is the result of domestic tradition—middle and lower ranking officials in Paris are used to seeing their initiatives countermanded by more senior political appointees. Partly, too, it reflects experience of the Delors Commission, where contacts between the Commission President and political leaders in Paris proved highly effective in shaping the EU agenda (Menon 1996: 236). Such an attitude, whatever its provenance, can prove counter-productive. As one senior businessman commented, the 'French think that a phone call to Jacques Delors can solve everything. They're wrong' (cited in *L'Expansion*, 3–19 Sept. 1992). For one thing, Delors is no longer there. Moreover, a focus on the upper echelons of the Commission limits French effectiveness in influencing the crucial drafting phases of legislative proposals. As one senior French Commission official put it, 'Les gens qui comptent sont ceux qui font les notes' (interview, European Commission, Brussels, May 1999; see also Schmidt 1996: 237). The tendency to deal directly with the Commission only once issues have become politicized, rather than to attempt effective upstream lobbying, can hamper attempts to shape legislative outcomes.

Moreover, concentration on appointments to senior positions has led to a concomitant failure to ensure that adequate numbers of French officials enter the administration at lower levels. Certainly things have changed since the time of de Gaulle when overt hostility towards the Commission was reflected in staffing policy.[5] Yet evidence exists that Paris still fails to treat the lower levels of the Commission seriously. A 1991 report pointed to a relative lack of French officials in the Commission overall: of 9,336 Commission officials in

---

[5] According to one story, Foreign Minister Couve de Murville, acting on instructions from the General, told his Directeur de Cabinet to ensure that there were 300 French officials in the Commission. When the latter protested that there were not enough good officials to go round, the reply came back, 'Alors, choisissez les plus cons'.

1988, only 975—or about 10 per cent—were French. Strikingly, however, the figure for Grade A officials was some 17 per cent (de Clausade 1991: 58, 60). Moreover, to the extent that any trends can be discerned from the figures regarding entrants to the Brussels administration, these show a marked preference for traditional 'French' specialties such as audio-visual and cultural policy (de Boisdeffre *et al.* 1996: 772). Such entrants do little to redress what officials see as the chronic under-representation of France in other sectors (interviews, FRANREP, European Commission, Brussels and SGCI, Paris, May 1999).

Finally, traditional suspicions of the European bureaucracy continue to shape relations between French officials and their Commission counterparts. Interviews with junior French officials in the Commission revealed a strong sense that they were simply not taken seriously by their predominantly ENA-educated counterparts in Paris; 'there seems to be a feeling', noted one, 'that French people enter the Commission because they failed to get into ENA' (interviews, European Commission, Brussels, July 1997, May 1999). The relative lack of ENA-trained applicants for the *concours* does little to improve this situation (Schmidt 1996: 231–2; de la Guérivière 1992). As a consequence of the disdain they suspect is felt towards them, junior French Commission officials are prone to 'couper les ponts' (interview, SGCI, 1999) with Paris: hardly a recipe for increasing French influence over that institution.

A further symptom of this mutual distrust is provided by the experience of those with experience of the Brussels bureaucracy who seek to return to the French administration. A recent report on the career path of former ENDs within the national administration found that the Direction Générale de l'Armament has the most effective structures for reintegrating former ENDs into the Ministry—hardly a testament to the effectiveness of those ministries which deal far more frequently with European affairs. Only a quarter of those returning to Paris were placed in positions requiring a detailed knowledge of EU affairs, while only half of them were promoted (Delpeuch 1999).

Conclusions

Paris has devised an administrative system in Brussels that functions reasonably well given the policy objectives that France has traditionally pursued and continues to pursue. Since the early 1990s, that system has been reformed in order to cope with the changing requirements imposed by the EC system. Major problems, such as a lack of interaction with private interests and under-representation in the lower reaches of the EU bureaucracy, have been directly addressed, if not with a uniformly high level of success. Paradoxically, the relatively slow pace of such reforms is partly linked to France's very successes over the years in shaping European integration. As one ENA report puts it, 'France, a founding member [of the EC] has for a long time been in the habit of making the majority of its opinions triumph' (de Boisdeffre *et al.* 1996: 764). France played the integration game very well and very successfully for many years. Consequently, it is perhaps no surprise that they have been relatively slow to adapt, preferring on occasion to rest on their laurels rather than respond to shifting conditions.

The relative success with which France manages to co-ordinate its administration in Brussels is perhaps all the more striking given the nature of the French administrative system which itself can undermine the efficacy of EU policy-making. Unlike the British system (see Menon and Wright 1999), the French administration is not based upon trust and habits of information-sharing. Divided between competing *grands corps*, which themselves on occasion serve merely to intensify interministerial rivalries, it has a culture of treating information as an 'instrument of power' (interview, Ministry of Finances, 1997). Such suspicions and rivalries hamper the ability of the French administration in Brussels to go about its tasks. One PR official commented that 'Paris n'aime pas la RP, le SGCI encore moins' (interview, FRANREP, Brussels, 1999). Similarly, tensions between the predominantly ENA-educated national civil service and their counterparts in the Commission have been alluded to above. Moreover, the absence of a culture of information-sharing can undermine co-ordination whilst also helping to account, in the minds of some, for the slowness with which the PR transmits its telegrams to Paris.

Recent developments within the EU have provoked a reassessment of the nature of the EU within France. No longer is European integration seen solely, or even primarily, as a project driven by interstate bargains, often negotiated at the level of head of state or government. The case of Justice and Home Affairs, where communitarianization has led to a role for the PR and a 'banalisation' of what was previously seen as core function of the 'État Régalien' is indicative of such evolutions. Administrative responses have focused on the need to cope more effectively with a system characterized in more and more sectors by bureaucratic interaction, routine policy-making, and the involvement of the supranational institutions.

Yet communitarianization and *banalisation* are not the same as a dilution of the perceived need to defend national negotiating positions within the EU. Certain authors have claimed that national administrations in Brussels have become somehow 'socialized' and hence less focused on the defence of perceived national interests. Thus Lequesne (1993: 200) speaks of the French PR as acting, at least in part, as 'the advocate of Community interests [in Paris] as much as the servant of Paris in Brussels'. The ambassador and his deputy, when negotiating in COREPER, feel 'as much guarantors of the Community (collective) interest as defender of (particular) national interests' (Lequesne

1993: 215; see also Spinelli 1966: 79). Such claims are easily made but difficult to substantiate. The interviews undertaken for this project indicate nothing of the sort. Certainly, PR officials are on occasion required to inform Paris that French negotiating positions are untenable, given the constellation of forces in the Council. This, however, is simply accepting the limits of national room for manœuvre, not some kind of conversion to the 'Community cause'. Similarly, whilst the importance of the supranational institutions has undoubtedly increased over the course of the last decade, Paris has responded not with abnegation, but with redoubled attempts to secure influence within the Commission.

As the scope, density, and complexity of European integration have increased, so too have the tasks of the French administration in Brussels. Perhaps typically, however, Paris has responded to the challenge not by accepting that the EU is taking on a life of its own, and developing into a semi-autonomous quasi polity in its own right, but by striving to ensure that, within this most complex and far-reaching instance of interstate co-operation, the French presence and French influence remain as strong as ever.

References

Carnelutti, A. (1992), 'L'Administration française face aux nouvelles échéances européennes', *Revue française d'administration publique*, 63: 459–89.

Cini, Michelle (1996), *The European Commission: Leadership, Organisation and Culture in the EU Administration* (Manchester: Manchester University Press).

Clamen, Michel (1996), *Bruxelles au jour le jour: Petit guide des négotiations communautaires* (Paris: La Documentation Française).

de Boisdeffre, M. *et al.* (1996), 'Le Travail gouvernemental et l'Europe', in D. Laurent and M. Sanson (eds.), *Le Travail gouvernemental* (Paris: La Documentation Française).

de Clausade, J. (1991), *L'Adaptation de l'administration française à l'Europe: Rapport au Ministre d'État, Ministre de la fonction publique et des réformes administratives et au Ministre des Affaires Européennes* (Paris: La Documentation Française).

de la Guérivière, J. (1992), *Voyage à l'intérieur de l'Eurocratie* (Paris: Le Monde Éditions).

Delpeuch, Jean-Luc (1999), 'Retour des experts nationaux détachés dans leur administration d'origine (période 1995–1998)' (Paris: SGCI), unpublished report.

De Richemont, Morel, Dobelle, and El Nouchi (n.d.), 'Permanent Representation', mimeo.

——(1994), 'Rapport final du Groupe de Travail conjoint SGCI-RP sure les instructions de SGCI A la RP', May.

Guyomarch, A., Machin, H., and Ritchie, E. (1998), *France in the European Union* (London: Macmillan).

Hayes-Renshaw, F., and Wallace, H. (1997), *The Council of Ministers* (London: Macmillan).

——Lequesne, C., and Mayor Lopez, P. (1989), 'The Permanent Representations of the Member States to the European Communities', *Journal of Common Market Studies*, 28/2: 119–37.

Hix, Simon (1999), *The Political System of the European Union* (London: Macmillan).

Jones, Christopher (1996), 'Aerospace', in H. Kassim and A. Menon (eds.), *The European Union and National Industrial Policy* (London: Routledge).

Lamy, Pascal (1991), 'Choses vues . . . d'Europe', interview with Denis Oliviennes, *Esprit* (10 Oct).

Lequesne, C. (1993), *Paris–Bruxelles: Comment se fait la politique européenne de la France* (Paris: Presses de la Fondation Nationale des Sciences Politiques).

Menon, Anand (1996), 'France and the IGC of 1996', *Journal of European Public Policy*, 3/2: 231–52.

——(1999), 'Power and Competition in the European Union: An Institutionalised Intergovernmentalist Approach', unpublished paper.

——(2000), 'France', in H. Kassim, G. Peters, and V. Wright (eds.), *The National Co-ordination of EU Policy: The Domestic Level* (Oxford: Oxford University Press).

——and Wright, Vincent (1999), 'The Paradoxes of "Failure": British EU Policy Making in Comparative Perspective', *Public Policy and Administration*, 13/4: 46–66.

Premier Ministre (1994), *Circulaire du 21 Mars 1994 relative aux relations entre les administrations françaises et les institutions de l'Union Européenne* (Paris: Premier Ministre).

Représentation Permanente de la France Auprès de l'Union Européenne (1999), 'La Representation Permanente de la France à Bruxelles', mimeo.

Robin, G. (1985), *La Diplomatie de Mitterrand ou le triomphe des apparences* (Paris: Éditions de la Bièvre).

Schmidt, V. A. (1996), *From State to Market? The Transformation of French Business and Government* (Cambridge: Cambridge University Press).

Spence, David (1997), 'Staff and Personnel Policy in the Commission' in G. Edwards and D. Spence (eds.), *The European Commission*, 2nd edn. (London: Cartermill).

——(1995), 'The Co-ordination of European Policy by Member States' in M. Westlake (ed.), *The Council of the European Union* (London: Cartermill).

Spinelli, Altiero (1966), *The Eurocrats* (Baltimore: Johns Hopkins University Press).

Westlake, M. (ed.) (1995), *The Council of the European Union* (London: Cartermill).

Wright, Vincent (1997), 'The National Co-ordination of European Policy-Making: Negotiating the Quagmire', in J. Richardson (ed.), *European Union Power and Policy-Making* (London: Routledge).

3

The German Case: A Key Moderator in a Competitive Multi-Level Environment

Andreas Maurer and Wolfgang Wessels

Conceptualizing a Janus-Faced Institution

A Janus-Faced Actor in Multi-Level Governance

Permanent representations are key players in a dynamic system of multi-level governance, which is characterized by an ongoing competition for access and influence in an expanding range of activities and across time. The process towards (Wessels 1990) and the path of (Pierson 1998) multi-level governance shapes the institutional terrain (Fligstein and McNichol 1998) of the Union and of the German politico-administrative system. The evolving institutional environment also shapes the roles and functions of permanent representations to a considerable extent. Permanent representations operate not only via delegation by 'their' government but also between different levels of governance. They act 'Janus-like' between and on behalf of two 'masters': the Council of Ministers and the member states' governments (Hayes-Renshaw and Wallace 1997: 224; Mentler 1996: 29). Of course, they are first and foremost responsible to their government and, to a limited extent, accountable before 'their' national parliament. As Hayes-Renshaw and Wallace put it, permanent representations are 'expected to articulate their government's point of view at all levels, including on informal and even social occasions' (1997: 224). However, permanent representations are not simply representative institutions of their country to the European Union. Being placed between Brussels—a polity beyond the nation-state—and their home country leads to a multiplication of communication flows and directions. Hence permanent representations do not simply deal with 'the Council' but with a multinational structure of decision-making. They lobby not only *between* 'Brussels' and their country, but also *within* a set of EU institutions (Council Secretariat,

Council substructures, other permanent representations, Commission *cabinets*, DGs, European Parliament, parliamentary committees, political groups, Committee of the Regions, ECOSOC), interest groups (located in Brussels and in the member states), as well as with third countries and organizations. All these actors operate on several levels and at different stages of the EU policy cycle.

Moreover, as far as the German case is concerned, we must add the legally fine-tuned and deeply institutionalized patterns of sectoral administrative arrangements and the specific network and intermediary structures in European policy-making of the Länder offices (sometimes themselves called 'representations') and the Bundesrat's representative institution, the 'Länder Observer'. Whereas the latter participates at each Council meeting, the Länder offices sometimes act (and since Maastricht to a growing extent) as competing permanent—parallel—representations on a 'single issue' orientation and a regionalist basis. The German permanent representation faces competition with the Länder—whether with regard to lobbying the European Commission or to those policy fields where the Länder execute their exclusive competencies directly *vis-à-vis* the European institutions.

The administrative institutions and mechanisms that connect the German government and its governmental agencies with Brussels have a reputation for performing poorly (Sasse 1975; Regelsberger and Wessels 1984; Bulmer and Paterson 1987; Bulmer *et al.* 1998; Janning and Meyer 1998). Compared to its French (Lequesne 1996; Szukala forthcoming) and British (Armstrong and Bulmer 1996, forthcoming) counterpart, the German European policy-making system suffers from horizontal and vertical fragmentation, old-fashioned and cumbersome procedures, institutional pluralism, and 'negative coordination' (Scharpf 1997; Maurer forthcoming; Maurer and Wessels 1999). These features are associated with strategic timidity, late preference-building and position-taking, and, as a result, minority positions in the Council of Ministers. In addition, the constitutionalized (vertical) division of power between the federal level and that of the Länder leads to a complex system involving not only a negotiating structure relating equivalent actors to each other, but also relationships across the hierarchies of governance which prevail at each level. Operating at both levels is a decentralized system of administrative interaction. Just as decision-making is organized in the EU Council of Ministers, with COREPER and working groups passing dossiers upwards, decision-making in internal and European affairs is filtered from the lowest towards the highest level with respect both to administrative and political issues (Gaddum 1994). Hence, Germany's EU policy capacity resides largely in problem-solving within bureaucratic networks at each level of governance and only to a limited extent in political solutions to be agreed upon by ministers.

The German permanent representation performs specific functions due to the special character of the EU, which 'normal' embassies of the Federal

Republic do not need to fulfil. The organizational set-up and behaviour of civil servants in Brussels depends on a multifaceted network of institutions and procedures at different layers of governance. In addition, the functional scope of European integration shapes the activities of member state representatives. Whenever permanent representations join the arena of EU governance, the practical options for exercising 'voice' differ according to the policy field in question. In other words, there is no single pattern for the role of the permanent representation. Its roles and functions depend on the policy field (legal bases), the phase of the policy cycle (decision preparation, negotiation, decision taking, implementation), and the policy arena (Council–COREPER–working group, Council–Parliament, comitology, etc.).

Theoretical Approaches

Discussion of the organizational and functional profiles of permanent representations necessitates a consideration of their institutional environment. Different theoretical conceptions of the Union lead to different perceptions of its actors—and thus also of the permanent representations. We consider the European Union (EU) to be a political system in a state of evolution. It is undergoing fundamental changes in respect to its functional responsibilities (the allocation and execution of powers conferred on it), as well as to its geographical scope (the accession of new member states), and organizational structure. Permanent institutional and procedural changes, the outcomes of subsequent Treaty reform, inter-institutional agreements and the European Community's secondary legislation provide the Union—its member states as well as its institutions—with an evolving set of rights and obligations. Many key issues have become subject to the European Union over the past fifty years. Whereas a high proportion of European citizens takes the increasing competencies and the significance of the Union for granted, serious concerns exist about the managerial performance of the EU, particularly with regard to those acting within the European bureaucracy (Wessels 2000).

Administrative policy-making plays a significant role in West European political systems, as it is an elementary part of the functioning of modern governments and governance. The administrative network surrounding 'Brussels' often arouses controversy. Major features determining this discourse are latent fears of an 'Archipelago Brussels', an ever-growing swamp which hosts a new class of 'Eurocrats' (Spinelli 1966). Beyond this popular scenario, analysing the role of administration and civil servants in the governing process has a long and extremely varied academic tradition in Western Europe, evoking stimulating research results in the fields of law, economics, and social sciences (Mayntz 1982: 75). However, most of these contributions focus on the national level. Although there has been a significant increase in the number of studies about European policy-making, administration in the European sphere has so far received only limited attention.

According to the governance school, which emerged in the late 1980s (Bulmer 1994; Caporaso 1996; Jachtenfuchs and Kohler-Koch 1996), interaction between administrations plays a particular role within the complex multi-level game of the EU. The EU polity is seen as a 'post-sovereign, polycentric, incongruent' arrangement of authority, which supersedes the limits of the nation-state (Schmitter 1996: 132). Some scholars of governance assume a non-hierarchical decision-making process overarching the geographical limits of the EU and its member states beyond. In this perspective, Brussels-based decision-makers do not (intend to) move the EU in a certain direction or transform its basic character and organization. Instead, they act as defenders of the—rather diffuse and vague—status quo. The permanent representations and COREPER matter, therefore, as arenas of collective decision preparation and making, indicating a new historical stage for both administrations and for the state.

Fusion theory (Wessels 1992, 1997) regards COREPER and the permanent representations as indicators of a permanent process by which national governments and administrations, as well as other public and private actors, increasingly combine and share public resources from several levels in order to adopt and implement binding decisions. Working groups and other bodies created under the authority of the Council and COREPER are the manifestation of a growing Europeanization of national and European administrations. In this view, the fifteen permanent representations are significant in the way the European Court of Justice has put it: if powers 'fall partly into the competencies of the Community and in part within that of the member states it is essential to ensure close co-operation between the member states and the Community institutions' (European Court of Justice 1994: 7–14). Thus, the permanent representations are examples of, and a main driving force behind, the merging of public instruments. They are to some extent a product of the increasing competition for access and influence in the EU policy cycle.

Applying fusion theory to our theme helps to identify interrelated processes of Europeanization both between the member states and EC/EU institutions and between national and European administrative systems. Both levels of interaction (Council Secretariat and permanent representations at the EU level and member state institutions and representatives from the national level) meet in a range of committee structures that co-ordinate the views and opinions of member state and EC/EU administrations on a given set of issues. Fusion theory would then expect that these arenas would act neither as the 'guard dogs' of national governments charged with controlling the European Commission nor as forums for exclusively intergovernmental bargaining. Rather, these structures (especially COREPER I and II, working groups, the Antici and Mertens Groups) behave as specialized bodies for joint action, not least because desk officers in the permanent representations tend to see Brussels as 'a more permanent fixture' (Westlake 1995: 289) of their professional career (technical postings are of longer duration than the traditional diplomatic ones from the Ministry of Foreign Affairs). Specific styles of interaction within the Council's substructures are to be expected: horizontally between its members and other committees (for example, between technical specialized COREPER I-related working group members, within the SCA, CREST, or between the ECOFIN working groups and the EC Employment committee) and vertically between its members and other specialized member state institutions or committees. These interactions socialize participants, producing a post-national ethos marked by constructive team spirit, a 'club atmosphere', effective collegiality, and not simply the strict interpretation of legal texts and formal rules.

Unlike this *horizontal/vertical fusion* which we generally expect to find in policy areas subject to the Treaty establishing the EC, *administrative co-operation* is more oriented towards and more dependent on the national level. A good example is the Art. 36 (formerly, the K4) Committee for Home and Judicial Affairs or the CFSP committee structure, where permanent representations are more likely to act under the auspices of the member state governments and in the interest of the 'conclusions' and 'joint strategic decisions' to be formulated by the European Council. The main characteristics are intergovernmental bargaining (as, for example, undertaken by permanent representatives in intergovernmental conferences), a diplomatic style of communication, and a rather strict interpretation of legal texts and formal rules, especially at times of conflict.

History and Evolution of the Organization: Growth and Differentiation

COREPER, which was legally recognized only in the Merger Treaty of 1965 (Art. 4), succeeded COCOR (Comité de Co-ordination) which itself was founded in February 1953 to prepare meetings of the ECSC Council of Ministers. Unlike COCOR, COREPER was installed as a permanent, Brussels-based organ. The German permanent representation was created in June 1958 (Westlake 1995: 286)—after Italy, Luxembourg (February 1958), Belgium, the Netherlands, and France had appointed their permanent representatives. The first permanent representative, Carl Friedrich Ophuels, headed the representation until 1961. The decision to appoint permanent representatives followed the agreement between the ministers of foreign affairs on 7 January 1958 to create a committee 'formé des Représentants des États membres'.

The German permanent representation to the EU is one of nine permanent representations of the Federal Republic to international organizations and organized roughly in the same manner (Table 3.1). The permanent representative to the EU is appointed by the Cabinet of the Federal government, on the basis of a proposal by the Ministry of Foreign Affairs. Indicating the joint responsibility of the Ministry for Foreign Affairs and the Ministry of Economics (since October 1998 the Ministry of Finance), the Ministry for Foreign Affairs must come to an agreement with the Ministry of Finance before nominating the head of the permanent representation. Accordingly, the deputy permanent representation is nominated by the Ministry of Finance in agreement with the Ministry of Foreign Affairs. The post of permanent representative is certainly one of the most prestigious jobs for diplomats. All have had a long career dealing with EC-related affairs. One, Jürgen Trumpf, became state secretary—an even higher position in the diplomatic service—and then secretary general of the Council. Two others retired from the job at the age of 65, one of whom later became the rector of the College of Europe.

Tenure in both positions has normally been long. Ten senior diplomats from the Ministry of Foreign Affairs represented Germany for 4.8 years on average. Interestingly, the German deputy permanent representative occupies his post much longer than any of his colleagues. So far, there have been only five deputy permanent representatives. Due to the transfer of the European co-ordination functions of the Ministry of Economics to the Ministry of Finance in October 1998, it is likely that Germany will nominate a new deputy permanent representative from the finance department.

The predominance of the two ministries is also reflected in the structure of the permanent representation. In 1998 the two core ministries for European policy-making—Foreign Affairs and Economics—occupied 57 per cent of the posts as against 43 per cent for the remaining technical ministries.[1] In view of the number of higher civil servants, the permanent representation in Brussels is the largest of all German permanent representations to international organizations. The staff has grown at around 3.3 per cent per year.

In view of the number of ministries that delegate civil servants, the permanent representation in Brussels is among the most 'representative' of German representations. Apart from the Ministry of Defence and the Chancellery, every Federal ministry has at least one civil servant at the Brussels permanent representation. The figures have changed with the Schröder government, as part of the Economic Ministry (BMWi) has been moved to the Finance Ministry (BMF).

The German permanent representation is structured along functional lines in view of the nature of the working of the Council. However, the

---

[1] This calculation is based on the data provided by the European Union's interinstitutional directory (Luxembourg: Office for official publications of the EC, March 1998).

TABLE 3.1. *Delegated higher civil servants of permanent representations of the FRG*

	EU	NATO Brussels	UN NY	UN, ILO Geneva	OSCE Vienna	OECD Paris	UN Vienna	FAO Rome	Council of Europe	TOTAL	% of Total
AA	10	10	24	10	7	4	4	1	3	73	49.6
ChBK	1					1				2	1.7
BMA	2			1						3	2.04
BMBau	1									1	0.7
BMBWFT	3						1			4	2.7
BMF	4	2	1	1		1				9	6.1
BMG	2									2	1.4
BMI	2	1								3	2.04
BMJ	1									1	0.7
BML	3							1		4	2.7
BMU	1									1	0.7
BMV	2			1						3	2.04
BMVg		15	2		5					22	14.97
BMWi	5	1	1	3		3	1			14	9.5
BMZ	1		1	1		1		1		5	3.4
TOTAL	38	29	29	17	12	10	6	3	3	147	

Source: Ministry of Foreign Affairs (Auswärtigen Amt: 1996).

Abbreviations: AA = Ministry for Foreign Affairs; ChBK = Chancellery; BMA = Ministry for Labour; BMBau = Ministry for Construction; BMBWFT = Ministry for Research, Science and Technological Development; BMF = Ministry for Finance; BMG = Ministry for Health; BMI = Ministry of the Interior; BMJ = Ministry for Justice; BML = Ministry for Agriculture; BMU = Ministry for Environment Affairs; BMV = Ministry for Transport; BMVg = Ministry for Defence; BMWi = Ministry of Economics; BMZ = Ministry for Economic Cooperation and Development; see also Wessels 2000.

TABLE 3.2. *Germany's permanent representatives and deputy permanent representatives, 1958–1999*

Year of nomination	Permanent representative	Deputy permanent representative
1958	Carl Friedrich Ophuls	M. Goers
1959		Eberhard Boemke
1961	Gunther Harkot	
June 1961	Hans Georg Sachs	
1973	Ulrich Lebsanft	
1976		Walter Kittel
1977	Helmut Sigrist	
1979	Gisbert Poensgen	
1985	Werner Ungerer	
1987		Jochen Gruenhage
1989	Jürgen Trumpf	
1993	Dietrich Von Kyaw	
1999	Wilhelm Schönfelder	

Source: Westlake 1995: 305; Interinstitutional Directory 1999.

predominance of the Ministries for Foreign Affairs and Economics/Finance is observable when looking at the organizational hierarchy. Hence, the personnel dealing with political affairs (institutional and procedural questions, and General Affairs Council) and those dealing with economic affairs are affiliated to directorates. The other departments are—hierarchically—one grade below and form a division each.

The quantitative involvement of the permanent representation can also be looked at in the cases of presidencies (Maurer forthcoming). Civil servants spent a large amount of time in working groups established by COREPER in order to clear the agenda of COREPER I and II. Although these co-ordination mechanisms are not officially established by law, they have a long tradition and structure the decision-making process of the Council to a considerable extent. Hence, the working-group level is the 'most vital' (Westlake 1995: 312) of all the Council's component parts. The ratio between Council and working-group meetings has nearly doubled from 1:12.6 in 1958 to 1:24.5 in 1995. Between 70 per cent (Hayes-Renshaw and Wallace 1995: 562; Barber 1995) and 90 per cent (Wessels 1991) of the Council's agenda is decided at this level (Beyers and Dierickx 1998).

If we compare previous presidencies with that of 1999 (i.e. the final draft plan of the Schröder government), we observe that the share of 'technical' presidencies—those who chair the relevant session—has increased to 33 per cent, whereas their share in regard to the German delegation speaker—those who then present the German position in the relevant session—decreased to

TABLE 3.3. *Structure of the German permanent representation (March 1999)*

Entity/Dept.	Number of Personnel	Minister Counsellor	Counsellor	Attaché	Secretary	Others (Adviser)
Political Affairs	16	1	6	1	7	1
Internal Affairs	5		2		3	
Justice	3		2		1	
Education	1				1	
Economic Affairs	15	1	3	3	7	
Environment	3		2		1	
Economic Co-operation	2				1	1
Finance	5	1	3		1	
Bundesbank	1					1
Agriculture	4		2		2	
RTD	3		2		1	
Transport	3		1		2	
Labour and Social Affairs	3	1			2	
Health	4	1	1		2	
Administration	17			14	3	
TOTAL	85	5	24	18	34	3

Note: The department names are those of the permanent representation.

TABLE 3.4. *Division of labour among presidents and representatives of the FRG in the working groups of the Council during German presidencies (first half of 1988, second half of 1994, and first half of 1999)*

Ministry	1988		1994		1999 (draft of 8/1998)		1999 (final draft of 12/1998)	
	PRE	SGD	PRE	SGD	PRE	SGD	PRE	SGD
Foreign Affairs	2	1	22	22	40	35	30	25
Economics	29	48	23	49	32	33	38	46
Agriculture	18	23	42	51	61	63	63	64
Finance	13	30	2	30	10	35	19	48
Justice	24	25	20	22	37	40	33	31
Interior	3	3	18	21	35	35	33	33
Labour	3	4	4	5	4	5	1	1
Transport	4	4	3	8	2	1	1	6
Youth, Family, and Health	3	13	23	28	34	26	35	28
Education, Science, Technology	1	2	4	6	1	0	2	0
Environment	2	3	2	6	5	5	8	8
Development and Economic Co-operation	0	5	0	4	0	2	1	1
Construction and Regional Planning	2	4	1	2	2	1	1	2
Permanent Representation	91	26	96	30	79	56	84	49
Others	2	3	4	13	2	1	2	1
TOTAL	197	194	264	297	344	338	351	343

Sources: For 1988 and 1994: Wessels and Rometsch 1996; for 1999: draft minutes of the European Delegates meeting of 15 December 1998, Auswärtiges Amt, Bonn, 18 December 1998; Bulmer *et al.* 2001.

Note: PRE = Presidency of the Council; SGD = Speaker of the German delegation in the Council.

32 per cent which is even below the 1988 rate.[2] Moreover, the share of the permanent representation as active participant in the Council—either as chair or as 'speaker' of the German delegation—has slightly decreased. However, for

[2] The main 'winners' are the Ministry of Finance (+17 presidencies, +18 speakers of delegation), the Ministry of Agriculture (+21 presidencies, +13 speakers), the Ministry of the Interior (+15 presidencies, +12 speakers) and the Ministry of Justice (+13 presidencies, +9 speakers). The 'losers' are all within the 'technical' ministries. Only the Ministries for Youth and Family, for Health, and for Environment affairs have increased their overall proportion.

each Council working group the Europe delegates nominate a correspondent in the German permanent representation in order to manage the information flow between the Council's bodies and the appointed speakers of the delegation.

These figures reflect not only the policy preferences of the European Commission and the Council of Ministers at a given time (the working groups are both a reaction to the European Commission's initiation new legislation and a mirror of the Council's activity with regard to the post-initiative stages in European decision-making), but they also indicate a shift in the competencies of the ministries within the German government and the growing desire of some core ministries to take over traditional tasks of the permanent representation. Comparing the 1994 and 1999 presidency drafts, we discover that the total share of involvement of the Ministries for Foreign Affairs remains rather stable at about 10 per cent, that the share of the Ministries for Finance and for the Interior has grown from 5 to 10 per cent, and that the share of the permanent representation in Brussels and of the Ministry of Economics have slightly decreased.

These observations are confirmed when looking at the division of labour during the last German presidency (January–June 1999). The Council's working groups are traditionally grouped together alongside the different Directorates General of its General Secretariat. Interestingly, DG B related groups (Agriculture–Fisheries) are exclusively composed of members of the Ministry for Agriculture. The only exception concerns working group 45 on AGRIFIN where a member of the permanent representation's finance division fulfilled the role of the Presidency. The same exclusivity granted to the national part of the German Euro-administration exists in relation to DG E working groups on CFSP (only the group of CFSP delegates is represented by the permanent representation at both the Presidency and the speaker level) and with regard to DG H working groups for Justice and Home Affairs ('reserved', with two exceptions—for the ministries of the Interior and of Justice). Transport policy working groups are exclusively handled (with one exception) by the respective members of the permanent representation, both with regard to the Presidency and the speaker of the German delegation. In the remaining working groups—DG C (Internal market), G (ECOFIN, Tax harmonization), I (Environmental and Consumer Affairs), and J (Social policy, Education, etc.)—the permanent representation usually shares its roles with national delegates.

As regards institutional questions and inter-institutional relations between the Council and other EU bodies, the permanent representation is responsible for preparing and clearing matters dealt with by the 'General Affairs Council' and for the preparation of European Council meetings. Accordingly, the head of the permanent representation directorate for political affairs—the 'No. 3'—acts as the German member of the Antici Group which clears the agenda of COREPER II. The head of the directorate for economic affairs, acting as the member of the Mertens Group, is responsible for the preparation of conciliation meetings called under the co-decision procedure. Unlike UKREP or the French permanent representation, the German representation has not established a special desk for relations with the European Parliament. Hence, the anticipation of the European Parliament's views and amendments as well as direct communication with MEP and the European Parliament's Secretariat of the Conciliation Committee is a responsibility of every ministry and permanent representation member concerned. Due to the fact that co-decision and co-operation procedures are generally used for the internal market, transport and telecommunication, research, environmental and consumer issues, the relevant units in both the Federal ministries and the permanent representation nominate at least one higher civil servant as 'relais' to the European Parliament.

The permanent representative of the FRG to the EU is the head of the PR hierarchy and can issue binding instructions based on those transmitted by the Ministry of Finance (acting as the instructing body of the Federal government). However, strict hierarchical lines function only to a limited degree, as the staff of other ministries maintain direct contacts with their 'home base' and with the relevant policy network in Brussels. Some areas concern the senior diplomatic staff more than others, and thus fall more directly under their control. Others are dealt with in more decentralized and fragmented ways. There is a routine meeting of all the PR staff every week.

The Tasks of the German Permanent Representation

The German permanent representation's roles and functions reflect the specific interaction styles of the German administration with regard to European integration. Germany is a federal state. Consequently different levels of government intervene in the political process. The Basic Law attributes to these levels specific competencies and functions. The vertical division of power between the federal level and that of the 'federated states'—the Länder—leads to a complex system of 'political interwovenness' or 'interconnectedness' (*Politikverflechtung*, see Hesse 1978; Reissert and Scharpf 1967; Scharpf 1988). There is no central decision-making actor but different levels participate in both the national and European decision-making processes. In addition to this formalized distribution of powers, we also observe a horizontal division of influence between the different ministries and institutions at each level (Derlien 1999; Rometsch 1996; Rometsch and Wessels 1996; Maurer forthcoming).

According to the principle of *ministerial autonomy* (*Ressortprinzip*), ministries at the Federal level are independent actors. Unlike in France or in the

United Kingdom, ministerial autonomy as a principle does hinder attempts by different branches of the German government, and notably the Chancellor, to impose co-ordination. However, the Chancellor enjoys a so-called 'guidance competence' (*Richtlinienkompetenz*),[3] which can be defined as the ability to *set strategic guidelines* for the Federal government and to *resolve interministerial disputes* (decisions of the Chancellor in this regard are binding on ministers).[4]

The principle and practice of ministerial autonomy has led several scholars to attach the following labels to German EC/EU policy-making: 'institutional pluralism' (Bulmer and Paterson 1987: 17), 'fragmented decision-making' (Siwert-Probst 1998: 15), 'institutional polyphony' or even 'institutional cannibalism'. These characteristics are very apparent in comparison to France and the United Kingdom. In brief, the powers conferred to the different levels of policy-making are not co-ordinated by a central agency responsible for formulating one coherent European policy overarching the specific interests of ministries and policy fields. These ongoing dynamics of administrative sectorization, institutional pluralism, and the potential for conflict between the various governmental actors dealing with EC/EU affairs suggest that co-ordination mechanisms and institutions across the different phases of the Brussels policy cycle are highly important.

Permanent Representation Participation in the National EU Policy Process

The co-ordination of EC/EU policy-making between the Federal government's institutions and the permanent representation is ensured by a set of formalized conferences, committees, and informal but regular contacts at the administrative level, which vary in importance and over time. In the absence of a centralized EU interface in Bonn/Berlin, channels of information, instruction, and communication have been established at each level of governance. Draft Commission proposals and other EC/EU documents are transmitted from the permanent representation to the Ministry of Economics—since October 1998 to the Ministry of Finance (Organizational Decree 1998). The proposals are then sent to those ministries which the Ministry of Finance considers relevant (*federführendes Ressort*). To instruct the permanent representation, the Ministry of Finance co-ordinates preparatory meetings in relation to COREPER I, whereas the Ministry of Foreign Affairs is responsible for the management of the Bonn/Berlin-based work in relation to

---

[3] See Article 65 of the German Basic Law.
[4] The rules of procedure of the Federal government define the Chancellor's *Richtlinienkompetenz* in §1 and §2.

COREPER II.[5] The retransmission of proposals and amendments, as well as the instructions for German delegations to the Council of Ministers and its subsequent bodies, is then the outcome of a complex co-ordination mechanism, which also involves the permanent representation.

First, the head of the permanent representation is a member of the Interministerial Committee of State Secretaries. This committee was set up in 1963 in order to free the Cabinet from controversies in relation to European affairs (Sasse 1975: 27). Meeting approximately on a monthly basis,[6] it brings together the state ministers and state secretaries of the Foreign Affairs Ministry, the Ministry for Economics, the Agricultural Ministry, and the Finance Ministry—the 'Four Musketeers' in European affairs—as well as the state minister responsible for European affairs in the Chancellery and the permanent representative of the FRG in Brussels. In addition, state secretaries outside this 'core' participate in the meetings when the chair (Foreign Affairs) considers it appropriate. Although the structure of this committee is flexible, entry as a permanent member is of political importance. The committee's main task is to settle controversial questions and to prepare dossiers of a political and strategic nature in advance of Council of Ministers meetings. Moreover, the committee deals with draft negotiating briefs for the German delegations to the Council's COREPER II. Committee decisions are taken by common accord and are politically binding on the ministries and legally bind the permanent representation (Sasse *et al.* 1977: 12). In consequence, the committee's main focus is on interministerial problem-solving and establishing coherent European policy strategies. It does not adopt a proactive approach on the basis of the Council of Ministers' agenda. This lack of willingness to advocate a coherent European policy approach across different policy areas provides the PR with considerable room of manœuvre (Bulmer and Paterson 1987: 19–20).

Secondly, the German deputy permanent representative participates in the meetings of the European delegates. In order to instruct COREPER I, and its working groups, each ministry has nominated a 'European delegate' (*Europa-Beauftragte*). From 1971 onwards, they have met irregularly—since the SEA roughly on a monthly basis—in the buildings and under the chairmanship of the Ministry of Economics. Since October 1998 the location and the

---

[5] There are exceptions: COREPER II meetings with regard to the Councils on ECOFIN, Budget, Finance and Tax policy are co-ordinated by the Ministry of Finance. The same applies to instructions for the German representative in COREPER II.

[6] Note that the frequency of meetings of the Interministerial Committee of State Secretaries on European Affairs varies. During the Grand Coalition between the Christian-Democrats and the Social-Democrats the Committee met virtually every week, illustrating its function as a clearing body for the component parts of the government. In contrast, it met on a monthly basis during the term of office of Helmut Kohl. During the 1999 Presidency, it only met three times.

chairmanship have been shifted to the Ministry of Foreign Affairs. Below the level of the European delegate, there are regular contacts between the heads of division (*Ressortleiter*) of ministries and the responsible civil servants in the permanent representation intended to resolve interministerial disputes that emerge from the Council working groups. The so-called 'Tuesday Committee', which meets on a weekly basis under the chairmanship of the Ministry of Finance, focuses on the technical aspects of dossiers. Both co-ordination among the European delegates and the informal meetings and contacts between civil servants of the divisions and directorates in the Tuesday Committee concern the settlement of disputes of a technical rather than political nature. As regards timing, these bodies focus on the working groups of the Council of Ministers. In general, meetings always include civil servants from the 'Four Musketeers'.

The Länder: 'Parallel European Policy' as a Complicating Factor

The German Länder possess—as legal entities with autonomous statehood— their own competencies and are thus able to structure politics and policies within their territory. In addition, they participate in the legislative and administrative process of the federation and thus play an important role in the decision-making system of the 'whole state' (*Gesamtstaat*). However, the 'process of European integration has posed a persistent challenge to the legal status of the Länder and their political quality as constituent states, and therefore also to the fundamental federal structure of the Federal Republic' (Hrbek 1999: 218).

Discussions over the establishment of a European Regional Development Fund (ERDF) in 1975 marked the first time that the EC took action that had a direct impact on the Länder's exclusive responsibilities. From that time, the Länder have attempted to assert greater influence over Germany's EC policies. In response to the SEA, the Länder developed direct channels of communication with Brussels and tried to strengthen their formal rights of participation in the internal discussion of EC matters. Considering the complex structure that characterizes European policy-making at the 'Brussels' as well as at the 'Bonn' level, it came as no surprise that the primary strategic response of the Länder was the establishment of a co-ordination mechanism both at the Federal State level and within the wider arena of policy-making in Brussels. As well as putting into place procedures for participation in EC/EU affairs (see Derlien 2000), the Länder have also developed various ways of entrenching their rights, and assuring themselves of an independent capacity for policy-making.

The Länder's 'Ear' in the Permanent Representation

In 1956, during the negotiations on the Rome Treaties, the Länder and the Federal government agreed on the institution of a 'Länder Observer' (*Länderbeobachter*), located in Bonn as well as in Brussels. The Brussels office is at the permanent representation with, however, a separate entrance. The main task is to provide information to the Bundesrat and the Länder (Dette-Koch 1997; Hrbek 1986: 26–7). The Länder Observer is entitled to participate in meetings of the Council of Ministers and reports on its proceedings to the Länder and the Bundesrat (Jaspert 1982: 24–6). However, due to its limited functions and the rather modest administrative support it enjoys—until 1990 there were only two full-time and one part-time civil servants working in its Bonn and Brussels offices—the Länder Observer did not become a key figure in the decision-making process between Brussels and the Länder governments.

As a result, and owing to the growing volume of EC legislation after the entry into force of the SEA, the western Länder opened information offices in Brussels between 1985 and 1987. Once the eastern Länder joined the Federal Republic, they followed this example. By 1992 every Land had its own representation or liaison office in Brussels. After initially being criticized by the Federal government as instruments of a 'parallel foreign policy' (*Nebenaußenpolitik*, see Hahn 1986), they quickly became a useful tool for the Länder in securing and passing on information about the European Commission and the German permanent representative during the decision-preparation phase. Moreover, they became instruments of the Länders' ambition to advance regional interests *vis-à-vis* the European Commission—especially with regard to the management of the structural and regional funds and to the settlement of disputes on state aid and the subsidies with the European Commission's Directorate General (formerly DG IV) for Competition. Unlike with the permanent representation, local government administrations and private industries consider the Länder offices as a tool for the economic promotion of their territory and for providing legal and practical assistance in the drafting of EC/EU-related projects. Compared with the Länder Observer, the Länder offices have considerably larger staffs: in autumn 1997, there were 141 civil servants working on the offices, out of which ninety belonged to the higher service (Von Ploetz 1998: 62).

The ratification of the Maastricht Treaty lead to very detailed and complex provisions setting out graded obligations on the part of the Federal government to observe the Länder's collective opinion (expressed by the Bundesrat) when acting in the Council of Ministers. Hence, whenever EC draft legislation involves the exclusive competencies of the Länder, the Federal Republic is represented in the Council of Ministers by a minister of a Land nominated by the Bundesrat. Moreover, the Länder are empowered to participate actively at the working-group level of the Council.

As far as the participation of Länder civil servants in the Council's and the Commission's working groups is concerned, Weber reported that, in April 1994, 250 Länder civil servants were nominated for Brussels-based working groups (Weber-Panariello 1996: 288). This number grew steadily from 354 in 1995 (Rometsch 1996: 90) to 450 in 1996. Since then, the internal workload of the Länder has lead to a reduction in the number of Länder representatives (Knodt 1998: 158). Hence, for the 1999 presidency, the Länder appointed officials for 314 working groups, of which 189 are attached to the Commission and its comitology network, and the remaining 125 to the Council's working groups. Accordingly, the Länder are present in 38 per cent of the Council's working groups (the German Presidency lists 327 operating working groups for the first half of 1999).

As regards co-operation between the Länder, the Federal government, and the permanent representation, the procedures set out in 1993 seem to function quite efficiently. However, the transfer of negotiation powers remained a matter of dispute on a case-by-case basis. During the 1994–8 legislature, the Federal government initially doubted the Bundesrat's view of

TABLE 3.5. *Participation of* Länder *representatives in Council and Commission working groups (first half of 1999)*

Policy fields	Commission's working groups	Council's working groups
Internal Market	22	15
Employment/Social Affairs	30	7
Agriculture	48	39
Transport	2	2
Environmental Affairs	38	3
RTD	27	2
Telecom.	8	4
Regional Affairs	5	2
Energy	1	2
Home and Judicial Affairs	—	27
Tax Harmonization	3	13
Financial Affairs	—	2
TOTAL	184	118

Source: Bundesrat: Vertreter der Länder in Beratungsgremien der EU, Jan. 1999.

the applicability of paragraph 5(2) and 6(2) of the Co-operation Law in twenty-six cases. In most of these, however, it proved possible to reach agreement either through mutual compromise or by offering the Länder participation in the Council of Ministers as joint members of the German delegation (Maurer 2000).

The European Centrality of the Permanent Representation

Given the specific features of German European policy-making, the German permanent representation orients its activities in six directions, each of them representing a separate, though not autonomous, arena of European policy-making:

1. Treaty-based (Art. 207 ECT, Art. 25 and 36 TEU and relevant provisions in the Council's Rules of Procedure) and nationally formalized communication between Bonn/Berlin and Brussels. Here, the permanent representation performs as the interface between the Council's General Secretariat and the German Government administration. It receives Commission, Council, and European Parliament documents, transmits all documents to the German Ministry of Finance (for CFSP matters to the Ministry of Foreign Affairs), receives instructions for COREPER I (from the Ministry of Finance), and II (from the Ministry of Foreign Affairs), and reports on the outcome of these meetings to one of two relevant ministries.

2. Treaty-based (Art. 207 ECT, relevant provisions in the Council's Rules of Procedure, Arts. 114, 130, 133 ECT and Art. 25 and 36 TEU, secondary legislation establishing special committees of the Council) communication within Brussels. The permanent representation functions as a correspondent institution of the Council Secretariat. It provides staff—in addition to those delegated by the German ministries concerned—to special committees of the Council, e.g. the SCA, the Article 133 Committee, the Committee for Monetary and Financial Affairs, the Political Committee, and the Art. 36 Committee Employment Committee—and communicates with the European Parliament and, to a lesser extent, with the Committee of the Regions and the Economic and Social Affairs Committee.

3. Formalized communication within Bonn/Berlin (based on government organizational decrees, *Organisationserlasse*). The permanent representative participates at the meetings of the Interministerial Committee of State Secretaries on European Affairs, the deputy permanent repre-

sentative participates in the meetings of the European delegates. As members of these national arenas, the two heads of the permanent representation sometimes even formulate the position of the German government, which is then agreed by common accord between all members of the committees.

4. Informal communication between the permanent representation and the Länder Observer as well as the Länder representation offices. The Länder Observer has a Brussels-based office in the building of the permanent representation. He or she participates at meetings of the permanent representation to prepare COREPER meetings. The permanent representation helps the Länder Observer in establishing and securing contacts with the EU institutions.

5. Informal communication between the permanent representation and the European Commission (DG and Cabinet level), the European Parliament (DG II units and individual MEP level). The permanent representation performs both as arena and actor. It provides an informal arena for staff members delegated from the ministries to deal with the Commission and the European Parliament. On the other hand, the permanent representation acts—on the basis of instructions and similar briefs from the capital—as a broker for German interests.

6. Informal communication between the permanent representation and Brussels-based interest groups. Although the permanent representation does not fulfil an official position in aggregating the interests of German industry, some staff members—especially those delegated from the Ministry of Economics and the Ministry for Labour—may act as 'lobby-lobbyists'.

Despite the general characteristics of autonomy, polyphony, and organized anarchy in German European policy-making, the German permanent representation cannot act on its own account. Instead, institutional pluralism and sectorization in European affairs proliferates within the permanent representation, where COREPER I representation is provided by the Ministry for Foreign Affairs and COREPER II by the Ministry of Finance. In addition, twelve other ministries have officials inside the PR.

Table 3.5 shows very clearly how busy the permanent representative and his deputy are. They participate in COREPER meetings (one to two days per week). The permanent representative is in charge of eighty-seven civil servants from twelve ministries and one from the Bundesbank. The total number of civil servants working in the permanent representation indicates an intensive involvement of the German administration. We take the total number of civil servants employed in the permanent representation as an indicator to measure the adaptation of member states to the EC/EU's range of competencies. A look at the size of the permanent representation from 1958 to 1998 indicates that

Germany's adaptation to the post-SEA period was less significant than the adaptation to the post-Maastricht period. In other words, the German permanent representation anticipated the enlargement of responsibilities brought about by the SEA. The Maastricht Treaty led to an increase in the personnel of all permanent representations under consideration. Only the Netherlands and Luxembourg, however, responded by sending more personal than Germany to Brussels.

The German permanent representative not only participates in COREPER meetings, but also has to assist his ministers in Council sessions (one on average per week); he has to attend meetings in Bonn; he keeps contact with the Chancellor and the other members of the German government (mainly the foreign minister); he meets with representatives from the Länder, with key members of the European Parliament (not necessarily German), and important lobbyists. According to his personal style, he gives lectures and participates on the cocktail circuit. His life is not easy: he has to present and defend the 'instructions' (*Weisungen*) transmitted by the Federal government which are often late and inconclusive due to internal bottlenecks among ministries in Bonn/Berlin. In order to make them more acceptable to his colleagues in COREPER, he sometimes feels not like the *Ständige Vertreter* (permanent representative) but the *Ständige Verräter* (permanent traitor, see Edwards 1996: 137; Mentler 1996: 109). The permanent representation faces problems that are mainly rooted in the internal European policy-making structure of Germany. Officials in the permanent representation from the Foreign Office, like those from the Chancellery and other ministries, maintain their own channels of information with political decision-takers and their respective European colleagues—be they in the Commission or in key positions of other national ministries.

The permanent representation's life has become even more difficult with the evolution of the European Union: the scope of policies have become broader; their relevance for political actors back in Bonn has increased; and the attention of political decision-makers has increasingly shifted to the Brussels arena. Moreover, the administrative network has grown considerably: in the mid-1990s, at least 1,500 committees and working groups were functioning in Brussels, involving at least one-quarter of all higher civil servants of the Federal ministries (Wessels 2000). Five hundred civil servants from the Länder are also involved in the Brussels policy cycle. The working groups of the Council, who clear COREPER's agenda, have increased in number from ten (1960) to 300 (1996); the number of their sessions increased from 500 (1960) to 2,300 (1995).

The permanent representation holds key positions for the EC part of the General Affairs Council's agenda, while for the CFSP the political directors of the Foreign Ministry play a major role. The same pre-eminence applies to the monetary aspects of the ECOFIN, where the representatives of the Finance

TABLE 3.6. *Evolution of staffing in the German permanent representation (total sum of civil servants) in comparison with number of days spent in the Council and its preparatory bodies*

	1958	1960	1969	1975	1988	1995	1998
Germany's permanent representation staff	5	19	28	39	42	59	87
Council meetings	21	44	69	76.5	117.5	98	94
meetings per civil servant	4.2	2.3	2.5	1.9	2.8	1.7	1.1
COREPER meetings	39	97	129	118	104	112	n.a.
meetings per civil servant	7.8	5.1	4.6	3.02	2.5	1.9	n.a.
Working-group meetings	302	505	1,412.5	2,079.5	2,000.5	2,364.5	n.a.
meetings per civil servant	60.4	26.6	50.4	53.3	47.6	40.1	n.a.

Sources: For 1960, 1975: Wessels and Rometsch 1996; for 1958, 1968, 1988–95: Hayes-Renshaw and Wallace 1997: 223; for 1998: European Union, Interinstitutional directory, Luxembourg (OOPEC) March 1998, Website of the Council, March 1999; Council: 43rd Review of the Council's Work, Brussels 1995; European Commission: General Report of Activities of the EU 1998, Brussels and Luxembourg 1999.

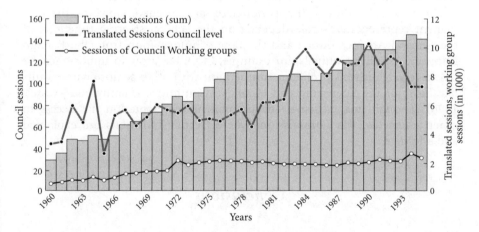

FIG. 3.1. Interaction trends in the Council

ministry and of the Bundesbank in the Economic and Finance Committee play a leading role. For the Agricultural Council the respective experts from that ministry struggle for access and influence. The same is apparently true for trade policy in the Council where the representatives of the Article 133 committee prevail over desk officers in the permanent representation. Given the nature of German administrative careers, most of these officials are long-serving, highly qualified civil servants with access running all the way to the political top. All of these 'national delegates' to the Council's working groups have their own networks (EC/CFSP/ex-Trevi/ex-Schengen). A proportion of their EC business is also kept out of the co-ordination process back home. Finally, the Chancellor and the ministries all have their own networks in which the permanent representation is not involved: at the informal luncheons of ministers, as with the sessions of the European Council, he is not present.

As to phases of the political cycle, the permanent representative is seldom involved in the 'groupes d'experts' advising the European Commission on the drafting of legislative initiatives or with the comitology committees in the implementation phase. The sheer size of this administrative network makes it impossible to be present everywhere or to control all groups.

The major asset in this multi-level and multi-actor game is the overview over crucial areas and privileged access to information. The permanent representation receives and transmits information to and from all relevant EC bodies, including documents that pertain to many sensitive areas. In view of his excellent contacts with other permanent representatives, the ambassador can offer advice about several sectors—what is at stake in each, what the positions of the key actors are, and what inter-sectoral bargains might be struck—though this is not necessarily heeded. However, the permanent representative's role depends on the general steering functions of the General Affairs Council and the flow of information from the Foreign Ministry. As other Councils, for example, ECOFIN, grow in importance, he has to re-establish his profile in competition with other senior civil servants like those of the Economic and Financial Committee (Hanny and Wessels 1998). Though not exclusive, the permanent representation has access to other actors like the Commission, where German positions are explained and advocated.

Conclusions

The Brussels arena is not a political space for an exclusive club of diplomats, nor has it replaced national political systems. The German administration has shaped and conquered the Brussels arena by means of an extensive and intensive network of formal and informal interactions. However, this process does not imply a 'rescue of the nation state' (Milward 1992) or a re-establishment of traditional 'Weberian' types of bureaucracies.

The permanent representation is a key link between Bonn/Berlin and Brussels. Comprised of officials from across all ministries (since 2000, the

Ambassador to the WEU and PSC has been located in the PR in Brussels) it articulates the Federal government's policies in various bodies which are within the Council hierarchy and where home-based officials or ministers are not in attendance. What are the distinctive features of the German permanent representation? First, ministerial autonomy is such that officials in the permanent representation act as if they are representatives of their ministerial department in Berlin/Bonn rather than as representatives of a government line. This element is aggravated by the fact that interministerial disputes may not be resolved until they reach the level of the Cabinet. Compared to the British approach to European policy-making, the German system tends to steer its final position on a given set of draft European law at a late stage. As a consequence, the permanent representation may be instructed to represent in Brussels a policy that has not been agreed upon domestically. Second, the autonomy of ministries may lead to situations where the permanent representation receives instructions from two of them. Given the Council's own system of agenda-setting, it is then up to the permanent representative to present some kind of a 'would-be' position and to defend this later back in Bonn/Berlin. The permanent representation is the representation of the Federal government, but there may be significant Länder interests to be taken into account.

All these circumstances frame the context in which the permanent representation can act. As a consequence, it has to conduct a diplomacy of improvisation, which contrasts especially strongly with the more choreographed diplomacy of its British and French counterparts (Bulmer *et al.* 2001). However, Germany's European policy machinery cannot be evaluated exclusively from this perspective. Vincent Wright reminds us that observing the machinery alone is insufficient: 'the effectiveness of a country's domestic EU co-ordinating capacity must be judged according to the issue, the policy type, the policy requirements and the policy objectives. Merely to examine the machinery of co-ordination is to confuse the means and the outcomes' (Wright 1996: 165). France or the United Kingdom may have better co-ordinating instruments and institutions for dealing with EU affairs, but that has offered no guarantee for a reliable European policy. We need to bear in mind the important shaping role that Germany has had on the integration project as a whole.

A puzzle therefore emerges with respect to the outcomes of German EC/EU policy-making. Despite all the apparent competitive disadvantages listed above, German preferences are reflected to a surprising degree in the structural and institutional fundamentals of the EU, as well as in most treaty amendments and revisions. This pattern goes well beyond the principles of a social market economy and monetary stability to encompass subsidiarity as well as the parliamentarization and the regionalization of the EU's institutional procedural system (Derlien 2000). A couple of explanations come to mind:

- A broad, but not exclusively utilitarian, pro-European consensus, together with Germany's considerable economic power and the committed engagement of the country's political class, determines outcomes despite administrative bottlenecks and complexities. In this respect, the *Kanzlerprinzip* can be mobilized when serious challenges loom (Siwert-Probst 1998). From this perspective, administrative bottlenecks might be understood as devices deliberately manipulated to keep players in the dark and reserve maximum influence for the political hierarchy.
- Linked to this first explanation is the suggestion that the German system is more effective at shaping 'polity' rather than 'policy' outcomes (Bulmer 1997; Derlien 1998). From this angle it could be argued that German actors are strong on issues of constitutional polity (e.g. the European Parliament, the Committee of the Regions, and the European Central Bank in Economic and Monetary Union), but rather weak with respect to routine policy issues (e.g. environmental affairs, education and youth policy).

Given the high vertical and horizontal pluralism of the national system, the German permanent representation faces more competition than the individual Federal ministries. On the other hand, given that the permanent representation is the only—however, 'out-sourced'—body of the German decision-making system which provides for an overall European policy approach, it is better equipped for timely anticipation of package deals in COREPER or the Council of Ministers. The fact of being 'out-sourced', at least physically, can provide more room for manœuvre for the permanent representative than those European policy structures which are organized in a more centralized manner at home. The permanent representation performs the role of a key moderator in a dynamic multi-level setting. Due to constitutional and historical constraints, it faces a flourishing network of actors which are competing for access to the Brussels arena. As part of, and a key actor within, an emerging machinery for joint problem-solving, the permanent representation is evidence of the existence of a decentralized system—both with regard to the European and the national level of governance.

References

Armstrong, Kenneth, and Bulmer, Simon (1996), 'United Kingdom', in Dietrich Rometsch and Wolfgang Wessels (eds.), *The European Union and Member States: Towards Institutonal Fusion?* (Manchester: Manchester University Press), 253–90.

———— (forthcoming), 'The United Kingdom: Between Political Controversy and Administrative Efficiency', in W. Wessels, A. Maurer, and J. Mittag (eds.), *Fifteen into*

One? The European Union and its Member States (Manchester: Manchester University Press).

Barber, Lionel (1995), 'The Men who Run Europe', *Financial Times* (12 Mar.).

Beyers, Jan, and Dierickx, Guido (1998), 'The Working Groups of the European Union: Supranational or Intergovernmental Negotiations?', *Journal of Common Market Studies*, 36/3: 289–317.

Bulmer, Simon (1994), 'The Governance of the European Union: A New Institutionalist Approach', *Journal of Public Policy*, 13/4: 351–80.

——(1997), 'Shaping the Rules? The Constitutive Politics of the European Union and German Power', in Peter J. Katzenstein (ed.), *Tamed Power: Germany in Europe* (New York: Cornell University Press), 49–79.

——and Paterson, William E. (1987), *The Federal Republic of Germany and the European Community* (London: Allen & Unwin).

——Jeffery, Charlie, and Paterson, William E. (1998), 'Deutschlands Europäische Diplomatie: Die Entwicklung des regionalen Milieus', in Werner Weidenfeld (ed.), *Deutsche Europapolitik: Optionen wirksamer Interessenvertretung* (Bonn: Europa Union Verlag), 11–102.

——Maurer, Andreas, and Paterson, William E. (2001), 'Das Entscheidungs-und Koordinationssystem deutscher Europapolitik: Hindernis für eine neue Politik?', in Mathias Jopp, Uwe Schmalz, and Heinrich Schneider (eds.), *Neue deutsche Europapolitik* (Bonn: Europa Union Verlag).

Caporaso, James (1996), 'The European Union and Forms of State, Westphalian, Regulatory or Post-Modern?', *Journal of Common Market Studies*, 34/1: 29–52.

Commission des Communautés Européennes (1960–95), *Activité du Service Commun Interprétation-Conférences* (Luxembourg: Office of Official Publications of the European Communities).

Derlien, Hans-Ulrich (2000), 'Germany: Failing Successfully?', in H. Kassim, B. G. Peters, and V. Wright (eds.), *The National Co-ordination of EU Policy: The Domestic Level* (Oxford: Oxford University Press).

——and Murswieck, Axel (eds.) (1999), *Der Politikzyklus zwischen Bonn und Brüssel* (Opladen: Leske & Budrich).

Dette-Koch, Elisabeth (1997), 'Die Rolle des Länderbeobachters im Rahmen der Mitwirkung der Länder an der Europäischen Integration', *Thüringische Verwaltungsblätter*, 4: 169–75.

Edwards, Geoffrey (1996), 'National Sovereignty vs. Integration? The Council of Ministers', in Jeremy Richardson (ed.), *European Union: Power and Policy-Making* (London: Routledge), 127–47.

European Court of Justice (1994), 'Rs. 1/94 (World Trade Organization) Summary', *Proceedings of the Court of Justice and the Court of First Instance of the European Communities*, 30: 7–14.

Fligstein, Neil, and McNichol, James A. (1998), 'The Institutional Terrain of the European Union', in Wayne Sandholtz and Alec Stone Sweet (eds.), *European Integration and Supranational Governance* (Oxford: Oxford University Press), 59–91.

Gaddum, Eckard (1994), *Die deutsche Europapolitik in den 80er Jahren: Interessen, Konflikte und Entscheidungen der Regierung Kohl* (Paderborn: F. Schöningh).

Hahn, Ottokar (1986), 'EG-Engagement der Länder: Lobbyismus oder Nebe-naußenpolitik?', in R. Hrbek and U. Thaysen (eds.), Die Dentschen Länder und die Europäischen Gemeinschaften (Baden-Baden: Nomos), 105–10.

Hanny, Birgit, and Wessels, Wolfgang (1998), 'The Monetary Committee: A Significant though Not Typical Case', in M. P. C. M. van Schendelen (ed.), EU Committees as Influential Policymakers (Aldershot: Brookfield), 109–26.

Hayes-Renshaw, Fiona, and Wallace, Helen (1995), 'Executive Power in the European Union: The Functions and Limits on the Council of Ministers', Journal of European Public Policy, 2/4: 559–82.

————(1997), The Council of Ministers (London: Macmillan).

Hesse, Jens Joachim (ed.) (1978), Politikverflechtung im föderativen Staat: Studien zum Planungs-und Finanzierungsverbund zwischen Bund, Ländern und Gemeinden (Baden-Baden: Nomos).

Hrbek, Rudolf (1986), 'Doppelte Politikverflechtung: Deutscher Föderalismus und Europäische Integration. Die Deutschen Länder im EG-Entscheidungsprozeß', in Rudolf Hrbek and Uwe Thaysen (eds.), Die Deutschen Länder und die Europäischen Gemeinschaften (Baden-Baden: Nomos), 26–7.

————(1999), 'The Effects of EU Integration on German Federalism', in Charlie Jeffery (ed.), Recasting German Federalism: The Legacies of Unification (London: Pinter).

Jachtenfuchs, Markus, and Kohler-Koch, Beate (1996), 'Regieren im dynamischen Mehrebenensystem', in Jachtenfuchs and Kohler-Koch (eds.), Europäische Integration (Opladen: Leske & Budrich), 15–44.

Janning, Josef, and Meyer, Patrick (1998), 'Deutsche Europapolitik: Vorschläge zur Effektiviening', in W. Weidenfeld (ed.), Deutsche Europapolitik: Optionen wirksamer Interessenvertretung (Bonn: Europa Union Verlag), 267–86.

Jaspert, Günter (1982), 'Der Bundesrat und die europäische Integration', Aus Politik und Zeitgeschichte, B12: 1–26.

Knodt, Michèle (1998), 'Auswärtiges Handeln der Deutschen Länder', in Wolf-Dieter Eberwein Karl Kaiser (eds.), Deutschlands neue Außenpolitik 4: Institutionen und Ressourcen (Munich: Oldenbourg), 153–66.

Lequesne, Christian (1996), 'France', in Dietrich Rometsch and Wolfgang Wessels (eds.), The European Union and Member States: Towards Institutonal Fusion? (Manchester: Manchester University Press), 185–96.

Maurer, Andreas (forthcoming), 'Germany: Fragmented Systems Fitting into the Union', in Wolfgang Wessels, Andreas Maurer, and Jürgen Mittag (eds.), Fifteen into One? The European Union and its Member States (Manchester: Manchester University Press).

————and Wessels, Wolfgang (1999), 'The Interagency Process in the Federal Republic of Germany', in Carl Lankowski (ed.), German Issue Briefs, No. II (Washington, DC: AICGS).

Mayntz, Renate (1982), 'Problemverarbeitung durch das politisch-administrative System: Zum Stand der Forschung', in Joachim Jens Hesse (ed.), Politikwissenschaft und Verwaltungswissenschaft (PVS-Sonderheft, 13: Opladen: Westdeutscher Verlag), 74–89.

Mentler, Michael (1996), Der Ausschuß der Ständigen Vertreter bei den Europäischen Gemeinschaften (Baden-Baden: Nomos).

Milward, Alan S. (1992), *The European Rescue of the Nation State* (London: Routledge).

Organizational Decree (1998), '*Organisationserlaß des Bundeskanzlers*', Bonn, 27 Oct. (including the 'Vereinbarung zwischen dem Auswärtigen Amt und dem Bundesministerium für Finanzen', Bonn, 20 Oct.).

Pierson, Paul (1998), 'The Path to European Integration: A Historical Institutionalist Analysis', in Wayne Sandholtz and Alec Stone Sweet (eds.), *European Integration and Supranational Governance* (Oxford: Oxford University Press), 27–58.

Regelsberger, Elfriede, and Wessels, Wolfgang (eds.) (1984), *The Federal Republic of Germany and the European Community: The Presidency and Beyond* (Bonn: Europa Union Verlag).

Reissert, Bernd, and Scharpf, Fritz W. (1977), *Politikverflechtung, Theorie und Empirie des kooperativen Föderalismus in der Bundesrepublik* (Kronberg/TS: Athenäum).

Rometsch, Dietrich (1996), 'The Federal Republic of Germany', in Dietrich Rometsch and Wolfgang Wessels (eds.), *The European Union and Member States: Towards Institutional Fusion?* (Manchester: Manchester University Press), 61–104.

——and Wessels, Wolfgang (eds.) (1996), 'Conclusion', *The European Union and Member States: Towards Institutional Fusion?* (Manchester: Manchester University Press).

Sasse, Christoph (1975), *Regierungen, Parlamente, Ministerrat: Entscheidungsprozesse in der Europäischen Gemeinschaft* (Bonn: Europa Union Verlag).

——Poullet, E., Coombes, D., and Deprez, G. (1977), *Decision-Making in the European Community* (New York: Praeger).

——(1988), 'The Joint-Decision Trap: Lessons from German Federalism and European Integration', *Public Administration*, 66/3: 229–78.

——(1997), 'Economic Integration, Democracy and the Welfare State', *Journal of European Public Policy*, 4/1: 18–36.

Schmitter, Philippe (1996), 'Imagining the Future of the Euro-Polity with the Help of New Concepts', in Gary Marks, Fritz W. Scharpf, Philippe C. Schmitter, and Wolfgang Streeck (eds.), *Governance in the European Union* (London: Sage), 121–50.

Siwert-Probst, Judith (1998), 'Die klassischen außenpolitischen Institutionen', in Wolf-Dieter Eberwein and Karl Kaiser (eds.), *Deutschlands neue Außenpolitik 4: Institutionen und Ressourcen* (Munich: Oldenbourg), 13–28.

Spinelli, Altiero (1966), *The Eurocrats: Conflict and Crisis in the European Community* (Baltimore: Johns Hopkins University Press).

Szukala, Andrea (forthcoming), 'The European Transformation of the French Model', in W. Wessels, A. Maurer, and J. Mittag (eds.), *Fifteen into One? The European Union and its Member States* (Manchester: Manchester University Press).

Von Ploetz, Hans-Friedrich (1998), 'Der Auswärtige Dienst vor neuen Herausforderungen', in Wolf-Dieter Eberwein and Karl Kaiser (eds.), *Deutschlands neue Außenpolitik 4: Institutionen und Ressourcen* (Munich: Oldenbourg), 59–74.

Weber-Panariello, Phillipe A. (1996), *Nationale Parlamente in der Europäischen Union* (Baden-Baden: Nomos).

Wessels, Wolfgang (1990), 'Administrative Interaction', in William Wallace (ed.), *The Dynamics of European Integration* (London: Royal Institute of International Affairs and Pinter), 229–41.

Wessels, Wolfgang (1991), 'The EC Council: The Community's Decision-Making Center', in Robert O. Keohane and Stanley Hoffman (eds.), *The New European Community: Decision-Making and Institutional Change* (Boulder, CO: Westview), 133–54.

——(1992), 'Staat und (west-europäische) Integration: Die Fusionsthese', in Michael Kreile (ed.), *Die Integration Europas* (PVS-Sonderheft, 23; Opladen: Westdeutscher Verlag), 36–61.

——(1997), 'An Ever Closer Fusion? A Dynamic Macropolitical View on Integration Processes', *Journal of Common Market Studies*, 35/2: 267–99.

——(2000), *Die Öffnung des Staates: Modelle und Wirklichkeit grenzüberschreitender Verwaltungspraxis 1960–1995* (Opladen: Leske & Budrich).

Westlake, Martin (ed.) (1995), *The Council of the European Union* (London: Cartermills).

Wright, Vincent (1996), 'The National Co-ordination of European Policy-Making: Negotiating the Quagmire', in Jeremy Richardson (ed.), *European Union: Power and Policy-Making* (London: Routledge), 148–69.

4

Italy

Giacinto della Cananea

A Neglected Theme

The Italian permanent representation has received very little academic or political attention. Indeed, there has been no explicit debate as to how this body should be shaped. Even when the central government decided that it should control all aspects of the formulation of EC policies—though delegating to regions their implementation in a number of cases (decree no. 616/1977)—the permanent representation was not even mentioned in the legislation. In the late 1980s, when a more elaborate framework for the co-ordination of EC policy-making was laid down by legislation (Cassese 1985; Chiti 1991; Franchini 1992), there was not a single paragraph about the permanent representation. The situation is no more encouraging in the academic literature. There is not a single book or essay on Italy's permanent representation, in spite of the considerable attention paid, say, to the European Parliament and its groups or even the Court of Auditors, with only few recent exceptions (Tizzano 1992).

This neglect, it is argued, is problematic for several reasons. First of all, although no body including national representatives was provided for in either the European Coal and Steel Community, created by the Treaty of Paris in 1951, nor within the EC, in both cases such bodies were set up as soon as the common institutions began fulfilling their tasks: the Commission de coordination, or Cocor as it was known from February 1953, a

An earlier draft of this chapter was presented at the conference on 'National Co-ordination in Brussels: The Role of the Permanent Representation', Oxford, Nuffield College, 14–15 May 1999. The author wishes to thank Prof. Sabino Cassese, for his comments on the earlier draft, and Prof. Antonio Tizzano, for his helpful insights into the activity of the permanent representation. Of course, the author alone is responsible for all omissions and errors.

few months after the Council of Ministers itself started working, and
COREPER from January 1958 (Tizzano 1992: 523). This was a unilateral
initiative, rather than a concerted one, as is so often the case in international
relations (Capotorti 1974). Secondly, although the EEC (now EC) Treaty
provided for the creation of a committee charged with the task of assisting
the Council of Ministers (vested with primary policy and law-making
powers), it was not at all clear that it should consist of the permanent representatives of the member states (for example, it could have consisted of
ad hoc members). However, this choice was made and never altered. Indeed,
the legal basis of COREPER was strengthened by the Merger Treaty of
1965 and was left untouched by the several constitutional amendments
which followed it. Eloquent testimony to the importance of the permanent
representations is given by the legal and political science literature, where
it clearly emerges that, in the broader context of the strengthened position
of national governments, the role of COREPER has gradually become crucial,
due to its capacity to influence the Council's decision-making process
and to either lend support to, or block, the Commission's proposals
(Gerbet and Pepy 1969; Sasse 1975; Wallace 1973; Hayes-Renshaw and Wallace
1997). Therefore, although the Council's own secretariat has widened,
the political role of the permanent representative has not been diminished
at all.

If overlooking the role of the permanent representation is a mistake, how
can its neglect be explained? As suggested elsewhere (della Cananea 2000),
membership of the European Community was the crucial and initially highly
controversial choice made by Italy's ruling élites in the second half of the twen-
tieth century (nowadays, however, a sort of consensus exists on this point,
although proposals aiming at introducing a specific European clause within
the Constitution have failed);[1] however, this choice was conceived in terms of
'high politics' and for a long time was not supported by adequate administrative machinery. Academic studies, too, with a few exceptions, shared this
broad vision of European integration, but neglected administrative bodies and
procedures (Cassese 1995: 429).

The discussion below is organized into four sections. First, a brief examination of the broader problem determined by the lack of a central authority
is undertaken. Next, both the functions of the permanent representation and
its organization and internal functioning will be considered. The concrete
division of labour between the central authorities and the permanent representation will then be examined. Finally, other networks which influence
Italian European policies will be discussed.

---

[1] A political scientist (Cotta 1998: 453) has recently stressed that the only time at which
Italy seemed to adopt a more sceptical view was during 1994, but that situation was rapidly
reversed.

The Lack of a Central Steering Authority

In order to understand the importance of the role played by the permanent representation, it is necessary to bear in mind the weakness which has constantly characterized the co-ordination of EC (and now EU) policies in Italy (Chiti 1991; Franchini 1992). Politically and symbolically important achievements in Italian EU policy, such as the Messina conference, or more recently the fulfilment of the criteria for access to the third stage of the European Economic and Monetary Union, were made possible by certain specific conditions, such as clear objections and strong popular support (Cotta 1998: 453) and a subtle mix of fiscal and financial measures (della Cananea 1997, 1998), hierarchically imposed by the then prime minister—Romano Prodi, who subsequently became President of the European Commission—and especially, the Minister of the Treasury, Carlo Azeglio Ciampi, later elected President of the Republic. This provides further proof that hierarchy, rather than loose co-ordinating tools, can be a very effective instrument of governance.

There are several causes of the weakness of co-ordination in Italy. The first is the absence of a central steering authority. In Italy, until recently, the President of the Council of Ministers was relatively weak in legal and political terms. Legally, the authority and legitimacy of the role was entirely derived from Parliament and the Constitution did not guarantee it a sphere of rule-making powers, unlike the case in France. In particular, according to the Constitution (Articles 95 and 97), even the organization of the prime ministers office and of the central departments had to be regulated by parliamentary legislation. Only since 1997, after the first two elections were carried out under the new mainly majoritarian system, have these constitutional clauses been interpreted in a less restrictive way, more consistent with the need for flexible organization of the executive, so as to be able to achieve the desired results. Politically, moreover, parliamentary majorities have traditionally been highly fragmented, though stable in terms of both political support (based on the same party from 1948 to 1994) and personal appointment to the Council of Ministers (a relatively limited number of people were appointed ministers in the years 1948–92), which resulted in frequent changes in the composition of the Council of Ministers.

These factors, however, are too general by themselves to provide a precise explanation of the deficiencies of co-ordination of European policies. To understand this, another element—the fragmentation of responsibility for dealing with European affairs—needs to be considered. Initially, and for a long time, the elaboration of EC policies was the primary responsibility of the Ministry of Foreign Affairs, the underlying idea being that European integration fell within the sphere of foreign policy. This explains the institutional relationship between the permanent representation and the Ministry of Foreign Affairs. The rules concerning the permanent representation were laid down in the ECSC in the context of the more general framework of the organization of the Ministry of Foreign Affairs (Monaco 1961) and this choice was confirmed both after the entry into force of the EEC Treaty (d.P.R. no. 16/1958) and in 1967. Since then, it has been a peripheral office within the Ministry of Foreign Affairs (Franchini 1992). The entire framework was based on two assumptions. The first is that the state is a monolith. This is the traditional view, according to which the state has a single interest, defined by the government and not by the Parliament, as in other areas of foreign policy. All policy decisions were, in fact, taken without any contribution, let alone binding decision, from the Parliament, which marks a striking difference from, for instance, Denmark (Greco 1989: 44). The preferences of the government were expressed by a specific body, the Ministry of Foreign Affairs (Ronzitti 1987; Tizzano 1992: 527). As the ministry did not have a specific directorate general (the basic administrative unit within ministries) in charge of European affairs, they were entrusted mainly to the directorate general in charge of economic affairs. The second assumption was that, since the ministry had to ensure external co-ordination (with EC institutions and other governments) and internal co-ordination (with all administrations involved in EC affairs)—this role was codified by the regulation adopted with the d.P.R. no. 18/1967—the permanent representation had to be its 'longa manus'.

This framework was consistent with the overall shape of EC policy-making, as EC policies were limited to negative integration, that is, to the suppression of obstacles to free trade among the member states. However, it became inadequate as soon as EC policies were directed towards positive integration, in the form of common policies, first in the fields of agriculture and external trade (mid-1960s) and later in new areas of activity, such as environmental protection and regional development, introduced in the early 1970s (Pinder 1968; Kapteyn 1979) and subsequently codified by the Single European Act of 1986 (Tizzano 1989: 61). This steady expansion of EC functions and powers had a series of consequences. At Community level, until the period of Jacques Delors's Presidency of the Commission, it was accompanied by a gradual shift of power, in terms of the ability to define the strategic direction of the EC, from the Commission to intergovernmental authorities, in particular the Council of Ministers and the European Council (Wallace 1973; Lenaerts 1991). At a national level, it required technical departments and regional authorities to be involved decision-making procedures. The former were asked to send senior officials to Brussels, so as to negotiate technical dossiers which diplomats were not able to deal with. An increasing number of experts therefore began flying regularly to Brussels to take part in the meetings of intergovernmental committees established either by the Council or by the Commission as part of the comitology system (della Cananea 1990). In this regard, it is necessary to mention the peculiar situation created by the fragmented nature of Italian central departments: controversial dossiers managed, for example, by the French Economic Ministry alone, were dealt with in Italy by three different ministries: Treasury, Budget, and either Finances or the *ad hoc* Ministry for Public Intervention in Southern Regions (abolished in 1993). The Italian regions initially played a very limited role. However, more recently they have been empowered to establish direct connections with EU institutions (Caranta 1997: 1222; D'Atena 1992).

In order to deal with this increased fragmentation, a limited number of reforms to the executive were introduced (and other, less significant, organizational changes occurred within parliamentary structures, with the creation of two specific committees). First, the most important committee of ministers, dealing with economic planning (*Comitato interministeriale per la programmazione economica*, Cipe), was entrusted with the task of formulating general guidelines on the national position within EC decision-making bodies. Secondly, from the early 1980s onwards, in most Council of Ministers meetings a minister without portfolio was given the task of co-ordinating national policies. This change was formally recognized in the late 1980s when legislation was introduced to adjust internal mechanisms so as to enable the minister to cope with the growing scope of EC law and policies. The minister was given a department (*Dipartimento per il coordinamento delle politiche comunitarie* 1994) within the prime minister's office. As it is a department rather than a ministry, it has well-specified competences but not the kind of autonomy that other units enjoy. Finally, the monitoring of financial activities was assigned to the Treasury, by way of a specific mechanism (*Fondo di rotazione per il coordinamento delle politiche comunitarie*).

These changes led to two further developments. On the one hand, they have gradually eroded the monopoly of the Ministry of Foreign Affairs. On the other, this monopoly has not been replaced by that of another central authority.

The idea behind attempts to reform the co-ordination of EC policies was to establish a sort of 'diarchy' with diplomats dealing with institutional issues (and the elaboration of new treaties) and the new department co-ordinating sectoral policies, especially in the context of the Single European Market. The result, however, has not been as clear cut, since the allocation of responsibilities has remained unclear and both institutions have sought to gain primacy. The department, though understaffed, profits from being part of the prime minister's office. In fact, two recent prime ministers, Prodi and D'Alema, have strengthened the role of the minister dealing with European issues. In March 1998, Prodi issued a directive[2] which enhanced the connection between the permanent representation (now redefined as '*Rappresentanza permanente*

---

[2] The directive is examined more fully in the next section.

presso l'Unione europea') and the department in the prime minister's office
(Franchini 1998: 889). D'Alema, for his part, has delegated a number of
powers to the minister.

The list of these powers, stated in the decree of January 2000, is quite
impressive, since the minister for the co-ordination of EU policies has: (*a*) to
ensure the coherence and promptness of national interventions on both
general EU initiatives and specific policies; (*b*) to prepare the annual bill (to
be adopted by Parliament) for the transposition and implementation of
European legislation on the basis of the opinions expressed by a committee
of regional representatives; (*c*) to ensure the respect of obligations undertaken
at the Community level; (*d*) to take part in meetings of the Council of
Ministers concerning the internal market; (*e*) to take all necessary actions to
prevent and deal with proceedings before the European Court of Justice; (*f*)
to decide whether it is useful to intervene in proceedings in which national
interests are at stake; (*g*) to lead a specific advisory committee on the internal
market (another committee has just been established to deal with procedures
related to European funds); (*h*) to take measures aimed at improving the
knowledge of EC law amongst civil servants; (*i*) to undertake to inform the
Parliament of developments in the EU.

If all the powers just mentioned were taken seriously, one might be tempted
to conclude that the *ad hoc* minister is now the steering authority. However,
there are several reasons to suspect that a more sceptical interpretation is
appropriate. The first, from a legal point of view, is that these powers are not
a ministerial prerogative: the prime minister has delegated them. This means
that the prime minister can exercise them directly. Moreover, with every
change in the composition of the cabinet (now less frequent than before 1995,
but still more so than in the other European democracies), different solutions
are likely to be adopted, depending on different points of view about how to
promote the national interest within the European arena.

Secondly, the department is entrusted with the task of overall coordina-
tions, but it still lacks well defined powers with regard to other administrations (Franchini 1998: 898). What happens, for instance, if conflict emerges
among administrations with distinct, or even opposing, interests? No hierarchy has been defined (such as the one which allows the state to overrule decisions taken by the regions whenever they fail to comply with EU law), which
suggests that the powers conferred on the department are more formal than
real. They exist on paper but not in reality.

Thirdly, as a matter of principle, strategic decisions are to be taken by Cipe.
Therefore it is highly significant that this committee is led by the minister of
the Treasury, which has absorbed most of the spending functions related to
the use of European funds by southern Italy. It has also merged with the
Budget Ministry and is expected to merge with the Ministry of Finances

(dealing with taxation) in 2001. The Italian case is not unique in this regard, as the strengthening of ECOFIN (in which this minister participates), as the main EU decision-making body for all economic and budgetary affairs, suggests.

Fourthly, the Ministry of Foreign Affairs has not given up its ambition to be in charge of European issues. In particular, while implementing the broad delegation obtained from Parliament in 1997, it proposed a governmental regulation, now adopted (no. 267/1999), which strengthens the units that deal with European issues. Not only was a specific directorate general set up, but its competences include both the elaboration of national positions *vis-à-vis* the institutions of the EU, and the conduct of negotiations relating to the process of integration (*direzione generale per l'integrazione europea*).[3] They also include the adoption of measures aimed at improving knowledge of EU rules and policies amongst civil servants—one of the tasks subsequently delegated to the Minister for the Co-ordination of EU Policies. According to the law, the decree must be interpreted in a manner consistent with legislative rules conferring functions on the prime minister, which can be delegated (Sico 1999: 844). Nevertheless, the general impression is inevitably one of persistent institutional rivalry, which is to a certain extent formalized. Moreover, from a political point of view, at least two issues should not be overlooked. One is that the same minister has led EU policy in the last three executives and has constantly sought to inspire governmental action with regard to all crucial European dossiers. The other is that while Prodi adopted a directive more favourable to the department, he did not appoint a minister, but rather an undersecretary of state (not even a junior minister, as is the case in the UK), which reduced both the department's status and its power. More generally, it is not easy to replace the Ministry of Foreign Affairs with the (still weak) Department for the Co-ordination of EC Policies: the former, at least, had and—to a certain extent—still has, a strong administrative tradition, high prestige in political terms, and high-quality staff from which, not by chance, Italian governments have selected EC Commissioners, such as Raniero Vanni d'Archirafi (for previous ones see Condorelli Braun 1972).

Finally, more than two-thirds of Italian ministries have specific units dealing with EC affairs (Cassese 1995: 420; Gnes 1997: 43). Moreover, other links between national and European institutions have gradually developed. The best example is that of the Bank of Italy. Other such instances are illustrated in the last section of this chapter.

---

[3] A glance at the areas covered by the units of the DG for European affairs is illuminating: economic policy (I), external relations (II), financial co-operation and aid to third countries (III), foreign and security policy (IV), justice and home affairs (V) and legal and institutional affairs (VI).

The Functions and Powers Conferred on the Permanent Representation

The functions of the permanent representation can be described in general terms as acting to promote the national interest, by (*a*) channelling information from the EU to Rome and vice versa; and (*b*) acting as a base for negotiators, whether they are formally included in the staff of the representation or simply have an *ad hoc* mandate. A more analytical description suggests that the permanent representation has three kinds of functions, while its powers are seldom clear.

A first function consists of transmitting to the Department for the Co-ordination of EC Policies all texts including policy guidelines (those which are listed are the Commission's annual plan of activity and those of the Council Presidency as well as the positions of the European Parliament) and draft legislation. Paradoxically, the Department for the Co-ordination of EU Policies then informs, *inter alia*, the Ministry of Foreign Affairs, which is the central administrative structure to which the representation belongs. This, however, is but one curiosity: another is the lack of attention paid to the Commission's non-legislative documents, which can be of some importance.

The second function works in the opposite way. Once the Council Presidency has obtained all the necessary observations from other institutions, it informs the permanent representation within thirty days about the positions which must be supported in the framework of EU negotiations. A specific procedure has to be followed by the Council in the case of draft regulations and directives, when EU procedures allow the decision to be altered at the request of one or more national governments. The department is also entrusted with the task of gathering observations from other central departments (including the Ministry of Foreign Affairs) as well as the two Houses of Parliament (both the Senate and the Chamber of Deputies have set up specific committees charged with the task of supervising governmental action and formulating guidelines) and regional authorities. The department then 'promotes' the elaboration of the governmental position and 'informs' the permanent representation (and, at the same time, the national Parliament) of the position to be presented to EU institutions. All this suggests that, as in the past, EU policy is still the responsibility of the executive and that the permanent representation is functionally, though not organically, attached to the department. In other words, it has a two-fold connection (*codipendenza*) with central authorities: a functional one with the department and both a functional and an organic one with the Ministry of Foreign Affairs. Indeed, the permanent representative is still appointed by the foreign minister and is accountable to him.

There is further evidence to support this conclusion. It is the task of the department to inform all national institutions about new EU legislation and to take all measures necessary to ensure their transposition and implementation. The department co-ordinates all the ministries and other administrations in order to ensure adequate and constant contact with the permanent representation. Once again, this may suggest that the department has taken over the old primary role played by the ministry. However, the reality is quite different, for reasons explained below.

Finally, besides channelling information and instructions, the permanent representation has to take care of the relationship with the Secretariat of the EU Council, the Commission, and other member states, with special regard to solving the (well-known and never-ending) controversies about the transposition and implementation of EU law. This is an aspect which has often been overlooked in the past, but it has attracted the attention of both policy-makers and academic observers since it became clear that the judicial process is frequently used as an alternative instrument to achieve policy (and sometimes even political) goals, and has been used for these purposes even by one member state (generally intervening in favour of the Commission in proceedings under Article 226, formerly Article 169, EC Treaty) against each other.

This description may suggest that, since all relationships must be channelled through the permanent representation, the state-as-monolith paradigm survives despite the decline of its traditional instrument, the administration of foreign affairs. It may also suggest that, after years of little or no attention being paid to the permanent representation, its functions and role have been well defined. Such conclusions would, however, be misleading.

The state-as-monolith paradigm was perhaps an adequate representation of reality when international relations were carried out exclusively through diplomatic channels, but it has become inadequate since these relations have come to involve sectoral or regional organizations. In the EU arena, in particular, experts from technical administrations constantly negotiate on a number of issues, of which only a few require political compromises among national permanent representatives. In addition, there are other networks among European and national institutions.

Moreover, the legal framework (which is not based on legislation, and is thus flexible and led by the executive without the need for parliamentary consent) introduced since the adoption of the directive of 1998 is little changed and inadequate. It has changed little because it simply codifies existing practices, adding a degree of transparency. Nor is it adequate: it is still based on the idea that documents circulate (only) on paper, while today information can easily be sent everywhere in an instant; it sets a deadline of thirty days, which is too long for problems which require a prompt solution. As a former legal adviser to the permanent representative observed some years ago: 'decisions are [taken] during the course of negotiations which . . . [leave] few or no possibilities for subsequent amendment' (Tizzano 1992: 527).

The Organization and Functioning of the
Permanent Representation

Having considered its responsibilities, we now turn to an examination of the organization and functioning of the permanent representation. The organization is characterized by four main features. First, a senior civil servant drawn from the ranks of diplomatic personnel has always headed it. Formally, the permanent representative has always enjoyed the rank and prerogatives of an ambassador; he consequently enjoys the privileges and immunities typical of the diplomatic career. If he differs from an ambassador, it is for other reasons: he has no need to receive the approval of either EC or Belgian authorities; he is included *ex officio* within the collegial body of national representatives (COREPER); moreover, in comparison with other ambassadors, he has more frequent contacts with national authorities.

Another notable feature of the PR is the rigidity of its administrative organization. This is based, like the traditional ministerial organization, on the hierarchical principle, rather than on the wide delegation of power introduced more recently in central departments and local governments. One reason for the rigidity of the organization is that it is regulated by secondary rules, which are binding on the government. The government may modify them, but not neglect them and any change requires the prior approval of the Council of State and of the Court of Auditors. The rigidity has been accentuated by a recent Act of Parliament, which limited the number of experts for all embassies, including that in Brussels: no more than twenty-nine people from the ranks of the Ministry of Foreign Affairs can be added to the personnel (Art. 58, l. no. 52/1996).

Thirdly, the representation in Brussels is slightly different from other embassies. It is bigger: there were thirty-five people at the end of the 1980s, now there are about fifty, but advisers and experts are added when necessary. There is also a deputy permanent representative, which is a consequence of the partial harmonization determined by the organization of EU bodies (COREPER has a committee of deputy representatives). Its staff, moreover, consists not only of diplomats and senior officers from specialized departments: the legal adviser to the permanent representative (a key role, especially with regard to controversial issues such as the identification of the proper legal basis of EU acts or the respect of procedures) has been, for some years, an academic who specializes in EU law.

Finally, the staff of the PR is heterogeneous. Until the 1970s, it was composed mainly of career diplomats. They form one of the subcommunities that, within the Italian civil service, have always been better trained, selected, and paid. Over the years, these features have gradually become more pronounced. Subsequently, the expansion of EC functions noted above resulted in a growing workload and, at the same time, in the need for technical expertise quite different from that possessed by diplomats. At present, half of the PR staff come from the Ministry of Foreign Affairs and the other half from other ministries dealing with EC policies in the agricultural or industrial fields, such as the Treasury, and from the Bank of Italy.[4]

These experts are chosen by their administrations, or, more precisely, by the administrative élite, though at least formally the Ministry of Foreign Affairs is required to approve their secondment to Brussels. There is also intervention from the Treasury for financial reasons. There is no specific procedure (let alone any kind of open competition) or set of criteria by which the staff are selected. However, current practice shows that officers coming from technical ministries have previously had some experience of EU negotiation in the framework of the myriad of advisory committees. Appointment to the PR has therefore become a kind of reward, which, not least, may improve the job prospects of officials once they return home. The problem that arises is that their choice is often influenced by political patronage, as is the choice of those who are sent from time to time to the committees of experts. Secondment, however, is limited by law to eight years (Art. 168, d.P.R. no. 18/1967).

If describing the features of the administrative machinery is a relatively easy task, it is less easy to give an account of its internal functioning and, most of all, of its performance. From the few studies available as well as some insiders' opinions, the permanent representation is characterized by at least three features. First, diplomats have a clear primacy over other administrators, even if they are younger. The permanent representative does not even meet experts coming from Rome, unless it is unavoidable. On the other hand, experts are a key resource: as the former legal adviser stressed, although they obey political guidelines, their negotiating skills are very useful, and often crucial. Moreover, diplomats could not replace them, since they lack adequate technical skills, for example, for the negotiation of banking directives, which has always been dealt with by officers coming from the Treasury and the Bank of Italy.

Secondly, those who have worked within the permanent representation describe its style as characterized by the 'utmost discretion' (Tizzano 1992: 522), as has traditionally been the case with diplomacy. This is another sign of the predominance of the working methods typical of the administration of foreign affairs.

Finally, the activity of the representation is highly fragmented, due to the sheer variety of dossiers and the limited human resources available: experts, once again, may offer valuable help, but this can easily accentuate

---

[4] In 1997, those who were not diplomats came from twelve ministries (three from the Treasury), the Bank of Italy, and two public bodies (Gnes 1997: 43).

fragmentation. There is the problem of ensuring 'consistency and . . . homogeneity in its work' (Tizzano 1992: 528).

The Permanent Representative as an Actor

In order to assess the role played by the Italian permanent representation it must be borne in mind that its strengths and weaknesses cannot be considered in isolation from the broader national context. For instance, the lack of continuity of governments and the 'kind of schizoid split in the conduct of the various institutions . . . inevitably hampers the achievements, and even tarnishes the image, of Italy's EC membership' (Tizzano 1992: 529). Nor is their action insulated from the environment within which it is carried out. Factors such as European procedures and the political majorities (the strength of the Franco-German *entente* or the support of the other Mediterranean countries) necessarily influence the capacity to produce the desired outcomes.

The personal prestige of the permanent representative is another key factor, though it is seldom or never explored. In this respect, although all of the permanent representatives to date have come from traditional diplomatic ranks, the type of individual chosen has differed over the years. Indeed, there is a striking difference between the appointment of people like Renato Ruggiero, who had worked in the Commission's staff (with the Dutch Commissioner Sicco Mansholt), and who therefore knew the European administration very well, had a strong personality, and significant prestige (which allowed him to be appointed minister, though for a limited time, and to become the first director general of the World Trade Organization), or Silvio Fagiolo, the present representative, who was previously deeply involved in all recent negotiations over both the institutional reform of the EU and its enlargement, and the appointment of a diplomat at the end of his career, after he concluded his office as diplomatic adviser to the President of the Council of Ministers. The appointment in this case comes as a sort of reward or even a bonus. Naturally, in the first two cases personal ability, prestige, and ambitions can contribute to the capacity to promote national interests, while in the latter case a routine role is more likely to be adopted.

With all these necessary caveats, some general observations may be made with regard to the role of the permanent representative and to the broader performance of the co-ordination of European policies within the Italian government.

First, if we adopt the oversimplified distinction of dividing permanent representatives into the two opposing categories of executors and policy-makers, the Italian case must certainly be included in the latter. On this point there is a significant convergence of opinions. Those who have worked within the permanent representation tend to emphasize that if 'Italy's diplomatic initiative has been often incisive, and sometimes . . . decisive, . . . the part played by the PRs must not be ignored' (Tizzano 1992: 528). An outsider with a privileged point of view (someone who had been the secretary-general of the European Commission for almost thirty years) confirmed that view, writing that one of the most solid pillars of the Italian EC policy-making was the permanent representative's capacity to take decisions with a margin of manœuvre unknown to his colleagues, due to the flexible directives coming from Rome and to the personal qualities of the senior officers who had to implement them (Noël 1989: 90). A different way of expressing the same opinion would be to point out that the view of the permanent representative as a policy actor, rather than an arena or an executor, largely stems from the ineffective co-ordination carried out by central authorities. Sometimes the ministries involved in the negotiation of technical dossiers have sent contrasting instructions. More frequently, such instructions do not arrive at all, as several official reports have shown in the last years (Senato della Repubblica 1992; Dipartimento della funzione pubblica 1994). Comparative analysis also reveals that Italian ministers are among those who attend Council of Ministers meetings least frequently, being replaced by either undersecretaries of state or the representatives themselves.[5] Seen in this light, the margin of discretion left to the permanent representative looks more like a remedy of other weaknesses than an asset. This also makes the personal qualifications and prestige of those appointed to this office more significant than elsewhere, although these are hardly likely to be considered as substitutes for a clear perception of national interests, for prompt instructions from politicians, and for a solid technical analysis from bureaucrats.

Besides personal prestige, direct political intervention is another key resource used when politically sensitive issues are at stake. For example, the successful negotiation in the European Union Treaty of the parameters on public debt and deficits and the subsequent European Council decision about the beginning of the third phase of EMU were both characterized by an unusually clear perception of national interests. They were also the product of a process long enough to permit an accurate perception of the implications of all possible options. Finally, negotiations were led by first-class diplomats and expert technicians, backed by two 'grands commis de l'État' with a solid international reputation, Guido Carli and Carlo Azeglio Ciampi (della Cananea 1998).

A more recent case, with a lower political profile, is that of the negotiation

[5] The data reported by a newspaper (*Corriere della sera*, 11 Dec. 1995) showed that under the executives led by Berlusconi (1994) and Dini (1995), of the twenty meetings of the ministers of foreign affairs and seventeen of financial ministers, in twelve cases (one-third), ministers were substituted because of other commitments, while the British Chancellor of the Exchequer did not miss a single meeting, although the UK was (and still is) outside EMU.

of agricultural product prices. In the past, Commission's proposals had been accepted, according to a parliamentary report, 'too quickly or superficially within experts' meetings of COREPER or the Council' (Camera dei Deputati 1982: 13), giving rise to the milk quota saga (with political and judicial conflicts). In 1999, however, a much better political compromise was obtained, by the prior formation of a coalition of interests within the Council of Ministers. Once again, however, this was the result of a political impulse from a specific minister, although others intervened in the preparation of the draft compromise.[6]

A different situation arises during the routine policy-making process, in areas such as technical rules or environmental protection. Expertise and domestic backing are key resources that are much more easily used when institutional issues are at stake than in the daily management of substantive EU policies (with the exceptions of the Treasury and the Bank of Italy). In this context, co-ordination is often left to informal procedures or even to personal initiatives, carried out by senior officers more accustomed to Brussels' working techniques, and thus compensating for the lack of political direction. This was the case with the Ministry of Public Education regarding the use of European funds, which provides an interesting case of administrative adjustment. First, some senior officers took the initiative in asking for EC financial resources, their unit then became the *chef de file* for all other units of that ministry, several committees were later created, and finally in 1997 a specific co-ordination unit and a committee of all directors were set up (Gnes 1997: 45).

The Growing Importance of Other Networks

The analysis carried out so far would be incomplete without at least a mention of the importance of other policy networks. Ten years ago it was claimed that the permanent representative 'is the Member States' ambassador to the EC, but he is also the Ambassador of the E.C. to the Member States' (Tizzano 1992: 531). This is no longer true, as a result of two converging phenomena.

The first is the demise of national boundaries for independent public institutions. The best example of this is that of the central bank, the Banca d'Italia. Even before the Maastricht Treaty, its senior officers were regularly involved in the activities of EC committees (Committee of Governors, Committee for Political Economy, and a number of advisory committees). The Bank is now outside the diplomatic framework, due to its inclusion in the

---

[6] In the interview given to the *Il Sole 24 Ore* (27 Mar. 1999), the minister emphasized that the governmental position had not been weakened by 'in the slightest', which led to an excellent result.

specific institutional network of the European system of central banks. This had internal consequences, like the creation of a co-ordination committee where all the services are represented. The creation of sectoral networks can also be found in other areas. For instance, both the authority that supervises the financial and stock exchange markets (Commissione nazionale per le società e la borsa, Consob) and the competition authority (Autorità garante della concorrenza e del mercato) have been authorized by an Act of Parliament to establish autonomous relationships with the Commission, to facilitate and enhance both the exchange of information and co-ordination of interventions in areas of common interest. The competition authority, in particular, is expanding connections of this sort, as a result of the increasingly decentralized implementation of competition rules envisaged by the EU Commission. The result is the gradual replacement of a single network, solidly in the hands of the Ministry of Foreign Affairs, with a set of networks. This is even more evident when these networks are not limited vertically to the relationships between the national authority and the Commission, but also have also a horizontal dimension with their national counterparts, as was specified for the Consob in 1991 and 1996.

The other phenomenon regards the regions. Even when they were not allowed to perform activities of a legislative character, regions acted as lobbyists in Brussels. Some of them, for this reason, created a their own equivalents of representations, though hiding their real nature: the *escamotage* was to do it indirectly, through the formation of a company whose shares belonged entirely to the region. More recently, the same Act of Parliament (art. 58, l. no. 52/1996) has meant that regional officers are assigned to the permanent representation and has authorized regions to establish their own *bureaux de liaison*, which act as channels of information and negotiation, though not of decision. However, in reality the borderline between these roles is rather unclear. The permanent representation is, therefore, no longer their 'ambassador', especially if several regions join in setting up a common information office in Brussels: five regions of central Italy have done so recently, by using a pre-existing structure, that of a financial company entirely in the hands of the Regione Toscana.

Both developments confirm that the old paradigm of the state-as-monolith can no longer be maintained, because there are new reasons for contact between public bodies which require direct relationships. It is worth mentioning that both needs have been dealt with simultaneously, by way of the same Act of Parliament (52/1996). The extension of the fields affected by European integration therefore has accentuated the steady demise of the old hierarchical structure of public powers within the state. This does not imply, of course, that there is less need for an efficient and prompt network for the exchange of information and instructions. On the contrary, the responsibility of the state to ensure 'unitary representation' within international organizations and the co-ordination of the relationship with the EU has recently been reaffirmed by the delegated legislation which has transferred an unprecedented number of functions and powers to regions and local authorities (d. lgs. no. 112/1998) (D'Atena 1992: 482). Politically, this means that, in spite of pronounced decentralization, the co-ordination of EU policies remains a state function. Moreover, the extension of EU intervention into new areas, especially in the field of Justice and Home Affairs, requires an increased efficiency in the traditional network which relies on the permanent representation. This generates the need to rethink more generally the allocation of responsibilities among central departments, in particular between the Ministry of Foreign Affairs and the department operating in the framework of the Presidency of the Council. It also implies that other administrative units will be involved in EU decision-making procedures, thus increasing the need to improve civil servants' training, for which today at least three governmental authorities have responsibility. It is the general responsibility of the Department of Public Administration and specific tasks are assigned, once again, to both the Ministry of Foreign Affairs and the Department for the Co-ordination of EC Policies, where a specific statute (no. 146/1994) set up a committee for the development of civil servants' training with regard to Community aspects. One broad reform has already been agreed. As a result of an unprecedented delegation of parliamentary power, a governmental decree (no. 300 of 1999), effective after the general elections of spring 2001, will reduce the number of ministries from eighteen to twelve. The reform strengthens the role of the prime minister—the main authority for deciding Italy's position on EU policies. It also gives the Treasury responsibility for managing EU funds, a task previously shared with the Department of EU policies. Thus, while the president takes charge of political choices, responsibility for administrative decisions about EU finances are assigned to the Treasury (Torchia and Pajno 2000).

References

Amato, G. (1997), 'The Impact of Europe on National Policies: Italian Anti-Trust Policies', in Y. Meny, P. Muller, and J. L. Quermonne (eds.), *Adjusting to Europe: The Impact of the European Union on National Institutions and Policies* (London: Routledge), 157–79.

Camera dei Deputati, Servizio delle relazioni internazionali (1982), *Direttive delle Comunità europee: Elenco delle direttive e stato di attuazione (1959–1981)* (Roma: Camera dei Deputati).

Capotorti, F. (1974), 'L'Administration italienne face aux organisations universelles', *Rivista di diritto internazionale*, 35: 74–93.

Caranta, R. (1997), 'I rapporti tra Regioni e Comunità europea: Un nuovo modo di tutela degli interessi nazionali', *Rivista italiana di diritto pubblico comunitario*, 1219–43.

Cassese, S. (1983), *Il sistema amministrativo italiano* (Bologna: Il Mulino).

——(1985), 'La regola e le deroghe: Il sistema politico amministrativo italiano e le directive comunitarie', in Cassese, S., *Studi in onore di Vezio Crisafuli* (Padua: Cedam).

——(1995), *Le basi del diritto amministrativo* (Milan: Garzanti).

——(ed.) (1997), *Funzione pubblica e integrazione europea* (Roma: Sipi).

——and della Cananea, G. (1992), 'The Commission of the European Economic Community: The Administrative Ramifications of its Political Development', in E. Volkmar Heyen (ed.), *Early European Community Administration* (Jahrbüch der Europaïsches Verwaltungsgeschichte, 4; Baden-Baden, Nomos), 75–94.

Chiti, M. P. (1991), 'L'amministrazione per il coordinamento delle politiche comunitarie nelle recenti riforme', *Rivista italiana di diritto pubblico comunitario*, 1: 11–32.

Condorelli Braun, N. (1972), *Commissaires et juges dans les Communautés européennes* (Paris: Librarie générale de droit et Jurisprudence).

Cotta, M. (1998), 'Le élite politiche nazionali di fronte all'integrazione europea', *Il Mulino*, 445–56.

della Cananea, G. (1990), 'Cooperazione e integrazione nel sistema amministrativo delle Comunitá europee: La questione della "comitologia" ', *Rivista trimestrale di diritto pubblico*, 4/3: 655–702.

——(1997), 'The Reforms of Finance and Administration in Italy: Contrasting Achievements', *West European Politics*, 1: 194–209.

——(1998), 'Riordino dei conti pubblici e "riforma" dello stato sociale', *Giornale di diritto amministrativo*, 2: 124–9.

——(2000), 'Italy', in H. Kassim, B. G. Peters, and V. Wright (eds.), *The National Coordination of EU Policy: The Domestic Level* (Oxford: Oxford University Press).

D'Atena, A. (1998), I rapporti tra Regioni e Comunità', *Le Regione*, 1401–26.

Dipartimento della funzione pubblica (1994), *La pubblica amministrazione e l'Europa* (Rome: Dipartimento della funzione pubblica).

Faro, S. (1997), 'Il tema della partecipazione dell'Italia all'Unione europea nei lavori della Commissione parlamentare per le riforme costituzionali', *Rivista italiana di diritto pubblico comunitario*, 6: 1323–30.

Franchini, C. (1992), *Amministrazione comunitaria e amministrazione italiana: La coamministrazione delle politiche comunitarie*, iv (Padua: Cedam).

——(1998), 'Integrazione europea e coordinamento delle amministrazioni', *Giornale di diritto amministrativo*, 897–9.

Gerbet, P., and Pepy, D. (eds.), (1969), *La Décision dans les Communautés européennes* (Brussels: Éditions de l'Université Libre de Bruxelles).

Gnes, M. (1997), 'Gli effetti dell'integrazione europea sull'amministrazione statale', in S. Cassese (ed.), *Funzione pubblica e integrazione europea* (Rome: Sipi), 27–96.

Greco, G. (1989), 'Profili di diritto pubblico italo-comunitario', in G. Greco (ed.), *Argomenti di diritto pubblico italo-comunitario* (Milan: Giuffrè), 19–90.

Hayes-Renshaw, F., and Wallace, H. (1997), *The Council of Ministers* (London: Macmillan).

Kapteyn, P. G. (1979), 'Outgrowing the Treaty of Rome: from market integration to policy integration', in *Mélanges Fernand Déhousse* (Paris: Éditions Labor), 45–63.

Lenaerts, K. (1991), 'Some Reflections on the Separation of Powers in the European Community', *Common Market Law Review*, 28/1: 11–35.

Monaco, R. (1961), 'L'organizzazione amministrativa delle Comunitá europee e la pubblica amministrazione italiana', *Rivista di diritto europeo*, 247–60.

Noël, E. (1989), 'Italia: Vizi e virtù di un membro fondatore', *Relazioni internazionali*, 22: 87–102.

Papisca, A. (1985), 'La Presidence du Conseil des Ministres des Communautés européennes: Rapport national sur l'Italie', in Colm O'Nuallain (ed.), *The Presidency of the European Council of Ministers* (London: Croom Helm), 163–86.

Pinder, J. (1968), 'Positive Integration and Negative Integration: Some Problems of Economic Union in the EEC', *The World Today*, 88 ff.

Ronzitti, N. (1987), 'European Policy Formulation in the Italian Administrative System', *The International Spectator*, 22/4: 207–14.

Sasse, C. (1975), *Le Processus de décision dans la Communauté européenne* (Paris: PUF).

Senato della Repubblica (1992), *Partecipazione dell'Italia alle fasi formativa ed applicativa del diritto comunitario* (Rome: Serato della Repubblica).

Sico, L. (1999), 'Note a margine della riforma del Ministero degli affari esteri', *Rassegna parlamentare*, 839–51.

Sinagra, A. (1988), 'Affari esteri (ordinamento amministrativo)', in *Enciclopedia giuridica* (Rome: Istituto dell'Encidopedia italiana).

Tizzano, A. (1989), 'Quelques observations sur le developpement des competences communautaires', *Pouvoirs*, 48: 59–71.

——(1992), 'The Permanent Representations of the Member States to the European Communities', in *1992: Public Administration and Europe* (Rome: Editoriale scientifica), 519–48.

Torchia, L., and Pajno, A. (2000), *La riforma del Governo* (Bologna: Il Mulino).

Wallace, H. (1973), *National Governments and the European Communities* (London: Chatham House).

5

Permanent Challenges? Representing Greece in Brussels

Calliope Spanou

Introduction

The rationale for the permanent representations, established in the early years of the European Communities, was to operate as mediators between national political-administrative systems and Community institutions. The intermediary role gives them a special place in the European administrative architecture *à cheval* between the national and European levels. Although an integral part of national administrations, through the COREPER they fully participate in the decision-making process of the EU (Hayes-Renshaw *et al.* 1989; Rutten 1992: 384). At the same time, permanent representations have to combine the political *and* technical dimensions of European policies decided by the Council. Each proposal has its own technical complexity and requires political choices (Wallace 1990: 217). Given that 85 per cent of all decisions on Council agendas will have been essentially agreed in advance of ministerial sessions (70 per cent in working groups and 10–15 per cent in COREPER I and II; Hayes-Renshaw and Wallace 1997: 78; Rutten 1992: 225), the importance of the permanent representation is beyond all doubt.

Both political and technical dimensions have developed considerably over the past forty years. The latter in particular have expanded substantially with the emergence of new European policy fields. The task of ensuring

The author gratefully acknowledges the financial support of the University of Athens Research Fund. The staff of the Greek permanent representation in Brussels also contributed greatly to the author's scientific endeavour.

coherent and consistent representation of national positions has become ever more demanding. In other words, co-ordination capacities appear all the more important. *Ceteris paribus*, the better the domestic co-ordination and the clearer the policy priorities, the easier it is for the permanent representation. Thus, the conditions of its performance are shaped by domestic factors as well as by the requirements at the EU level.

In terms of organizational arrangements there is little to differentiate the various permanent representations from each other. To a large extent, their organizational scheme is shaped by their functions within the EU system, and especially the preparation of decisions for the Council. In light of this 'isomorphism' (see Introduction, above), diversity in the national representations may be seen as an example of how domestic factors introduce variations into an organizational structure that is basically similar, thereby demonstrating how individual countries can respond very differently to the same co-ordination challenges and requirements.[1] These differences arise from country-specific factors such as the pattern of relations between different national actors (political, administrative, and interest groups), the domestic political-administrative style and culture, as well as the pattern of ambitions, resources, and constraints defining the way a member state positions itself *vis-à-vis* the EU (Wright 1996).

The Greek administrative system is characterized by a set of parameters: sectorization and fragmentation, low co-ordination, centralization and hierarchical structure, importance of informal networks and personal strategies, as well as weak institutionalization of horizontal and staff functions. Deficient steering at the top and lack of clearly set priorities are deeper reasons for co-ordination deficiencies at the national and sectoral level. In that sense, the co-ordination scheme can be seen as a 'truncated pyramid' (Spanou 2000), even though, more recently, major national priorities represent an exception to the rule (EMU, for example).

Greece features among smaller EU member states whose major interests fall within the scope of Union action. Its capacity to promote its interests, however, is tested, as is shown below. The permanent representation is an important piece of the puzzle. This chapter argues that the EU environment and its functional imperatives put pressure on the Greek permanent representation to compensate for defensive attitudes and domestic administrative weaknesses, while at the same time being affected by them.

---

[1] 'Although each of the delegations has the same functions to perform, and each conforms to a basically similar model, the organization, functioning and status of Member-states representations will differ according to national attitudes, practices and priorities' (Hayes-Renshaw *et al.* 1989: 120; Hayes-Renshaw and Wallace 1997: 219).

Organization

Following practice elsewhere (Hayes-Renshaw *et al.* 1989: 123), the Greek permanent representation was established in 1962, soon after the ratification of the association agreement. It was placed under the authority of the Ministry of Co-ordination, later Ministry of National Economy (MNE), where it remained until 1980. The 'freezing' of the accession process during the 1967–74 dictatorship, delayed accession until it finally started on 1 January 1981. A law of 1980 (no. 1104), designed to prepare Greece for full membership, introduced a number of organizational changes. Among them, general responsibility for representing Greece *vis-à-vis* the EC—'outward' representation—was transferred to the Ministry of Foreign Affairs (MFA). The permanent representation became—and still remains—an external service of the MFA which constitutes its main, if not exclusive, official correspondent and channel of communication between Brussels and the Greek administration.

At the same time, however, the MNE was entrusted with a co-ordination role—'inward' representation—concerning the elaboration of economic policy in the European context.[2] This division of labour meant that the MNE was to co-ordinate technical ministries and monitor adjustment policies. In addition, it brought about tension and antagonism not only between the two leading ministries, but also between the technical ministries and the MNE (Spanou 2000), which is further reflected in the permanent representation's operation.

The permanent representation comprises the following organizational units:

(1) external relations and Common Foreign and Security Policy (second pillar);
(2) economic policy (ECOFIN, EMU, EURO);
(3) agricultural policy;
(4) other policies;
(5) legal affairs;[3]
(6) third pillar and Schengen issues (Justice and Home Affairs);

---

[2] The MNE deals with ECOFIN matters and the implementation of Community support frameworks.
[3] The head of the legal affairs unit is appointed by the MFA. He follows the legal action of the Commission or other member countries against Greece and informs the special legal service of the MFA and the corresponding ministries. The unit informally performs as the legal advisor of the permanent representation. More recently, legal affairs have been separated from third pillar issues due to the broadening scope of Justice and Home Affairs.

(7) institutions, European Parliament, Economic and Social Committee, Committee of the Regions;
(8) organization and administrative affairs.

The Greek permanent representation is headed by a full ambassador, proposed by the MFA and approved by the Council of Ministers. Unlike some other permanent representations, the deputy is also a diplomat rather than a technical expert (Hayes-Renshaw and Wallace 1997: 219). The division of labour corresponds to the dossiers treated by the COREPER II and I respectively. After approval by the minister responsible for European affairs, the ambassador decides on the internal organization of labour and assigns duties to the personnel under his authority.

The post of economic adviser, initially established in 1980, is a reflection of the dualism of leading ministries. Equally, it underscores the expansion of economic policies. The place of the MNE in the hierarchy of the permanent representation is substantially different from other ministries, since the rank of the economic adviser is equivalent to the deputy and his role is to co-ordinate economic and technical ministries as head of the Economic Policy Unit. Unlike other positions, this post is filled by contract. An expert from the Ministry of Agriculture based in Brussels heads the Agricultural Policy Unit and participates in the Special Committee on Agriculture (CSA). Ministries represented in the permanent representation include Foreign Affairs, Economy and Finance, Agriculture, Development (Industry, Energy, Technology and Trade), Transports and Communications, Labour and Social Security, Health, Education, Merchant Marine, Environment, Physical Planning and Public Works, Justice, Public Order and Press.

The intermingling of political and technical dimensions is reflected in the presence of diplomatic personnel as well as experts. The work of permanent representation is very different from that of bilateral embassies, since most dossiers require the presence of specialists from technical ministries (Hayes-Renshaw and Wallace 1997: 224). The presence of non-diplomats increased dramatically as a result of the widening of EU policy responsibilities and the demand for technical expertise,[4] leading to diversity in the ministerial origin, status, and expertise of personnel. The number of posts at the permanent representation has been increased in successive waves, but without an overall plan in terms of the organizational structure. Positions were simply created and attached either to the MFA, the MNE, or the sectoral ministries. Once posted to Brussels, officials are considered part of the MFA and placed under the authority of the ambassador. In 1999, the permanent representation employed ninety-four people, including fifty-five administrators (the permanent representative and deputy included) involved in policy issues. Only

---

[4] Nevertheless, they all enjoy diplomatic status.

thirteen were diplomats[5]—a ratio that is below the 40 per cent average across all permanent representations (Lequesne 1993: 196; Hayes-Renshaw and Wallace 1997: 221–3).

Though the number of higher officials and diplomats has been relatively stable since 1985,[6] the Greek permanent representation is among the largest in terms of personnel. Two reasons are generally put forward to account for its size. First, the distance of EU decision-making centres from Athens makes it difficult to have frequent contacts with sectoral ministries. Second is the desire of sectoral ministries to have their own representatives in Brussels, so that they can get information first-hand and not have to rely on diplomats in the permanent representation (Stephanou 1986: 7 n. 64; Makridimitris and Passas 1993: 55). In that sense, the number of personnel in the permanent representation may reflect the competition between horizontal and sectoral ministries and a determination on the part of the latter to bypass the MFA or MNE. There is also a third reason. This has to do with the role that the permanent representation plays in order to compensate for weaknesses at the domestic level. More than distance and departmentalism, the large size of the Greek permanent representation is to be explained by a function that it performs informally.

Secondment is the usual method of recruitment for postings to Brussels and is decided jointly by the MFA and the relevant technical minister. Only in exceptional circumstances is recruitment explicitly made for the permanent representation. This is the case, for example, with the head of the Economic Relations Unit, who is hired on contract by the MNE. To a large extent, staffing relies on civil service resources and procedures.[7]

The expertise required for permanent representation staff has to be seen in the light of the political and technical, domestic, national, and European dimensions of their role. Though they represent a national administration, familiarity with European procedures and multilateral negotiation, as well as linguistic capacities and a thorough knowledge of the policy issues and their implications, is important (see Gonzalez Sanchez 1992). This multifaceted expertise is not easy to develop. The diplomatic career may be as remote

[5] This is out of twenty-one MFA officials including diplomats. The personnel of the MFA comprises diplomats and experts (non-diplomats).

[6] It ranges from forty-five in 1985 to fifty-five in 2000. Presidencies tend to increase the number of personnel serving at the permanent representation. During the first Greek Presidency in 1983, the personnel reached the 'record number' of 105 persons, declining afterwards to seventy-five in 1985. Out of these seventy-five, forty-five were higher officials and diplomats (Stephanou 1986: 7).

[7] In response to patronage and favouritism, recruitment in the civil service tends to be characterized by uniformity, rigidity, and a low degree of differentiation. Selection procedures allowing appreciation of individual qualities are suspected for partiality and give rise to heated debates between government and opposition.

from it as any technocratic or administrative career. The importance of the selection process cannot be overstressed.

The lack of a systematic approach to staffing is related to problems in the selection process. The high status and prestige associated with the post, as well as the financial advantages involved, as well as the *ad hoc* nature of appointments by secondment, make personal and political networks extremely important. For a long time, appointments were made *ad personam* and *ad hoc*, personal networks over-riding expertise, experience, specialization, and other necessary skills.[8] More recently, it seems that, though political support is still important, possession of the appropriate qualifications is not neglected. Concerning the length of service, the current norm is four years for diplomats, three to four years for secondments, and up to six years for support staff. In the past, many officials would stay for longer, since there was no maximum time limit.

There still is no systematic effort to establish a 'European' career trajectory. This applies to all kinds and all levels of staff. For diplomats, appointment even to the position of ambassador or deputy ambassador does not require any previous EU experience. And by the same token, they can be appointed to posts unrelated to European affairs. The exception concerns experts from the MFA's non-diplomatic staff who may be 'recycled' between similar positions in the ministry or in Brussels, not due to any effort on the part of the Ministry, but because of the motivation and career perspectives of this group of civil servants. Contract employees are not integrated in the civil service and are, therefore, 'lost' so far as the Greek administration is concerned, since no one knows where they end up. No previous experience or familiarity with EU decision-making is required for secondment by sectoral ministries. Moreover, it is far from guaranteed that the expertise they have acquired will be used upon return. On the contrary, they may receive any position or even be intentionally marginalized in the service since their appointment to Brussels is seen as an envied privilege. In such a context, tenured civil servants may be interested in prolonging their stay and pursuing a career in the Commission or being appointed, with the help of the government, as a 'national expert'. If they are successful in this, they are unlikely ever to return to Greece. This applies mostly to officers from sectoral ministries, given that they have nothing to expect in terms of career advancement in their home department.

The idea of rotating personnel between the national administration and EU institutions is intended to expose more civil servants to the EU policy-making process and enable domestic ministries to take advantage of the

---

[8] On the practice of political and personal selection criteria at the expense of merit, see the comments of T. Pangalos (in Tsoukalis 1993: 281), Pierros (1991: 23), and Giataganas (1990: 262–2).

experience and contacts gained during the tenure at the permanent represen-tation. This implies an awareness of the European policy arena and the pos-sibilities to advance domestic policy priorities. The very fact that data concerning the number of Greek civil servants that have worked in the permanent representation are not available shows, however, that there is no systematic policy in this respect. The neglect of the opportunities pre-sented is part of a more general failure to build the necessary policy expertise in an important area of the Greek administration. The fact that Greek gov-ernments do not seem to have realized the importance of a consistent per-sonnel policy for the permanent representation and the need to take advantage of their EU expertise and networks once they are back reveals both the low priority attributed to EU matters by individual ministers and the Greek administration in general[9] and a more general disregard of staff functions and policy expertise. A significant number of departments whose policies are directly affected by EU action do not place a high premium on European expertise and offer no encouragement to officials to follow a European career path.

Though the diverse origins of its personnel are far from being an exclusive feature of the Greek permanent representation, it is difficult to speak of an administrative 'melting pot' (*creuset administratif*, according to Lequesne 1993: 190; Hayes-Renshaw *et al.* 1989: 129). The diversity is preserved within the permanent representation, enhanced by the mutual suspicion between ministries, the competition between corps of civil servants, and the strong vertical links to the centre. Moreover, the diversity of the personnel is symp-tomatic of the diverse range of policy issues.

Tasks and Functions

The role of the permanent representation is to manage the interface between Brussels and the domestic administration. The functions involved are usually described along three interconnected axes: information-gathering, the presentation of national concerns, and negotiation of national positions in Brussels. Networking with other institutions is an important precondition for all three (Lequesne 1993; Wright 1996: 159). However, the performance of these functions is influenced by the deficiencies of domestic co-ordination, as well as the uneven distribution of European priorities within and across sectors and ministries.

---

[9] Opportunities offered by personnel exchange programmes are not used sufficiently (Passas 1994; Giataganas 1990).

Communication with the Centre

The permanent representation's main correspondent is the MFA, which ensures further communication with other ministries. The ambassador has regular contacts with the MFA at the level of the minister or junior minister, meeting them once a month in Athens. There is also contact with the Ministers of Foreign Affairs and the National Economy before the meetings of the General Affairs Councils and the ECOFIN. He also meets the Prime Minister, though less often. Contact takes place once every three months, ahead of the European Council, where issues of 'high politics' are discussed (institutional reform, for example). However, though desirable and useful, there are no systematic contacts with the Cabinet or cabinet committees (for EU affairs), nor with Parliament.

The permanent representation has the primary function of informing the national government of what is happening in Brussels. This is mainly a downstream process. Officers involved in sectoral negotiations follow the working groups and report back to ministries about their progress and the decisions taken by the Council of Ministers. More than mere transmission is involved. As well as acting as a 'central postbox' for documentation, the permanent representation plays the role of 'benevolent censor' (Hayes-Renshaw *et al.* 1989: 129) and interpreter of developments in Brussels. The information transmitted to the centre must be accurate and thorough, but it also has to be contextualized. Communications from the permanent representation, therefore, include intelligence and additional information gathered in Brussels from relevant sources. Wider considerations concerning the policy environment, advice about realistic alternatives, and an assessment of implications for the country's interests and domestic sectoral policies form an important part, above and beyond the official EU texts. Officials play a crucial role and their expertise on the subject-matter is vital, but their interest and capacity to gather information are also extremely important.

Information is normally transmitted through the MFA, which is the main—formally, the only—domestic correspondent of the permanent representation. However, the volume of information, the technicality of the issues, and the quantity of accompanying documents make direct contacts with the ministries involved necessary.[10] In spite of the MFA's claim to a monopoly, there are other channels of communication between the mission in Brussels and the administration at home. For example, there is close and regular contact between the head of the Economic Policy Unit in the permanent representa-

---

[10] From the permanent representation in Brussels to the MFA and then to the technical ministries, the communication chain seems quite long and time-consuming. In the past, sometimes it could not be supported by sufficient technical infrastructure (Minakaki 1992; Stephanou 1986). Information overload is a real risk for the MFA.

tion and the MNE and the body of economic experts in Athens, mainly by telephone or other means, though not visits to the capital. Similarly, the agricultural sector unit is, to a large extent, an extension of the home department. Equally, officials from the line ministries are in constant touch with their ministries, either in their role of information-gathering or to suggest policy positions. The tendency to bypass the MFA is stronger among the representatives of sectoral ministries due to the technical nature of the issues and the limited capacity of the MFA to intervene effectively. In practice, the MFA risks losing its communication monopoly in a wide range of policy areas.

In order to defend the monopoly of the MFA and the intermediary role of the permanent representation, direct contact between sectoral officials and the home ministries is not permitted, except in emergencies, according to a ministerial decision of 1994. Communication with the domestic administration should pass via the ambassador or his deputy, who control the flow of information to sectoral ministries. Though effective co-ordination is the objective, such a centralizing procedure generates dysfunctions and reflects suspicion of direct communication between sectoral ministries and seconded officials in Brussels, bypassing the MFA and the diplomatic hierarchy. Furthermore, officials tend not travel to Athens to attend meetings or discuss issues directly with their ministries, even though elsewhere this is regarded as necessary in order to sensitize and mobilize home services towards EU policy priorities.

Internal Functioning and Working Methods

There is a formal provision for a meeting of the ambassador and his deputy with the heads of the organizational units for mutual information and co-ordination to take place at least once a week. Meetings also take place on an *ad hoc* basis, collectively or individually, with the advisers for specific issues (for example, briefings by the Antici Group representative or in the area of foreign relations or economic relations). Meetings—one or two at least—are also held the week before the COREPER as well as the day, or even the hour, before it is scheduled to convene, in case last-minute instructions are forwarded from Athens.

Normally, disagreement over policy positions between the MFA and another ministry has to be solved in Athens. However, rivalries between the two lead ministries MFA and MNE and with the sectoral departments originating in Athens continue within the permanent representation. Though there is nothing original or new about inter-sectoral conflicts and departmentalism (see Lequesne 1993: 185–99 and 203), the extent to which sectoral perspectives are integrated may vary. Unlike in France (Lequesne 1993: 198; Hayes-Renshaw *et al.* 1989: 129; Menon, this volume), where staff co-operate rather well, despite their varying origins, segmentation within the Greek permanent representation is marked. The ministerial provenance of the permanent representation employees is striking. The loyalty of officials to their ministry of origin is also an important factor (Hayes-Renshaw *et al.* 1989: 127).

The mode of operation is hierarchical and centralizing, since all business must pass through the ambassador and his deputy, but also fragmented, since segmentation along sectoral lines is deeply entrenched. In agriculture, the existence of the Special Committee for Agriculture may be seen as providing an institutional reason for relative autonomy of the sector, but the same insularity extends to other sectors as well. More generally, the complexity of technical co-ordination as well as departmental resistance to it have increased as sectoral ministries become more assertive and claim primacy in their area of responsibility. The weakening of the co-ordination role of the MFA undermines the corresponding role of the permanent representation. The sectorization of policy is further enhanced by vertical dependence on the central department of origin and, very often, the political level (minister and cabinet). Staff appointed on an *ad hoc* basis and *ad personam* maintain, and are keen to maintain, close links with the political leadership of their ministry, since the latter can provide them with the necessary support to perform their duties. By contrast, dependence upon, and loyalty towards, the head of the permanent representation is weakened.

Co-ordination differs between the two COREPERs. Where issues fall within the competence of the MFA or the MNE priority is clear. Matters are more complicated in the case of sectoral polices (COREPER I). Apart from *ad hoc* meetings for the preparation of the agenda with the relevant officers who point out the critical issues to the deputy, there is a lack of internal, horizontal information and co-ordination. Depending on the personal style of the deputy, horizontal meetings may take place more or less systematically. However, the lack of effective cross-sectoral co-ordination at the European level is not confined only to the Greek permanent representation, but is evident in other national missions (see, for example, Maurer and Wessels, Müller, this volume) and is a feature of the EU system as a whole (Wallace 1990: 215–16 and 224). The fragmented character of the issues and of the EU policy-making system favours sectoral perspectives. The number of ministries involved and sometimes the lack of clear priorities (see below) at an early stage tend to reinforce a rather reactive style. As a result, the importance of technical negotiations may be underestimated. Last, the lower visibility of technical issues, compared with high politics, limits awareness of their medium- and long-term implications.

In such a context, permanent representation officers tend to concentrate on their area of sectoral expertise. They attend the working groups, contact their home ministry, and co-operate with colleagues from other permanent representations and the Commission. They seek information by their own means (personal contacts) and consult colleagues on their own initiative. Information-sharing is therefore not systematic, but *ad hoc* and uneven. In practice, experts make their choices about their own policy areas, informally institutionalizing vertical expertise.

Officials regret that more information is not widely circulated. This is especially important for the interrelations between policies—for example, external relations and sectoral policies, transport and environment, health, consumer protection and agriculture. Lack of information concerning national positions across sectors may lead an official to shape his or her negotiation tactics in an inappropriate way or to be unaware of a position taken by colleagues in a different working group that restricts his or her margin of manoeuvre. An important negative side effect is the undermining of his or her credibility in the eyes of colleagues from other countries.

Horizontal co-ordination is lacking due to the inadequate preparation of policy priorities and strategies at the domestic level. This is the case not only with EU policy, but is true of domestic policy too, and is a feature of Greek administration. At the governmental level, the lack or relative inertia of co-ordinating mechanisms have to be linked to the absence of clear strategic priorities concerning Greece's overall participation in the EC/EU—a situation that has only recently begun to change. Fragmentation and *ad hoc* co-ordination are byproducts of the absence of a clear referential framework and insufficient steering at the top. This is why the domestic co-ordination system can be qualified as a 'truncated pyramid' (Spanou 2000). In the absence of strong domestic co-ordination, it is not possible at the permanent representation level to put pressure on individual ministries and contain sectorization, because of insufficient political weight. Inter-sectoral integration in Brussels is further complicated by the technicality and complexity of the issues. The role of the ambassador and his deputy is not simple, having to reconcile and overcome differences of perspective and sectoral-departmental loyalties, and also mutual suspicion. Of course, at the COREPER it is the ambassador or the deputy who presents the national position, and who is, therefore, able to introduce a horizontal view and reserve some bargaining latitude.

Transmission of National Positions and Instructions

Presenting a clear national position in Brussels, is 'relatively easy when one is received from a Foreign Office which in turn is presenting a position formulated in a centralised agency' (Wright 1996: 160). An important issue is therefore the capacity of the domestic administration to study the implications of, and to react to, a policy proposal. This capacity is unevenly distributed within the Greek administration. European policy priorities do not always permeate home departments.

An important distinction can be made between two groups of policy areas. The first includes those sectors where priorities are more or less clear and consistent. This applies to foreign affairs (Ioakimidis 1993: 218–19) and also to macro-economic policy (EMU), where decisions are mainly elaborated in Athens by the relevant ministries. In these cases, priorities are much clearer and centrally defined as part of the national interest. Merchant shipping is also a sector marked by policy consistency and clarity due to the nature and structure of economic interests. Agriculture, as the oldest common European policy, is in addition a policy field where guidelines are sent from home, though allowing some flexibility. The second involves sectors where domestic preparation is poor and last-minute decisions in Brussels are common practice. This is the case with most sectoral policies. Such a situation automatically increases the importance of officials in the permanent representation. Ministries tend to rely more on them, not only for information, but also for suggestions as to which positions should be defended at various stages of decision-making, from the working group to the COREPER and the Council.

For a number of sectoral policies the expertise of MFA personnel in Athens to co-ordinate strategies and objectives is inadequate. But domestic co-ordination is weak because of a more general absence of clear sectoral priorities. This undermines the co-ordinating role of the MFA,[11] while at the same time sectoral departments claim an autonomous capacity to be present in Brussels. In such circumstances, the entire co-ordination system is affected, since national positions are not formulated early or in time, and they are not clear or realistic. The over-riding majority of domestic co-ordination takes place through *ad hoc* meetings, personal contacts, and, as a means of last resort, before the meetings of the COREPER at a rather advanced stage of negotiations either at the MFA or in Brussels (Passas 1997: 27).[12]

From the point of view of the permanent representation, domestic weaknesses may be seen as a lack of appropriate institutional backing. This is often visible in the timing and quality of instructions. In order to allow informal contacts and discussions with group members, instructions have to be sent as early as possible. Delays prevent active participation from the start of the discussions and might even lead to contradictory positions (González-Sánchez 1992: 393). Consistency, coherence, clarity, and flexibility, as well as discretion, are important qualities that facilitate the operation of officials at the perma-

---

[11] For a short time only, this process was subjected to scrutiny by the MFA in the framework of the preparation of the COREPER meetings and the obligation that any communication with the permanent representation should pass through the MFA. Gradually both fell into inertia and direct communication was established (Ioakimidis 1993: 219).

[12] At the same time, the co-ordinating role of the MNE is either doubled by the MFA or both expect competent ministers to take the initiative for their respective policies (Passas 1997: 28).

nent representation. Either oral or written instructions must be the result of dialogue between the representative and the national authorities (González-Sánchez 1992: 394).

The quality of guidelines and instructions depends upon clear sectoral priorities and the definition of realistic alternative scenarios. Given the deficient policy capacity in many sectoral ministries, it may happen either that national positions are decided in the last minute between the representative in the permanent representation and the ambassador or that there are no clear and/or realistic national sectoral priorities. In both cases, the role of staff at the permanent representation is important. Officers representing the relevant ministry may act as a complementary link between the ambassador and their home department, using their personal contacts, relations, and access to the minister to explain negotiation constraints and to table realistic alternatives. Corrective suggestions are submitted by the ambassador or the deputy or other officers.

For politically sensitive issues, there are always written instructions. These may be the result of informal communication with the cabinet of the minister, which is subsequently officially sent to the permanent representation via the MFA. When no instructions arrive before the final decision-making stage, the practice is that the officer drafts a position and submits it to the relevant ministry asking for reactions or approval. Silence is then interpreted as agreement.

Absence of clear priorities and instructions increases the latitude and the role of officials in Brussels. Still, the absence of a general policy framework makes initiatives rather risky and the access to the political level may be an important parameter determining how far officials can go. If they have the political support, they can take initiatives that commit the country to a specific position, even though that may involve imposing constraints on the sectoral ministries (for a Council decision or for a preparatory conference). Such initiatives may then be accepted, tolerated, and may even be beneficial, but the balance is rather fragile.

There is a close link between this need to fill the gaps in Brussels and the tendency of officials to address themselves directly to the political level (minister or cabinet). To a certain extent, this can be explained by the aforementioned departmental loyalty, as well as personal or political networks. An additional reason has to do with the functions performed. If the official has to improvise, he or she will need some political approval or backing. This is an expression of a wider deficiency in terms of clear (sectoral) strategy and priorities in EU affairs that is solved by centralization and *ad hoc* policy decisions. Positions tend to be shaped at the highest political level with the help of the official based in Brussels. However, when positions are decided in the last minute at a high political level, they do not pass through the services. Changes at the top may result in a lack of awareness of related issues, commitments, the continuity of negotiations, and adjustment of priorities.

The absence of instructions is the clearest sign of the lack of strategy and domestic sectoral priorities and, further, of the low expertise, policy capacity, and interest in EU policies of domestic administration. In many ways, officials at the permanent representation representing home departments may remain alone in dealing with the issues for most or all of the decision-making process. In order to compensate for this deficiency, they *de facto* develop the expertise (concerning negotiations, networking, but also technical aspects) that allows them to perform their duties. In this context, they will also have an important role in shaping national positions. They take initiatives ('improvise') in order to cope with EU procedures and constraints. Thus, in some cases the permanent representation *de facto* shapes policy. Whether the centre provides insufficiently clear guidelines or no instructions at all, the permanent representation is the means of last resort where the gap can be filled.

Presentation and Negotiation of National Positions

Loose policy frameworks defined by the capital are supposed to allow wider discretion (Wright 1996: 161; Lequesne, 1993: 215; Nugent 1994). When the permanent representation does not receive the necessary support from the centre, there is a wide scope for personal interpretation and handling of the situation, but also the possibility for mistakes or miscalculations.

For many sectoral policies, the permanent representation operates with little or no institutional support. At the working-group level, experts coming from home departments are often absent. Officers based in Brussels try to fill the gap with variable efficiency. Reasons accounting for the 'empty seats' include lack of corresponding expertise, low awareness of the importance of participation, or financial restrictions. Though there is some variation, this seems to be the general rule. The importance of discussions at working-group level exceeds the technical character of the issues. It is at this level that a consensus can be reached on a Commission proposal or on some aspects of it (González-Sánchez 1992: 392). The quality of the representatives in working groups can modify the real weight of the member state within the EC/EU (González-Sánchez 1992: 393).[13]

The distinction between policy areas is often linked to the degree of flexibility and latitude left to the permanent representation in presenting and

---

[13] The staff of the permanent representation attempt to compensate for the insufficient or the non-systematic representation of national ministries in various committees with their own personnel. Telephone contacts are used as a substitute for direct representation (Minakaki 1992: 45).

negotiating a position. When positions are formulated and transmitted from the centre, they may be more binding and allow less margin for negotiation. This is often the case in 'high politics' issues, closely linked to political priorities. Of course, the role of the permanent representation is not mere transmission. The information gathered, its interpretation, and the assessment of the European policy environment may lead the ambassador or the officers in contact with home departments to suggest adjustments. The situation is different regarding working groups for sectoral policies, where there is a *de facto* latitude, due to frequently absent or unclear positions at the domestic level, further enhanced by the reduced visibility of EU policies implications in the short run.

According to some authors, Greece figures among member states that 'tend to have less room for manœuvre in working parties, and in the COREPER and are generally reluctant to negotiate on policy issues below ministerial level', leaving them only technical matters (Nugent 1994: 414). In practice, the degree to which instructions from the centre are binding varies according to the issue. In the case of extremely salient political issues positions are strictly defined, allowing no discretion or latitude (for example, the Protocol for Finance to Turkey). In such a case, the exchange of information takes place at the political level between the capital and the ambassador. For sectoral issues, however, the situation is less clear-cut. Much depends on the individual official who deals with the issue and his or her relationship with the centre. Generally, Athens allows a margin of manœuvre, especially in sectors where communication between the permanent representation and the ministry or minister is good.

Networking

Networking is an important prerequisite for successful performance of the above tasks and functions. Sensitizing EU institutions and policy actors to the policy concerns and constraints of the country may have an influence on the agenda of the EU (Peters 1994). Further, the exchange of information it allows contributes to the realistic assessment of opportunities and constraints in a multilateral environment, the promotion of policy ideas and priorities at an early stage, and the formation of alliances. The advisory function towards the capital requires 'sensitive antennae' (Wright 1996) and the establishment and maintenance of close contacts with important actors at the European level.

The extent to which the Greek permanent representation is a nodal point for communication is rather limited. This may be seen in the insufficient search for alliances and avoidance of isolation during negotiations. It seems, however, that a new approach is emerging that favours alliances and promoting a more active role in the negotiations. For priority issues, preparation of the ground *vis-à-vis* other member states is more developed. At the same time, alliances are sought mostly with Southern European countries facing similar problems (e.g. for agricultural issues).

At the working-group level, the success of national representatives depends on their 'effective integration'. Friendships and informal relations are as important as active participation in the work (González-Sánchez 1992: 393). Adequate language skills and familiarity with the working methods in international fora play an important role. Though networking depends very much on personal initiative, interest, and capacities and therefore varies, it may be more or less institutionally encouraged as part of a normal way of 'doing business'. At the personal level, networking is practised and seen as important, but institutional encouragement is lacking. Financial support for social contacts is not provided, given the lack of special budgetary provisions to cover public relations expenses.

Contacts with Greek nationals working in the Commission are good but rather limited. Once again, it is more a matter of personal initiatives on the part of individual officials than a consistent policy. Institutional support for the development of contacts (e.g. organization of social events for Greek nationals) is lacking. The same applies to the absence of a policy[14] for promoting Greek nationals to higher posts in the Commission. To a large extent the achievements of Greeks working in EU institutions are a result of their own personal effort. With the Greek Commissioners and their *cabinets*, relations are generally good and exchange of information seems smooth. However, despite anticipated links (Nugent 1994; Franchini 1991), co-operation on the grounds of common national origin is neither particularly close nor systematic. The use of these unofficial channels is therefore rather limited. The capacity of the permanent representation to exercise influence during the informal stages of policy formation is not sufficiently developed (see e.g. Louloudis 1993; Galatsinou 1996; Passas 1994).

Contact between the permanent representation and the European Parliament was only occasional until 1993.[15] Both sides considered the exchange of information to be insufficient. The role of promoting Greek interests and positions was played by the MFA. The systematic monitoring

[14] Greece does not have a policy of following the career and placements of Greek nationals in the various institutions of the EU (Commission and various DGs, Secretariat of the Council, etc.). Giataganas (1990: 260–1) notes the under-representation of Greece in terms of numbers as well as of importance of positions for Greek nationals in the Commission. The insufficient interest shown by the Greek government in this respect contrasts with the important potential of this channel for informal influence.

[15] Pierros (1991: 24) notes the lack of systematic co-operation between MEPs, domestic administration, the government and the permanent representation, leading to the fragmentary and elliptic approach of the issues by Greek MEPs in the EP.

of the EP is a relatively recent phenomenon (Passas 1997: 29). It currently falls within the scope of a special unit, which transmits information to and from MEPs, as well as members of ECOSOC and the Committee of the Regions. Given the wide range of issues and the heavy agenda of the EP (plenary sessions and working groups), following its activities is necessarily selective, according to the 'degree of interest for Greece' (Rammou 1997). Direct contacts with the ambassador and the deputy or more junior officials also take place. Staff at the permanent representation are increasingly aware of the importance of the EP, given the extension of its legislative role. Co-decision may allow a more efficient defence of national interests in the EP arena than in the Council one. Thus, contacts and mutual information with the Greek MEPs may further develop. But, despite high expectations on the part of MEPs, their requirements are sometimes seen as an extra burden that comes on top of a heavy professional schedule (Rammou 1997).

Last, but not least, contacts with interest group organizations are also limited. The official mistrust of the Greek administrative culture towards interest groups is one general reason. Interest groups may use the relevant ministry in order to promote certain demands (e.g. the Technical Chamber and the Ministry of Public Works, or ship-owners and the Ministry of the Marine). It is important to note, however, that Greek interest groups—for example, SMEs and Chambers—are generally small, competitive, and weak in terms of organization and expertise. Due to the structure of the economy, the sectoral interests at stake, as well as the incentives for mobilization, are not strong. Of course, there are notable differences between interest groups. The Union of Greek Industries or the Union of Greek Exporters (SEV, EEE) are more active than the labour unions. Against this background, the role of the permanent representation is peripheral.[16]

Unlike other countries, there is no systematic support and promotion of Greek interest groups. And, inversely, these do not seek regular links with the permanent representation. Only on specific issues might there be contacts with the ambassador or deputy. (A recent example concerns the feared impact on Greek products of the proposed agreement between the EU and South Africa.) Officials in the permanent representation may have *ad hoc* contacts with interest organizations. The same applies to local governments and their representatives and NGOs. To the extent that institutions such as the ECOSOC

---

[16] The SEV has established a bureau in Brussels for its representation in the UNICE, which has developed independent links with EU institutions, the Commission, the permanent representation, the Economic and Social Council, and the EP (Tsinisizelis 1996: 248–9; Sidjanski 1990; Aligisakis and Papadopoulos 1990). The Farmer's Union (PASEGES) equally has an office in Brussels, but its poor financial situation limits its potential (Tsinisizelis 1996: 246). Certain regions and public corporations also have their own representatives in Brussels.

or the Committee of the Regions have only an advisory role, contacts with their representatives remain occasional and based on their initiative. The Greek permanent representation cannot therefore be described as a nodal point of a network promoting Greek interests of various sorts—interest groups, local government organizations, economic actors, and NGOs—at the EU level. Interest promotion is not seen as an integral part of the permanent representation mission.

Assessment and Conclusion

'The games played in Brussels', as Helen Wallace (1990: 215) quite rightly observes, 'are linked to the outcomes of games played in national capitals'. Thus, the 'truncated pyramid' of the Greek co-ordination system extends to the permanent representation and affects the way it performs its functions. While at the domestic level there may be weaknesses or inadequacies, the whole policy and co-ordination system is tested at the EU level, where the real competition of interests takes place and where gains and losses are incurred. In Brussels, the question is not anymore one of mere co-ordination (means), but of influence on the decision-making process (ends).

Greek administration exhibits weak responsiveness to the EU policy system. To a large extent, it relies on the permanent representation and its staff, which are thus caught between the twin pressures of insufficient institutional support, on the one hand, and EU procedures and requirements on the other. Seen in this light, the permanent representation in fact performs better than one might reasonably expect. It combines the role of representative, transmitter of EU concerns, and advocate of EU policies towards the domestic administration with that of policy-shaping. It seems, none the less, that EU priorities do not permeate the ministries at home. Central departments are generally absorbed by their domestic concerns and appear less sensitive to the European logic, rhythms, conditions, and constraints.

The analysis of the functions informally performed by the permanent representation may also explain its size. As noted above, its size reflects its importance as the last resort for Greek ministries to participate in and follow EU policy-making and development. Administrative deficiencies have pushed not only co-ordination, but also policy formulation, upwards to the permanent representation level. This increases its importance and grants it a role beyond its initial task and actual capacity. To the extent that sectoral ministries do not have the information, interest, expertise, and readiness to produce policy positions, they tend to rely heavily on their representatives in the permanent representation. Apart from their normal tasks, they have to compensate for domestic deficiencies, going as far as drafting the position to be subsequently adopted for negotiation.

If the role of the permanent representation is to be qualified as arena or actor, the latter would seem more appropriate. It is an actor to the extent that it has to compensate for the insufficient policy framework and priorities for EU policy-making at the domestic level. But this takes place more in a sectoral than a horizontal perspective. Nevertheless, it is doubtful that horizontal, cross-sectoral co-ordination is really possible, given the sectorized nature of the EU environment.

Formal and informal opportunities for the Greek government to seek influence at the EU level (Nugent 1994: 412 ff.) are not sufficiently used and are hindered by the lack of clear policy priorities and the absence of strategy. The lack of institutional backing creates scope and opportunity for individual initiatives and strategies. Success is often attributed to these informal dynamics and personal commitment. As a working method, however, it does not ensure predictability and continuity, nor does it shape the conditions under which these initiatives can be effective.

The permanent representation has partly to remedy the shortcomings of previous policy stages, by containing fragmentation and sectorization, by developing the horizontal and European dimension, and by paying attention to the technical character of the issues that often determines the outcome in political terms. The permanent representation is thus caught in a vicious circle. The reasons for its demanding role, as well as the difficulties it has to overcome, stem from the wider characteristics of the Greek political-administrative system, of which it forms an integral part.

References

Aligisakis, M., and Papadopoulos, I. (1990), 'L'Insertion des groupes d'intérêt Grecs dans la Communauté Européenne', in D. Sidjanski and U. Ayberk (eds.), *L'Europe du Sud dans la Communauté Européenne* (Paris: Presses Universitaires de France), 85–114.

Ciavarini Azzi, G. (1985), 'Les Experts nationaux: Chevaux de Troie ou partenaires indispensables?', in J. Jamars and W. Wessels (eds.), *Community Bureaucracy at the Crossroads* (Bruges: De Tempel, College of Europe), 99–104.

Franchini, C. (1991), 'Les Problèmes de relations entre l'administration communautaire et les administrations nationales', *Politiques et management public*, 9/2: 37–50.

Galatsinou, M. (1996), 'Organizational and Operational Adjustments of Greek Administration for the Co-ordination of Agricultural Policy in the EU', University of Athens, Department of Political Science and Public Administration (unpublished Masters thesis).

Giataganas, X. (1990), *Europe and the Left* (Athens: Themelio).

González-Sánchez, E. (1992), 'La Négociation des décisions communautaires par les fonctionnaires nationaux: Les Groupes de travail du Conseil', *Revue française d'administration publique*, 63: 391–9.

Hayes-Renshaw, F., and Wallace, H. (1997), *The Council of Ministers* (London: Macmillan).

Hayes-Renshaw, F., Lequesne, C., and Mayor Lopez, P. (1989), 'The Permanent Representations of the Member States to the European Communities', *Journal of Common Market Studies*, 28/2: 119–37.

Ioakimidis, P. C. (1993), 'Greek Administration and European Policy Formation', in L. Tsoukalis (ed.), *Greece in the EC: The Challenge of Adjustment* (Athens: EKEM and Papazissis), 209–30.

Lequesne, C. (1993), *Paris–Bruxelles: Comment se fait la politique européenne de la France* (Paris: Presses de la FNSP).

Louloudis, L. (1993), 'CAMAR Project: The Greek Report', Agricultural University of Athens, Department of Agricultural Economics (unpublished paper).

Makridimitris, A., and Passas, A. (1993), *Greek Administration and European Policy Co-ordination* (Athens: Sakkoulas).

Minakaki, T. (1992) 'The Communication of Central Administration with the EC and the Role of the European Affairs Units of the Ministries in Greece', *Administrative Reform* (Dioikitiki Metarrithmissi), 51–2: 33–56.

Nugent, N. (1994), *The Government and Politics of the European Union* (London: Macmillan).

Passas, A. (1994), 'National Administrations and their Relations to the European Parliament', *Parliamentary Review* (Koinovouleftiki Epitheorissi), 17–18: 162–9.

——(1997), 'L'Expérience de la Grèce en matière de réforme de l'administration publique dans la perspective de l'intégration Européenne', Multi-country seminar, SIGMA–OECD, Athens, 8–10 Oct. (unpublished paper).

Peters, G. B. (1994), 'Agenda-Setting in the European Community', *Journal of European Public Policy*, 1/1: 9–26.

Pierros, P. (1991), 'The Administrative Lethargy of Greece and the EEC', *Ikonomikos Tachydromos* (28 Nov.), 23–4.

Rammou, D. A. (1997), 'The Role of the Permanent Representation', University of Athens (unpublished paper).

Rutten, Charles (1992), 'Au Cœur du processus de décision européen: Le Comité des représentants permanents (COREPER). Entretien avec C. Rutten', *Revue française d'administration publique*, 63: 383–90.

Sidjanski, D. (1990), 'Les Groupes d'intérêt de l'Europe du Sud et leur insertion dans la CE', in D. Sidjanski and U. Ayberk (eds.), *L'Europe du Sud dans la Communauté européenne* (Paris: Presses Universitaires de France), 235–64.

Spanou, C. (1996), 'On the Regulatory Capacity of the Greek State: A Tentative Approach Based on a Case-Study', *International Review of Administrative Sciences*, 62/2: 219–37.

——(1998), 'European Integration in Administrative Terms: A Framework for Analysis and the Greek Case', *Journal of European Public Policy*, 5/3: 467–84.

——(2000), 'A Truncated Pyramid? Domestic Co-ordination of EU Policy in Greece', in H. Kassim, G. Peters, and V. Wright (eds.), *The National Coordination of EU Policy: The Domestic Level* (Oxford: Oxford University Press), 161–81.

Stephanou, C. (1986), 'La Préparation des décisions communautaires par l'administration nationale: Le Cas de la Grèce', Athens (unpublished paper).

Tsinisizelis, M. (1996), 'Greece', in D. Rometsch and W. Wessels (eds.), *The EU and the Member States: Towards Institutional Fusion?* (Manchester: Manchester University Press), 216–52.

Tsoukalis, L. (ed.) (1993), *Greece in the EC: The Challenge of Adjustment* (Athens: EKEM and Papazissis).

Wallace, H. (1990), 'Making Multilateral Negotiations Work', in W. Wallace (ed.), *The Dynamics of European Integration* (London: Pinter and RIIA), 213–28.

Wessels, W. (1990), 'Administrative Interaction', in W. Wallace (ed.), *The Dynamics of European Integration* (London: Pinter and RIIA), 229–41.

Wright, V. (1996), 'The National Co-ordination of European Policy Making', in J. Richardson (ed.), *European Union. Power and Policy Making* (London: Routledge), 148–69.

6

The Portuguese Permanent Representation in Brussels: The Institutionalization of a Simple System

José M. Magone

The Context

Portugal is a small country in the European Union. The country's ambition is to protect as efficiently as possible its vital interests. The Portuguese political élite is committed to the advancement of the European integration process, which is regarded as being in the national interest. This attitude has been consistent since the adoption of the Constitution of 1976. Despite some divergence of opinion about the outcome of this process, none of the four main parties wants to reverse what has already been achieved. This has consequences for public administration and the national co-ordination of EU policy.

Civil servants dealing with EU matters are in a privileged situation in relation to other parts of the administration. Portuguese public administration had to overcome the culture of an authoritarian public administration which tended to be patrimonial, where clientelistic and patronage networks prevented the establishment of a modern, Weberian universalist administration. Such efforts were started only with the advent of democracy in 1974. Despite the good intentions of the political élite and sections within the public administration, reform attempts before 1986 failed due to governmental instability. Between 1976 and 1985 Portugal had nine governments, but then, in the same year that the Single European Act was signed, Anibal Cavaco Silva emerged as Prime Minister. For nearly a decade (1986–95) Cavaco Silva was able to

I would like to thank the Research Support Fund of the Faculty of Social Sciences at the University of Hull for financing my research trip to Brussels in February 1999.

tackle the long-term reform of the public administration. Important in this context was the establishment of the Secretariat for Administrative Reform (Secretariado para a Modernização Administrativa), which was created to improve the quality of public services, and to reform the structure and culture of public administration by tackling the duplication of services, the lack of co-ordination between ministries, and the inefficient use of personnel. Problems in the implementation stages still remain, however, particularly in the linkage between central and local government. The creation of an Institute of National Administration (Instituto de Administração Nacional, INA) was designed to raise the standards of public service.

While public administration entered a period of instability and change after 1976, national structures for the co-ordination of EU policy remained stable. Until 1985, the Secretariat of European Integration (Secretariado de Integração Europeia, SIE), located between the Finance Ministry and the Ministry of Foreign Affairs, co-ordinated negotiations with Brussels. It moved in the mid-1980s to the Ministry of Foreign Affairs, which became the centre for EU policy co-ordination. Weekly meetings of representatives of the other ministries in the Directorate-General for Community Affairs (Direcção-Geral de Assuntos Europeus, DGAC) has since then assured an efficient system of presenting the Portuguese position with one voice.

Policy continuity has been possible since 1986, because the political opportunity structure does not hinder the EU policy coordination process. The four political parties—the Socialist Party, the Social Democratic Party, the People's Party, and the Communist Party—do not tend to interfere in what is considered to be an essentially administrative domain. 'Europe' is one of the rare issues that is above party politics. Indeed, discussions about European integration only take place when a new treaty is ratified, such as, for example, happened in 1992 with Maastricht.

The Assembleia da República, the Portuguese Parliament, is kept informed by the government about EU policy co-ordination. The government has to submit an annual report to the Committee of European Affairs. The government's submission is scrutinized by several parliamentary committees, and a report produced by the Committee of European Affairs with comments on, and criticisms of, the policy performance of the government. This *ex-post-facto* scrutiny is a weak instrument for the opposition to use against the government (Magone 1995, 2000).

With respect to the basic structure of the state, unlike the Austrian, German, and Belgian systems, Portugal has only two levels of government, central and local. Although regionalization was enshrined in the Constitution of 1976 and has been debated over the past twenty-five years, a referendum on 8 November 1998 led to a rejection by the majority of the voters. The EU policy co-ordination system is, thus, considerably simpler than it might otherwise be. On the whole, the permanent representation in Brussels has to deal with an extremely simple system of decision-making in Lisbon. The centralized, flexible, and administrative character of EU policy co-ordination enhances the performance of the permanent representation considerably.

Organization: Adjusting and Learning from Other Member States

The Portuguese permanent representation is regarded as an important part of the national system for EU policy co-ordination. The Portuguese administration tends to send its best officials to the mission in Brussels. The Portuguese permanent representation was created after Portugal became a member of the European Union in 1986. From the very beginning the permanent representation was influenced by the missions of other member states. The main models were the permanent representations of France and the UK. The special relationship of Portugal to these countries shaped the organization and operation of the Portuguese permanent representation. These lessons learnt were not so much related to the structure, which is similar to those of other member states, but more to the skills and the way the members of permanent representation do their jobs. This is related to the experience of those civil servants in the French and British administrations before they were sent to the permanent representation.

The main preoccupation in the first six years was the organization of the permanent representation. Only after the Portuguese presidency in the first half of 1992 did the permanent representation become more consolidated and established. Since its creation, it has won high esteem and a strong reputation in Lisbon. The knowledge of the European institutional framework displayed by officials in Brussels increased their importance to Lisbon. The longevity of officials serving at the permanent representation was a factor that played a large part in enhancing its status. The presence of a permanent core group in Brussels allowed knowledge to be accumulated and enduring links with officials of the European Union institutions and other representations to be established, which further strengthened the reputation of Portugal's permanent representation in the national capital.

The importance of the permanent representation in the Portuguese case cannot be overestimated. Indeed, the distance from the national capital makes the permanent representation an indispensable element in responding adequately to legislative proposals or negotiations. This can be seen in its recent move from the rue Marie-Therese near the rue de la Loi where the Royal Palace is located, to a building in the avenue Cortenberg, closer to the European institutions. The six-floor building was bought by the Portuguese government and completely renovated. This is certainly a sign of the growing importance that the Portuguese government attaches to its permanent representation, and an indication that this small country on the fringe of south-western Europe is keen to increase its influence upon the EU policy-making process.

Although formally subordinate in relation to the national capital, the permanent representation's position is enhanced by its relations with officials of EU institutions and other member states. This is where the real importance of the permanent representation lies in the Portuguese case. It is able to transmit opinions and outline decision-making possibilities to Lisbon, because of its detailed knowledge and understanding of the state of play in Brussels for any dossier. The success of any member state's permanent representation can be orientated towards blocking the success of legislation that any government wants to avoid, so its work is very often informal or secretive. The Portuguese case is not very different from other countries.

Officials are a transmission belt of the Ministry of Foreign Affairs and as such they are subordinate to the decision-making process in Lisbon. This fact makes it very difficult for outsiders to recognize patterns or even structures within the permanent representation. The internal structure of the permanent representation mirrors the flexible and fluid nature of its work. Since it cannot investigate the internal operation of the Portuguese permanent representation in detail, this chapter attempts to map out its main boundaries and features.

The Portuguese permanent representation is the successor to the Portuguese Mission to the European Communities, which was originally established in 1977 following Portugal's application for membership on 14 March. It was put on a new footing by decree law no. 185 of 20 June 1979, which defined it as the supporting organ in Brussels of the Commission of European Integration (Secretariado de Integração Europeia, SIE), the central co-ordinating body in Lisbon. After the positive opinion by the Commission of the European Communities on the membership application by Portugal, negotiations started formally on 17 September 1978. The establishment of a mission to the European Community was regarded as important for co-ordinating its position during negotiations, which started in 1980, but in advance of which the Portuguese administration wanted a structure in place. According to the decree law, the mission received instructions from two ministries. On foreign policy issues, instructions were to be sent from the Ministry of Foreign Affairs (Ministro de Negócios Estrangeiros, MNE). On all technical issues, however, instructions would be received from the Vice Prime Minister for Economic and European Integration Affairs, via, directly or indirectly, the Commission of European Integration. The Vice Prime Minister was obliged to inform both the Minister of Foreign Affairs and the President of the Commission on European Integration of technical instructions conveyed to the mission (DAR, 20 June 1979, I-Serie, no. 140: 1347). Shortly before accession, the mission became the permanent representation in Brussels.

Decree law 526 of 31 December 1985 overhauled the entire system for the national co-ordination of EU policy. The permanent representation was integrated into the Ministry of Foreign Affairs. Thus, officially, all instructions must go through the General-Directorate of the European Communities (Direcção-Geral das Comunidades Europeias, DGCE) (DAR, 31 Dec. 1985, I-Serie, no. 301: 130) This formal monopoly is, of course, complemented by informal linkages between officials in the permanent representation and individual ministries. Nevertheless, the decree law ended the bicephalous nature of the institutions of policy co-ordination, bringing Portugal into line with most other member states.

The Portuguese permanent representation has a flexible structure that encourages teamwork and is characterized by non-hierarchical relations. The mission is headed by a permanent representative who comes from the diplomatic corps. He is assisted by the diplomatic permanent representative, who is responsible for liaising with officials and is a pivotal figure in internal co-ordination. The division of responsibilities changes according to the different topics discussed in COREPER or other institutions of the European Union. The flexibility and quality of response is the most important aspect emphasized in the Portuguese permanent representation. Due to the volume of business that confronts the permanent representation, teamwork and a non-hierarchical approach enables Portugal to define a position on most issues. Such a position can, of course, be a non-position as well, meaning that Portugal in conjunction with other countries may block proposed legislation for years. The work of the permanent representation is very difficult to assess, because of its interface nature, its Janus face between national and supranational level. Sometimes the work may be very positive, but on controversial questions the permanent representation may use a negative strategy to delay or block new legislative proposals. In this sense, its flexible, non-hierarchical structure prevents the establishment of an organogram (interview with Manuel Carvalho, permanent representation, Brussels, 8 Feb. 1999).

When it was established, the Portuguese permanent representation was small, comprising only twenty-four persons. The number of people working for the permanent mission more than doubled between 1986 and 1992. It was at its largest when Portugal held the Presidency in 1992, when fifty people worked in the permanent representation. After 1992 the number stabilized at forty-seven, which is comparatively large. In terms of composition, eleven departments were represented in the mission in 1986—a number which grew to fifteen in 1988. The restructuring of portfolios inside the permanent representation continued until 1992, but even in 1991 a stabilization was

TABLE 6.1. *Composition of the Portuguese permanent representation, 1986–1998*

	1986	1987	1988	1989	1990	1991	1992	1993	1994	1995	1996	1997	1998
Political and External Affairs	8	9	12	11	11	12	14	11	12	12	12	12	12
Agriculture	2	6	4	5	5	5	4	4	4	5	4	3	5
Fisheries	1	—	1	1	1	1	1	1	1	1	1	1	1
Internal Market	—	—	—	1	1	1	1	1	1	1	1	1	1
Industry and Trade	3	4	4	4	4	5	6	6	6	6	4	4	4
Economic and Finance Policy	1	6	6	5	5	5	5	5	5	5	5	5	5
National Bank	—	1	1	1	1	—	—	—	—	—	—	—	—
Social Affairs	3	2	2	2	2	2	2	2	2	2	1	2	2
Regional Policy	—	3	1	1	1	1	1	3	3	3	3	3	3
Transport and Telecommunications	—	1	—	1	1	1	1	1	1	1	1	1	1
Environment	—	—	1	1	1	1	1	1	1	1	1	1	1
Research and Civil Protection	1	—	2	2	2	2	2	1	1	1	1	1	1
Information Technology	—	—	—	—	—	—	—	—	—	—	—	—	—
Press and Tourism	1	1	1	1	1	1	2	1	1	1	1	1	1
Chancery	2	2	2	3	3	3	3	3	3	3	3	3	3
Staff and Administration	—	—	—	—	—	—	—	—	—	—	—	—	—
Protocol	1	1	1	1	1	1	1	1	1	1	1	1	1
Legal Affairs	—	2	2	2	2	2	3	4	3	3	4	4	5
TOTAL	23	37	38	41	42	43	47	45	45	46	43	44	47

Source: General Secretariat of the Council, *Guide to the Council of the European Communities* (Luxembourg: Office for Official Publications of the European Communities, 1986–93); European Commission, *Who's Who in the European Union: Inter-Institutional Directory* (Luxembourg: Office for the Official Publications of the European Union, 1995, 1998); Vacher, *Vacher's European Companion* (Berkhamsted: Vacher's Publications, various dates).

evident and only minor changes took place thereafter. Some policy areas, such as regional, agricultural, and environment policy, have developed autonomy over time. After 1992, the number of personnel dealing with regional policy increased, which may reflect the importance attached by Portugal to the structural funds.

More generally, the growth in complexity of EU policy co-ordination led to a strengthening of the permanent representation. The increase in the number of personnel and the singling out of certain policy areas which are relevant for the Portuguese economy became the most salient features of the adjustment of this interface between the Portuguese government and the European institutions. Several officials of the permanent representation became specialists in areas such as Schengen or relations with the ACP states and the Lomé Convention. In many ways, the Portuguese permanent representation has strong similarities with the UK permanent representation in terms of its organization.

Personnel: Professionalization and Stability

The officials of the Portuguese permanent representation are recruited from the home civil service and the diplomatic service. Ministries, typically, send their best experts on European affairs to the permanent representation. A position in the permanent representation is regarded as very prestigious within the Portuguese civil service. Usually, the best prepared and most knowledgeable civil servants are sent to Brussels. Even members of the judiciary have been seconded to the Portuguese permanent representation to deal with issues that raise difficult legal questions. In general terms, most civil servants are extremely experienced in their technical area and belong to the senior echelons of public administration. They come directly from ministries, and maintain a privileged relationship with the ministry of origin. The specialists work closely with the minister responsible for the particular area and so keep the informal contact with the ministry of origin.

One of the key functions of the permanent representation is to support ministers from Lisbon when they fly out to Brussels. The distance between the Portuguese capital and Brussels is one of the reasons accounting for the comparatively large size of the mission. While some member states, including the United Kingdom, Germany, Belgium, and Luxembourg have smaller staffs in Brussels and fly officials out from the capital to attend meetings, Portugal, like Greece, decided to have a large permanent representation in Brussels to compensate for the distance from their capital.

Until the early 1990s, staff turnover was very high, but this has declined subsequently. Until the Presidency, the number of newcomers each year was

TABLE 6.2. Staff continuity and change in the Portuguese permanent representation, 1986–1998 absolute (%)

	1987	1988	1989	1990	1991	1992	1993	1994	1995	1996	1997	1998
1986	17 (45.9)	15 (39.5)	11 (26.8)	10 (23.8)	10 (25.3)	9 (9.14)	9 (20)	7 (15.6)	9 (19.6)	8 (18.2)	8 (8.2)	7 (14.9)
1987	20 (54.1)	14 (36.8)	14 (34.5)	13 (31)	12 (28)	11 (23.4)	6 (13.3)	6 (13.3)	4 (8.7)	4 (9.1)	4 (9.1)	4 (8.5)
1988		9 (23.7)	8 (19.5)	7 (16.7)	6 (14)	6 (12.8)	5 (11.1)	5 (11.1)	5 (10.9)	4 (9.1)	4 (9.1)	4 (8.5)
1989			9 (22)	9 (21.4)	9 (21)	9 (9.2)	4 (8.9)	4 (8.8)	4 (8.7)	4 (9.1)	4 (9.1)	4 (8.5)
1990				3 (7.14)	3 (7)	1 (2.1)	1 (2.2)	1 (2.2)	1 (2.2)	1 (2.3)	1 (2.3)	1 (2.1)
1991					3 (7)	3 (6.4)	1 (2.2)	1 (2.2)	1 (2.2)	1 (2.3)	1 (2.3)	1 (2.1)
1992						9 (19.2)	5 (13.3)	5 (11.1)	5 (23.9)	2 (4.6)	2 (4.6)	2 (4.3)
1993							11 (24.4)	11 (24.4)	11 (23.9)	10 (23.3)	10 (22.7)	6 (12.8)
1994								3 (6.7)	3 (6.5)	3 (6.4)	3 (6.8)	3 (7)
1995									3 (6.5)	3 (6.4)	2 (4.5)	2 (4.3)
1996										3 (6.4)	3 (6.8)	3 (6.4)
1997											2 (4.5)	2 (4.3)
1998												8 (17)
	37	38	41	42	43	47	45	45	46	43	44	47

Source: General Secretariat of the Council, Guide to the Council of the European Communities (Luxembourg: Office for the Official Publications of the European Union, 1989–93); European Commission, Who's Who in the European Union: Inter-Institutional Directory (Luxembourg: Office for the Official Publications of the European Union, 1995, 1998); Vacher, Vacher's European Companion (Berkhampsted: Vacher's Publications, various dates).

between 5 and 6 per cent. In 1993, it reached a dramatic high of 34 per cent, then fell back to 3–6 per cent. It only began to rise again in 1998, when 20 per cent of staff were replaced. The stability of personnel is particularly evident in certain policy areas, such as internal market, regional policy, social policy, education and health, and especially, agriculture and fisheries. Expertise is a major criterion that keeps the turnover rate at relatively low levels. Generally, most civil servants in permanent representation stay for a period of five to six years, but about one-third of the officers have spent more than nine years in the permanent representation. Among this group, a substantial number—many in agriculture and fisheries—began their posting in the late 1980s and have simply not been replaced. Sections dealing with internal market, social affairs, legal affairs, and transport and communication also include long-serving officials.[1] The high level of stability has created a pool of expertise in the permanent representation, without disrupting long-term strategies adopted in the COREPER and different other committees.

Portuguese civil servants tend to remain in public administration after leaving the permanent representation. Their European expertise is regarded

TABLE 6.3. *Portuguese permanent and deputy permanent representatives, 1986–2001*

Permanent Representatives	
Fernando Manuel da Silva Marques	1986
Leonardo Mathias	1987–1989
Carlos Alberto Soares Simoes Coelho	1989–1991
Jose Cesar Paulouro das Neves	1991–1996
Jose Gregorio Faria Quiteres	1996–1998
Vasco Valente	1998–
Deputy Permanent Representatives	
Luis Octavio Roma de Albuquerque	1986
Pedro Jose Ribeiro de Menezes	1987
Vasco Valente	1987–1993
Joao Vallera	1993–1998
Maria Margarida de Araujo Figueiredo	1998–

Source: General Secretariat of the Council, *Guide to the Council of the European Communities* (Luxembourg: Office for the Official Publications of the European Union, 1989–93); European Commission, *Who's Who in the European Union: Inter-Institutional Directory* (Luxembourg: Office for the Official Publications of the European Union, 1995, 1998); Vacher, *Vacher's European Companion* (Berkhampsted: Vacher's Publications, various dates).

---

[1] An exception is the section responsible for political and foreign affairs—also the largest—which has experienced the highest levels of staff turnover.

as an important asset for the different ministries and assists in career advancement. They may even return at a later stage to the permanent representation. The attractiveness of leaving the public administration and the opportunities for selling EU expertise to the private-sector economy are small in Portugal, where lobbying and information-related skills are still at an early stage of development. Civil servants tend, therefore, to remain in the administration, which is regarded as prestigious in the Portuguese context and particularly if it is related to European integration issues (interview with Manuel Carvalho, permanent representation, 8 Feb. 1999).

While technical experts tend to stay for longer periods in Brussels, the permanent representative and the deputy—both diplomats—serve relatively short terms. The permanent representative may stay for two years, while the deputy tends to stay longer to ensure a degree of continuity. The permanent representative in post at the time of writing had already served in the mission. Ambassador Vasco Valente was deputy permanent representative between 1987 and 1993 and was a crucial figure in the preparation for the Portuguese Presidency. In his late fifties, he began his diplomatic career under the authoritarian regime, and served in London and Africa. Much of his career was spent in the Ministry of Foreign Affairs where he worked in the Asian and African department. He was seconded to the permanent representation as deputy permanent representative in the late 1980s (*The European Companion* 1992: 449–50).

The deputy permanent representative, Maria Margarida de Araújo Figueiredo, has worked in the mission since 1994, when she was appointed minister plenipotentiary in the political and foreign affairs section. Her promotion to deputy representative shows that diplomatic officials dealing with European Union affairs have become more integrated in the recent past. Mme Margarida de Araújo Figueiredo had worked in the Commission as assistant to Commissioner João Deus Pinheiro between 1992 and 1994 (interview with Manuel Carvalho, permanent representation, 8 Feb. 1999). The former deputy permanent representative João Vallera was born in 1950 and is a representative of the new generation of Portuguese diplomats. He started his diplomatic career in the Ministry of Foreign Affairs in 1974 and, after serving as secretary in the Portuguese Bonn embassy, became a member of the Portuguese mission to the EEC between 1979 and 1984. He returned in 1991 as assistant to the permanent representative and Portugal's representative in the Antici Group. Two years later, he was promoted to deputy permanent representative and, according to the pattern of recruitment, he may return as permanent representative in the future (*The European Companion* 1994: 139–40).

By 1993, Portugal had developed a core of EU specialists. Today, the permanent representation consists of highly experienced officials, who have spent on average six years in the permanent representation—some even longer.

Recruitment patterns have become more stable and structured. A body of experienced diplomats and technical experts are able to socialize newcomers quickly and effectively. The permanent representation is, therefore, an important repository of experience and expertise.

Internal Functioning and Working Methods: Teamwork and Flexible Arrangements

All diplomats and technical experts sent to permanent representation have experience in European matters and most are senior level officials, which creates cohesion and reinforces an *esprit de corps* among its staff. The non-hierarchical nature of the internal functioning is regarded as a prerequisite for responding quickly to the demands of COREPER. According to Manuel Carvalho, there are only two levels in the Portuguese permanent representation: the ambassador and all other officials. This naturally leads to co-ordinated teamwork. Liaison between the two levels is the responsibility of Portugal's Antici Group member, who co-ordinates the position of Portugal for meetings of COREPER.

The flat structure seems always to have been a feature of the permanent representation. Some issues are of an interdepartmental nature and call for an environment that permits flexibility and co-operation. This is one reason for the lack of hierarchy in the Portuguese case (interview with Manuel Carvalho, permanent representation, 8 Feb. 1999). Another is that the technical experts come from different line ministries and, even if they are on loan to the Ministry of Foreign Affairs, they retain linkages to their ministry of origin. Furthermore, socialization with officials of the permanent representation in other countries through the various working group and COREPER structures enhances their autonomy in relation to nationally orientated hierarchical structures. Officials become part of a transnational culture of working methods, which is shared with other similar permanent representations of other member states.[2]

Role: Arena or Actor? A Peripheral Actor

According to a recent much acclaimed book by former Belgian permanent representative, Philippe de Schoutheete, the present European Union is best

---

[2] Here, there was effectively a changeover in 1993. Though a large team, the Portuguese permanent representation has been able to create a climate of teamwork which, according to Helen Wallace, is more usually found within smaller missions (Wallace 1973: 63).

conceived as a network which is permanently changing. The web of relations and flows is characterized by asymmetrical density and thickness of relationship, which are well developed in some parts and less so in others (Schoutheete 1998: 53–74). The transnational Janus nature of COREPER, which transmits, mediates, and negotiates between national governments and the supranational institutions, makes it a pivotal area of study. COREPER can be regarded as an interface between national and supranational networks, bringing both together in a single transnational network. In recent research on COREPER, the network approach has been studied in detail, with the relative influence and importance of some actors over others. The Portuguese permanent representation emerges as a junior partner, while the larger countries are identified as the key players in this web of relationships.

This picture is confirmed at working-group level, as a study conducted by Jan Beyers and Guido Dierickx during the Belgian Presidency in 1993 illustrates. There were about 170 groups, composed of diplomats and technical officials, at the time of their research, and these groups met frequently. For example, in 1994, they met on 2,580 occasions, compared with 125 for the Council and 117 for COREPER.[3] As a result of their frequent interaction and stable membership, Beyers and Dierckx concluded that working groups establish a common culture or *esprit de corps*, and have undergone a process of formalization in relation to COREPER and the Council (Beyers and Dierickx 1998: 290–1). Moreover, working groups are important. Between 70 and 90 per cent of all decisions are taken informally at this level with the remainder agreed in COREPER and the Council. According to the authors, the Portuguese permanent representation is regarded as peripheral within this system. The core actors are Germany, France, and the United Kingdom. Only Germany is interested in keeping strong linkages to the periphery, while France and the United Kingdom tend to neglect the periphery and work with other northern European countries or together. The second group, of small northern European states, is still in the making. It includes the Benelux countries, Ireland, and Denmark, and probably, since 1995, Finland, Sweden, and Austria. The third group, which is composed of southern European member states, includes Italy, Spain, Greece, and Portugal. Their weak linkages to the centre make them peripheral (Beyers and Dierickx 1998: 305–6). This categorization of member states emerges from a snapshot view based on communication flows during the Belgium presidency and probably only tells part of the story. Configurations may vary from presidency to presidency and are

[3] According to Wolfgang Wessels, there were *c.*1,150 committees in 1994: 600 Commission working groups, 270 working groups of the Council, and 280 Commission implementation committees. In 1990, over 1,000 German civil servants were involved in these committees, sometimes two or three committees at the same time (Wessels and Römetsch 1996: 105–6 n. 58). According to the Council Guide, there were, in 1995, 287 Council working groups and committees (Council Guide, 1996: 91–104).

likely to change depending on the dossiers or issues under discussion. Also, until the early 1990s, Portugal was still learning to deal with the spider's web and adjusting its administration, including the permanent representation, to deal with the complex challenges presented by EU membership. As part of this process, modern telecommunications systems between Portuguese embassies and the Ministry of Foreign Affairs had to be set up (Pereira 1996: 210–17; Magone 2000).

The Portuguese permanent representation is one of fifteen within a transnational community. Though their allegiances are national, officials inevitably become part of wider networks. The experience of former permanent representatives, such as Philippe de Schoutheete of Belgium or Pierre de Boissieu of France, or stalwarts, such as the German deputy Jochen Grünhage, socialize the newcomers, and introduce them to the norms and conventions of the 'club' (Lewis 1998: 488).

As its experience has grown and it has become accustomed to the ways of Brussels, Portugal's permanent representation is no longer merely the transmission belt for instructions from the national capital. With maturity, it has gained a reputation in the national capital which lends authority to the advice on feasible positions that it transmits to the main interministerial committee, the Interministerial Committee of Community Affairs (Comissão Interministerial de Assuntos Comunitários, CIAC) which meets every Friday morning in the Ministry of Foreign Affairs in Lisbon. Although, in theory, permanent representations act under instruction from the national capitals, in reality, they are actors in their own right, shaping the decision-making process. Like other permanent representations, the Portuguese permanent representation tends to follow the four generic patterns recognized by Jeffrey Lewis (1998: 490–1).

1. Departing from Recommendations and Making 'Recommendations'

In some cases, instructions from the capital set out the wrong approach for negotiation, and the permanent representation may send recommendations to change them. This practice has become more common, and produces a dialogue, sometimes very informal, about the approach that a national delegation should take in a particular situation.

2. The National Capital Signals that a Margin of Manœuvre Exists

The permanent representation can draw on the talents of the best diplomats and technical officials from the Portuguese administration. Their expertise in negotiations gives them a special status in the co-ordination of EU policy. They are able to use the margin of manœuvre to achieve a realistic outcome for the Portuguese delegation.

3. There is a Political Need to Minimize Confrontation

Portugal tends to take a consensual approach. The avoidance of confrontation has been its style. As a small state, the Portuguese administration, through the permanent representation, prefers to seek compromise.

4. The National Capital Cannot Make up its Mind

The distance from the negotiating arena and to the dynamics among the different actors within COREPER strengthens the position of the permanent representation as the real source of its own instructions. The reports received in Lisbon from permanent representation may come back to Brussels as instructions, because the Portuguese CIAC trusts the expertise and knowledge of the permanent representation (interview with Josefina Carvalho, DGAC, 22 Sept. 1998).

Thus, CIAC's agenda is normally drafted by the permanent representation to reflect what is likely to be discussed at the next meeting of COREPER. The dialogue between Brussels and Lisbon is overwhelmingly dominated by the permanent representation, which asks for instructions or makes recommendations.

In the Council forums, Portugal is more reactive than active. Portugal has no agenda-setting capacity, and this is normally left to the larger member states. In relation to the capital, the permanent representation has the power of knowledge, so that the flow of information is dominated by Brussels rather than Lisbon. The power of knowledge is also used informally by the individual ministries. The main task is also to support the ministers and officials who come for meetings in Brussels before the Council meetings. The prestigious position of the permanent representation within the Portuguese administration reflects the latter's awareness that Brussels-based officials have privileged knowledge of, and links within, COREPER. The Portuguese permanent representation becomes more active in aspects related to structural funds, regional policy, and social policy. The discussion about the financing of Agenda 2000 led to a tougher negotiating position to assure that Portugal was able to retain the maximum level of structural funds amounts until 2006 (Manuel Carvalho, permanent representation, Antici Group, 8 Feb. 1999).

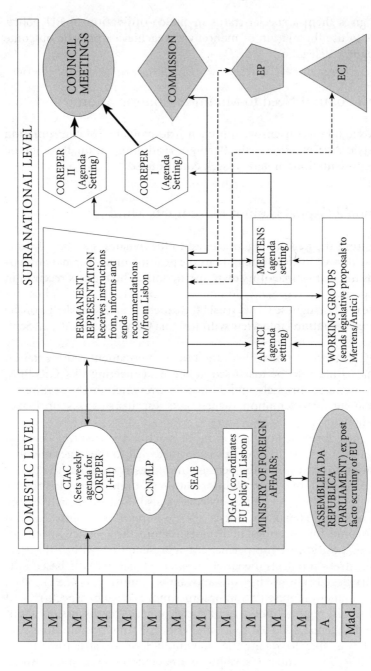

FIG. 6.1. The National Co-ordination of EU Policy: The Case of Portugal

CIAC Interministerial Committee for Communitarian Affairs; M Representative of Ministries, including A Acores and Mad. Madeira; CNMLP National Co-ordination of Free Movement of People in European Space; DGAC Directorate-General for Communitarian Affairs; SEAE State Secretary for European Affairs; ECJ European Court of Justice; EP European Parliament

Capacity to Implement Ambitions: A Realistic Approach

The Portuguese permanent representation is designed to be the interface between the national government and the supranational institutions. Its capacity to implement ambitions very much reflects political will in Lisbon. Portuguese civil servants dealing with EU policy co-ordination are well aware that there are limitations to the country's ambitions in EU policy-making. As already noted, the Portuguese permanent representation normally reacts to agenda-setting by the larger member states. In this respect, Portugal shares the same outlook as other small states such as the Netherlands, Denmark, Austria, Greece, Sweden, Finland, Belgium, and Luxembourg, which have to try to use any opportunity to further national interests. The six-month Presidency is probably the best way to bring Portuguese-specific issues onto the agenda, but, in reality, even business under the Presidency is dominated by the Commission or other member states. Thus, for example, in the first semester of 1992, Portugal had to sacrifice its agricultural interests to achieve a reform of the CAP (Magone 1997).

Although the permanent representation represents Portugal in relation to other European institutions, particularly the European Parliament and the European Commission, most of its work is concentrated on the Council. The permanent representation does act as a liaison between the Commission's Directorate Generals and national civil servants that come to Brussels, but its work is very much dominated by the pattern of relations adopted by the Council for COREPER in relation to the other European institutions (General Secretariat 1996: 35–41). Whatever contacts are established are related to work in the Council or demands originating in Lisbon. There is no autonomous contact-building. According to Vitor Martins, the former state secretary for European affairs, there is no systematic co-operation between Portuguese members of the European Parliament and permanent representation. On the whole, the permanent representation tends to neglect contacts with other institutions. Any contacts are of a sporadic nature and related to work in the Council (question to Vitor Martins, 7 July 1999).

The establishment of a strong network of Euro-groups was one of the most dynamic elements of the European integration in the 1990s. The lack of a tradition of lobbying in the Portuguese case explains why very few interest groups approach the permanent representation. For example, in 1997, seventy-nine national associations were represented at European level. Four of them were Portuguese—in other words, 5 per cent of the total. Countries such as Finland, Spain, Denmark, Belgium, Norway, and the Netherlands have even fewer (Gray 1998: 285; Greenwood 1998). In 1994, there were 1,674 pressure groups, which comprised corporate EU offices (17 per cent); law firms (9 per cent); trade associations (35 per cent); political consultants (5 per cent);

national associations (5 per cent); regions (6 per cent); conferences (2 per cent); international organizations (5 per cent); trade unions (1 per cent); think-tanks (1 per cent); business and industry (1 per cent); interest groups (8 per cent); association chambers of commerce (1 per cent); and chambers of commerce (2 per cent) (Gray 1998: 283). Inevitably, the Portuguese permanent representation is regularly lobbied by some pressure groups. However, in Portugal, the administration is confronted by a very weak civil society and lobbying is underdeveloped (Manuel Carvalho, permanent representation, Antici Group, 8 Feb. 1999).

In terms of coalition partners, Portugal has no privileged relationship with any particular member state(s). The Portuguese permanent representation attempts to keep good relations with all member states. Only on issues related to structural funds, industry, and agriculture are temporary and informal coalitions forged with countries with similar interests. In recent years, however, there has been a closer relationship between Spain and Portugal, leading, for example, to the solution of long-standing problems between the two countries, such as the question about shared rivers. With respect to European Union financing, as well, Portugal and Spain have similar interests. Nevertheless, at the level of COREPER the Portuguese permanent representation clearly tends to keep good relations with all member states, because the process of negotiations is a process of changing coalitions.

The expertise of the permanent representation is perhaps Portugal's strongest asset at the European level. The aim is not so much to be ambitious in the policy-making process, but to be moderately successful in policy areas where there is a strong national interest, such as structural funds, industry, social policy, education, agriculture, and fisheries. In these areas, the permanent representation spends its time preventing a negative outcome for Portugal. The introduction of the Ioannina formula in 1994, under which a group of countries can block a qualified majority with twenty-three to twenty-five votes and force further negotiations, was regarded as positive for the protection of the small states.

Success: Upstream and Downstream

The Portuguese permanent representation has a good reputation both in Lisbon and within the European Union. The crucial milestone was the Presidency in 1992, where in spite of difficulties, such as the process of Treaty ratification and the emerging war in Bosnia-Herzegovina, Portugal was considered to have been well-organized and to have performed successfully. The Presidency is taken extremely seriously in Portugal and preparations for its term in 2000 began in 1998.

The permanent representation has been used by the Portuguese adminis-tration to give civil servants experience of the EU (Pereira 1996). A position in the permanent representation fosters career advancement of both in the diplomatic and home service. Permanent representation officials also play an important role in shaping the community of policy-makers dealing with EU affairs in Lisbon. Indeed, according to Wolfgang Wessels, the fifteen perma-nent representations are able to create, through their linkages to the various ministries in each country, a transnational network of 25,000 civil servants (quoted in Lewis 1998: 488). These connections are an important, but only partially visible, element of European integration.

Comparative Dimension: Centralization and Flexibility

The Portuguese permanent representation was established in a period when the European integration process was receiving a new impetus. In 1986, Portugal was due to assume the Presidency of the European Community in the second half of the year, but due to its inexperience, the government asked to be passed over and wait until the first half of 1992 (Pereira 1996: 214). This strategy paid off. Between 1986 and 1992, Portugal strengthened its co-ordination structures and learnt from the experiences of other countries. It also studied the conduct of EU business and the structure of EU institutions. The organization of the Council was regarded as particul-arly important, and the channelling of business through COREPER I and COREPER II was a feature that attracted particular attention.[4] In addition, the adoption of the SEA brought about an increase in the number of Council working groups and Commission consultative committees. Both provided invaluable sources for training for Portuguese officials. At the same time, national co-ordination structures were adjusted to suit the demands of a small state. The Portuguese permanent representation experienced problems of adjustment in its early days, but it gained a firm, stable, but at the same time flexible, structure by 1992.

---

[4] For an insider's view on the genesis of COCOR and COREPER see Meulen (1966). While COREPER I deals mainly with technical issues, COREPER II is concerned with polit-ical issues (see Mentler 1996: 51–7). The agendas of COREPER I and COREPER II are pre-pared by the Mertens Group and the Antici Group respectively (Council Guide, 1996: 20). The division of labour between the two is as follows: COREPER I deals with Internal Market, Energy, Research, Industry, Telecommunications, Fisheries, Transport, Environ-ment, Consumers, Labour and Social Affairs, Health, Education, Culture, Tourism and Agriculture (veterinary and plant-health questions); COREPER II deals with institutional matters, preparation of General Affairs, ECOFIN, Development, Justice and Home Affairs, and Budget Council Meetings (Council Guide, 1996: 18).

In comparative perspective, the Portuguese permanent representation is part of a very simple system of co-ordination. Interest groups are weak, regional government apart from the autonomous regions of Madeira and Acores is absent, and, last but not least, limited scrutiny by the Parliament strengthens the role of the Portuguese administration in EU policy co-ordination. The Portuguese permanent representation does not include any other interest than that put forward by the different ministries of the public administration. The Portuguese public administration is highly centralized and tends to emphasize the need to speak with one voice.

The Portuguese permanent representation is a formal part of the co-ordination structures located in the Ministry of Foreign Affairs. All other ministries have to go through the CIAC, the interministerial committee, to send instructions to the permanent representation. Only technical issues are dealt with directly and informally with the responsible ministry, but this has to be reported to CIAC. Like other permanent representations, the Portuguese permanent representation was able to gain autonomy in shaping instructions by sending recommendations to the national capital, which normally are accepted in Lisbon. This situation is reinforced by the fact that, since 1985, Portuguese governments have been either absolute majority governments or strong single-party minority governments, which strengthens the centralization of the decision-making process and reduces the time spent in domestic negotiations, unlike the Dutch and German experiences (Wessels 1997: 85–92). There is no bicephalous structure, as is partly the case in Belgium, and very clear in France and Greece (Lequesne 1997), and no regional tier, as in Belgium, Germany, or Spain (Wessels and Römetsch 1996: 88–90; Morata 1998: 385–401). Moreover, the Portuguese representation never has to ask for a 'parliamentary reservation'[5] in COREPER meetings, as Denmark and the UK sometimes have to do, since the Portuguese Parliament only has the power of *ex-post-facto* scrutiny. Nor does the government have to seek instructions from Parliament, as the Danish government is compelled to do with respect to the Folketing (Munro 1996: 93–4; Norton 1995, 1996; Jensen 1996: 43). Consequently, the co-ordination of EU policy in Portugal is an extremely straightforward process.

---

[5] Permanent representatives have different ways of dealing with instructions and delaying the progress of a dossier: a 'reservation' or 'scrutiny reservation' can be put down, so that the proposal can be studied further in the national capital; 'ad referendum' means that the permanent representative agrees with proposed legislation, but awaits the final approval by the national capital; and a 'waiting reservation' is where formal approval by the national capital is anticipated, but needs to be secured definitively. In some cases, the permanent representative cannot signal approval, but indicates that it will 'recommend' to the national capital to accept it. Such is the prestige that the Portuguese permanent representation enjoys in the national capital that recommendations are usually accepted. Last but not least, the 'parliamentary reservation' may be entered by permanent representatives of nations where there are strong parliaments, who need to secure the approval of the latter (Zwaan 1995: 192–3).

The regularization of the administration achieved since the Cavaco Silva government that was elected in 1985, and continued by the Guterres government that came to power in 1995, has strengthened its reputation and credibility. The recruitment of the Portuguese permanent representation is less dominated by clientelism, as has been the case in Greece, where such practices throughout the 1980s and 1990s led to a very unstable and heavy permanent representation. Recruitment to the Portuguese mission has been meritocratic, driven by the belief that it is crucial to have the best people in Brussels. Moreover, concern to defend vital Portuguese interests in certain key domains ensures that officials feel that they are fighting for a common cause.[6]

The simplicity and efficiency of national EU policy co-ordination in Portugal, and the place of the permanent representation, should not be extrapolated to the field of EU policy implementation. There is clearly a gap between the macro-level of EU policy co-ordination and the meso- and micro-level of implementation coordination. This question goes beyond the scope of this chapter, but is clearly noteworthy. The élitist approach towards EU policy co-ordination, which is legally strong in implementation, but weak in real implementation, differs markedly from practice in Germany, the Netherlands, Sweden, and the United Kingdom. The weakness of Portuguese interest groups, the weakness of local and regional civil societies, and soft parliamentary control creates a democratic deficit with regard to action taken by the government and administration on behalf of the population, even if this deficiency is what makes national EU policy co-ordination in Portugal simple and efficient,[7] and makes the job of the permanent representation considerably less complex than it might otherwise be.

Conclusions

Realism and flexibility characterize the work of the Portuguese permanent representation. The Portuguese administration took the decision to send its

---

[6] Fiona Hayes-Henshaw and Helen Wallace (1997: 221) identify four groups of permanent representations according to size and number of departments represented: Group I (all 15): Foreign Affairs and Economic and Financial Affairs; Group II (14/15): Agriculture and Fisheries and Justice and Home Affairs; Group III (9–13/15): Transport and Communications, Health and Social Affairs, Employment and Labour, Education and Research, Industry and Trade, Energy and Environment; Group IV (in only a few): Regions, Taxation and Customs questions, National Bank, Cultural Affairs and Merchant navy, The Portuguese permanent representation clearly belongs to Group III according to this categorization.

[7] An attitude characterized by Morlino and Montero (1995: 252) as 'democratic cynicism'.

best civil servants to Brussels early on. Officials seconded to the permanent representation by the different ministries have become part of a transnational community of officials, though one where national allegiances have been retained. The functional differentiation of areas within the Portuguese permanent representation stabilized in the 1990s. Currently, fifteen areas are covered by civil servants specializing in these areas. Some areas were able to gain more human resources, such as agriculture, industry, trade, economic and financial affairs, and regional policy. On the whole, the Portuguese permanent representation is extremely well-integrated in the national EU policy co-ordination system, which is characterized by centralization, weak civil society, and *ex-post-facto* parliamentary control.

References

Beyers, Jan, and Dierickx, G. (1998), 'The Working Groups of the Council of the European Union: Supranantional or Intergovernmental Negotiations?', *Journal of Common Market Studies*, 36/3: 289–317.

European Commission (1995, 1998), *Who's Who in the European Union: Inter-Institutional Directory* (Luxembourg: Office of the Official Publications of the European Union).

Falco, Tortora de (1980), *Il Comitato dei Rappresentanti permanenti dai Trattati istitutivi alla prassi Comunitaria* (Naples: Giannini Editori).

General Secretariat of the Council (1986–1994), *Guide to the Council of the European Communities* (Luxembourg: Office of the Official Publications of the European Communities).

——(1997), *Council Guide*, 3 vols. i. *The Presidency Handbook*; ii. *Comments on the Council's Rule of Procedure*; iii. *The Delegates' Handbook* (Luxembourg: Office of the Official Publications of the European Communities).

Gray, Oliver (1998), 'The Structure of Interest Group Representation in the EU: Some Observations of a Practitioner', in Paul H. Claeys and Corinne Gobin (eds.), *Lobbying, Pluralism and European Integration* (Brussels: European Interuniversitary Press), 281–302.

Greenwood, Justin (1998), 'Corporatism, Pluralism and the Capacities of the Euro Groups', in Paul H. Claeys and Corinne Gobin (eds.), *Lobbying, Pluralism and European Integration* (Brussels: European Interuniversitary Press), 83–109.

Hanf, Kenneth, and Soetendorp, Ben (eds.) (1998), *Adjusting to European Integration: Small States in the European Union* (London: Longman).

Hayes-Renshaw, Fiona, and Wallace, Helen (1997) *The Council of Ministers* (Basingstoke: Macmillan).

Jensen, Jorgen Alboek (1996), 'Prior Parliamentary Consent to Danish EU Policies', in Eivind Smith (ed.), *National Parliaments as Cornerstones of European Integration* (London: Kluwer Law), 39–48.

Lequesne, Christian (1997), 'French Central Government and the European Political System: Change and Adaptation since the Single Act', in Yves Mény, Pierre Muller, and Jean-Louis Quermonne (eds.), *Adjusting to Europe: The Impact of the European Union on National Institutions and Policies* (London: Routledge), 110–20.

Lewis, Jeffrey (1998), 'Is the "Hard Bargaining" Image of the Council Misleading? The Committee of Permanent Representatives and the Local Elections Directive', *Journal of Common Market Studies*, 36/4: 479–504.

Magoné, Jose M. (1995), 'The Portuguese Assembly of the Republic: Discovering Europe', in Philip Norton (ed.), *National Parliaments and the European Union* (London: Frank Cass), 151–67.

——(1997), *European Portugal: The Difficult Road to Sustainable Democracy* (Basingstoke: Macmillan).

——(2000) 'Portugal', in Hussein Kassim, Guy Peters, and Vincent Wright (eds.), *The National Coordination of EU Policy: The Domestic Level* (Oxford: Oxford University Press), 141–60.

Martin, Araceli Mangas (1980), *El Comité de Representantes Permanentes de las Comunidades Europeas* (Madrid: Centro de Estudios Constitucionales).

Martins, Vitor (1999), 'Portugal na Uniao Europeia 1986–1999', paper presented at the course, 'Between Africa and Europe: The Foreign Policy of Democratic Portugal', Summer University in the Convent Arrabida, 7 July.

Mentler, Michael (1996), *Der Ausschuss der Ständigen Vertreter bei den Europaischen Gemeinschaften* (Baden-Baden: Nomos).

Meulen, J. van der (1966), *Meditations sur le rôle et le statut du Comité des representants permanents et des représentations permanentes dans le cadre des Communautés européennes instituées par le Traité de Rome*, mimeo.

Morata, Francesco (1998), *La Union Europea: Procesos, Actores y Politicas* (Barcelona: Ariel).

Morlino, Leonardo, and Montero, José Ramon (1995), 'Legitimacy and Democracy in Southern Europe', in Richard Gunther, P. Nikiforos Diamandouros, and Hans-Jürgen Puhle (eds.), *The Politics of Democratic Consolidation: Southern Europe in Comparative Perspective* (Baltimore and London: The John Hopkins University Press), 231–60.

Munro, Colin R. (1996), 'The UK Parliament and EU Institutions: Partners or Rivals?', in Eivind Smith (ed.), *National Parliaments as Cornerstones of European Integration* (London: Kluwer Law), 80–99.

Norton, Philip (1995), 'United Kingdom: Political Conflict, Parliamentary Scrutiny', in Philip Norton (ed.), *National Parliaments and the European Union* (London: Frank Cass), 92–109.

Norton, Philip (1996), 'National Parliaments in Western Europe', in Eivind Smith (ed.), *National Parliaments as Cornerstones of European Integration* (London: Kluwer Law), 19–35.

Pereira, Pedro Sanchez da Costa (1996), 'Portugal: Public Administration and EPC/CFSP—A Fruitful Adaptation Process', in Franoc Algieri and Elfriede Regelsberger (eds.), *Synergy at Work: Spain and Portugal in European Foreign Policy* (Bonn: Europa Union Verlag), 207–29.

Schoutheete, Philippe de (1998), *Una Europa para todos: Diez ensayos sobre la construccion europea* (Madrid: Alianza Editorial).

Vacher's *European Companion* (various), (Berkhamsted: Vacher's Publications).

Wallace, Helen (1973), *National Governments and the European Communities* (London: Chatham House and PEP).

Wessels, Wolfgang, and Rometsch, Dietrich (1997), 'German Administrative Interaction and European Union: The Fusion of Public Policies', in Yves Mény, Pierre Muller, and Jean-Louis Quermonne (eds.), *Adjusting to Europe: The Impact of the European Union on National Institutions and Policies* (London: Routledge), 73–109.

Wright, Vincent (1996), 'The National Coordination of National European Policy-Making: Negotiating the Quagmire', in Jeremy Richardson (ed.), *European Union: Power and Policy-Making* (London and New York: Routledge), 148–69.

Zwaan, Jaap W. de (1995), *The Permanent Representatives Committee: Its Role in European Union Decision-Making* (Amsterdam: Elsevier).

7

The Belgian Permanent Representation to the European Union: Mailbox, Messenger, or Representative?

Bart Kerremans and Jan Beyers

Introduction

Belgium is one of the six founding member states of the European Union, and has historically supported a federal conception of European integration. For the Belgians, the process of European integration is primarily a political project—a project that can help a small state like Belgium in the defence of peace and prosperity, and the pursuit of its own interests on the international stage. Without the EU, Belgium would have been a small state among many others and squeezed—either virtually or literally—between its bigger neighbours.

But the EU is special for Belgium in still another way. Most of its main institutions are located in, or operate from, the Belgian capital, Brussels. The EU is therefore not in Belgium's backyard; it is in its drawing room, its kitchen, even its bedroom. The EU is not an organization with a remote headquarters located overseas, but announces its presence with its sometimes questionable architecture in the capital. Its well paid officials live not only in the outskirts of Brussels, but from Ostend to Liège, and from Antwerp to Charleroi. The direct benefits that are brought to the Belgian economy should not be forgotten.

If Europe is right at the centre of Belgium—both politically and geographically—why does Belgium need a permanent representation to the European Union? Why do the Belgians have something as odd as an embassy representing Belgium located in Belgium itself? The answer is obvious: it is not at Belgium's insistence, but due to the EU. It is simply the way the EU works and participating in it means that a member state needs to have the necessary structures. A permanent representation is part and parcel of this.

The question needs, therefore, to be rephrased: if Belgium needs its own permanent representation in the streets of its own capital, next door to its own national ministries and alongside EU institutions, what kind of role does this representation play? Is it merely doing what any member state has to do, and no more? Is it just there for the sake of the Union, responding to the need of the EU institutions to have a local mailbox in each of the member states? Or is there something more? Maybe even more than one would expect from a traditional embassy?

The purpose of this chapter is to examine the role of the Belgian permanent representation to the European Union from two angles. The first is sceptical. What role does the Belgian permanent representation play beyond that of postbox, of transmitter of messages between the EU and Belgium and vice versa? This viewpoint is sceptical because of the presence of all federal Belgian institutions—including the federal Foreign Ministry—in Brussels. One would expect that they—and especially the federal Foreign Ministry—would be able to provide for the co-ordination, preparation, and defence of Belgium's EU policies. So what would be left for the permanent representation? The role of postman?

The second viewpoint is quite the opposite. This is the perspective of high expectations. Being in Brussels and representing Belgium's interests in the same city could be beneficial. A local presence could provide added value to the work a permanent representation traditionally plays or is expected to play. What would be that added value, and does the Belgian permanent representation provide it? The answer will come from looking at the general benefits— and the extent to which they are used productively by the Belgian permanent representation—and at the particular dividends it pays within the context of the Belgian federal political system.

Looking at the role and the function of the Belgian permanent representation raises the question of internal organization, and the position of the mission in the Belgian co-ordination system. It is to these questions that we will turn first before embarking on a discussion of the added value and role of the Belgian permanent representation in relation to its presence inside the country it is supposed to represent.

Inside the Belgian Permanent Representation

Personnel and Organization

Composition of the Belgian permanent representation

The Belgian permanent representation to the European Union was created in 1951. It began operations in 1952 when the European Coal and Steel Community Treaty entered into force. Given its presence in Brussels, close to the ECSC institutions, the permanent representation was set up as a representation, not only of Belgium as such, but also of its federal ministries. For that reason, it was organized as a service composed of diplomats and specialists from different ministries. That is still the case today. About half—eighteen out of thirty-eight—of its officials are professional diplomats, while the remainder come from the technical ministries. With the state reforms of 1988 and 1993, when Belgium was reformed from a more or less centralized state into a fully fledged federal one (cf. Beyers and Kerremans 1995), the communities and regions have their own representatives in the permanent representation as well (Kerremans and Beyers 1996). These representatives are called 'attachés'. There are *inter alia* an environmental attaché, a social attaché, a financial attaché, an agricultural attaché, an attaché of the Flemish Community and an attaché of the Walloon Region (see Table 7.1).

The most senior positions in the permanent representation are occupied by professional diplomats. This is the case for the permanent representative (the ambassador), his deputy, the Antici Group representative, and the Mertens Group representative.[1]

TABLE 7.1. *Composition of the Belgian permanent representation*

Ministry	No. of officials in the Belgian permanent representation to the EU	
	1992	1996
Ministry of Foreign Affairs[a]	20	18
Ministry of Economic Affairs	2	3
Ministry of Agriculture	2	1
Ministry of Communications	1	1
Ministry of Telecommunications	0	1
Ministry of Employment and Labour	1	2
Ministry of Finance	5	5
Belgian National Bank	1	1
French Community	1	2
Flemish Community	0	1
Walloon Region	1	2
Brussels Region	0	1

[a] Including the ambassador and his deputy.

[1] The function that the Mertens Group representatives play with regard to COREPER I is analogous to that of the Antici Group representatives in COREPER II (see Introduction, above).

Although it is difficult to discern an overall pattern in the employment at the different permanent representations to the EU in Brussels (see Kassim and Peters, this volume), the Belgian mission is one that has a relatively large proportion of professional diplomats. The availability of specialists from the specialized ministries close by—mostly accessible by foot or by metro—is an important reason for this, in addition to the respect for ministerial autonomy—with its concomitant acceptance of the large involvement of the specialized ministries in EU decision-making—and the autonomy of the regions and communities. Because of this autonomy, the Belgian Foreign Ministry cannot monopolize EU decision-making inside Belgium and is required to engage in extensive consultations with the specialized ministries and the regions and communities whenever issues falling within their competence are at stake. In Belgium, this can happen by engaging in close contacts with representatives from these ministries that work in their respective ministries, without needing to have them permanently in the mission. For other member states that work according to the same tradition or model, such a permanent presence is needed more because of the geographical distance between their permanent representation and these ministries in their capitals.

The comparison between 1992 and 1999 indicates, however, that despite the advantage of being in Brussels itself, many specialized ministries and Belgian regions and communities have found it to be important to have their own representatives at the Belgian permanent representation. Research by Beyers (1994) indicates that this is matter of investment and added value. Ministries that are not represented inside the Belgian permanent representation tend to be more dependent on other sources—such as the federal Foreign Ministry and the secretariat of the EU Council—to get information. Ministries that are represented directly, however, have access to the large array of information available inside the permanent representation.

As far as the size of the Belgian permanent representation is concerned, it will be no surprise that it is a relatively small service compared with most other EU member states. As a matter of fact, with its thirty-eight officials (not including administrative personnel), it is smaller than the average. Only two member states (Ireland and Luxembourg) have smaller permanent representations. This figure still is surprisingly high, however, given the proximity of all the Belgian federal ministries, and an indication therefore that the permanent representation plays a role that is qualitatively distinct from that of the specialized ministries.

Recruitment

As far as recruitment is concerned, one has to make a distinction between the professional diplomats and the attachés of the technical ministries. The recruitment of professional diplomats depends on the Foreign Ministry. As is the case for all Belgian diplomats, officials are posted to the permanent representation for a period of normally three or four years at maximum. After three years in a diplomatic post officials are entitled to a 'permutation' or transfer to another position. After four years, this happens automatically.

In a typical diplomatic career, efforts are made to send diplomats abroad for two successive periods (which means between six and eight years) after which they have to return to Belgium for one period (three years, four at maximum) in order to allow them to 'stay in touch with the country' and to avoid them 'going native'. The Belgian permanent representation is one of these special posts, as is the Belgian permanent representation to NATO and the Foreign Ministry itself. The higher one goes in the diplomatic hierarchy of the permanent representation, however, the more prominent those with experience of the EU become. The current diplomats at the level of ambassador, deputy ambassador, Antici representative, and Mertens Group representative all have previous (sometimes extensive) experience of the Union. Where this has not been the case—as, for example, with the previous Belgian permanent representative to the EU—the incumbents have been in posts where negotiating was a major part of the job.

The most senior posts in the permanent representation to the EU are curious in a further sense. Normally, the four-year rule does not apply to the Belgian ambassadors. They serve longer periods in office, normally six years. But for the Belgian permanent representatives to the EU, experience shows that on average they stay much longer. Since the Belgian permanent representation began, it has had only five permanent representatives. All—except the first and the current incumbent—served for at least ten years. And for the current ambassador, it is generally expected that this will also be the case. Table 7.2 gives an overview.

The fact that an exception is made for the Belgian permanent representatives to the EU—in the sense that they stay in office for a longer time than their fellow ambassadors do—is not a coincidence. It is a deliberate policy that starts from the assumption that experience and seniority are especially important in the European Union. Experience is important not just because of the jargon and the complexity of the EU, its institutions, its procedures, and its

TABLE 7.2. *Belgian permanent representatives to the EC/EU (1958–1999)*

Ambassador	Period at the Belgian PR	Ministry of Origin
Baron de Spinoy	1951–1958	Foreign Affairs
Jan Van der Meulen	1958–1979	Economic Affairs
Pierre Nôtre-Daeme	1979–1987	Foreign Affairs
Philippe de Schoutheete	1987–1997	Foreign Affairs
Frans Van Daele	1997–	Foreign Affairs

policies, but also because the diplomatic network in Brussels is highly competitive. It is a network consisting of experienced diplomats and experts from the different member states and of experienced officials from institutions such as the Commission, the Council, and the European Parliament (the latter is important, given the increasing importance of the co-decision procedure). It is equally a network where negotiating skills are tested, almost on a daily basis.

The attention that is paid to experience in the case of the Belgian top diplomats at the permanent representation can be illustrated by the permanent representative, Frans Van Daele, who was appointed to the post in 1997.[2] Ambassador Van Daele started his career in 1971 with his diplomatic training after he passed the diplomatic examination. His training (internship) brought him under the wing of the then Belgian political director, Etienne Davignon. This was when Davignon was playing an important role in launching European Political Co-operation (EPC). After completing his training, Ambassador Van Daele began his professional career at the Belgian permanent representation to the EU (1972–7). In 1977 he moved to Athens where he worked at the Belgian embassy during the accession negotiations with Greece. In 1984 he returned to the Belgian permanent representation to the EU, this time as the Antici Group representative. Between 1984 and 1986, he was spokesman for Leo Tindemans, the foreign minister at the time. In 1986 he was sent to Rome where he was not directly involved in EC matters. In 1989, he was sent to New York, when Belgium began its two-year term in the United Nations Security Council. Intensive negotiating was an important part of the job as deputy ambassador to the United Nations during the Gulf War (1990–1). In 1993, he returned to Belgium where he became deputy political director, responsible for the implementation of the Maastricht Treaty and for Yugoslavia. In the second semester, he was closely involved in Belgium's presidency of the European Union. In 1994 he became political director and a member of the Belgian negotiating team in the 1996–7 Intergovernmental Conference. When Ambassador de Schoutheete, Belgium's permanent representative during the 1991 IGC and the 1996 IGC, retired in September 1997, Van Daele succeeded him.

Permanent representatives and their deputies are top-ranking diplomats with considerable experience in negotiating. Having been a deputy permanent representative to the EU opens the door to other important diplomatic functions. Jan De Bock, the previous deputy PR, subsequently became the secretary general of Belgium's Foreign Ministry—the highest position in the foreign office. Clearly, working at the Belgian permanent representation as a professional diplomat is not a run-of-the-mill entry on one's CV. Within the

---

[2] Thanks to Ambassador Frans Van Daele, who allowed us a long interview on this matter.

Belgian diplomatic *corps*, it is an appointment reserved for the best. The prestige of the job has a political consequence, however, known in Belgium as 'the Belgian disease'. Political considerations are taken into account in making appointments. It is not that somebody of a particular political colour has more chance of becoming ambassador or deputy ambassador, but in the act of balancing different important and prestigious diplomatic functions between different political colours and, critically, between the two language groups, the permanent representative to the EU is considered to be one of the 'high-fliers'.

The recruitment of the specialized attachés is very different, and depends on the ministry sending the attaché to the permanent representation. Neither the permanent representative nor the Foreign Ministry is involved in this process. It is an internal matter for the ministries, and appointments are decided by the highest officials—directors general and secretary general— and the minister and his cabinet.[3] In all cases, however, attachés are relatively high-ranking officials and work in close collaboration with the federal or the European correspondent of their ministry.[4] As these correspondents are responsible for following up the implementation of EU rules inside their ministries, this is not unimportant. The recruitment of the attachés by their own ministries is important in understanding the way in which the Belgian permanent representation works, especially as far as the preparation of Belgium's point of view at the three Council levels—Council, COREPER, and working group—is concerned (see below).

With regard to appointment decisions, EU-related experience plays a role, as does possession of negotiating skills, but there is no uniform system through which such recruitment takes place. Much depends on the interest and priorities of particular officials in the different ministries. The importance attached to these functions also differs from ministry to ministry. It is a job reserved, however, for middle-ranking to senior officials—the current attaché for finances is an inspector general, which is a very senior post—compared to the middle ranks of the current attachés for social affairs and communications. The difference between the different ministries can partly be explained by the importance of the European Union for their activities. The more important the EU, the higher the rankings of the attachés will be. The seniority of attachés usually goes hand in hand with an active 'policy of presence' in EU co-ordination in Belgium, which basically means that the attaché will act

---

[3] In Belgium, the term 'cabinet' refers to the team of personal collaborators of the minister.

[4] The European correspondent is the official in each federal (and regional) ministry who is responsible for the follow-up on EU decision-making for issues relevant for his/her ministry. The federal correspondents also play a central role in Belgium's internal co-ordination on EU issues.

as part of a specialized team inside his own ministry and as an important participant—together with colleagues from his own ministry—in Belgium's internal co-ordination system.

Ministries that attach less importance to the EU focus their representation on their attaché inside the permanent representation and are inclined to reserve middle-ranking officials for that function. Among the various ministries, agriculture and finances attach a tremendous importance to the EU and work with larger teams inside their ministries, inside Belgium's system of domestic co-ordination, and inside the permanent representation itself. Ministries such as communications and telecommunications work with smaller teams and with single attachés inside the Belgian permanent representation. Whenever more people are needed for EU issues, that is, whenever many matters related to their activities reach the Council agenda at the same time, *ad hoc* methods come into play.

Equally, in the regions and communities, appointment procedures for the job of attaché are internal matters. They tend to be more visible, however, not least because these attachés act as the 'permanent representatives' of their region or community in the Belgian permanent representation and play an important internal advisory role (inside their region or community) on EU issues.

Internal Operation of the Permanent Representation

It is difficult to summarize briefly the *modus operandi* of the Belgian permanent representation. It is neither completely hierarchical nor completely horizontal, but a combination of both. The operative assumption seems to be that the ambassador and his deputy know what happens in all the working groups of the Council,[5] but in reality this is simply not possible. In addition, at least in theory, the ambassador and his deputy should know all the Commission proposals that come into the permanent representation. In practice, however, this is not possible. In consequence, a certain division of labour exists. This is not a surprising or particularly impressive conclusion, but, in the case of the Belgian permanent representation, the specialized attachés deal with technical matters that fall within the remit of their home department. Their function is in the first place to inform and to represent their ministry, not to work for the ambassador or his deputy. Moreover, it is not because a ministry has an attaché in the permanent representation that this woman or man represents Belgium in a Council working group. It is completely and wholly the sovereignty of the ministry concerned to decide who will participate in these working groups. A few ministries, such as environment, tend to select their

---

[5] This implies that the permanent representation is not involved in issues related to the implementation of EU law by Belgium. This is a question reserved to J12, a service that operates as part of the legal service of the federal Foreign Ministry.

attachés. Some, for example, agriculture, almost always send officials directly from their ministry. Others, like finance, combine the two, depending on the issue under discussion.

On the other hand, whenever issues shift from the working groups to COREPER, and from COREPER to the Council of Ministers, the role of the ambassador or his deputy becomes much more important. When a dossier reaches COREPER, the specialized attachés act as advisers to the ambassador or his deputy, depending on which COREPER is concerned. This process works in two directions. The ambassador or his deputy needs the technical input from the specialized attachés. They also need information on the bargaining process, such as who is close to conceding what, where Belgium stands, what chance there is of a compromise being struck, and whether this augurs well for Belgium. On the other hand, the attachés—and their ministries—depend on the ambassador or his deputy as far as the negotiations in the COREPER are concerned. They depend on the minister when the talks are taking place in the Council. But in the Council, the ambassador or his deputy is an important adviser to the minister. The consequence is a certain interdependence between the ambassador (or his deputy) and the specialized attachés. The ambassador cannot negotiate effectively without a certain technical input. The attaché needs the ambassador in order to be sure that he is going to defend the interests of his ministry (or the interests as perceived by his ministry) as well as possible in the COREPER, or that he is going to brief the minister to do this. In other words, the EU Council decision-making system, with its different layers, promotes, even stimulates horizontal co-ordination—that is, co-ordination between the federal Foreign Ministry, the permanent representation, and the specialized ministries (both federal and subnational)—inside Belgium.

It is difficult, if not impossible, to separate this process of co-operation between the ambassador and the specialized attachés from the wider context of co-ordination in Belgium. In most cases, issues that will be dealt with in COREPER—and in all cases issues that will be dealt with in the Council—are discussed in advance in Belgium's internal co-ordination system. That system does not operate inside the permanent representation—it operates inside the Foreign Ministry in the so-called P.11 Meetings (Kerremans and Beyers 1997; Lejeune 1995)—and the permanent representation is just one of the participants and more one that listens than talks.[6] It advises—on the feasibility of political-strategic choices—rather than defending particular interests.

[6] The ambassador is, however, a formal member of the P.11 Co-ordination. Most ministries participate only in these meetings when issues of interest to them are on the agenda. Only a limited number of participants are entitled to attend all the meetings. The ambassador is one of them. Others are the representatives of the federal Prime Minister, the federal deputy prime ministers, and the minister-presidents of the regional and community governments.

In practice, therefore, whenever the ambassador or his deputy have to negotiate a particular issue in COREPER, a meeting of a limited number of persons
takes place at the offices of the permanent representation in Brussels. The participants are, depending on the subject-matter, the ambassador or his deputy,
the Antici or the Mertens Group representative, and the specialized attaché or
attachés, where matters fall—partly or wholly—within the competencies of
the regions or communities. The attachés inform the others about the state of
negotiations and brief them on the technical aspects of the outstanding issues.
In the ensuing meeting, a discussion takes place on the possible politically
strategic options. The two main questions in this discussion are: what is
Belgium's interest in this matter, and what negotiating position is feasible,
given stance struck by the other member states? Based on his or her informal
contacts with the other member states and knowledge of the state of play in
the working groups, the attaché will look, together with the other participants,
for a way to approach the talks in COREPER.

In cases where more than one ministry or more than one level of government is involved—as is often the case—several attachés participate in these
meetings. The purpose is not to define a mandate for the ambassador—that
is done in Belgium's internal co-ordination process at the Foreign Ministry—
but to see how this mandate can best be defended and fulfilled in the EU.
Whenever the strategic discussion results in the conclusion that the mandate
needs some adaptation, the question will be referred back to the Foreign Ministry for co-ordination unless a consensus on minor issues can be reached
informally among the participants. In most cases, the need for adaptation does
not come as a surprise, since the different specialized attachés talk to each
other inside the permanent representation whenever they feel that adjustments to the mandate will be necessary, or simply for additional advice or
input. This informal way of working is emphasized quite strongly by those
involved in this process (see also Pijnenburg 1993: 165). Telephone calls can
resolve many outstanding issues quite quickly whenever necessary. But the role
of this way of working—and this is emphasized in the permanent representation itself—is neither to repeat nor to replace the official channels of co-
ordination at the Foreign Ministry; it is rather meant to see how the mandate,
as defined there, can best be defended, given the political-strategic situation
of the negotiations with the other member states. An important aspect of this
is the Commission's position on the issue, as Belgium tends to follow the
Commission on most occasions.

The conclusion as far as the internal operation of the permanent representation is concerned is that there is no strict hierarchy inside the representation. This simply would not work given the relative autonomy of each of the
specialized attachés—which fits into the tradition of ministerial autonomy—
and the wide autonomy of the regions and communities. Although the ambassador formally heads the permanent representation, it would not work if

he decided to impose a hierarchical system. The way of working is much more focused on political-strategic co-ordination and on the informal exchange of strategically important information among people from different ministries that share offices next to each other in the buildings of the Belgium's permanent representation in Brussels. To some extent, one could say that the internal operation of the permanent representation is characterized by fragmentation. There are never any meetings which all the attachés of the permanent representation attend, unlike the 'morning prayers' that take place in the Dutch permanent representation (see Soetendorp and Andeweg, this volume) or the weekly meeting held in the UK permanent representation (see Kassim, this volume). Contacts between the different people working at the permanent representation take place in two ways: either at a meeting of a limited number of people with the ambassador or deputy, or informally by talking directly to each other on common problems that they have to face. Moreover, neither the ambassador nor deputy is kept informed on every position that the specialized ministries take in the different working groups. Whenever the need is felt, the specialized attaché will briefly consult or inform the ambassador. This occurs when it is expected that the matter will be dealt with in COREPER or the Council.

The Belgian Permanent Representation and the Belgian Co-ordination Process

The Belgian Permanent Representation as a Participant in the Co-ordination Process

Since detailed accounts of the Belgian internal co-ordination process and its complexities exist elsewhere (Beyers and Kerremans 1995; Lejeune 1995; Kerremans and Beyers 1996, 1997; Kerremans 2000), only a brief general outline, sufficient to highlight the role of Belgium's permanent representation, is offered here. As indicated above, the federal Foreign Ministry plays a central role in the internal process through which Belgium's position in the EU is determined, but it is not the only ministry that does so. A distinction must be drawn between decision-making on issues that are dealt with in the Council of Ministers and COREPER and those dealt with in the Council working groups. With respect to the former, the federal Foreign Ministry plays a central role through its directorate on European affairs (P.11), though 'central role' means that the ministry acts as the organizer of meetings in which Belgium will determine its position. It prepares the agenda of those meetings—based on the issues that will be dealt with in the Council and COREPER in the coming week—and invites the various participants. Every Friday, such a meeting—the so-called P.11 Meeting—takes place in the buildings of the federal Foreign Ministry in Brussels. In many cases, additional *ad hoc* meetings are organized during the week. In the course of September–October 1999, for instance, special meetings took place on the Tampere European Council and on the preparation of the Belgian position for the 2000 IGC.

The participants in these meetings are representatives of the various ministries, both federal and subnational.[7] The precise composition depends on the items on the agenda of the Council and COREPER. If environmental and agricultural Councils are due, for example, representatives from both the federal and regional environmental and agricultural ministers attend. There are, however, a small number of permanent members that are invited to all of them. They include the representatives of the federal Prime Minister, his subnational counterparts (the ministers president), representatives of the federal deputy prime ministers, and a representative from the permanent representation to the EU, which in most of the cases means the ambassador himself, his deputy, the Antici Group representative, or the Mertens Group representative.

The P.11 Meeting takes its decisions by unanimity, which is especially important for the subnational participants. Since no federal law or executive decision can overrule a subnational law or executive decision, reaching consensus on issues where the subnational authorities have competencies is a constitutional requirement. If P.11 fails to reach such a consensus, the issue can be put on the table of the federal government, the Interministerial Conference for Foreign Policy, or even of the Concertation Committee. The Interministerial Conference consists of the federal foreign minister and his subnational counterparts. The Concertation Committee consists of the federal Prime Minister and his subnational counterparts.

As has been indicated, the P.11 Meetings aim at defining the Belgian position in the Council and COREPER. This means that they decide on the instructions that will be transmitted to the Belgian representatives in these bodies and, sometimes, the need to adapt them. Before the P.11 Meeting does this, a lot of preparatory work has to be done in the EU and inside the Belgian co-ordination system. In the EU, this takes place in the Council

---

[7] 'Subnational' refers to the regions and communities. Communities are responsible for social or person-centred issues, such as family policy, social welfare, education, and culture, whereas the regions are responsible for territorially related matters, such as the economy, road construction, and the environment. As a consequence, Belgium currently consists of three communities, each with their own parliament and government (the Flemish Community, the French Community, and the German Community) and three regions, equally with their own parliaments and governments (Flanders, Wallonia, and Brussels). The institutions of the Flemish Community and Region have been merged into the Flemish Parliament and Flemish Government.

working groups, and, in Belgium, in systems of specialized co-ordination. The word 'systems' is somewhat misleading, because it suggests that they are institutionalized. In some sectors, for example, the environment, agriculture, and transport, this is indeed the case, but in others, such as social affairs, they are not. In the former case, co-ordination takes place through the meetings of middle-ranking and high-ranking officials from the different competent specialized ministries (both federal and subnational). An important role is played here by the specialized attachés at the Belgian permanent representation.

In the second of the cases distinguished above—that is, at the working-group level—co-ordination takes place through telephone calls or informal information-gathering. The kind of system that is used depends on the choices made by the specialists involved or their ministers. Whatever kind of system they choose, the outcome of their work is reported to P.11, which puts it on the table of the P.11 Meetings whenever the issue will be dealt with in COREPER or the Council.

Given these co-ordination systems, what is the role of the co-ordination that takes place inside the permanent representation? It is important to emphasize that the latter's role is not to repeat this co-ordination inside the walls of its own offices, despite the fact that—technically speaking—it could do so. Indeed, most federal ministries, and regions and communities, have their attachés inside the permanent representation itself. But as has been indicated above, the permanent representation perceives its role in the first place as political-strategic and restricted to what happens in COREPER and the Council. The working groups are, in principle, left to the specialized co-ordination systems and, if the specialized attaché believes this to be necessary or useful, to informal contacts among attachés at the permanent representation or between these and the ambassador. But once again, the purpose of these is political-strategic, not to change instructions. It is important to emphasize this because none would accept otherwise. The P.11 co-ordination process is relatively open. Every ministry, federal or subnational, that has a stake in a dossier on the agenda of COREPER or Council of the upcoming week is entitled to participate in P.11. For that reason, P.11 is not only open—every ministry that might have an interest receives the agenda of the P.11 Meetings—it is also all-encompassing as it includes all ministries.

Co-ordination at the permanent representation works completely differently. It is, from a formal point of view, much less open. As a matter of fact, it is relatively closed. Co-ordination takes place among a limited number of participants inside the ambassador's (or his deputy's) office whenever the need is felt. There is also co-ordination—but on an even more *ad hoc* and informal basis—among the attachés in the permanent representation. The fact that these only focus on political-strategic aspects of the negotiations—besides functioning as a way to brief the ambassador or his deputy—has as its main advantage that the number of participants remains limited and that the talks only focus on the purpose for which the permanent representation has been created: to represent Belgium to the best of its ability in the EU. Inside the permanent representation, there is a clear resistance to any co-ordination that goes further. It is considered to be dysfunctional—as it would duplicate the P.11 co-ordination—and counter-productive, as it would harm the necessary confidence the different ministries have in the permanent representation as their representative at the higher layers of the Council decision-making. In restricting its internal co-ordination, therefore, the permanent representation protects itself.

The fact that the permanent representation does not need to play a duplicate role in co-ordination is due to the geographic proximity of the permanent representation to the place where the P.11 co-ordination takes place. Both are located in Brussels, which allows the permanent representation to participate—not only with its ambassador but also with other personnel—directly in the P.11 co-ordination. This makes additional co-ordination that would duplicate the P.11 process an unnecessary waste of time. Moreover, geographic proximity also makes it possible to organize meetings between the leading officials in the federal Foreign Ministry, the permanent representative, his deputy, and the Antici Group representative, and for the members of the cabinet of the minister himself to meet each other on a weekly basis in order to prepare the agenda of the P.11 co-ordination or to fine-tune strategic choices if necessary.

The Permanent Representative as a Representative of Belgium in the EU

Downstream communication: Belgian interests in the EU

It is obvious that the role of the permanent representation involves representing Belgium in the EU. Two consequences follow. First, it has to participate in the decision-making of the Council—at different levels—and that it needs, therefore, the ability to negotiate. Consequently, although instructions for the Belgian representatives tend to be determined in advance through the Belgian co-ordination process, the representative needs some leeway in order to be able to negotiate whenever the situation requires this. In the Belgian context, this is not simple. The permanent representation represents a country that divided on many issues (cf. Lijphart 1981; Huyse 1986) and where those with a stake in the matter look carefully at the extent to which their interests are protected by Belgium's representatives in the Council. This places a tremendous responsibility and burden on the shoulders of those who actually take part in negotiations in the Council (or COREPER or working groups). In taking this responsibility, it is essential for a representative to be able to make a distinction between what is considered to be an essential interest for Belgium and what is of secondary importance only. When we talk about decision-making at the level of the Council and at the level of COREPER, the fact that the permanent representation is located in the same city as the different ministries is a great advantage. Through its participation in the P.11 co-ordination process, the members of the permanent representation are able to find out what is considered to be essential and what is not by federal ministries, the regions, and communities. In addition, through its meeting with the representatives of these different ministries and levels of government, the members of the permanent representation get the chance to get to know them personally, which makes it easier to contact them informally whenever problems in the negotiations in the Council or COREPER arise.

Downstream communication: EU compromises in Belgium

The permanent representation clearly has the opinion that negotiating in the EU may require concessions to be made that go beyond the limits of the mandate as defined by the P.11 co-ordination in Belgium. Even if, according to the permanent representation itself, this happens only rarely, provision has to be made. First, neither the ambassador nor ministers ever participate in the EU meetings on their own. They are always accompanied by an attaché in the case of COREPER and by the ambassador or an assessor in the case of the Council.[8] The latter are able to consult other federal ministries or the governments of the regions and communities whenever they believe that the negotiations require them to go beyond the limits of their negotiating mandates.

Second, going 'beyond the limits of the mandate' requires that the ambassador or deputy, or the minister, who can consult the ambassador who sits next to him in the Council, know how risky such an endeavour is going to be. This is relevant in two types of situation. One is where the required concession is of only minor importance, so that calling everybody would be an overreaction. In such cases, the minister (Council), the ambassador (COREPER II), or his deputy (COREPER I) 'take responsibility' and explain the reasons for their behaviour later to their counterparts inside the Belgian co-ordination process. The second is where the required concessions are so

---

[8] The assessor is a minister from another government level, who joins the minister representing Belgium in the Council. In some areas, the assessor will be a minister from one of the subnational governments accompanying the federal minister representing Belgium. In others, the assessor will be a member of the federal government who accompanies a subnational minister representing Belgium. This system has been created in response to the far-reaching federalization of Belgium in four consecutive constitutional reforms in 1970, 1980, 1988, and 1993.

fundamental to specific Belgian interests that either the ambassador or the minister cannot expect the question to be resolved by a few phone calls to the concerned ministries (federal and subnational). In such cases, they ask the other members of the Council or COREPER to postpone the issue or to accept a reserve. Whether an issue is fundamental or not for Belgium is a question of personal judgement, and this judgement is based on the substantial array of information that the personnel of the permanent representation has gathered both in the domestic co-ordination process, and in contact with the various interest groups, political parties, and business executives in Belgium. In addition, officials at the permanent representation are deeply involved in the process of informal co-ordination that takes place among the specialized ministries—both federal and regional—inside Belgium (Kerremans and Beyers 1997: 28). According to the permanent representation itself, the fact that the permanent representation is located in Belgium's capital is a tremendous advantage in this. It allows it to fully grasp the sensitivities concerning EU issues in Belgium itself, but whatever the permanent representation does in these EU meetings, it will have to explain this *ex post* in Belgium. This fact highlights the other function that the permanent representation has to exert. It not only represents Belgium in the EU, but has also to represent the EU— at least to a certain extent—in Belgium.

It is perhaps strange to talk about the permanent representation as the representative of the EU in Belgium. It is perhaps better to talk about the permanent representation as the representative of EU decisions in Belgium. Indeed, the permanent representation not only defends Belgium's positions on EU issues in the EU, but also the reasons for its own actions in the EU, whether in the Council or COREPER.

(i) Advisory role in decisions taken

Whenever the minister or the ambassador decide to 'take their responsibilities' or to ask for a reserve in the Council, they will have to explain this to those ministries (both federal and subnational) that did not participate in the relevant EU meeting, but they will usually have the benefit of the doubt. Since they were present, they know the political-strategic arguments much better than the absentees. That gives the permanent representation considerable responsibility in the internal co-ordination process and makes it even more important for it to be aware of sensitivities on the part of the concerned parties. Because of its presence inside Belgium, it is materially able to do so.

(ii) Advisory role on future decisions

Rather than resolving a problem after it has happened, the permanent representation tries to avoid them by trying to anticipate when they might arise. This enhances the importance of the role of the specialized attachés and their informal briefings of the ambassador and his deputy, and the role of the

ambassador in the P.11 co-ordination in Belgium. The permanent representation is expected to anticipate the concerns of other member states and the
feasibility of advancing Belgian's preferred position given these stances, and
to offer a full briefing and advice to other participants in P.11 co-ordination.
In this sense, the permanent representation has the task of bridging the gap
between the internal Belgian co-ordination process, and decision-making in
the EU. Anticipation is better than cure, since it allows the other participants
to prepare themselves mentally for concessions that may have to be made or
for the consequences of cases where Belgium will refuse to do so. The permanent representation's ability in this regard affects its credibility inside
Belgium and the trust that other actors in the Belgian co-ordination process
are prepared to grant it.

Upstream communication and the advisory role

It is clear that playing the role of adviser in the sense as described above
requires more than simply participation in the EU decision-making process.
It also requires the development of networks between the permanent representation and other participants in the EU. For that reason, members of the
permanent representation have been assigned the task of specifically staying
in touch with the relevant directorate generals and cabinets inside the European Commission, with their counterparts in the other member states, and
with members of the European Parliament, especially Belgian MEPs. However,
it is admitted by the Belgian permanent representation that their personnel
sometimes lacks the resources (especially in terms of time) to fully respond
to these requirements.

Networking inside the EU institutions is facilitated to a large extent by the
fact that almost half of the personnel of the permanent representation consists of specialized attachés. For that reason, they are not only specialized
advisers of the ambassador and his deputy, but also important players in the
preparatory processes in their respective specialized ministry. One of the consequences of this is that they benefit from the specialized networks that are
built and maintained by their ministry with the EU institutions and with the
other member states. This is in the first place the case for networks with the
directorates general in the European Commission since a lot of energy is put
in maintaining and developing these. In many cases the specialized attaché is
a central figure here. The directorates general with which the networks are
constructed depend on the areas for which the respective ministries are
responsible. There is no indication, however, that in building such networks
Belgian nationals are targeted.

As far as the contacts with the members of the Commission and their
cabinets are concerned, the ambassador and his deputy play the key
roles. Although personal acquaintances promote informal contacts—which

certainly helps in getting in touch with the Belgian member of the European Commission and most members of his cabinet—there is no indication, and certainly not an explicit policy, of attempts to persuade the Belgian member to defend the position of Belgium in the European Commission. During Karel Van Miert's tenure as Commissioner, this would certainly have had the opposite effect, since he was adamant at keeping his independence as European Commissioner responsible for a sensitive area, namely, competition policy.

It is difficult to measure the effectiveness of the contacts developed by the Belgian permanent representation and its specialized attachés with the European Commission. It is generally believed that such contacts are useful only in the sense that they allow Belgium better to anticipate to the positions and proposals that the European Commission is going to defend in the EU. For that reason, the specialized ministries—although not all to the same extent—try to be involved in the preparatory stages of the definition of a Commission proposal as soon as possible, but this is something that is in the first place important for the specialized ministries, much less for the permanent representation itself.

Sensing the interests of the others by developing informal networks is not only limited to the EU. Members of the permanent representation are also asked to stay in touch and to cultivate contacts with interest groups (unions, employers, agriculture) inside Belgium. In addition, contact with the press is considered to be increasingly important. For that reason, the permanent representation organizes a press conference every Friday afternoon in which issues on the EU agenda of the coming week are discussed.

The fact that the permanent representation itself operates in Belgium gives it an advantage. Also, as many interest representatives realize that the permanent representation plays an important role in defining Belgium's positions in the EU and in the adaptation of these positions whenever the EU negotiations require this, they have taken the initiative in establishing contact with the relevant members of the Belgian permanent representation.

Conclusion: The Added Value of a Belgian Permanent Representation inside Belgium

The fact that the Belgian permanent representation to the EU is located in, and operates from, its own capital offers a number of advantages. That is the reason why Belgium operates through its permanent representation, when it needs to be represented in the EU Council structure, and not through the federal Foreign Ministry. There are two principal benefits. The first is that the permanent representation is considered to be separate from the Foreign Ministry itself. Rather than being part of a ministry, it is a place where representatives from the different specialized ministries and from the regions and communities can work. This would have been much more difficult if the federal Foreign Ministry had tried to exert that function. In that sense, the permanent representation acts in the same way as all other Belgian embassies. They represent Belgium, not one ministry, and, indeed, as in some foreign embassies, specialized attachés can be at work alongside career diplomats. For example, at the embassy in Washington, DC, one can find attachés from the finance ministry (covering the IMF and the World Bank), the defence ministry, and the regions and communities.

Second, as a separate but relatively small structure, the Belgian permanent representation is a highly recognizable institution. This is not only the case for the different authorities inside Belgium, but also for the other member states, the European Commission, MEPs, and interest groups. This is not only an advantage for the permanent representation but also an opportunity, especially as far as interest groups, the specialized ministries, the regions, and the communities are concerned. Because it is 'in the middle of it', the permanent representation has the possibility of checking the 'mood of the country' itself and, indeed, it is expected to do so. In a highly divided country like Belgium, with its tradition of ministerial autonomy and with regions and communities that are anxious to safeguard their rights and prerogatives, this is very important. It allows the permanent representation not only to check these concerns through the formal co-ordination process, but also to feel them through the multiple informal networks through which a considerable part of decision-making in Belgium takes place.

It may be a coincidence that most European institutions are located in Brussels, but at the same time it saves Belgium a lot of resources and time to enable itself as a decentralized and divided country to be represented in Europe. The Belgian permanent representation is the instrument that makes this possible.

References

Beyers, J. (1994), 'De structuur van besluitvorming in de Raad van Ministers van de Europese Unie', *Res Publica*, 36: 381–98.

——and Kerremans, B. (1995), 'De plaats van de federale overheid, gewesten en gemeenschappen in de Europese Unie: Consequenties van de staatshervorming en de wijziging van artikel 146 EU', *Tijdschrift voor Bestuurswetenschappen en Publiek Recht*, 11: 647–57.

Huyse, L. (1986), *De gewapende vrede: Politiek in België na 1945* (Leuven: Kritak).

Kerremans, B. (2000), 'Belgium', in H. Kassim, B. G. Peters, and V. Wright (eds.), *The National Co-ordination of EU Policy: The Domestic Level* (Oxford: Oxford University Press), 182–200.

——and Beyers, J. (1996), 'The Belgian Sub-National Entities in the European Union: "Second" or "Third" Level Players?', *Regional and Federal Studies*, 6: 41–55.

————(1997), 'Belgium: The Dilemma between Cohesion and Autonomy', in K. Hanf and B. Soetendorp (eds.), *Adapting to European Integration: Small States and the European Union* (London: Longman), 14–35.

Lejeune, Y. (1995), 'The Case of Belgium', in S. A. Pappas (ed.), *National Administrative Procedures for the Preparation and Implementation of Community Decision* (Maastricht: EIPA), 59–112.

Lijphart, A. (1981), *Conflict and Coexistence in Belgium: The Dynamics of a Culturally Divided Society* (Berkeley, Calif.: Institute of International Studies).

Pijnenburg, B. (1993), 'Belgium: Federalized EC Lobbying at Home', in M. P. C. M. van Schendelen (ed.), *National Public and Private Lobbying* (Aldershot: Dartmouth), 155–82.

8

Dual Loyalties: The Boundary Role of the Dutch Permanent Representation to the EU

Ben Soetendorp and Rudy B. Andeweg

'It cannot be denied that national traditions and idiosyncrasies have repercussions on both the formal attributes and the behaviour of these missions . . .

(Hayes-Renshaw *et al.* 1989: 135)

Hayes-Renshaw *et al.* did not include the Dutch permanent representation in their analysis, but there is no reason to assume that their observation could not apply to the small but growing staff at Hermann Debrouxlaan 48 in Brussels. If so, what should we expect to find there? The Dutch political and administrative system has been described as fragmented, and lacking a clear hierarchical structure: politically, it is a country of minority parties governed by coalition; administratively, it is characterized by departmental autonomy and strong policy networks (Andeweg and Irwin 1993: 164–86, 229–40). EU membership has undoubtedly led to the gradual development of procedures for the domestic co-ordination of the Dutch position in Brussels, but Van den Bos still concluded (1991: 85) that 'EC policy co-ordination in the Netherlands can best be regarded as a patchwork of more or less distinctive patterns of co-ordination lines across substantive fields of policy'. These are 'the national traditions and idiosyncrasies' that may be reflected in the organization and style of the Dutch permanent representation.

It should be emphasized, however, that the permanent representation to

The authors would like to thank Dr Bernard Bot, permanent representative, and Professor Jaap W. De Zwaan, former legal adviser to the Dutch permanent representation and now professor of EU Law at Erasmus University, Rotterdam, for their valuable information and comments.

the EU is integrated not only into the national, but also into the European administrative machinery: in our interviews it was stressed repeatedly that officials from the various member states' permanent representations are in close contact with each other, in a network that is characterized by both the formal procedures of COREPER and other committees, and informal socialization experiences (Lewis 1998: 486–8). Although the Dutch permanent representation is not located in the immediate vicinity of the Council building where most of the other permanent representations are found, all permanent representations have offices in the Council building, and it is there that the officials spent most of their working day (Hayes-Renshaw and Wallace 1997: 218–19). As a result, national differences are muted and the organization and role of the Dutch permanent representation may be less idiosyncratic than one would expect on the basis of national political and administrative traditions. If so, should we expect some 'contamination' by the often more hierarchical modes of co-ordination used by other EU member states? Is the Dutch permanent representation forced to compensate for the functional segmentation back home?

Organization

The Dutch permanent representation to what is now known as the European Union is as old as Dutch membership. Being one of the six founding members of, then, the EEC, the Dutch permanent representation was set up in 1958, after the decision of the foreign ministers in January of that year. With the rank of ambassador, and residing in Brussels, the Dutch permanent representative and his staff were responsible for the preparation of the meetings of the Council of Foreign Ministers on behalf of the Dutch government. From the start, the Dutch government appointed as its permanent representative one of its most highly qualified diplomats. Representing the cream of Dutch diplomacy, successive permanent representatives have been able to turn their position into one that is accorded great importance and influence. Hence, the post is the most coveted one for senior Dutch diplomats. It is now considered even more prestigious than the post in Washington. As we shall discuss below in more detail, the permanent representative is a key player in the domestic co-ordination process, and he enjoys easy access not only to his 'own' foreign minister, but also to all Cabinet ministers including the Prime Minister.

Over the years, the Dutch permanent representation has increased in size, but the development has not been a gradual one, even apart from the temporary enlargements during Dutch Presidencies. Starting with five diplomats in 1958, the permanent representation had already grown to comprise nineteen officials in 1968, but it remained quite stable at that level until after the signing of the Single European Act (SEA) in 1986 (Hayes-Renshaw and Wallace 1997: 223). With the increase of the range of issues dealt with by the EC/EU following the implementation of the SEA and the final implementation of the Treaty on European Union (TEU) in 1993, the number of officials almost doubled during the following decade. Today, the Dutch permanent representation numbers 48 officials and an almost equal number of auxiliary staff.

While the permanent representative and his deputy, as well as some of the other officials, are career diplomats from the Foreign Office, a large number of the officials staffing the permanent representation actually come from other, sectoral, ministerial departments, and are attached to the permanent representation. Since the mid-1980s, the balance within the permanent representation has shifted significantly to the sectoral departments. Currently, eighteen officials, or 38 per cent, are from the Foreign Office. Roughly speaking, they can be divided into three categories. Some of them are involved in the co-ordination of the permanent representation's work, such as the Antici and Mertens counsellors. Other officials from the Foreign Office carry out horizontal or staff functions. The permanent representation's legal adviser, for example, always comes from the Foreign Office, as does the press officer. A third group of FO officials takes care of various policy areas; they are responsible for foreign affairs, enlargement, etc., or look after the interests of departments that have not yet set up their own division within the permanent representation.

The permanent representation has a divisional structure that closely resembles the departmental structure in the Hague; even the names of most divisions are identical to those of the ministerial departments from which the officials come. The composition also reflects the state of European integration: the only ministerial department that has no division within the permanent representation is Education; the largest divisions are now Economic Affairs, Agriculture, and more recently (EMU!) Finance. The youngest additions and still relatively small units are the 'third pillar' divisions for Justice and Home Affairs. Furthermore, as a consequence of the European Council's decision to further develop the Common European Security and Defence Policy, the permanent representation now also includes the Dutch representative to the interim Political and Security Committee, and an official from the Ministry of Defence. Note also that the Prime Minister's Office, the Department of General Affairs, is not represented within the permanent representation.

The organizational structure of the permanent representation is not based on any conscious preference for a particular model, but is the result of Dutch administrative traditions. There is no unified civil service in the Netherlands. Despite attempts to increase interdepartmental mobility of the highest levels of the Dutch bureaucracy (*Algemene Bestuursdienst*), ministerial departments are still largely autonomous. In the absence of a general entrance examination, each department sets its own standards for the recruitment of personnel, sharing only a psychological test as entrance requirement, and the conditions of service. Each department is surrounded by strongly integrated networks of interest groups and advisory councils. Departments have developed distinct policy-making cultures, so that jurists refer to various departmental 'legal families'. It is this departmental segmentation that is reflected in the divisional structure of the permanent representation. This also affects the position of the permanent representative: on the one hand, he is considered to function as the head of all officials at the permanent representation, regardless of which ministerial department they come from; on the other hand, his formal authority is limited to the Foreign Office officials. The permanent representative cannot dismiss non-FO officials, but he does assess them, and if he reports a problem the official involved is usually recalled by his department. A similar ambivalence characterizes the non-FO officials themselves. They are expected to remain loyal to their home base, and to consider the interests and instructions of that department as their first point of reference. After all, this is presumably where they go back to after their stint in Brussels. In practice, most of them are quickly socialized to become 'true PRs' with a dual loyalty.

In summary, Dutch departmental autonomy is reflected in the organization of the permanent representation, but its impact is subdued by the reality of working in a relatively small unit, away from the home department, in the very different environment of EU decision-making. The net result is a relatively flat organization with a permanent representative and a deputy permanent representative placed at the top. This absence of an elaborate hierarchy is further illustrated by the ranking among the officials at the permanent representation. With the exception of the Foreign Office diplomats, who bear titles according to the usual administrative ranking at Dutch embassies, officials from the other ministerial departments are ranked either as counsellor (*Ambassaderaad*) or attaché for the specific policy area for which they are responsible.

Personnel

As mentioned above, there is no centralized recruitment procedure for the Dutch administration, and this aspect of departmental autonomy is carried over to the staffing of the permanent representation in this respect. Each department is allowed to send its own chosen people to Brussels and follows its own personnel policy in this respect. Occasionally, a department invites the permanent representative to participate in the selection process, but usually his involvement is limited to a meeting with the department's permanent secretary when a vacancy arises, and a visit to the permanent representative of departmental nominees before their appointment is finalized. It happens, albeit rarely, that the permanent representative disapproves of a departmental nomination after such a visit. If the department then persists, the permanent representative may even take the matter to the Prime Minister. The permanent representative does not always emerge as the winner of such conflicts, but it should be emphasized that this kind of disagreement is exceptional.

Despite departmental autonomy in this respect, the recruitment policies of the various departments seem to converge. The Foreign Office, for example, recruits its officials in the permanent representation from either its staff in the Hague, or from any of the Dutch embassies. In this way, it conforms to the personnel policy that it introduced some years ago, which abolished the distinction between officials in the Foreign Office itself, and officials in the diplomatic service. However, although the integration of the diplomatic service into the overall structure of the Foreign Office has made every official available, and eligible, for every vacancy whether at home or abroad, those responsible for filling the vacancies have quickly learnt that the principle of rotation has its disadvantages as well. The demanding tasks at the permanent representation require from Dutch diplomats based in Brussels quite different qualifications than those necessary for a posting in Beijing or Bogota. Excellent negotiating skills, an understanding of the politics of all other member states, and an intimate knowledge of the formal and informal rules of the game in Brussels are all considered imperative for a diplomat posted to the permanent representation. The Foreign Office therefore actually selects its people at the permanent representation from a network of qualified officials who have built their European expertise through rotation between the European directorate of the Foreign Office, Dutch embassies at the major European capitals, and the permanent representation itself. Thus, a Dutch FO official in the permanent representation will usually start his first turn at the permanent representation in a relatively junior position, to return at a later stage of his career in a more senior position, spending time in between as a civil servant at the European directorate in the Hague or as a diplomat in the capital of one of the other member states. Gone are the days of a diplomat being recruited to the permanent representation directly from an embassy in, say, Africa, although there are still exceptions.

A similar development can be seen at the other ministerial departments. They started to participate in European decision-making at different points of time, but all of them have build up a team of European experts by now, who rotate between the European desk of their own sectoral department and the permanent representation in Brussels. As many, although not all, of the ministerial departments have their own representatives placed in the Dutch embassies in the major member states as well, these officials, like the professional diplomats, will have an opportunity to learn about their European counterparts on the spot. Occasionally, officials who are selected by the sectoral department for a posting at the permanent representation have also spent some time as officials within the relevant directorate of the European Commission or Council. In the past, the Dutch government was reluctant to send its own officials on secondment to the Commission or Council, for the very simple (and very Dutch) reason that these officials remain on the Dutch payroll. It took some time for the Dutch government to recognize the benefits of having one's 'own men' not only at the permanent representation, but also within the European Union's institutions. In this way, the officials learn the rules of the game in Brussels at first hand, they build a network of useful contacts within the Commission and Council Secretariat, and they are an important source of information for the ministerial departments in the Hague and their officials in the permanent representation. At present, such secondments are seen as a long-term investment, which pays off when the official returns to his Dutch department.

As far as we have been able to ascertain, recruitment to the permanent representation is not politicized. Although there are significant exceptions, it is rather unusual for the governing parties in a Dutch coalition to appoint only fellow party members to high-level administrative positions. Appointments to the permanent representation are no exception. Permanent representative Bot, for example, is a Christian Democrat, and he was first appointed by a Christian Democrat foreign secretary in a government dominated by Christian Democrats, but his mandate was easily renewed by a Conservative-Liberal foreign secretary in a 'purple' coalition (of 'reds' and 'blues', Social Democrats and two Liberal parties). Within the Dutch bureaucracy, politicization of appointments takes a different form. It was one of the tacit rules of Dutch consociational democracy that the various subcultures should be represented in the bureaucracy more or less proportionally. This tradition is still visible: to the extent that party affiliation plays a role in Dutch administrative recruitment, it is primarily to ensure a rough political balance among high-level officials. In this respect the permanent representation does constitute an exception: this form of proportional representation does not seem to affect its composition.

Data on the average length of a tour of duty at the Dutch permanent representation are not available. Since the appointment of Linthorst Homan as the first permanent representative in 1958, there have been seven permanent representatives, resulting in an average stay in Brussels of six years. Two of them (Jan Lubbers and Charles Rutten) had been deputy permanent representative before. However, there has been considerable variation in the length of time permanent representatives have stayed in office, with the current permanent representative, Bernard Bot, being one of the longest serving. The average duration of appointments to other positions in the permanent representation is almost certainly less; from our interviews we estimate it at roughly four to five years. We cannot distinguish between FO and other officials in this respect (Hayes-Renshaw and Wallace (1997: 223) report a tendency for officials from the Foreign Office to stay for shorter periods than officials from other departments, whereas De Zwaan (1995: 23) seems to imply the opposite). There is a tendency for officials from the department of Economic Affairs to serve somewhat longer. After leaving the permanent representation, the officials go back to their own department in the Hague. However, one of the former members of the permanent representation we interviewed noted signs that some senior officials are becoming hesitant about returning to their home base. Some have tried to extend their stay by joining one of the Commission's directorates, although, without taking the exam, this is only possible in the highest ranks or for short periods.

Internal Functioning and Working Methods

The divisional structure of the permanent representation already suggests a strict division of labour among its officials. Each of them carries full responsibility for the specific policy area to which he has been assigned. The final responsibility for the work within COREPER rests with the permanent representative and his deputy, but all other preparatory work is carried out by officials from the ministerial departments most concerned, whether in the specialized working groups of the Council or in the permanent committees that prepare the work for a specific Council of Ministers, such as the Special Committee on Agriculture (SCA), the Article 113 Committee (on trade), the Political Committee, the Financial Committee, or the K4 Committee (on justice and home affairs). They will receive their instructions directly from their department in the Hague, or they will be joined by colleagues coming over for a specific meeting. FO officials sometimes claim, with some exaggeration, that their colleagues from other departments 'are always on the phone' to their departmental superiors in the Hague.

However, each working day starts with an informal meeting of all officials at the permanent representation, chaired by the permanent representative or his deputy. This practice was started by the first permanent representative, and is known as the *Ochtendwijding*: 'matins' or 'morning prayers' (cf. De Zwaan 1995: 23). As far as we are aware, none of the other permanent representations uses this mechanism for informal co-ordination. Where a similar meeting takes place, as it does in the missions of Ireland, Germany, Sweden, and the UK, it is less frequent (usually, once a week) and certainly less informal: officials in the Dutch permanent representation come in with their coffee and croissant, read briefs or newspapers, while listening to the discussions. The primary function of these meetings is to serve as a forum for an informal exchange of information and views among all the officials. The general policy lines and goals are discussed, as well as the strategies and tactics to achieve those goals. While the current dossiers that are dealt with by the Dutch officials are not discussed in detail, officials do inform each other on these dossiers so that all of them gain a broader view of what is going on in Brussels at that moment. During these meetings officials also seek advice from each other on how to handle a specific problem they might face. The problem may be with counterparts from other countries, but also with superiors at the ministerial department. As the meeting is confidential and no minutes are taken, officials burdened with what they regard as an impossible instruction from the Hague (a rather common complaint within the permanent representation) may seek advice from their colleagues on how to get more leeway for manœuvre. Such problems may lead the permanent representative to exercise his influence in Brussels or back home. Through these meetings officials are able to search for a common solution and less experienced officials have an opportunity to learn from older hands. Moreover, the daily morning service offers officials a venue to bridge occasional departmental differences, such as on tobacco advertising between the economic affairs division and the public health division (Deputy permanent representative Oostra, quoted in Van Schendelen 1993: 301). In this sense national co-ordination in Brussels does occur. For the permanent representative himself, morning prayers constitute one of the few occasions where he is in a position to exercise some leadership over his staff as a whole, and to become acquainted with dossiers long before they reach COREPER. As many of the participants testify, these short daily meetings have become a crucial factor in the creation of an *esprit de corps* and a sense of a common mission shared by all Dutch officials at the permanent representation.

Thus, morning prayers provide an important counterforce to existing centrifugal tendencies. Such tendencies arise not only out of the tacit rule of mutual non-intervention that guides Dutch administrative behaviour at home and in the permanent representation (although it certainly aggravates the problem), but also result from the simple fact that after the meeting each official returns to his own business, to what his own department has instructed him to do. His focus narrows as his main concern becomes the proper handling of a particular dossier within the relevant Council working groups. His interactions are more with his counterparts from other permanent representations, and with his departmental colleagues in the Hague, than with the other officials in the Dutch permanent representation. Although most specialists realize that their dossier has to pass COREPER and their own permanent representative sooner or later, there is a risk of them losing sight of the overall Dutch strategy. The daily morning prayers cannot prevent this from happening, but they mitigate its effects and generally cause officials to be open to their colleagues about their exploits so that, according to those we interviewed, a collegial attitude in the working relationship prevails.

Role

Notwithstanding the occasional resolution of interdepartmental differences at morning prayers, the Dutch EU position is co-ordinated in the Hague and not in or by the Dutch permanent representation. The permanent representative as well as the officials from the various ministerial departments act on instructions that are formulated domestically. They are not, however, passive recipients of these instructions. Domestic procedures for co-ordination of the Dutch position in EU decision-making have several characteristics (Van den Bos 1991; Harmsen 1999: 93–8) that differ from Dutch policy co-ordination in general. First, Dutch governments invariably comprise more than one political party so that two types of co-ordination are needed: of ministerial departments and their associated interests, and of the governing parties and their associated ideologies. However, so far European integration has never been politically controversial, at least not among the *Koalitionsfähige* parties. Moreover, even if a particular EU dossier deals with a policy area on which the parties are divided, the need 'not to be out of step with the rest of the EU' is often sufficient to depoliticize the issue. Occasionally, EU proposals may even be designed for this purpose: 'One of the ancillary reasons for the ambitious targets of the common energy programme was to help member-states such as the Netherlands in overcoming their internal opposition (to nuclear energy)' (Van der Doelen and De Jong 1990: 66). As a consequence, EU co-ordination is primarily interdepartmental co-ordination, carried out by officials rather than politicians. On the one hand, this strengthens the position of the permanent representation because, being officials, its members have easier access to departments than to parties. On the other hand, as the permanent representative himself warns, special efforts are needed to ensure that politicians participate in the process, to keep them informed and committed (Bot 1993: 61). A second difference between policy co-ordination in general and co-ordination of EU positions is that, apart from the preparation of the budget, there is probably no other type of co-ordination in Dutch government that is as institutionalized and as streamlined as EU co-ordination. Van den Bos (1991) emphasizes in this respect that the EU sets the timetable, creating pressure to arrive at a common negotiating position.

However, in another important respect EU co-ordination conforms to the characteristics of Dutch policy co-ordination in general: it is inclusive (in that all interested parties can participate) and it is relatively non-hierarchical

(Gans and Meerts 1995: 151). The procedures for EU co-ordination follow the different stages of European decision-making, with varying opportunities for the permanent representation to intervene.

Dutch EU policy is still predominantly reactive (Schout 1999: 31), and the long cycle of national co-ordination starts only when the permanent representation sends to the Foreign Office a proposal to be put before the EU Council of Ministers by the Commission. Such a proposal is then discussed in the BNC working group, the interdepartmental working group to assess new Commission proposals, set up only in 1989. The BNC is chaired by an official from the Foreign Office's European directorate and consists of officials from all ministerial departments. The permanent representation itself is not represented, but this is not a major disadvantage: the main function of the BNC is pigeonholing: deciding which ministerial department is most concerned and should take the lead in handling the dossier, and which departments are also immediately affected and should be consulted by the lead department. For the permanent representation the only implication of this decision is that it determines which two or three officials from which divisions within the permanent representation will be assigned to the dossier. In the Hague, the lead department will then produce a *fiche*, outlining the financial and legal implications for the Netherlands, the relation to subsidiarity, and the position to be taken in the Council working group. When this *fiche* (and subsequent position papers for the working-group stage) is prepared, the relevant specialists within the permanent representation are obviously involved. Occasionally, their input consists of some substantial 'pre-co-ordination', and they will also provide tactical advice, especially when QMV applies. The BNC discusses the *fiche* and monitors progress of the dossier in the working group, but substantial co-ordination takes place elsewhere, between the lead department and the few other departments involved in the policy area (if at all). When the department determines its position for the pre-negotiations in the working group, its officials both in the Hague and in the permanent representation will sound out their counterparts in Brussels and in the other capitals. The department most concerned will also decide whether its officials in the permanent representation will conduct the negotiations in the working group on their own, or whether they should be accompanied for that purpose by one or more specialists on the issue from the department in the Hague (note that Brussels is only a two-hour train ride from the Hague).

Once the dossier reaches COREPER stage, domestic co-ordination takes place in the 'Instruction Meeting', convened each week on the day before COREPER meets, also chaired by a senior official from the FO European directorate. Again, the permanent representative does not participate directly in this meeting, but his instructions are usually based on a first draft prepared by the ministerial department that had taken the lead in the working-group stage. The permanent representation has been involved in this draft, if only because it cannot but reflect the negotiating results thus far. During the Instruction Meetings, interdepartmental conflicts may come to the surface. In the Netherlands, such conflicts can only be resolved by Cabinet, but there is no time to wait for a Cabinet decision. The Foreign Office will attempt to mediate, but lacks the power to arbitrate. Such cases usually result in rather vague compromise instructions, giving more discretion to the permanent representative. During Instruction Meetings, participants will also get a first opportunity to relate the negotiations on the dossier concerned to ongoing negotiations on other dossiers, to suggest linkages and package deals that fit in an overall strategy (Soetendorp and Hanf 1998).

During COREPER I and COREPER II meetings, the deputy permanent representative and the permanent representative are strictly bound to the instructions issued by the Instruction Meeting. This applies not only to the 'A Points' on which complete agreement has already been reached in the working groups, but also to the 'B Points' on which the permanent representatives still have to reach agreement. With regard to these B Points, however, the situation is more complicated than the formal lines of command suggest. Some of the instructions may already be outdated when they arrive in Brussels, due to last-minute changes in the positions of other member states who also formulate their negotiating position just before the COREPER meeting. Even if this is not the case, instructions may become outdated as the process of give and take during the negotiations changes the original positions. The permanent representative will occasionally interpret his instruction 'in a creative way', establishing for that purpose direct contacts with the relevant senior officials or even Cabinet ministers in the Hague. As many experienced officials in the Dutch permanent representation argue, European policy usually has a long decision-making cycle that generates its own dynamics and makes one-way communication from the national capital to the permanent representation impossible. Actually, there is a permanent feedback process between the Hague and the permanent representation, in which the instructions for COREPER meetings constitute one moment, but not the final one; according to the officials we interviewed it continues right through COREPER meetings.

The same observation applies to the co-ordination of the Dutch position during the next and final stage, the meetings of the general and sectoral Councils of Ministers. Every proposed negotiating position in any Council meeting needs the seal of approval of the Dutch Cabinet. To prepare such Cabinet decisions, a cabinet committee has been set up. In the past, this Cabinet Committee for European Affairs, REZ (*Raad voor Europese Zaken*), like all Dutch cabinet committees, included a large number of officials in addition to the ministers. The permanent representative was a member and usually attended the meetings. In 1996, the system of cabinet committees was reorganized. REZ was merged with a few other cabinet committees on international affairs into REIA (Raad voor Europese en Internationale Aangelegenheden). This was largely cosmetic, as the committee meets in a separate composition to discuss European affairs: REIA–EA. Each minister is allowed to bring only one official along, and the permanent representative is no longer an official member (*Staatsalmanak* 2000). It is not much of a loss, however, because the permanent representative has a standing invitation to attend the cabinet committee's meetings (as does the Dutch Commissioner). The importance of the Cabinet Committee on European Affairs should not be overestimated, as cabinet committees have no delegated powers in the Dutch system, and as they tend to meet infrequently (although the Cabinet Committee on European Affairs has known periods of relatively frequent meetings). What is more important is that, like any cabinet committee, REIA–EA has an interdepartmental co-ordination committee to act as 'antichamber' (*ambtelijk voorportaal*) and to prepare its meetings. In this case, the antichamber is the Co-ordination Committee for European Integration and Association Issues, known as 'Co-Co'. Co-Co meets weekly and when there is no REIA–EA meeting, it reports directly to Cabinet. It is probably more important for the co-ordination of the Dutch EU position than the cabinet committee itself. It is chaired by the junior minister (*Staatssecretaris*: minister of state) for European affairs, the only junior minister with the right to attend each meeting of Cabinet. The permanent representative is a member of Co-Co and used to attend most of its sessions. Because of the widening scope and intensification of EU policy-making, the frequency of EU Council meetings has increased as well, and it has become more difficult for the permanent representative to leave Brussels for Co-Co meetings that are held in the middle of the week. The same developments have also increased Co-Co's workload and the average rank of the officials attending Co-Co meeting has become lower, making it less interesting for the permanent representative to attend. A separate committee has been set up, consisting only of the most senior officials, also chaired by the junior minister for European affairs, meeting less frequently than Co-Co, but dealing with long-term European developments and related decisions. The permanent representative is also a member of this 'Co-Co HAN' (HAN for *Hoog Administratief Niveau*, or high administrative level). In recent years the practice has grown of the permanent representative rarely attending ordinary Co-Co meetings, being represented there by a senior official from the permanent representation, but participating in most Co-Co HAN meetings. Permanent Representative Bot is in the Hague each Friday, the day of the weekly Cabinet session, to meet Cabinet ministers and high-level officials. At the end of Friday afternoon he always has a meeting with the junior minister for European affairs to synchronize their the Hague and Brussels watches.

Co-Co discusses a draft negotiating position for the coming Council meeting prepared by the Foreign Office. The draft will usually propose a choice between the options listed by the permanent representative, based on the outcome of the relevant COREPER meeting. This will happen in close co-operation with the leading ministerial department on that particular dossier, which in turn will consult its officials in the permanent representation. Since the views of both the permanent representative and the departmental officials in the permanent representation thus find their way into the draft that is presented to Co-Co, one might argue that co-ordination within Co-Co takes place not only in the Hague, but also within the permanent representation in Brussels.

In Council as in COREPER, the Dutch representative, in this case a Cabinet minister, has to stay within the limits of the negotiation mandate as it is determined by Cabinet on a proposal of Co-Co directly, or indirectly via the cabinet committee. Again, the negotiating position that a minister brings to Brussels, may be outdated by the time he arrives there. With the assistance of the permanent representative and his own officials at the permanent representation, the minister must adjust his strategy to the latest negotiating positions of his counterparts from other member states. Occasionally, this has to be done on the spot, during the actual negotiations, sometimes necessitating direct consultations with the Prime Minister whenever the minister has to go beyond the mandate given by Cabinet.

In conclusion, it appears that the permanent representative and the other officials at the permanent representation act primarily as a transmitter of the national interest to the EU, rather than as a conduit for communication of EU concerns to the Hague. In general, however, it is often difficult to distinguish the two, as European integration is generally perceived to be in the Dutch national interest. As (former) Deputy Permanent Representative Ate Oostra put it: 'For the Permanent Representation, an important condition for defending sectoral interests is that the general interest of the Netherlands benefits. *And that general interest is: European integration*' (quoted in Van Schendelen 1993: 301; our emphasis and translation). When Dutch national interests and European integration are at odds, it is clear where the permanent representation's loyalties lie as illustrated by the 1998–9 Dutch campaign on the Dutch contribution to the EU. The Dutch government considered a reduction of its contribution to the EU budget necessary and instructed its permanent representative (and all ministers) to take an uncompromising position towards any proposal that would have undesirable financial consequences from the Dutch perspective, meaning that expenditure increases beyond an inflation rate of 2 per cent were to be blocked. On the whole, Permanent Representative Bot and his officials conformed to these instructions, although they were well aware that this made them unpopular with their counterparts as the unprecedented inflexible Dutch position delayed or prevented final decision-making in the Council of Ministers on several occasions.

However, officials in the Dutch permanent representation also emphasize that they do not serve as robotic messengers, as their national masters' voice in Brussels, but 'are wearing two hats' (cf. the 'Janus face' attributed to EU permanent representations in general by, for example, Lewis 1998: 483). First, straddling the Dutch and EU administrative machines, they clearly function also as the Hague's 'eyes and ears' in Brussels. Their daily contacts with their counterparts in the other permanent representations, in and outside the Council meeting rooms, provide invaluable information that often leads to adaptations in the Dutch negotiating position. When politicians and officials ignore such intelligence from the permanent representation, they often come to regret their stubbornness. During the Dutch Presidency in 1991, the European directorate of the Foreign Office produced a draft for the Maastricht Treaty. Permanent Representative Peter Nieman repeatedly warned the ministers and officials involved that the draft was much too supranational for the taste of practically all other member states. His warnings went unheeded, and the Dutch draft was humiliatingly defeated on what is known as 'Black Monday' in Dutch diplomatic history. Second, and less neutrally, the officials in the permanent representation also try to impress the importance of European integration on the domestic policy-makers. 'The Hague still thinks very provincially', according to one senior official, and they seek to remedy that situation: 'A member of the Dutch delegation claimed their presidency would be used to "re-educate the national administration into Europe", to really go deep; this involves participation of some 500 to 600 people.'

Capacity to Implement Ambitions

It has never been the ambition for the permanent representation to replace or complement domestic co-ordination of the Dutch EU position. If the permanent representation occasionally does reconcile departmental differences, it is because the edge is taken off fragmentation by its relatively small size, being housed in the same building, and the famous morning prayers.

The official ambition is to be both the Hague's voice in Brussels, and its eyes and ears. Unofficially, many officials in the permanent representation have the ambition of promoting Europe in the Hague. For all these purposes, the permanent representation seems well equipped. The same composition that makes internal co-ordination difficult ensures that the permanent representation is extremely well integrated into domestic networks. Through their daily contacts with counterparts from other permanent representations the officials remain abreast of the views and interests of the other member states.

It is increasingly realized that the permanent representation needs to build similar confidential working relationships with the Commission and, to a lesser extent, with the European Parliament. A good working relationship with the relevant officials in the Commission is essential to any official in the permanent representation who has to know what goes on within the Commission, so that his department in the Hague is able to anticipate proposals coming from the Commission at an early stage. Since the Commission usually puts a proposal before the Council only after it has become convinced that it will enjoy sufficient support from member states, it has proven to be crucial, according to the officials we interviewed, to exercise one's influence before the Commission issues its proposal, especially after the introduction of QMV. Hence, much of the time of an official at the permanent representation is spent lobbying and networking on behalf of his department. In this respect, much has changed. In the past, regular contacts between the Dutch permanent representative and the Dutch Commissioner, or between Dutch officials in the permanent representation and Dutch officials in the Commission were rather exceptional and to some extent frowned upon (Gans and Meerts 1995: 153). Nowadays, keeping in touch with the Dutch Commissioner and *cabinet*, maintaining regular contacts with Dutch officials seconded to the Commission or the Council Secretariat, organizing informal gatherings of officials in the Commission or the Council Secretariat who carry a Dutch passport, have all become legitimate instruments for extracting the necessary information and exercising indirect influence.

A similar development has taken place with regard to Dutch MEPs, as former Permanent Representative Rutten testifies: 'Par exemple j'avais l'habitude d'inviter tous les quinze jours tous les deputés européens d'origine néerlandaise pour un déjeuner où l'on discutait de ce qui se passait au Conseil; j'expliquais la position du gouvernement néerlandais et ils m'informaient sur le déroulement des travaux du Parlement européen' (quoted in Ziller 1992: 390). As a result of the co-decision procedure such contacts have intensified. They involve the permanent representative as well as the junior minister for European affairs. Within the permanent representation an official has been designated as liaison with the European Parliament, and these contacts are no longer confined to Dutch MEPs. As one experienced official in the permanent representation put it in the interview, while one half of one's time is devoted to the Council meetings, much of the other half is spent on contacts with officials in the Commission and members of the European Parliament.

Less is known about the relationship of the permanent representation with pressure groups. The Dutch permanent representation does serve as a centre of expertise for Dutch lobbyists coming to Brussels. They will be informed about the current stage of decision-making on the dossier, about the line-up of actors, and an official from the permanent representation may even help them on their way by accompanying them to their first contacts. The permanent representative is a guest at the regular 'Egmont lunch', convened by twenty of the most important of the approximately 2,000 Dutch lobbyists stationed in Brussels. Occasionally, the permanent representation will not get involved, as on high-definition television (HDTV), because the lobby is perceived not to be in the Dutch interest. However, these relations with pressure groups seem to be directed primarily at funds and contracts. For this purpose, the permanent representation even set up a separate division for the assistance of private enterprise in the early 1990s; it was the first permanent representation to do so. When it comes to influencing EU policy, Dutch pressure groups seem to seek out the assistance from the permanent representation considerably less (Deputy Permanent Representative Oostra, quoted in Van Schendelen 1993: 300, 313). The permanent representative has taken the initiative for a meeting with trade union leaders and representatives from the employers' organizations, but there is little evidence of the permanent representation forging coalitions with Dutch pressure groups. On the other hand, pressure-group contacts are not really needed for information and expertise. Even when the specialized officials within the permanent representation's divisions lack the necessary expertise, the geographical distance is such that it is quite easy to summon support from the Hague.

Effectiveness

It is difficult to assess the permanent representation's effectiveness in an objective way. All that can be said is that the Dutch permanent representation appears to have a good reputation, both at home and within the EU. As mentioned earlier, the Dutch permanent representatives have always been highly qualified senior diplomats of great personal authority at home and with their counterparts. Before being stationed in Brussels, the current permanent representative, for example, was permanent secretary at the Foreign Office, the highest administrative position within the department. The officials from the other departments too have usually served in very senior positions before moving to the permanent representation. This clearly contributes to their authority in the Hague and in Brussels. Due to their long experience of European decision-making, many of them have become true EU insiders. In addition, the language skills of Dutch officials in the permanent representation contribute to their effectiveness inside and outside the meeting rooms of the Council. Permanent Representative Bernard Bot, for example, often speaks French at COREPER meetings, which wins him sympathy from the Southern member states and opens avenues to France, which is regarded as a key country for the building of any coalition. The Dutch have learnt from experience how pivotal French support is for achieving any result within the EU.

It should also be taken into account that the role of the Dutch permanent representation is eased by the fact that European integration is still not controversial in the Netherlands. In the exceptional case of the budget fight in the context of Agenda 2000, which led to a reduction of the effective Dutch contribution to the EU at the Berlin summit, the Dutch permanent representation got a taste of what it means when your government is trying to sail against the tide of European integration. However, in normal circumstances, the Dutch can allow themselves to be flexible, and are thus in a situation to mediate between the conflicting views of other member states.

As a result, the Dutch feel that they have been able to leave their fingerprints on many EC/EU policies. The Common Agricultural Policy, which still consumes a large part of the Union's budget, has always served Dutch agricultural interests well. Although the Dutch government failed in its attempt to move the EU in a more supranational direction in the intergovernmental negotiations on the TEU, it was nevertheless able to conclude the long process of two IGCs leading to the Treaties of Maastricht and Amsterdam, the two most important EU treaties of recent years. The appointment of the President of the Dutch Central Bank, Wim Duisenberg, as the first President of the European Central Bank is regarded as a Dutch success by officials from other member states, including France. Generally speaking, the Dutch officials at the permanent representation do not have the impression that their role in working groups, COREPER, and Council meetings is ineffective or marginal.

References

Andeweg, R. B., and Irwin, G. A. (1993), *Dutch Government and Politics* (London: Macmillan).

Bot, B. (1993), 'Coordinatie van Buitenlands Beleid, Diplomaten en Buitenlandse Dienst', *Internationale Spectator*, 47: 56–61.

De Zwaan, J. W. (1995), *The Permanent Representatives Committee: Its Role in European Union Decision-Making* (Amsterdam: Elsevier).

Gans, R., and Meerts, P. W. (1995), 'De Nederlandse Onderhandelaar in de Europese Unie', *Internationale Spectator*, 49: 150–4.

Harmsen, R. (1999), 'The Europeanization of National Administrations: A Case Study of France and the Netherlands', *Governance*, 12: 81–113.

Hayes-Renshaw, F., and Wallace, H. (1997), *The Council of Ministers* (London: Macmillan).

Hayes-Renshaw, F., Lequesne, C., and Mayor Lopez, P. (1989), 'The Permanent Representation of the Member States to the European Communities', *Journal of Common Market Studies*, 28: 119–37.

Lewis, J. (1998), 'Is the "Hard Bargaining" Image of the Council Misleading? The Committee of Permanent Representatives and the Local Elections Directive', *Journal of Common Market Studies*, 36: 479–504.

Schout, A. (1999), *Internal Management of External Relations: The Europeanization of an Economic Affairs Ministry* (Maastricht: European Institute of Public Administration).

Soetendorp, B., and Hanf, K. (1998), 'The Netherlands: Growing Doubts of a Loyal Member', in K. Hanf and B. Soetendorp (eds.), *Adapting to European Integration: Small States and the European Union* (London and New York: Longman), 36–51.

Staatsalmanak (2000), *Staatsalmanak voor het Koninkrijk der Nederlanden 2000* (The Hague: SDU).

Van den Bos, J. M. M. (1991), *Dutch EC Policy Making: A Model-Guided Approach to Co-ordination and Negotiation* (Utrecht: ICS).

Van der Doelen, R. C. J., and De Jong, J. H. (1990), 'Energy Policy', in M. Wolters and P. Coffrey (eds.), *The Netherlands and EC Membership Evaluated* (London: Pinter).

Van Schendelen, M. P. C. M. (ed.) (1993), *Nederlandse Lobby's in Europa* (The Hague: SDU).

Ziller, J. (1992), 'Au cœur du processus de décision européen: Le Comité des Représentants Permanents (COREPER). Entretien avec M. Charles Rutten, Ancien Représentant Permanent des Pays Bas auprès des Communautés Européennes', *Rêvue française d'administration publique*, 63: 383–90.

9

Ministerial Government at the European Level: The Case of Austria

Wolfgang C. Müller

Introduction

Although Austria applied for full membership of the EC in 1989, and has been a member of the European Union only since 1995, it observed European integration closely from the very beginning and has had a mission for handling relations with the European Coal and Steel Community since the mid-1950s (Table 9.1). The mission was gradually adapted both to European integration and Austria's place in it. Until the late 1980s, the Austrian mission was essentially an observation unit. It then became actively involved in the negotiations that led to Austria's participation in the European Economic Area (EEA), completed in 1991. Much of the co-ordination with other EFTA members was conducted by the mission. It then played an important role in the preparation and conduct of the membership negotiations that were opened in 1993 and successfully completed in 1994. Accordingly, the Austrian permanent representation was not deliberately modelled upon a foreign equivalent. Nor was there a masterplan of how the permanent representation should be organized, once Austria had achieved membership. Rather the existing structure was continuously adapted to perceived demands which resulted from the integration process. In the words of one official,[1] it is the

---

[1] This chapter draws heavily on twenty-three interviews with members of the Austrian permanent representation which were conducted in April and June 1999 on the understanding that they were not personally attributable. In order to maximize anonymity I make reference to both sexes when I cite from the interviews. The chapter also draws on a smaller number of interviews with capital-based civil servants and EU officials. I am most grateful to the interviewees for providing their time so generously and sharing their insights with me.

TABLE 9.1. *The permanent representation of Austria, 1955–2000*

Year	Institution	Ministry in charge of mission or representation	Head of mission or permanent representation	Additional duties as head of mission
1955	European Coal and Steel Community (ECSC)	Foreign Affairs	Ernst Lemberger	—
1962	European Economic Community (EEC)	Foreign Affairs	Ernst Lemberger	ECSC, Euratom
1964	EEC	Trade and Economy	Ernst Lemberger	ECSC, Euratom
1966	EEC	Trade and Economy	Karl Herbert Schober	ECSC, Euratom
1968	European Communities (EC)	Trade and Economy	Karl Herbert Schober	—
1970	EC	Trade and Economy	Franz Leitner	—
1974	EC	Foreign Affairs	Rudolf Reiterer	—
1976	EC	Foreign Affairs	Georg Seyffertitz	—
1984	EC	Foreign Affairs	Manfred Scheich	—
1987	EC	Foreign Affairs	Wolfgang Wolte	—
1993	EC, European Union	Foreign Affairs	Manfred Scheich	—
1999	EC, European Union	Foreign Affairs	Gregor Woschnagg	—

Source: *Amtskalender der Republik Österreich 1955–1999/2000.*

product of 'the development of our own experience, and also out of our knowledge of how other member states are organizing their permanent representations'.

Although this chapter touches on the long-term development of the Austrian permanent representation, it concentrates on the time since Austria has been a member of the EU. The first two sections deal with the organization and personnel of the permanent representation. The following section locates the permanent representation in the co-ordination process. A discussion follows of the limits to co-ordination which are inherent in the set-up of the Austrian institutions, and a brief discussion of activities and strategies. The conclusion attempts to situate the empirical findings in the context of models of government.[2]

---

[2] Research for this chapter was completed before the coalition of the People's Party and Freedom Party formed in Feb. 2000, which triggered very negative reactions from the other fourteen EU member states.

Organization

The permanent representative is a senior ambassador. His two deputies and the largest single group of officials come from the Foreign Ministry. However, the vast majority of staff members belong either to other ministries or to non-ministerial organizations. Technically, they are attached to the Foreign Ministry for the duration of their service in the permanent representation and the permanent representative is their superior (*Dienstaufsicht*).[3] In reality, the Foreign Ministry has no influence on the recruitment of these staff members,[4] the length of their service in Brussels, or most of their actual work. All ministries and organizations represented in the permanent representation share the costs proportionally.

Only one ministry, the Ministry of Defence, is not represented in the Austrian permanent representation.[5] The permanent representation's staff includes delegates of non-ministerial organizations, including the National Bank, the joint organizations of the Länder, cities, and local communities, as well as the major interest groups. The National Bank has an important role in monetary policy and has been represented in the Austrian mission since 1975. The Länder, cities, and local communities are important domestic actors, with constitutional rights concerning Austria's participation in EU bodies.[6] Beginning with a joint Länder department in 1990, they have established themselves in the permanent representation. Eight of the

[3] The representatives of the Ministry of the Economy enjoy a special status. They are directly delegated by their own ministry. Nevertheless the ambassador is their formal superior. This construction parallels that of the trade delegates (*Außenhandelsdelegierte*) in Austrian embassies all over the world. It also reflects the special role of the Department of the Economy in matters of foreign trade and business relations. Indeed, this department had been in charge of relations with the EEC for many years (see Table 9.1).

[4] Indeed, sometimes new staff members from line ministries show up in Brussels before the Foreign Ministry, or the Foreign Ministry part of the permanent representation, has been officially informed about their appointment.

[5] The Ministry of Defence is strongly represented in the Austrian observer mission to the West European Union, of which Austria is not a member. The Minister of Women's Affairs and Consumer Protection also has no separate section in the permanent representation. However, she did not head a ministry but was a minister in the Chancellery, which does have a relatively large sections in the permanent representation. This minis-terial position was abolished in the change of the ministerial structure introduced by the incoming government of the People's Party and Freedom Party in 2000.

[6] See Bundes-Verfassungsgesetz Art. 23c and Art. 23d (*Bundesgesetzblatt*, 1013/1994). These actors nominate Austria's representatives in the Committee of the Regions (formal appointment by the Cabinet) and they are entitled to issue opinions on all EU proposals which affect their domestic competencies. In the case of the Länder, the national government is bound to this opinion and may deviate from it only for 'cogent foreign and integration policy reasons'. For details see Unterlechner (1997) and Müller (2000) and the literature cited there.

nine Länder, in addition, have their own small representations in Brussels (cf. Unterlechner 1997: 86).[7]

The major interest organizations, which have had a presence in the permanent representation since the late 1980s, also have constitutional rights regarding Austria's participation in EU bodies. They represent Austria in the Economic and Social Committee of the EU. In addition, they have the right to be informed about all proposals that aim at making rules at the EU level and to be heard on these matters. Moreover, they are members of advisory boards on EU affairs and participate in the domestic process of EU policy co-ordination in advance of meetings of COREPER. All non-ministerial actors have the right to join the Austrian delegations in EU bodies (without the right to speak or vote).

The permanent representation is the single largest Austrian representation abroad. It employed around 130 persons overall in early 1999. This figure includes all representatives of all institutions mentioned above. With the exception of interest-group representatives, all officials enjoy diplomatic status. Table 9.2 shows staff in 'A' grade posts—positions that normally require university training[8]—according to their home ministry or organization. Compared with most other member states, the foreign service, which provides about a third of the staff, is slightly under-represented (though France, Germany, Portugal, and Greece have a lower share of diplomats) (de Zwaan 1995: 282–4). However, if the members of the second co-ordination department, the Chancellery, are counted as diplomats (and some actually are), then Austria occupies a middle position in terms of 'departmentalization'.

The figures in Table 9.2 are partly inflated; the 1999 column includes most of a temporary staff increase for the Austrian Presidency in the second half of 1998. Altogether the number of 'A' posts was increased by twenty-two for a maximum period of one and a half years that ended in June 1999. The normal number of 'A' posts is about fifty. According to de Zwaan (1995: 282–4) of the EC12 only Greece and the United Kingdom had larger staffs. However, the same author (1995: 22) also notes that new member states tend to have larger staffs in the first years after accession.

The structure of the pre-membership mission changed according to the functions it had to carry out. During the EEA and membership negotiations, the mission's output was very focused. The negotiations tended to concentrate on a limited number of topics at any given time. This allowed the mission to act exclusively through its foreign service members, while those departments already represented in the mission were restricted to providing input into the negotiations. Once membership was achieved, the permanent representation

---

[7] These Land representations consist of one to four people, half of whom are representatives and secretarial staff.
[8] See Liegl and Müller (1999) for details.

TABLE 9.2. *Departmental background of the permanent representation's officials (March 1999 and March 2000)*

	Number of staff	
	1999	2000
Foreign Affairs	18	15
Chancellory	6	5
Finance	4	4
Interior	2	2
Justice	2	2
Labour, Health, and Social Affairs	5	4
Environment, Youth, and Family	2	2
Education and Cultural Affairs	1	1
Agriculture and Forestry	3	3*
Science and Transportation	5	3
Economy	5	5
Subtotal of Government Departments	53	46
National Bank	2	2*
Länder	2	2*
Cities	1	1
Local communities	1	1
Subtotal of Subnational Authorities	4	4
Business Chamber	6*	5
Chamber of Labour	3*	3
President's Conference of Agricultural Chambers	1	1
Trade Union Congress	2	2
Federation of Industry	3	3
Subtotal of Interest Organizations	15	14
TOTAL	74	66

Note: 'A' positions only, i.e. university graduates or equivalents.
* Including one position which is currently vacant.

had to adapt to the working methods of the Council. This meant that the permanent representation was further enlarged, external relations were no longer monopolized by the diplomats, and a flexible pattern of work-sharing developed between the ministries in Vienna and the permanent representation.

Figure 9.1 shows the internal organization of the permanent representation in 1999, which has remained largely the same since 1995. There are three features which need to be stressed. First, the permanent representation is very strongly compartmentalized. The departments which represent the individual line ministries are primarily linked to their home institutions. When

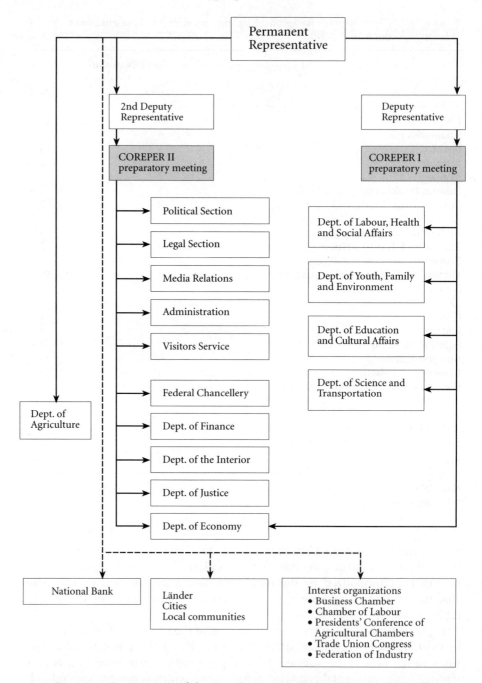

FIG. 9.1. Organogram of the Austrian permanent representation (1999)

it comes to policy-making in their domain, the chain of command is a direct one from their home ministry (rather than from the top of the permanent representation) to the departments in the permanent representation (*Fachauf-sicht*). In their daily work they have much closer contacts—either personal (in the working parties) or by telephone, e-mail, or fax—with civil servants of their ministry than with members of other departments of the permanent representation. The line ministries also have their own secretarial staff. However, the permanent representation has a centralized filing system, so that the permanent representative—in principle—can take note of all formal business between the permanent representation, ministries at home, and EU institutions.

The second important feature is the almost complete functional division of the permanent representation along the lines established by COREPER I and II. In practice, the permanent representative works with one group of line ministries and his first deputy with the another group. This distinction becomes blurred when the division of work between the COREPER I and II does not fully correspond with the division of labour between the two groups of ministries, but this situation does not arise very frequently. The permanent representation's department of agriculture relates to the Special Committee on Agriculture and is normally not included in these two groups of ministries.

The third important feature is the big gap separating those elements of the permanent representation which belong to the central administration (including the National Bank) and the others. The representatives of the Länder, cities, and local communities act as *rapporteurs* for their home institutions more than they play an active part in the co-ordination game. This parallels the largely passive role of their home institutions in the domestic co-ordination process (Falkner and Müller 1998; Falkner *et al.* 1999).[9] The representatives of the interest organizations take a more active part, both inside and outside the permanent representation. Internally, they interact almost exclusively with the departments responsible for the policies that matter most to them, that is, the socio-economic ones.

Personnel

Figure 9.2 shows how staff numbers have developed over time. When Austria was conducting EEA negotiations and preparing for membership, the staff of

[9] While the Länder occasionally table a joint opinion on EU proposals which considerably affects their domestic competencies, they lack the capacity to update their opinion through the various stages and versions through which EU dossiers usually go.

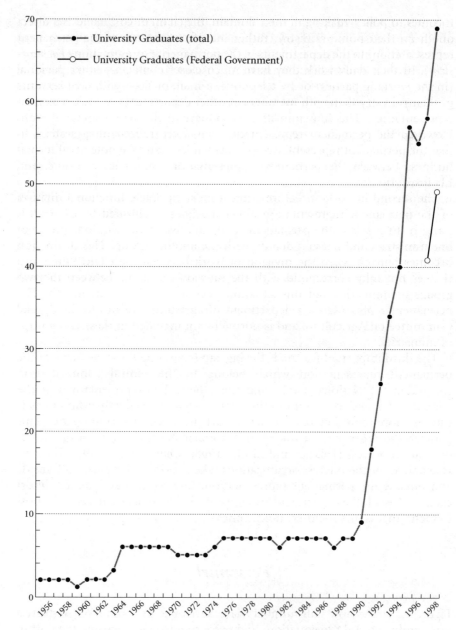

FIG. 9.2. Number of staff in the Austrian permanent representation (1955–1999)

the mission was gradually increased. When formal membership was achieved, another increase occurred, but the majority of positions had already been established. Initially, it was not easy to find civil servants in the line ministries who wanted a Brussels appointment. At this time it was left to the individual ministries to determine how many civil servants they wanted to have in the permanent representation. Later there was a rush to Brussels. The individual ministries wanted to increase their presence and obviously it became easier to find qualified candidates for these jobs. Some ministries wanted to add full-time positions even for tasks that required a half-time employee or less. For budgetary reasons, the number in the permanent representation was frozen in February 1995 by a cabinet decision. Accordingly, each ministry has a maximum quota of positions in the permanent representation. With one exception—the Foreign Ministry, which had one empty slot at the time of writing—all ministries make full use of their quota. Figure 9.2 also includes the temporary increase for the Austrian Presidency mentioned above. The quota system certainly keeps unreasonable departmental demands for positions in Brussels at bay, but it has the drawback that it does not allow for flexibility. Given that demands for participation in working parties are cyclical in most policy areas, temporary variations in the size of the individual ministries' staff in Brussels would be more appropriate (though more difficult to arrange) than the fixed quota system.

As in other multinational diplomatic posts, members of the permanent representation have longer appointments than in bilateral embassies (cf. de Zwaan 1995: 17). When the research for this chapter was done, the service periods were particularly long because there was a halt on reshuffles one and a half years or more before the first Austrian Presidency (in the second half of 1998). After completing their term, most members of the permanent representation return to their home institutions. It is too early to evaluate the career impact of working in the permanent representation. The limited evidence collected in the research for this chapter is mixed. Service in the permanent representation is most likely to be favourable for diplomats. While the foreign minister visits important embassies no more than once a year and less important ones perhaps once in a decade, he or she comes to Brussels every month. Thus the permanent representation is a kind of showcase for ambitious diplomats. Also bilateral embassies in EU member states should be keen to get assignments of diplomats with EU experience. The career expectations of civil servants from line ministries appear to be less good. Only one of my interviewees claimed that her/his ministry would honour good service in Brussels: 'I am sure that I will get an interesting position in my ministry when I return, provided that the political situation [i.e. the party holding the ministry] has not changed.' However, the same civil servant was quick to point out that most other departments tend to see it as a kind of 'treason' to leave the ministry for Brussels. Indeed, one of my interviewees had to give up a position as head of a division (*Abteilung*) in order to go to Brussels. At the planned end of this official's stay there was no suitable vacancy in his/her home department and hence he/she remained in the permanent representation. Two other interviewees returned after a relatively short stay in the permanent representation in order to maintain, or secure appointment to, such a leadership position. For them, staying in Brussels would have meant either stepping down the career ladder or missing a step upward. According to the view from the permanent representation, the general attitude among civil servants who remain in Vienna is that people who go to Brussels have a great time there and so it is only right that they should have to queue up when they return.

Thus, service in the permanent representation is not attractive for mid-career civil servants of line ministries. In the Foreign Ministry, the most recent reform of civil servant salaries (Liegl and Müller 1999) has made service in Brussels (as well as other multinational posts such as Geneva and New York) less attractive financially than positions elsewhere, especially for more senior diplomats. As a consequence, the civil servant members of the Austrian permanent representation on average are quite young compared to those of the other member states. If age equals experience and if experience is an advantage, then Austria is currently at a disadvantage. This, however, may turn into an advantage in the long run, if the civil servants with EU experience are kept in the civil service. Currently, this seems to be the case. Only a few 'A' grade officials (two in the 1996–8 period) have taken the exit option and found appointments in the European Commission. More interest-group representatives have taken this career track and there has been a considerable movement of secretarial staff to the Commission. The latter, of course, is an administrative nuisance rather than one that affects network building.

Given the importance of the permanent representation, appointment to senior positions is considered a political issue by the government parties. The choice of the first permanent representative in 1994 was a foregone conclusion. Manfred Scheich had been the head of the Austrian mission before membership negotiations started and then had been the Austrian chief negotiator. Making him the first permanent representative was an obvious choice after the successful completion of the membership negotiations. Political considerations came into play when the post of the deputy permanent representative was filled. Since 1945, the two major parties, the ÖVP and SPÖ, had agreed that the foreign service should not be monopolized by one party. While at the beginning this meant the inclusion of some Social Democrats, later this meant that the most important embassies should not all be held by adherents of one party but rather should be divided among conservatives (but not necessarily card-carrying members of the People's Party) and Social Democrats. This informal arrangement survived all changes of government. While a 'natural' choice, the first permanent representative was considered a man of the People's Party and a confidant of foreign minister, Alois Mock. The Social Democrats had also accepted the nomination of the People's Party minister of agriculture, Franz Fischler, as the first Austrian Commissioner. Given the importance of the permanent representation in general, and access to information about EU matters and the relevance of the bottle neck, COREPER, in particular, the Social Democrats claimed the office of deputy permanent representative. Initially, this claim was resisted by the foreign minister, but in the end a compromise was found: it was decided to have two rather than one deputy permanent representative. Two career diplomats were appointed, each of whom had—besides merits—also a close relationship with one of the two government parties. While the first deputy permanent representative is in charge of COREPER I, the second works closely with the permanent representative and is in charge of much of the internal organization.

The party-political game continued when the first permanent representative of Austria retired in 1999. There were two excellent candidates for his succession, one sponsored by the People's Party (ÖVP) and one sponsored by the Social Democratic Party (SPÖ). The case was an interesting example of coalition politics. Over a period of months, the ÖVP foreign minister's cabinet proposal for appointments of ambassadors to a number of countries—twenty-nine positions altogether—was removed from the cabinet agenda week after week at the SPÖ's request. The Foreign Minister had nominated the SPÖ-sponsored candidate for the position of permanent representative for another senior ambassador post, aiming to remove him as a candidate before the Brussels post appeared on the cabinet agenda (which was deliberately delayed). The Social Democrats, in turn, demanded that all ambassador positions should come up for decision at the same time and insisted on their candidate. For a while they even linked it to the Austrian nomination of a Commissioner in the Prodi Commission, claiming that no party should make the nomination for both positions. However, after the package had been removed twenty-two times, the SPÖ and its candidate in particular tired of this war of attrition. The package of ambassadors was accepted and hence the way to Brussels was cleared for the People's Party's candidate. Apparently the Social Democrats were promised compensation with regard to EU-related appointments in the Foreign Ministry (*Der Standard*, 29 June 1999).

Co-ordination

Quantitatively the most important task of the permanent representation is to participate in working groups of the Council. This task is carried out by specialists from the individual departments. There is no uniform pattern with regard to fulfilling this task between the various departments of the permanent representation. Some departments manage to attend most meetings of working groups in their realm, leaving only very technical ones to experts from Vienna. Working groups tend to be more technical in the early parts of their life. In several areas the number of working group meetings is too large to allow the staff of the permanent representation to attend all of them. Attaché meetings and meetings of informal working groups, which are called at short notice, are attended by members of permanent representation exclusively.

Moreover, the permanent representation's various sections have developed different attitudes towards attending these meetings. Some, in principle, aim to attend all meetings, even if representatives of their home ministry come for this purpose. They do so in order to maintain an overview of the development of individual dossiers, which will be handed over to them at COREPER stage at the latest. Several of my interviewees complained about the uneven quality and delay of written reports about these meetings by their colleagues from the capital. As one interviewee has put it: 'There are still individuals who do not understand the working of the EU and believe it is like the United Nations. When you attend a UN meeting and write a report three weeks later, it's OK. But this is not the case here. Here you need a report on the next day, because the matter goes on immediately.' Not attending the meetings hence may result in an informational disadvantage. Other sections have a more restrictive policy and attend meetings only if no one is due to come from Vienna, or attend meetings only if their home ministry has provided them with clear instructions on what position to take ('I am not attending just to listen and write a report'). Many factors account for the different patterns between the ministries. These include, on the one hand, the number of staff members and, on the other hand, the number and technicality of working parties.

One interviewee estimated that roughly a third of all working groups are attended by members of the permanent representation exclusively. According to another, about 50 per cent of the working groups are the exclusive domain of civil servants flying in from Vienna for that purpose. These are particular frequent in the second pillar, although this may change now that the Treaty of Amsterdam has become effective. Taking the two estimates at face value and putting them together, there remain about 20 per cent of the working groups with mixed composition.

Position-taking in working groups is done by civil servants of the ministry in charge, who can be either Vienna-based or Brussels-based. Where more than one ministry is affected by the dossier, one department takes the lead. In practice, it is not always clear which this should be. Resulting conflicts are normally settled in Vienna, but occasionally they are carried into the permanent representation. In any case, lead ministries are expected to consult not only all other ministries in Vienna, but also the major interest groups and other privileged actors before deciding what position to take (Morass 1996; Karlhofer and Tálos 1996; Luif 1998; Müller 1997, 2000). For that purpose interministerial co-ordination groups have been established that meet regularly. Being the lead ministry is, of course, an advantage when it comes to determining the Austrian position. Although the ministries and the other actors aim to work out a truly national position, remaining differences tend to be settled according to the preferences of the lead ministry. Given conflicting interests (e.g. between the Economy and Environment Ministries) and the time constraints which are typical for EU decision processes, a full consensus cannot always be achieved (Falkner and Müller 1998; Falkner *et al.* 1999).

The civil servants of the line ministries in the permanent representation co-ordinate their taking of positions in working groups with their home ministries. As long as technical questions prevail in the working groups, it is sufficient to remain in contact with the specialists in the ministries' subdivisions. When it comes to policy decisions, heads of divisions, subdepartments, and departments come into play, with the level depending on the relevance of the decisions to be made. In many ministries, the EU department is involved in all stages of the decision process and more so toward its end. If required, the heads of the Brussel departments may also contact the personal *cabinet* of the minister or the minister himself.

Civil servants of line ministries also have contacts with their minister when he or she comes for the Council meetings. In some ministries, in particular the Ministries of Foreign Affairs, Finance, and Agriculture this is frequently the case (Hix 1999: 67; Nugent 1999: 147). Otherwise, the main instrument of co-ordination is the telephone. According to the permanent representation's accounting system, some of its members have work days with telephone lines busy for ten hours. Although not all of these calls connect the civil servants with their home department, many do. Faxes, e-mails, and conventional paperwork, including reports on the meetings of working groups, which is transmitted by DHL, are other daily means of communication. Finally, members of the permanent representation also visit their home ministries on a regular basis. My interviewees reported a considerable variation of the frequency of these visits, ranging from one visit per month to one per quarter or even less. There seems to be a clear negative correlation between the frequency of the presence of high-ranking ministerial delegations in Brussels and the frequency of the civil servants' professional visits to Vienna. Diplomats, who are used to long-distance communication with their department, tend to travel even less than even those civil servants from line ministries with frequent opportunities to meet their superiors and colleagues in Brussels. While most of the line ministries' travel to the capital occurs in preparation for

242   *Wolfgang C. Müller*

Austria

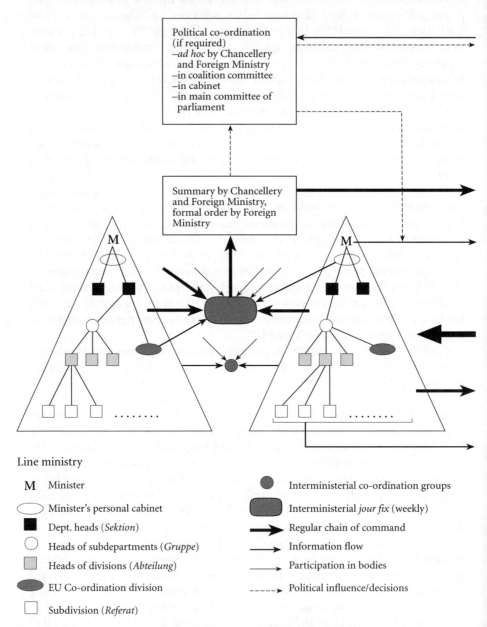

Fig. 9.3. The co-ordination process

European Union

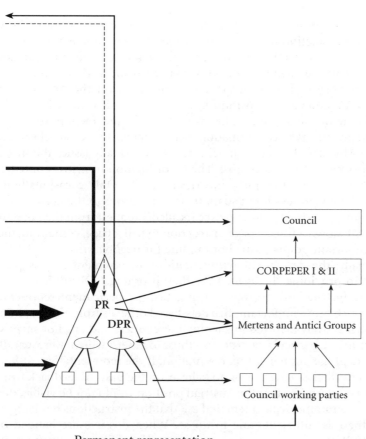

Permanent representation

PR Permanent representative

DPR Deputy permanent representative

⬭ Co-ordination meeting before COREPER

▢ Departments of line ministries

↑ Flow of dossiers

Council meetings, it also has the function of maintaining contacts with those important civil servants who normally do not come to Brussels, that is the heads of the personnel and finance departments and those civil servants who are too senior to travel.

Once dossiers move up to COREPER, they are processed at the weekly central co-ordination meeting at official level in the capital, the *jour fixe*—on Tuesday (Müller 2000). The meeting again includes all relevant domestic actors and aims to achieve for a consensus. Also, the lead ministry can choose what stance should be adopted if no agreement on the Austrian position emerges. Of course, the position is somewhat predetermined by the stance taken in the working groups. The instructions for the line ministries are summarized by the two co-ordination departments, the Chancellery and the Foreign Ministry. The Foreign Ministry then formally issues the instruction to the permanent representative. The co-ordination ministries only transmit what they get from the line ministries as a rule. Only occasionally do they request the line ministries to adapt their instructions to the needs of decision making in Brussels. One interviewee recalled a request from the Foreign Ministry to cut down a fifteen-page instruction to half a page, containing the three most important points as the bottom line for negotiations.

Formally, the permanent representation's involvement in this process is limited to providing the agenda for the upcoming COREPER meeting and receiving instructions. However, in practice the permanent representation's role is much more important. Brussels-based officials from the line ministries have been actively involved in shaping these orders and are 'not surprised' by them. This is particularly true for those dossiers which were handled by members of the permanent representation. If the representatives of line ministries nevertheless have reason to believe, on the basis of feedback from their foreign counterparts, that the Austrian position would not be viable, they may contact their home department and ask that the instructions be changed, provided there is sufficient time to do so. When dossiers are handed over to COREPER, the permanent representative and the first deputy representative become involved. They too try to influence the content of the order from Vienna. They do so in particular if they identify problems on the basis of their paperwork on the agenda items against the background of their general information. Given the often 'economic' reporting on meetings that are attended by Vienna-based civil servants of line ministries, this may be the first time that the diplomats learn about important aspects of these dossiers and the respective negotiations. However, 'economic' reporting appears to be less a deliberate strategy to preserve the line ministries' monopoly on policy-making than an indication that they have not yet fully adapted to the needs of multi-level policy-making.

In most cases the underlying problem behind instructions which 'do not fit' is that they do not reflect the most recent developments in Brussels. There negotiations go on while the Austrian co-ordination mechanism deals with the 'final' draft version of a dossier. This situation has become a regular feature, occurring about every second week and often involving several cases. Another cause of instructions that 'do not fit' is that representatives of line ministries, particularly those who are Vienna-based, are not completely familiar with the diplomatic language (in particular of their French counterparts) and/or tend to see their dossiers in splendid isolation. Thus the positions of some member states or their firmness may be misrepresented and package deals not anticipated. This sometimes makes the specialists who attend the working groups overly optimistic about the viability of the Austrian position. Another reason for instructions that are not viable, that is, have no chance of getting qualified majority support, is that 'someone wants to demonstrate that he is fighting until the last drop of blood and then was voted down'. That is, a qualified majority decision is anticipated, and it is considered more important to be able to distance oneself from this decision than to shape its content marginally.

There are also cases in which the co-ordination process in Vienna has failed. In these cases the order to the permanent representative may contain conflicting positions of line ministries on the same dossier. According to my interviewees, this problem has become less severe with the routinization of the co-ordination procedure in Austria, though it still occurs. One of my interviewees estimated that Austria does not have a position with regard to 5 per cent of the COREPER items due to failed co-ordination in Vienna. The permanent representation is not entitled to decide these jurisdictional conflicts, nor does it want to. As a senior official has put it: 'I am not willing to interfere in fights between departments. This would conflict with the mood and climate of the permanent representation. The mission of the permanent representation is to represent a unified Austrian position. Conflicts must be solved in Vienna.' If there is no national position, the Austrian representative will not speak and vote on this item in COREPER. While in principle it is a disadvantage to abandon the chance of exercising influence, the permanent representation has learnt to live with such situations, as long as it does not see vital national interests negatively affected. Sometimes remaining silent is preferred to representing a non-viable position which is considered 'a muddle'.

Co-ordination problems are much more frequent between 'technical' ministries, such as Environment, Economics, and Traffic–COREPER I matters. These conflicts are typically about the subject-matter of EU legislation, for instance higher versus lower environmental standards. They are the more likely, the quicker the working group's proposals have reached the COREPER level. These conflicts reflect both the 'mission' of the ministries involved and their party-political make-up. Conflicts also occur between the Finance Ministry and the other ministries. For instance the Ministry of

Agriculture in the 'Agenda 2000' negotiations wanted to secure the best possible result from the point of view of Austrian farmers and was less concerned about the overall costs, while predictably the Ministry of Finance had a clear base line concerning the financial side of any solution. The same applies to the attempts to start an EU employment policy, which are much more popular in the Labour and Social Affairs Ministry than in the Finance Ministry, despite the fact that both were headed by Social Democrats. Conflicts between the Ministry of Finance and line ministries are also most common in the domestic arena, where the Ministry of Finance exercises enormous influence. In a similar vein one interviewee stated: 'In my personal experience most conflicts are those between the Ministry of Finance and the other ministries, and the Ministry of Finance wins.' Thus, in many respects the Ministry of Finance fulfils the same functions as at the national level and *de facto* is a t hird ministry involved in the 'negative co-ordination' which is characteristic of Austrian domestic preparation of position-taking in EU bodies (Müller 2000).

Another problem which occasionally is not filtered out by the co-ordination process in Vienna is where positions on individual dossiers (which are shaped by individual ministries) conflict with strategic positions Austria has taken. To provide an example: while it may be attractive for a line ministry to protect a policy by exempting it from scrutiny by the European Court, the Austrian strategy has always aimed at the strengthening of this institution.

As a rule, the orders for the permanent representation contain some leeway. If time permits, representatives of line ministries may work out fall-back scenarios which are then included in their instructions.[10] It nevertheless happens frequently that the first order from the capital is considered insufficient by the people in the field to achieve their task.

Ideally, instructions for the permanent representative arrive in time for the meetings of the Mertens and Antici Groups (see de Zwaan 1995: 100). These constitute another opportunity to check whether the Austrian position is viable. If not, the affected line ministry or the two co-ordinating departments are informed and advised on how to change the order to maximize the Austrian impact on the decision to be made. The findings from the Mertens and Antici Groups also inform the discussions in the preparatory meetings which are held separately for COREPER I and II on the following day. These meetings are chaired by the first deputy permanent representative and the permanent representative respectively. Normally, they are attended by those civil servants of the line ministries who have been in charge of the dossiers which are now items on the agenda. However, the meeting is open to all members

---

[10] The British administration is generally admired for providing its EU representatives with guidelines containing fall-back options under many different scenarios.

of the permanent representation, including interest-group representatives. Attempts to adapt the orders from Vienna to the changing state of the decision-making process in the EU are continued after this meeting. This is not always easy. The civil servants of the line ministries who are in charge of the dossiers often have to get the approval of their superiors in the administration or even their political masters, who may be difficult to contact at short notice. If more than one ministry is involved, the problem is even worse. If the regular bureaucratic processes are seen as taking too long or unlikely to produce a result, the Brussels team frequently tries to short-circuit it by appealing to department heads, the minister's private *cabinet*, the minister, or the two co-ordination departments. In particular the permanent representative and first deputy permanent representative have easy access to decision-makers in Vienna.

These contacts often result in the orders being revised, sometimes during COREPER meetings. If this does not happen, Austrian is likely to be outvoted where decisions are taken by qualified majority. In matters which require unanimity, the rule is to resort to placing a waiting reserve on the respective dossier (see Westlake 1995: 118). In practice this means that Austria leaves it to the other member states to shape the decision. Occasionally, Austrian representatives find themseves in situations in which they find it in the national interest not to follow the instructions. (Under the Habsburg monarchy, when acting against an order turned out to have been the best cause of action, such conduct was honoured by the Maria Theresa medal.)

At the Council stage the permanent representation is involved in several ways. To begin with, it organizes the technical aspects of the ministers' stay in Brussels (transport from the airport, accommodation). Civil servants from the line ministries contact their minister and other high-ranking officials. In the Council the minister is accompanied by the permanent representative or the first deputy representative, depending on the respective section's link to either COREPER II or I. Ministers participate in EU decision-making with varying degrees of interest. Sometimes it is only then that a minister discovers the policy priorities of his or her ministry ('Why I do want this?'). It seems that the role of the permanent representation is more limited in this stage of decision-making than preceding ones.

The general picture of co-ordination provided here in practice varies considerably according to policy area. The most interesting variation is agriculture, which is only partly processed through COREPER and through the Special Committee on Agriculture (SCA) and which leaves much more real decision-making to the Council (see Peterson and Bomberg 1999: 134–8). Most of the variation is a general feature of this policy area and not typical of Austria. What is worth mentioning, however, is that the national representative in the SCA is not a staff member of the permanent representation, but flies in from Vienna for the meetings of this committee.

Thus far, discussion has concentrated on the 'normal' conduct of business. Attention will now be turned briefly to the permanent representation's role during the Austrian presidency in the second half of 1998. The interviewees agreed that this was a time of both very hard work and great excitement. The latter derived from two sources. First, all civil servants who had chairperson functions were not subject to orders from Vienna. Even those civil servants who continued to represent Austria in EU bodies, were not kept on a 'short leash'. This was the perfect environment for creative working. However, there was a second factor accounting for the excitement. Being in the Presidency, Austria for once was in the middle of the game. In the words of one of my interviewees:

Normally, we stand before a pulled-down curtain and do not recognize that a play is performed behind it.[11] Only when the final applause comes do we recognize that there has been a play. When we held the presidency, we were involved in the play. . . . We have learnt a lot during the presidency of what is going on in terms of interventions and what you can try to do.

Thus the Presidency was an eye-opener with regard to the functioning of the EU and it has revealed the limited impact Austria has had so far on decision-making.

Will the Presidency have any lasting effect? Yes, concerning understanding the decision-making process in the EU. As for contacts established during the Presidency, these are personal and likely to last as long as the respective people remain in their positions. As for the leeway given to the permanent representation, it is hard to say. One interviewee claimed that, since it had worked out so well, there is no need to put the Brussels people on 'a short leash again'; others were less optimistic.

Finally, I will briefly discuss the role of those departments in the permanent representation which are not part of the ministerial structure. The Länder department shares responsibility for attending those working parties of the Council which affect the interests of Länder with joint representatives of the Länder who fly in from Austria. Currently there are around 100 joint Länder representatives for a wide range of questions, however it is unclear how much they actually participate in meetings. In any case the Austrian delegation in the working party is led by civil servants from federal ministries. Representatives of the Länder department also participate in COREPER and Council meetings in an observation mission whenever the agenda contains items which affect the interests of the Länder. The other major task of the Länder department in the permanent representation is to scrutinize EU

---

[11] As another interviewee has pointed out: 'It is difficult to know how often package deals occur. There is much trade, but it is hard to know why a country changes its position. Is it because it has made a deal or because it does not want to hold back the decision process?'

papers and to inform the Länder about potentially relevant topics. This short-cuts the imparting of official information via the federal ministries and gives the Länder more time to co-ordinate between themselves in order to arrive at a joint position. Another task of the Länder department is to notify the Commission of Land legislation that implements EU directives.

The National Bank has a stake in making decisions about Economic and Monetary Union (EMU). The Austrian position is co-ordinated between the National Bank and the Ministry of Finance. In the case of conflicting positions, the Ministry can impose its will. The National Bank has one slot in the Austrian ECOFIN delegation and its Brussels representatives participate in specific working parties of the Council and attend the relevant subcommittee of the EP. During the Austrian Presidency, the National Bank was more involved and provided chairpersons for working groups.

Representatives of the interest groups are hardly involved in the co-ordination process described above. While the major interest groups have a stake in the co-ordination process in Vienna, their Brussels representatives are largely restricted to providing information for that purpose and about other EU-related matters. However, they are in close, and in some cases even daily, contact with those departments of the permanent representation which correspond most closely with their interests. Civil servants and interest-group officials exchange information gathered in their respective networks and both sides claim to profit. Even the diplomats, who do not have much contact with interest-group representatives find their presence in the permanent representation useful since they can provide background information on Austrian economic interests which is not available via the official channels. Occasionally interest-group representatives also attend meetings of EU bodies in order to check that the national position which reflects their input is indeed upheld. However, given the number of potentially relevant meetings and the limited personnel resources of the interest groups, as well as their numerous other tasks, there are clear limits to this activity.

Limits to Co-ordination

There are two structural limits to co-ordination, the Austrian ministerial structure and the lack of strong central co-ordination. First, the Austrian ministerial strucure has not been adapted to the structure of the Council.[12] This

---

[12] The incoming ÖVP–FPÖ government changed the ministerial structure thoroughly in 2000. This reform is not discussed here. However, it was triggered by domestic considerations rather than any attempt to adapt the ministerial structure to the structure of the Council.

has led not only to very imbalanced demands on Austrian ministers in terms of participation in Council meetings, but also to many differences in the jurisdiction of the Council and the corresponding ministries. There are ministers who sit in four different Councils but there are also topics which involve three or four ministries. Large ministries—such as Finance, Economy, and Science and Transportation—allow for a good deal of co-ordination within their own boundaries. While it may be difficult enough to achieve this (see below), it is certainly easier than interministerial co-ordination. Of course, it would be no solution to the co-ordination problem to push the size of departments to an extreme. The Minister of Science and Transportation, Caspar Einem, complained about the demands made on his time by having to sit in four Councils. Several interviewees have complained about the mismatch of organizational structure between Austria and the European Union, and have suggested that Austria should adapt to the European Union.

The problem is aggravated by the lack of 'a strong central co-ordination institution, as France and Britain have it'. These two countries are indeed widely considered as positive examples of EU co-ordination among Austrian civil servants. They are considered to have an 'excellent apparatus which can provide very elaborate positions at short notice' and which speaks with one voice: 'In France and Britain, it does not make a difference to whom you talk. If you talk to the last dwarf in a line ministry, to the minister's private *cabinet*, or to the minister himself—each one will tell you exactly the same. In Austria, each one will tell you something different.'

One consequence of the co-ordination problems identified above is that Austria hardly participates in package deals, that is, deals which go beyond one particular dossier. The interviews conducted as part of the research for this chapter confirm anecdotal evidence from other sources (Müller 2000). Accordingly, 'package deals do exist in large numbers, but mostly Austria is not included', is only 'rarely included', or 'we are almost never on board'. As one diplomat has put it: 'Package deals are a constant feature of decision-making in the EU. Spain is the world champion and others also quite good at making these deals. We are certainly not world champions.'

These statements relate particularly to package deals which go beyond the boundaries of individual ministries. While civil servants and politicians make deals within the scope of their own ministry, those which go beyond ministerial boundaries are off limits. In my interviews I have identified only a single package deal beyond ministerial boundaries. It had been made by diplomats without prior consent from the negatively affected ministry and has caused considerable conflict since it was discovered by the line ministry (which had aimed to 'sell' the same concession for its own purposes). Indeed, most civil servants have never been involved or learnt about a package deal with their dossiers: 'Package deals which go beyond my department may happen somewhere, but several steps above me, for instance in the General Council when discussing "Agenda 2000" '. Indeed, only grand issues—such as the Treaty of Amsterdam, or 'Agenda 2000'—are mentioned in this context. These matters are considered 'high politics'. Consequently, they are discussed at cabinet level and between the coalition partners well before the negotiations start.

One of the problems in making deals is non-simultaneous exchange (Weingast and Marshall 1988), that is, the parties which engage in a deal receive their benefits at different points in time. In order to make such a deal both sides must be able to make credible commitments. As one interviewee put it: 'Occasionally, you cannot offer a compensation for supporting your position at the time being. However, then you are in the position of not being able to say "no" three month later.' The capability to engage in non-simultaneous exchange would require even more centralization than simultaneous exchange. While it may be possible to get a negatively affected ministry to agree *ad hoc* on a package deal, it would be high risk taking for the diplomats to anticipate such agreement and to enter non-simultaneous package deals.

As Nugent (1999: 430) has observed, 'Of all the Councils, the Agricultural Council is perhaps the most reliant on issue linkages and package deals for the conduct of its business.' This indeed seems to be the case and Austria has learnt to play according to these rules. The following example is again strong evidence for the compartmentalization or ministerial government thesis. Despite not having banana farmers in the country, nor former colonies which grow this fruit, as part of a package deal Austria helped to defend the banana trade regime against an attempt to scrap it in 1999. This, in turn, led to conflict with the United States (Peterson and Bomberg 1999: 108–9) and made Austria a target of US retaliatory measures. This particular package deal was not generally welcomed. As a representative of the industrial sector put it, 'The luxury we afford with respect to our farmers is enormous.'

There are 'objective' reasons why Austria does not regularly participate in day-to-day package deals. Austria has only four votes in the Council and in many cases these are not required for building majorities. So other member states have little incentive to involve it. Nor does Austria belong to one of the informal alliances of member states, the Franco-German coalition, the Benelux countries, the 'Nordic bloc', or the 'cohesion bloc' (cf. Hix 1999: 71). While Germany may look like a 'natural' ally to observers, the two countries clearly have different interests whenever the size of member states impinges on position-taking. However, there are also 'subjective' reasons, which relate to co-ordination problems, in particular to the slow pace of decision-making and the difficulty in overcoming ministerial and party-political egotisms. As one of my interviewees has put it: 'In order to be successful in Brussels it is absolutely required to speak in different working groups with one voice about the same dossier'. This is not the case with Austria.

We cannot relate different matters across the fields . . . In all other member states it is common practice to have an easy-to-survey documentation of all reservations which had been made in order to make deals across dossiers and working parties. . . . In our department we are in the process of gradually building up the capacity for making package deals. This is not easy since I have to convince the respective head of department in each case that it costs less than we gain. With a . . . number of departments this is not an easy task.

Activities and Strategies

Members of the permanent representation occasionally also serve in working groups of the Commission, however, the tendency is to leave this task to civil servants based in the capital. Regarding working with the Commission, the problems of a newcomer are still visible. On the one hand, the Presidency has revealed how many contacts have not yet been made. On the other hand, interviewees have agreed that, besides holding the Presidency, national ties are helpful in making these contacts. Here the permanent representation faces the problem that Austrians are still under-represented in the EU bureaucracy. For top positions, the national quota has not been reached. Moreover, for a small country even an exhausted national quota would not mean representation in all parts of the bureaucracy, particularly given the high degree of specialization. It seems that Austrians have a stronger hold in areas which are less important from a national point of view, such as EU foreign policy, but can hardly be found in the areas of competition or tax policy, which are generally considered more relevant nationally. This may be due to the fact that neither the Austrian government nor the Austrian Commissioner have tried to supervise and influence recruitment of Austrian citizens to EU institutions, something other member states are said to do.

All interviewees with whom this question was raised have pointed out that that the Austrian Commissioner is very 'correct' and 'European' also in other respects. While the Commissioner is held in high esteem it is also clear that he is not a national lobbyist nor does he provide information about plans of the Commission at an early stage. Both types of activities are said to be carried out by other Commissioners. The difference between the Austrian Commissioner and his colleagues from other member states is explained as a mix of rational adaptation of a newcomer, personal correctness, and problems in the 'personal chemistry' between the Commissioner and the first permanent representative.

When the interviews for this chapter were conducted, contacts with the European Parliament did not figure prominently in the activities of permanent representation members. Contacts had intensified during the Austrian

Presidency in the second half of 1998 and a further intensification was generally expected due to the Amsterdam Treaty's co-decision procedure. The general policy is that the representatives of the individual ministries remain in charge of dossiers as they proceed through the European Parliament, though it is the permanent representative or the first deputy permanent representative who formally represent the country in the Conciliation Committee. Contacts with the European Parliament concentrate on national MEPs, in particular members of the government parties (that is, the SPÖ and ÖVP, when the interviews were conducted). Naturally, individual civil servants concentrate on the members of the committees which correspond with their area. While national MEPs are considered good first contacts, the *rapporteurs* are seen as the most interesting potential contacts.

Conclusion

Austria's permanent representation is a mirror image of the ministerial structure back home. While there are differences in the functions the individual departments of the permanent representation perform for their home institutions, there is no doubt about loyalties. The co-ordination mechanism in Vienna gives individual ministers a very strong position: in contrast to national policy-making, where any legislative proposal must be unanimously accepted by the Cabinet before it is introduced in Parliament, they are not constitutionally bound by collective Cabinet decision-making in the case of position-taking on EU legislation. Only the Parliament can issue binding directives to ministers (Müller 2000). As this chapter has demonstrated, the strong role of ministers and ministries is reflected in the organization and working of the permanent representation. It is thus possible to speak of ministerial government at the European level.

The concept of ministerial government has been forcefully promoted by Michael Laver and Kenneth Shepsle (1996) as a realistic description of domestic politics. They argue that the executive branch's powers of agenda control privilege the Cabinet *vis-à-vis* Parliament, but also pervade the organization of the executive branch itself. In their words, 'the agenda and implementation power that the cabinet exercises vis-à-vis the parliament is in turn exercised vis-à-vis the cabinet by individual ministers and their civil servants' (Laver and Shepsle 1996: 281). According to their theory, parliamentary democracies reach policy decisions by granting jurisdictionally specific 'property rights' (ministerial discretion) through the assignment of Cabinet portfolios.

The concept of ministerial government already contains a kernel of truth in the Austrian domestic arena (Müller 1994). However, there are mechanisms to ensure co-ordination between ministries and political parties. These include collective Cabinet decision-making on issues of major salience, cross-cutting responsibilities of ministers, co-ordination functions of the Chancellor and the finance minister, and detailed coalition agreements which map out the content of policies and the mode of decision-making. In short, there is a variety of governance structures in which authority is not decentralized to the extent that ministerial government implies (Strøm and Müller 1999; Müller and Strøm 2000).

While some of these mechanisms have been adapted to position-taking in EU bodies (Müller 2000), ministerial government is the dominant feature there. It is the characteristics of the policy process in the political system of the European Union which strengthen ministerial against Cabinet (that is, more collegial) government. These characteristics include agenda control by third parties, in particular the Presidency, strict time constraints, and the fact that decisions are shaped to a considerable extent at a lower level which is hard to control even by the ministers in whose names they are prepared, let alone their Cabinet colleagues. Once these decisions reach the political level, the decision-making process in the EU tends to be too advanced for demands for major reversals to succeed.

While the permanent representation cannot overcome these features which are inherent in EU decision-making on the one hand and the problems in the domestic co-ordination on the other hand, it nevertheless has an important function in the Austrian co-ordination process. Although the boundaries of its influence are narrowly drawn, it is important for identifying problems which result from 'compartmentalization' and for suggesting workable solutions.

References

De Zwaan, Jaap W. (1995), *The Permanent Representatives Committee: Its Role in European Union Decison-Making* (Amsterdam: Elsevier).

Falkner, Gerda, and Müller, Wolfgang C. (eds.) (1998), *Österreich im europäischen Mehrebenensystem* (Vienna: Signum).

——*et al.* (1999), 'The Impact of EU Membership on Policy Networks in Austria: Creeping Change Beneath the Surface', *Journal of European Public Policy*, 6/3: 496–516.

Hix, Simon (1999), *The Political System of the European Union* (Houndmills: Macmillan).

Karlhofer, Ferdinand, and Tálos, Emmerich (1996), *Sozialpartnerschaft und EU: Integrationsdynamik und Handlungsrahmen der österreichischen Sozialpartnerschaft* (Vienna: Signum).

Laver, Michael, and Shepsle, Kenneth A. (1996), *Making and Breaking Governments* (Cambridge: Cambridge University Press).

Liegl, Barbara, and Müller, Wolfgang C. (1999), 'Senior Officials in Austria', in Edward C. Page and Vincent Wright (eds.), *Bureaucratic Élites in West European States* (Oxford: Oxford University Press), 90–120.

Luif, Paul (1998), 'Austria: Adaptation through Anticipation', in Kenneth Hanf and Ben Soetendorp (eds.), *Adapting to European Integration: Small States and the European Union* (London: Longman), 116–30.

Morass, Michael (1996), 'Österreich im Entscheidungsprozess der Europäischen Union', in Emmerich Tálos and Gerda Falkner (eds.), *EU–Mitglied Österreich: Gegenwart und Perspektiven: Eine Zwischenbilanz* (Vienna: Manz), 32–48.

Müller, Wolfgang C. (1994), 'Models of Government and the Austrian Cabinet', in Michael Laver and Kenneth A. Shepsle (eds.), *Cabinet Ministers and Parliamentary Government* (Cambridge: Cambridge University Press), 15–34.

——(1997), 'Das Regierungssystem', in Herbert Dachs *et al.* (eds.), *Handbuch des politischen Systems Österreichs* (Vienna: Manz), 71–83.

——(2000), 'Austria', in Kassim Hussein, B. Guy Peters, and Vincent Wright (eds.), *EU Policy Co-ordination: The National Dimension* (Oxford: Oxford University Press), 201–18.

——and Strøm, Kaare (2000), 'Die Schlüssel zum Zusammensein: Koalitionsabkommen in parlamentarischen Demokratien', in Jan van Deth and Thomas König (eds.), *Europäische Politikwissenschaft: Ein Blick in die Werkstatt. Mannheimer Jahrbuch für Europäische Sozialforschung 4* (Frankfurt am Main: Campus), 136–70.

Nugent, Neill (1999), *The Government and Politics of the European Union*, 4th edn. (Houndmills: Macmillan).

Peterson, John, and Bomberg, Elizabeth (1999), *Decision-Making in the European Union* (Houndmills: Macmillan).

Strøm, Kaare, and Müller, Wolfgang C. (1999), 'The Keys to Togetherness: Coalition Agreements in Parliamentary Democracies', *Journal of Legislative Studies*, 5/3–4: 255–82.

Unterlechner, Josef (1997), *Die Mitwirkung der Länder am EU-Willensbildungs-Prozeß* (Vienna: Braumüller).

Weingast, Barry R., and Marshall, William J. (1988), 'The Industrial Organization of Congress; or, Why Legislatures, Like Firms, are Not Organized as Markets', *Journal of Political Economy*, 96/1: 132–63.

Westlake, Martin (ed.) (1995), *The Council of the European Union* (London: Cartermill).

10

The Swedish Permanent Representation to the EU: Melding National and Collective Interests

Sonia Mazey

Introduction

The organization, role, and working methods of the permanent representations are to a significant degree dictated by the administrative structure, routines, and rhythm of meetings imposed upon them by COREPER and the Council of Ministers. However, national political contexts, administrative structures, and cultures also remain important sources of influence upon the European policy-making process. This is particularly true with respect to the permanent representations of the member states, whose *raison d'être*, formally speaking, is to defend the views and policy preferences of their national governments in EU level negotiations.[1] Thus, in order to evaluate the role of the Swedish permanent representation we need first to establish the policy ambitions and co-ordination needs of the Swedish government. However, the following analysis of the Swedish permanent representation also suggests that the role played by the Brussels-based officials in the EU decision-making process is more complex than intergovernmentalist theories suggest (Moravscik 1993, 1998). As several authors have observed, the intergovernmentalist assumption that national

This publication is linked to the Swedish research project, 'Democracy in Transition', directed by Professor Gunnel Gustafsson, University of Umeå, funded by the Swedish Council for Research in the Humanities and Social Sciences. The author would like to thank the Council for its generous research funding. The author would also like to thank all those Swedish officials in Stockholm and Brussels who assisted in the preparation of this chapter. She would also like to thank Jeremy Richardson for his comments on an earlier draft.

[1] For an overview of the Council of Ministers and COREPER see Hayes-Renshaw and Wallace (1997); Westlake (1995).

preferences are determined and fixed at the domestic level ignores the impact of transnational relations and the involvement of supranational actors, notably the European Commission (Beyers and Dierickx 1998: 292; see also Hayes-Renshaw and Wallace 1995; Kerremans 1996; Lewis 1998). These sociological and institutionalist critiques of the intergovernmentalist approach stress instead the degree to which national interests are refined during the decision-making process, as actors 'learn new rules, develop new identifications and new patterns of mutual trust and regard' (Lindberg 1970: 98). In this context, COREPER is 'an institutional mechanism where member-states internalize EU membership into their "self"-interest calculations. The officials share a collective rationality based on the dual responsibility to deliver the goods at home and collectively at the EU level' (Lewis 1998: 484). Thus, in evaluating the effectiveness of the Swedish representation, we need to evaluate not only its ability to defend national instructions in Council committees, but also its capacity to 'interpret' the two different cognitive worlds of Brussels and Stockholm in order to meld together national and transnational interests.

The chapter is divided into two parts. The first part of the discussion provides the contextual backdrop to the detailed study of the Swedish permanent representation which follows. The argument presented here is twofold. First, it is argued that effective co-ordination of EU policy at both the national and EU levels is regarded as extremely important by the Swedish government for at least two related reasons: the high political salience of EU matters in Sweden; and the Social Democratic government's determination to be an influential actor in the EU policy arena. The specific EU policy ambitions of the Swedish government derive from its long-standing preference for intergovernmental co-operation, the need to assuage widespread public Euroscepticism and a (related) desire to transfer key elements of the Swedish model of Social Democracy—an active employment policy, sex equality, and government transparency—to the EU policy arena. Secondly, it is argued that, although Swedish administrative adjustment to EU membership has been relatively unproblematic in the short term, the process of adaptation is not yet complete. The initial belief that EU matters could simply be incorporated into the Swedish system of ministerial consultation has, in practice, proved problematic. Meanwhile, the volume and pace of EU policy-making has placed considerable strains upon the limited resources of these ministries, and might yet prove to be incompatible with embedded elements of the Swedish policy style (Mazey and Richardson forthcoming). In an attempt to address these problems, the government introduced in 1998 new co-ordinating structures designed to streamline central EU policy co-ordination and strengthen political leadership on EU policy.

The second part of the chapter examines how the Swedish permanent representation fits into this wider picture. It highlights the composition, role, and working methods of the Brussels-based administration and evaluates its effectiveness, bearing in mind the co-ordination needs and policy ambitions of the Swedish administration. The picture that emerges from this study is one of a technically specialized, functionally segmented, and non-hierarchical bureaucracy, which, after five years, is nevertheless still evolving as an administration. Given the Swedish government's specific EU policy goals and its general ambition to be viewed as a significant, albeit small, member state, the Swedish permanent representation appears to have been effective thus far, though any such evaluation is necessarily subjective. Moreover, evidence suggests that the Swedish officials in the permanent representation have in a relatively short space of time internalized EU decision-making and bargaining norms. As such, they are often better informed about EU decision-making procedures and have a stronger sense of what is feasible politically than national officials, many of whom still have no personal experience of EU level negotiations. Indeed, the fact that the Swedish administration has not yet achieved a critical mass of officials familiar with EU decision-making processes constitutes a significant problem for the officials. Thus, it is argued that the effectiveness of the Swedish permanent representation in delivering national policy ambitions is as much a reflection of its capacity to influence the national administration as of its diplomatic role in Brussels.

Sweden in the EU: The National Context

Swedish accession to the EU in 1995 marked the culmination of a long period of economic integration and co-operation with the EU. Sweden had signed a free trade agreement with the EC in 1972 and had been a member of the European Economic Area (EEA) created in 1992. The application for full membership was made by the Social Democratic government in July 1991 and the accession treaty was duly signed at the EU summit in Greece in 1994 by the then non-socialist Prime Minister Carl Bildt. The issue of EU membership was finally resolved by a positive result in a national referendum on entry to the EU in November 1994. This period of Swedish–EU relations and the reasons for the decision to seek membership have been extensively analysed elsewhere (Eckengren and Sundelius 1997; Miles 1996; Milner 1994; Sundelius 1994; Lawler 1997) and no attempt is made here to discuss it in detail. For the purposes of this study, the following points about Swedish–EU relations are pertinent.

The Political Context

Swedish accession to the EU was prompted by economic and political pragmatism, rather than any deeper commitment to European federalism.

The application for membership represented a recognition on the part of the government that as a small, peripheral, Nordic state, Sweden 'needed to trade not only autonomy for wealth but also sovereignty for voice' (Gstöhl 1996: 61). Sweden is a 'reluctant European' in the sense that it is opposed to any further European political integration which might weaken national democratic processes. The Swedish government has repeatedly stated that EU co-operation should strengthen democracy in the member states, not erode it. This minimalist stance constitutes the starting-point for understanding Swedish EU policy ambitions, particularly with respect to EU institutional reform.

Secondly, EU membership has been a politically divisive issue in domestic politics. In the 1994 referendum on Swedish entry to the EU, just 52.3 per cent of the participants voted 'yes' and 46.8 per cent voted 'no' (Swedish Institute 1996). Moreover, subsequent public opinion polls indicate increasing levels of Euroscepticism among the Swedish people. In autumn 1995, 43 per cent of Swedes believed that their country would benefit from EU membership, compared to 41 per cent who believed it would not benefit. By autumn 1998, these figures were 27 and 53 per cent respectively (European Commission 1996, 1998). Two of the seven parliamentary parties, the Left Party and the Greens, have consistently advocated withdrawal from the EU. Moreover, since the 1998 parliamentary elections, the minority Social Democratic government has been reliant upon both of these parties for support. The other parties are divided over the critical issue of Swedish membership of EMU and half of the Swedish MEPs elected in 1995 were opposed to EU membership. Though there is some evidence that public opinion has recently begun to move in an 'EU positive' direction, the EU remains an important issue in Swedish politics (Lindahl 2000). Swedish ambivalence towards the EU derives in large part from a concern that the progressive Swedish model of social democracy, characterized by open government, a strong commitment to high levels of public welfare, social equality, and state intervention might be eroded by the legal, financial, and fiscal obligations of EU membership (Lawler 1997). Concerns that Sweden's rigorous environmental and consumer-safety standards might be compromised by EU membership are also widespread.

The high political salience of EU issues on the domestic political agenda, a proportional electoral system, and a multi-party system means that, for the government, effective political co-ordination and presentation of EU policies is essential. In addition, Swedish governments need to be able to demonstrate to a sceptical electorate that EU decision-making procedures are compatible with the Swedish policy style of open and transparent decision-making. Clear and effective government co-ordination of EU policy is obviously important in this context. Moreover, this national political opportunity structure has further helped to define the specific EU policy ambitions of successive governments. In an attempt to convince a sceptical electorate of the benefits of

EU membership the Swedish government has (with some success) sought to embed key aspects of the Swedish model into EC policies. Thus, since 1995, Sweden has been proactive in advocating the development of stronger EU employment and social policies, greater openness and transparency in EU decision-making, and more (and tougher) EC regulation in the areas of EU environmental and consumer policy (Johansson 1999). As a Nordic country with security and trade interests in the Baltic region, Sweden has also campaigned strongly for enlargement of the EU into the Baltic States as well as Eastern and Central Europe (Lawlor 1997; Hamilton *et al.* 1996).

National Political and Administrative Co-ordination of EU Policy

Swedish adaptation to EU membership has been relatively unproblematic in terms of routine administrative co-ordination, for the reasons outlined below. Nevertheless, since 1995, central co-ordination of EU policy has been at the forefront of the political agenda for two reasons. First, it became apparent that the initial assumption that EU matters could be dealt with by traditional government co-ordinating mechanisms was proved wrong. Secondly, the government recognized that effective central co-ordination of EU policy was important in maximizing Swedish influence within the EU decision-making arena. As Eckengren and Sundelius note, 'national co-ordination of prioritised policy positions is presented as a substitute for material resources and political weight for a small but ambitious member state' (Eckengren and Sundelius 1997: 137). These pressures culminated in the creation in 1999 of new political and administrative co-ordinating structures designed to streamline and strengthen central co-ordination of EU policy. Meanwhile, five years of membership have also exposed some important underlying tensions between certain, traditional, and embedded aspects of the Swedish politico-administrative system and that of the EU. Specifically, the cumbersome and often time-consuming consultative structures associated with the Swedish policy style, embodied in the *remiss* system are ill-suited to the faster pace of EU decision-making. EU membership has also placed considerable strains upon the small and relatively inexpert ministries and prompted debate about the legitimate EU policy-making role of the quasi-independent, administrative agencies, which in Sweden are responsible for policy implementation and regulation. More generally, there has been a clash between the pragmatic and non-hierarchical Swedish administrative culture and the more legalistic EU culture of extensive negotiation and political compromise (SOU 1996; Eckengren and Sundelius 1997).

National level administrative and political co-ordination of EU policy in Sweden has been facilitated by the formal and informal centralizing pressures exerted by a unitary state and a parliamentary system of government, within which executive power rests with the Cabinet, headed by the Prime Minister and the heads of the ministries. The strong principle of collective responsibility is reflected in weekly meetings of the Cabinet and the daily, private lunches of Cabinet members in the Government Office, where major policy issues are freely discussed. Collective responsibility and central co-ordination is further reinforced by the formal absence in Sweden of ministerial rule and joint preparation of government policy between ministries. Individual ministers must acquire the support of their colleagues for their legislative proposals. The fact that all bills to be presented and important ministerial announcements to be made in Parliament on behalf of the government must be circulated beforehand to all ministers for written comments also allows for exchange of information and discussion between Cabinet ministers and officials. Significantly, Swedish ministries are small units, typically comprising some 150 people (Larsson 1995). This feature of Swedish government is attributable to the fact that the enforcement of government decisions lies not with the ministries, but with the central administrative agencies, whose director generals are appointed by the government, but which operate independently of the government. Officials working in the agencies are appointed on the basis of their specialized knowledge and technical expertise in their respective fields and, in reality, often work closely with the ministry concerned, supplying information and participating in policy formulation (Larsson 1995). However, the concentration of technical expertise inside the autonomous agencies has become more problematic as a result of EU membership. The ministries are generally acknowledged to be too small and insufficiently expert to send representatives to Council working groups, formulate clear and timely instructions to Swedish representatives in Brussels, and simultaneously develop longer term EU policy objectives. Meanwhile, as the work of the regulatory agencies has become increasingly Europeanized, they have inevitably been drawn into the EU policy-making process. While this blurring of the distinction between government and administration existed before 1995 (Mazey and Richardson forthcoming), EU membership has exacerbated and exposed this co-ordination weakness in the Swedish model and raised questions about the political accountability of the agencies. Since 1995, the government has sought to address this problem through increased funding for the central ministries, greater efforts to improve co-ordination between the agencies and ministries, and some redistribution of personnel from the administrative agencies to the ministries (Ruin 2000).

The Swedish model of social democracy is not merely about policy substance; it also refers to the way in which policy is determined. In this context, the Swedish policy style implies a commitment to openness and extensive public consultation. Traditionally, on important policy issues, it has been normal practice for the government to call upon a group of experts to serve on a commission of inquiry, whose terms of reference are set by the government. Members may include members of Parliament, representatives of labour and employers' organizations and other relevant interests, and scientific experts from the agencies or elsewhere. Commission reports are then sent by the ministry concerned to all relevant administrative agencies and interest groups for their comments. The material thus collected forms the basis for government bills to Parliament and further public discussion. In reality, this aspect of the Swedish model has, since the mid-1970s, been somewhat eroded as a result of endogenous change. Thus, their terms of reference have narrowed and they sit for much shorter periods (Mazey and Richardson forthcoming). However, to the extent that structured consultation remains part of the Swedish model, the practice can be cumbersome and time-consuming and as such fits uneasily into the much faster pace of EU policy-making, which is often beyond the influence or control of the Swedish authorities, or indeed, any single member state.

Prior to EU membership, the preparation of EU issues was dealt with jointly by the Cabinet Office, the Ministry for Foreign Affairs, and the Ministry of Finance. Since accession, EU issues have become an extension of domestic policy-making and, as such, are handled in the first instance by the relevant ministry. Co-ordination of EC policy takes place within the Ministry for Foreign Affairs, though the latter's dominant position in EU matters has been increasingly challenged by other ministries who have developed their own bilateral relations with Brussels. Until 1999, administrative co-ordination of EU policy took place within the EU co-ordination secretariat in the Ministry for Foreign Affairs, which also contained a policy-oriented European integration department. Political co-ordination of EU policy takes place within the normal government co-ordinating structures outlined above. In addition, in 1995 a senior level Co-ordination Group for EU Relations (EU-beredningen) was set up to resolve interministerial conflicts over EU policies and to co-ordinate EU policy positions. This permanent committee, which meets once a fortnight, comprises the state secretaries of the Cabinet Office, the Ministry for Justice, and the Ministry for Finance. Until the 1999 reforms (see below), this committee was chaired by the state secretary for European affairs in the Foreign Ministry (Eckengren and Sundelius 1997: 138; interview, 13 August 1999).[2] The election of a new Social Democratic government in March 1996 heralded the introduction of a series of reforms designed to strengthen central (and prime ministerial) co-ordination of EU affairs (Ruin 2000; Johansson 1999; interviews, May 1998).

---

[2] In Sweden, state secretaries are political appointees. Between 1995 and summer 1999, the state secretary to the Minister for European Affairs with responsibility for EU questions in the Foreign Ministry was Mr Gunnar Lund. In March 1996, the post of Minister for European Affairs was abolished, though the state secretary's post was retained. In March 1999, a state secretary for EU affairs was appointed to the PM's office, and now chairs this committee.

First, in 1999 in the Foreign Ministry the EU co-ordination secretariat was merged with the European integration division to create a single, large department for EU affairs, comprising some fifty officials and headed by a senior civil servant, the director for EU affairs. Within this department, there is an EU Co-ordination Group composed of fifteen officials (headed by a director for COREPER co-ordination), who constitute the principal link between the Swedish permanent representation in Brussels and the national ministries.[3] Members of the Co-ordination Group are responsible for ensuring that Swedish standpoints are prepared for all items on upcoming Council agendas, and for finalizing and transmitting official instructions to representatives for COREPER and Council meetings. In Stockholm, instructions are finalized in the weekly meetings each Friday of another group—the Fredagsgruppen— comprising high-level civil servants from the Prime Minister's Office and the Ministries of Finance and Foreign Affairs. Members of the permanent representation also fly home for these meetings which are chaired by the director of the department for EU affairs. The Co-ordination Group is also responsible for informing the Advisory Committee on EU Affairs in the Swedish Parliament (*Riksdag*) of the Swedish government's position on EU policy issues. Formally, the powers of this committee are limited since it is an advisory body. As such, it cannot (unlike the Danish Parliament) commit a minister to a certain position. Nevertheless, there is an expectation that the relevant minister(s) and his or her advisers will attend the (closed) Friday meetings of the committee to discuss the issues to be dealt with in the Council the following week. Moreover, if a minister does not follow the advice given by the committee, theoretically a vote of no-confidence could be taken in the Parliament (Johansson 1999; Hegeland and Mattson 1997; Bergman 1997). In reality, this has never occurred.

Secondly, increasing awareness of the need to develop a pro-active, political-strategic European policy and a desire to further strengthen central co-ordination of EU policy prompted the introduction of new and stronger co-ordinating mechanisms within the Prime Minister's Office. The State Secretary for EU Affairs within the Ministry for Foreign Affairs was replaced by a State Secretary with responsibility for EU matters and international questions generally, based in the Prime Minister's Office. This State Secretary heads a unit comprising six political advisers, who are jointly responsible for developing a long-term EU strategy and resolving EU policy conflicts between ministries. The unit was also responsible for planning for the Swedish EU presidency in 2001 (interviews, Stockholm 26–7 May and 13 August 1999). The main body for Swedish co-ordination of EU relations and policy positions remains the Co-ordination group for EU relations. However, since 1999,

[3] Other constituent groups include EU enlargement, EU institutional matters and Nordic affairs.

this committee has been chaired by the Prime Minister's 'own' state secretary; the special state secretary for EU and international matters is a member of the committee (Ekengren and Sundelius 2001).

As yet, it is unclear how these changes will affect Swedish EU policy co-ordination. The increasing concentration of EU-oriented activities within the Prime Minister's Office will probably weaken the role of the Ministry for Foreign Affairs with respect to establishing strategic, political objectives. However, the Ministry for Foreign Affairs will continue to play a key role with regard to routine co-ordination of EU policy and in the Council of Ministers. Moreover, the Foreign Ministry can claim exclusive authority in forging a national position in the area of common foreign and security poicy (CFSP). Thus, in the absence of clear lines of responsibility, the fact that EU policy co-ordination is now shared between individual ministries, the Foreign Ministry and political advisers in the PM's office is unlikely to improve significantly, the administrative tensions surrounding Swedish EU policy co-ordination (Ekengren and Sundelius 2001; Ruin 2000).

The Swedish Permanent Representation to the European Union

In several respects, the organization, working methods, and role of the Swedish permanent representation are similar to those of other EC member states—evidence of the degree to which European integration has prompted a degree of administrative convergence between member states. However, in other respects, its functioning and effectiveness can be explained only by reference to the national political context and administrative culture. Equally, the fact that Sweden has been a member of the EU for such a short time means that the permanent representation is still evolving as an administration. Swedish officials are still internalizing the cultural norms and rules of the 'Community method' of decision-making. Swedish policy networks between members of the representation and other EU institutions and with interest groups based in Brussels are also (according to members of the representation interviewed) as yet less dense than those of other representations. Nevertheless, the representation is a highly professional, competent administration whose members share a common sense of purpose as representatives of the national government in Brussels. However, as highlighted below, this agency role is certainly not considered to be incompatible with attempting to shape and, where necessary, refine national positions. On the contrary, representatives believe this to be a necessary part of their job.

Organization

The Swedish permanent representation was established at 30 Square de Meeûs in September 1995, following Sweden's accession to the EU. There was no particular model for the representation. Rather, it evolved out of and replaced the Swedish mission to the EC, which was created in the early 1960s and attached to the Swedish embassy in Brussels. Between 1995 and 1999, the size of the permanent representation increased from thirty-nine to fifty-two officials,[4] thirty-one of whom were senior officials (attaché, counsellor, or minister[5] level). In terms of provenance, twenty-four members of the representation in 1999 were career diplomats from the Ministry for Foreign Affairs. Others were seconded from the Ministries of Finance, Agriculture, Industry, Employment and Communications, Education and Science, Environment, Justice, Health and Social Affairs and Culture. The only government ministry not represented in the permanent representation was the Ministry for Defence. The senior officials were supported by thirty-nine administrative assistants and other support staff, bringing the overall size of the permanent representation to ninety-one (European Communities 1995, 1999).

When Sweden took over the EU presidency in January 2001, the total number of people in the permanent representation was 121, sixty of whom were senior officials (attaché, counsellor, or minister level) (European Communities 2001). In addition, some thirty civil servants have been seconded to the permanent representation for the duration of the Swedish presidency (interview; January 2001). The additional personnel were required to assist the representation with the task of organizing and chairing some 1,500 meetings of Council working groups in Brussels and Luxembourg during the six-month presidency. Though one of the smallest EU member states, Sweden has one of the largest permanent representations in Brussels. The representation is also Sweden's largest overseas delegation. A number of reasons were offered by interviewees for the relatively large size of the representation. Several interviewees stressed the importance of the Brussels delegation as a learning site for national officials unaccustomed to the EU policy-making process. Other reasons given included the need for Sweden as a small member state, which none the less wishes to be an influential EU policy actor, to have a strong negotiating presence in Brussels. The geographical distance between Sweden and Brussels was also cited as a factor that necessitated a larger representation, as it is difficult for national officials to commute routinely to and from Council meetings.

[4] This figure does not include the permanent representative and deputy representative.
[5] Ministers are senior officials whose diplomatic rank is between that of a counsellor and an ambassador.

In terms of internal organization, the Swedish permanent representation is structured along functional lines and replicates the national administrative structure both in terms of lack of hierarchy and informality. The representation is headed by the ambassador (since summer 1999, Mr Gunnar Lund) and deputy ambassador (since 1995, Mr Olof Lindgren), both of whom are career diplomats from the Foreign Ministry, and who are responsible for representing the Swedish government at meetings of COREPER II and COREPER I respectively. Beneath this level are the senior officials—attachés, counsellors, and ministers—who have responsibility for their functional areas and may have managerial responsibilities for more junior staff (first and second secretary). The division of responsibility reflects the work of the Council, with fragmentation into different policy areas and Council structures. Individual representatives have responsibility for particular EU policies and/or policy sectors and report upwards directly to the ambassador or deputy ambassador and downwards to their ministry and the Ministry for Foreign Affairs. A Foreign Affairs official is responsible for representing Sweden at the Antici Group and a counsellor from the Justice Ministry is a member of the Mertens Group, the two committees which prepare the agendas for the meetings of COREPER II and I. The only exception to this flat structure is the agricultural division of the representation, which has a head of section.

Personnel

Members of the representation are with few exceptions (see below), recruited from the relevant domestic ministries on the basis of their technical expertise and experience of international affairs. There are no uniform, formal recruitment procedures; individual ministries determine who goes to Brussels. All interviewees stressed the need for members of the representation to have considerable experience of having worked first in the domestic administration in the relevant policy sector. Most representatives are therefore senior level officials in mid-career. Occasionally, members of the representation are recruited from national agencies on the proposal of the relevant ministry and subject to the agreement of the ambassador and the Foreign Ministry. Thus, one of the three representatives currently responsible for environmental policies was recruited from the Swedish Environmental Protection Agency. Similarly, the current representative with responsibility for issues relating to the Schengen agreement, who was nominated by the Justice Ministry, is a member of the Police Board. While they are members of the permanent representation, individuals recruited from the agencies enjoy diplomatic status and are the administrative responsibility of the Foreign Ministry, just like other representatives.

One consequence of Sweden being a new member state has been, until recently, a high turnover of staff within the representation. In the first two

years of EU membership, many officials left the mission after just a
few months for permanent posts in the Commission and the European
Parliament. Nowadays, the average length of time spent in the representation
is four years, after which period officials normally return to the ministry from
which they came. Several people interviewed expressed the view that
working in the permanent representation represented an important (and
increasingly necessary) career opportunity for national officials to learn about
EU policy-making and to gain knowledge and experience which could then
be applied back in Stockholm. By this process, the Swedish administration is
gradually acquiring a reservoir of expertise in EU policy-making. After four
years as the Mertens Group representative, for instance, one official has
returned to a senior position in the EU legal section of the Ministry of Justice.
Similarly, in a senior level 'job swap', Frank Belfrage, permanent representative to the EU since 1995, returned to Stockholm in summer 1999 to take up
the post of director general for EU affairs in the Foreign Ministry. He was
replaced by Mr Gunnar Lund, former state secretary for EU affairs in the
Foreign Ministry.

Internal Functioning and Working Methods

The Swedish permanent representation's internal functioning and working
methods are non-hierarchical and sectorally fragmented along departmental
lines. The non-hierarchical character of the representation is reflected in the
fact that relatively junior members of the administration are often responsible for major policy areas and are expected to carry heavy workloads. Again,
this is a typical characteristic of the organizational culture of the Swedish civil
service. The functional organization of the administration along sectoral
lines mirrors the Swedish system wherein individual ministries are the lead
departments for EU policy matters in their domain. Members of the representation tend to maintain close contact with their home ministry not only
to exchange information regarding EU policy developments, but also because
this is the institutional base from whence they came and to which they will
eventually return. At a more formal level, vertical co-ordination between
Stockholm and Brussels is further assisted by weekly meetings every Friday in
Stockholm of the permanent representative and senior members of the Ministries of Finance, Justice, and Foreign Affairs. These meetings, which were
introduced in September 1998 as part of the reforms discussed above, are
chaired by the state secretary for EU affairs in the Prime Minister's Office.
Meanwhile, in Brussels, individual members of the representation enjoy
considerable autonomy over the organization of their work and their relationships with both the domestic administration on the one hand and the
ambassador/deputy ambassador on the other. In essence, contact takes place

on a 'need to know' basis and the frequency of such communication is dictated in large part by the rhythm of Council meetings, which vary from sector to sector. Each functional specialist services the relevant Council committees, monitors EU policy developments in the Commission and the European Parliament, and maintains close links with his/her ministerial counterparts in Stockholm. Occasionally, agency personnel attend the Council working groups, particularly in highly technical/specialized policy areas such as agriculture. In such cases, the agency representative is expected to liaise first with the ministry to ascertain the Swedish policy stance. However, there tends to be a division of labour between the ministries and agencies, with the latter concentrating on participation in Commission working groups. As discussed in more detail below, the relationship between ministries and agencies has become more problematic as a result of EU membership, prompting widespread debate about the effectiveness of this aspect of the Swedish politico-administrative system.

There are few formal, horizontal co-ordinating mechanisms inside the representation. A weekly meeting of all departments is held on Monday mornings to discuss the agenda for the coming week (Council working groups and COREPER). The other principal sources of horizontal co-ordination are the Antici and Mertens Group representatives who prepare the agendas for the COREPER meetings and who brief the permanent representative and deputy permanent representative before COREPER. The permanent representative holds a regular briefing session with all members of the representation before the weekly COREPER meeting. The deputy representative also meets representatives involved in the preparation of items of the COREPER I agenda individually prior to the meeting.

Though most people interviewed expressed satisfaction with the above arrangements, the internal organization and working methods of the representation have recently been a subject of considerable debate, a debate prompted in part at least by Sweden's turn to take up the Presidency in the first six months of 2001. At the request of the government, the Swedish agency for administrative development, Statskontoret, conducted a review of the organization and working methods of the Swedish permanent representation, the results of which were published in a report, *Översyn av Sveriges ständiga representation vid EU*, in October 1998. Having compared the Swedish representation with that of other EU member states (especially Denmark, Finland, and the UK), the report concluded that the Swedish representation was too large, lacking an effective hierarchical structure, and excessively fragmented. The report recommended that the ambassador should have more authority to deploy staff more flexibly between policy sectors. This would imply the introduction of a more integrated system of internal working arrangements between officials from different ministries. The report, which was prompted by a desire on the part of the government to have an effective structure in place for the Swedish Presidency in 2001, also recommended that officials from the national ministries should be more involved in the work of the representation. Notwithstanding these recommendations, the size of the representation increased at least temporarily during the Swedish Presidency, since all ministries indicated a need to send more officials to Brussels for this period. As highlighted in other contributions to this volume, the management of the Council Presidency is a major task for a permanent representation and often has longer term consequences in terms of size and internal functioning.

Role: Actor or Agent?

There is considerable debate among EU scholars about the policy-making role played by national officials involved in EU level negotiations. Intergovernmentalist or rationalist explanations of the EU policy-making process argue that EU policy preferences are determined at the domestic level by national governments, which also control EU policy outcomes. According to this view, members of the permanent representation are instrumental, utility maximizers, and agents of the national government in the Brussels arena. Policy outcomes are the outcome of power and bargaining (Moravscik 1993, 1998). By contrast, sociological or institutionalist models of the EU policy process stress the importance of both the cultural-institutional context of policy-making and the constructed identity of actors (Hall and Taylor 1996; Pierson 1996). According to this model, policy preferences are reshaped during the policy-making process as a result of policy learning, exposure to new 'frames of meaning' (Hall and Taylor 1996) and actor socialization into the 'Community method' of decision-making (Lewis 1998).

Advocates of this approach have thus argued that national officials who are immersed in the complex reality of transnational negotiations internalize collective norms (including a commitment to supranationality) and policy objectives which may conflict with those of their national government. Such arguments are not new; Leon Lindberg (1963: 79) observed that: 'The permanent representatives defend national points of view, but at the same time are influenced by their participation in Community affairs and often argue back to their national capitals in favor of Commission proposals, or in favor of making concessions to another Member State in order to achieve agreement.' Detailed analysis of the Swedish permanent representation provides further evidence of the ambiguous role played by COREPER officials in the European integration process. On the one hand, members of the Swedish permanent representation clearly perceive their primary role to be that of representing the Swedish government in Brussels. However, they also acknowledge that they spend a lot of time convincing national officials and politicians of the need to define Swedish interests in terms of a broader EU policy agenda, the need to be taken seriously by other member states during negotiations, and the need for political compromise.

There is a strong sentiment among members of the representation that the principal *raison d'être* of the representation is to represent the views and instructions of the Swedish government within the Council. All interviewees explained that EU policies and packages are formulated in Stockholm and relayed to the Brussels-based officials in the form of instructions which clarify the Swedish negotiating position. Thus, in keeping with the intergovernmental model, officials in the permanent representation do perceive themselves as agents of the Swedish government. A number of representatives also said that working-group meetings often involved hard bargaining between member states and competing national interests. However, several representatives acknowledged that the principal–agent model only partially captures their role. In particular, several representatives said that they believed they were influential in shaping national preferences and instructions in the first place. As one representative explained: 'the work of the committee is so specialized that the Ministry relies upon me to decide what we should do' (interview, May 1998). Other representatives commented that national instructions often arrived too late or not at all. In these circumstances, the representatives said they tended to rely upon their own judgement in Council negotiations rather than seek to delay proceedings and risk irritating other member states (interviews, April 1999). Another senior level respondent said that his minister trusted him to negotiate within a broad negotiating framework, adding that, without this leeway, his job would be impossible (interview, April 1999). In reality, the degree of autonomy and discretion enjoyed by members of the permanent representation varies between sectors and between officials. Members of the representation are often better informed about the minutiae of current negotiations and changes in other member states' positions than national officials and thus 'by default' may enjoy considerable autonomy and discretion. In highly technical areas, the representative (or agency official) may also have a better understanding of the dossier than generalists in Stockholm. Similarly, in areas where the Swedish policy stance is clearly defined in general terms, the officials in Brussels enjoy some discretion within a broad 'negotiating framework' (interview, April 1999). However, in 'high politics' areas and/or issues which are politically sensitive domestically (e.g. EMU, CFSP), negotiating mandates are generally much less permissive.

Contact between the representatives and Stockholm is frequent and regular: most members of the representation have daily e-mail, fax, and telephone contact with their ministry in Stockholm to brief national officials on negotiations and discuss national instructions. However, communication is very much a two-way process and information relayed to Stockholm by the representatives is itself influential in helping to shape national preferences. Such reports—their contents and recommendations—play an important role in bridging national and EU 'policy frames' (Schön and Rein 1994). As one representative remarked: 'It is our job to make people in Stockholm aware of the need for EC policies to address everybody's concerns, not just Sweden's' (interview, April 1999). Further evidence of the degree to which Swedish representatives have internalized collective decision-making norms is highlighted by the following comment from a senior member of the representation: 'When we first joined the EU we thought other member states should adopt Swedish environmental standards. But we have had to learn that other countries have other more important problems and different views about how to solve environmental problems. Now we think it is more important to listen and to find small areas of agreement' (interview, April 1999).

Yet, though the officials freely acknowledge their dual role as interpreters of two different cognitive worlds and may enjoy some discretion, they are generally subject to effective political control. Moreover, their institutional identity is clearly centred upon the Council and the associated activity of detailed policy negotiation, rather than with agenda-setting and policy formulation. Contacts with other EU institutions are, in consequence, considered to be of secondary importance. The most important points of contact beyond the Council are with the Swedish Commissioner and her cabinet and members of relevant Commission working groups. Generally speaking, contacts with the European Parliament are not well-developed, though as one member of the representation responsible for environmental policy remarked, the extension of co-decision to new policy areas has made such links increasingly important. The representation has one person who is responsible for relations with the European Parliament.

Conclusion: Effectiveness and Capacity to Implement Ambitions

The key issue to be addressed here is the extent to which the permanent representation is capable of producing effective co-ordination of EU policy. Unfortunately, there is no straightforward answer to this question, not least because there is no objective way of measuring effectiveness. Moreover, the capacity of the permanent representation is a function not only of its own internal characteristics, but also of its position within a much wider policy-making environment. Specifically, the co-ordinating capacity of the permanent representation is affected by the effectiveness of national co-ordinating structures and by links with other EU institutions and policy actors, including private interests. Moreover, all of these variables are dynamic and thus subject to change. The meaning of the term 'co-ordination' is also ambiguous. As highlighted above, the officials are not merely concerned with administrative co-ordination. Rather they are also crucial actors in the process of the political co-ordination of national and European interests.

In terms of administrative co-ordination, the functioning of the Swedish permanent representation provides further confirmation of the relative ease with which Sweden has coped with the demands of EU membership. Indeed, the Swedish policy style of rational, pragmatic, consensual decision-making has proved extremely helpful to representatives in Council working groups, where rational arguments based on knowledge rather than political arguments count (SOU 1996: 75). In terms of internal characteristics, the potentially dysfunctional fragmentation of the permanent representation along sectoral lines is to some extent countered by its collegial administrative culture and shared commitment to defending Swedish interests. The administrative and political co-ordinating capacity of the representation has also benefited from the existence of relatively strong centralizing pressures at the national level. As a small, centralized, unitary state, Sweden has never experienced the co-ordination problems of federal member states such as Germany. Moreover, the recent politico-administrative reforms outlined above (which were inspired partly by the UK system) have further strengthened national EU policy co-ordinating structures. The clearly defined EU accession policy agenda of the Swedish government has also provided the permanent representation with a sense of negotiating direction up until now (though it is not clear what will replace this increasingly dated agenda). The close and regular links between members of the permanent representation and the national administration also increase the co-ordinating capacity of the former. These institutional and cultural norms, together with the Swedish government's need to demonstrate effective central co-ordination of EU policy, provide the basis for national political accountability of the permanent representation.

Yet, the co-ordinating capacity of the Swedish representation is limited in some respects. First, the Swedish permanent representation does not (like the UK permanent representation) constitute the centre of a powerful, national policy network in Brussels. It is not always the first port of call for national officials (either from the ministries or the agencies) coming to Brussels to attend Commission working groups. Nor are members of the representation particularly pressured by Swedish interest groups. Again, this contrasts with the UK representatives, who have been aptly described as 'the lobbied lobbyist' (Spence 1993). Moreover, it seems to be the case that the Swedish permanent representation does not have access to such a dense system of national networks within Brussels as the representations of some other member states. There are several reasons for this. First, Sweden is a new and a small EU member state. As such, it still lacks a critical mass of administrative personnel with expertise in EU matters. Sweden also has fewer nationals working in the Commission and the European Parliament than several other member states. The hostility of many Swedish MEPs elected to the European Parliament in 1995 has also hindered the development of links within the

European Parliament. However, this situation has improved recently: in the 1999 European elections, the number of Green and Left Party Swedish MEPs fell to seven (out of twenty-two Swedish representatives). A number of interviewees also suggested that cultural factors were also important: most Swedes are not good at informal networking. The relative weakness of such networks is significant in two respects. First, it limits the degree to which the Swedish permanent representation is able to monitor potentially significant policy developments in the Commission and/or Parliament. Secondly, it reduces the capacity of the permanent representation to play a more proactive role in the EU policy-making process, either inside the Commission or the Parliament. This may in turn reduce its capacity to realize national policy ambitions.

Secondly, links with EU pressure groups are also acknowledged to be rather weak by members of the representation. Paradoxically, a frequently cited reason for this is the Swedish administrative tradition of extensive, formalized consultation with interest groups in the national policy-making process. Thus, some officials in the permanent representation believed that, given this practice, there was no need for them to develop personal links with Swedish interest groups. Asked more generally whether they had links with interest groups of any type, several officials remarked that, in the Swedish context, it is not really considered appropriate for public officials to talk informally to groups to the extent that the officials of some other member states do. This attitude seems to have inhibited the development of networks with groups at the European level, though there is some evidence to suggest that some members of the representation (especially those who have spent longer periods in Brussels) now realize the potential benefits of such networks in mobilizing advocacy coalitions for Swedish policy objectives and have begun to internalize this practice (interviews, May 1998 and April 1999).

Thirdly, the effectiveness of the permanent representation is, according to all those interviewed, adversely affected by the lack of expertise in EU affairs in the domestic administration. In particular, everyone interviewed commented that most national officials and politicians had little idea of the fast pace of EU policy-making. Several people interviewed gave examples of instances in which instructions had arrived from Stockholm either very late, or not at all. In some cases, such delays were a consequence of the Swedish policy-making system, with its emphasis upon consultation. However, a number of people believed that it was also attributable to a more general failure on the part of some national officials to regard EU matters as urgent. More than one official complained that the lack of interest in EU matters on the part of some national politicians at ministerial level resulted in a lack of political support for the work of the representation, which in turn weakened the negotiating position of Sweden inside the Council working groups (interviews, Brussels, May 1998 and March 1999). Arguably, the more fundamental problem is that the ministries are simply too small to cope with the additional demands placed upon them by EU membership. As one national civil servant remarked, 'EU issues come in on top of everything else. EU stuff tends to be seen as "slave work" on top of the rest of one's job' (interview, May 1999). There was also general agreement that few officials in Stockholm appreciated the need for political compromise and for civil servants in the representation have more flexible mandates.

The strains placed upon the ministries by EU membership has, of course, been exacerbated in the Swedish case by the concentration of technical expertise in the much larger administrative agencies. Even where (as is often the case) relations between the ministry and the agency are good, the separation of technical and policy-making expertise can be problematic, especially if there is high staff turnover in the ministry. In the context of EU policy-making, the problems are greater. The tendencies for agency representatives to attend the Commission working groups and for ministry officials to attend Council working groups create discontinuity. Though the work of the regulatory agencies has become increasingly Europeanized, they lack the political authority to speak on behalf of the government and have to work with and through the ministry. Thus, the agency system, a key element of the Swedish politico-administrative system, is ill-suited to the EU decision-making system.

To some extent the above limitations to the effectiveness of the Swedish representation are attributable to its status as a new member state. Over time, it is likely that Swedish officials will acquire more expertise and understanding of EU policy-making. Similarly, as Swedish civil servants continue to internalize EU policy-making procedures, it is likely that they will develop closer links with other EU institutions and interest groups. Arguably, it is the policy-making system and style back home which might prove to be the Achilles' heel. The trajectory of change internally is influenced by an amalgam of exogenous and endogenous factors. As argued elsewhere (Mazey and Richardson forthcoming) there are endogenous changes taking place which suggest that some of the disadvantages under which Sweden has operated in the EU may be lessening over time. Thus, there is now widespread recognition among political and administrative élites of the importance of national EU policy co-ordination, of the need to strengthen the resources of the ministries and tackle the agency problem. Historically, Sweden has been the model of an adaptive state and is often cited as the ultimate example of the small, *smart* state. Thus, there is every reason to believe that it will rise to the EU challenge.

References

Bergman, T. (1997), 'National Parliaments and the EU Affairs Committees: Notes on Empirical Variation and Competing Explanations', *Journal of European Public Policy*, 4/3: 373–87.

Beyers, Jan, and Dierickx, G. (1998), 'The Working Groups of the Council of the European Union: Supranational or Intergovernmental Negotiations', *Journal of Common Market Studies*, 36/3: 289–318.

Eckengren, Magnus, and Sundelius, Bengt (1997), 'Sweden: The State joins the European Union', in K. Hanf and B. Soetendorp (eds.), *Adapting to European Integration: Small States and the European Union* (London: Longman), 131–48.

——and Sundelins, Bengt (2001), 'Sweden', in Brian Hoching and David Spence (eds.), *EU Member State Foreign Ministries: Change and Adaptation* (London: Macmillan), 165–76.

European Commission (1996 and 1998), *Eurobarometer*, 44 and 50 (Luxembourg: Office for Official Publications of the European Communities).

European Communities (1995, 1999, and 2001), *Who's Who in the EU? Interinstitutional Directory* (Luxembourg: Office for Official Publications of the European Communities).

Gstöhl, S. (1996), 'The Nordic Countries and the European Economic Area (EEA)', in Lee Miles (ed.), *The European Union and the Nordic Countries* (London: Routledge), 32–46.

Hall, P., and Taylor, R. (1996), 'Political Science and the Three New Institutionalisms', *Political Studies*, 44/4: 936–57.

Hamilton, C., Jakobsson, U., Jonung, L., Lungren, N., and Thyesen, N. (1996), *Swedish Strategies at the European Union Intergovernmental Conference* (Stockholm: SNS Economic Policy Group, Occasional Paper, 76, Mar.).

Hayes-Renshaw, F., and Wallace, H. (1995), 'Executive Power in the European Union: The Functions and Limits of the Council of Ministers', *Journal of European Public Policy*, 2/4: 559–82.

——(1997), *The Council of Ministers* (London: Routledge).

Hegeland, H., and Mattson, I. (1997), 'The Swedish Riksdag and the EU: Influence and Openness', in M. Wiberg (ed.), *Trying to Make Democracy Work* (Stockholm: Bank of Sweden Tercentenary Foundation), 70–107.

Johansson, K. M. (1999), 'Europeanisation and its Limits: The Case of Sweden', *Journal of International Relations and Development*, 2/2: 169–86.

Kerremans, B. (1996), 'Do Institutions Make a Difference? Non-Institutionalism, Neo-Institutionalism and the Logic of Common Decision-Making in the European Union', *Governance*, 2: 217–40.

Larsson, T. (1995), *Governing Sweden* (Stockholm: Statkontoret).

Lawler, Peter (1997), 'Scandinavian Exceptionalism and European Union', *Journal of Common Market Studies*, 35/4: 565–94.

Lewis, Jeffrey (1998), 'Is the "Hard Bargaining" Image of the Council Misleading? The Committee of Permanent Representatives and the Local Elections Directive', *Journal of Common Market Studies*, 36/4: 479–504.

Lindahl, Rutger (2000), 'Swedish Public Opinion and the EU', in Lee Miles (ed.), *Sweden and the European Union Evaluated* (London: Continuum), 97–126.

Lindberg, Leon (1970), *The Political Dynamics of European Economic Integration* (Stanford, Calif.: Stanford University Press).

Mazey, Sonia, and Richardson, Jeremy (forthcoming), 'The Swedish Policy Style: From Saklighet to Normal European Politics?'; in J. Richardson (ed.), *Sweden: Consensual Governance under Pressure* (Cheltenham: Edward Elgar).

Miles, L. (ed.) (1996), *The European Union and the Nordic Countries* (London: Routledge).

——(1997), *Sweden and European Integration* (London: Ashgate).

Milner, H. (1994), *Social Democracy and Rational Choice: The Scandinavian Experience and Beyond* (London: Routledge).

Moravscik, A. (1993), 'Preferences and Power in the European Community: A Liberal Governmentalist Approach', *Journal of Common Market Studies*, 31/4: 473–524.

——(1998), *The Choice for Europe: Social Purpose and State Power from Messina to Maastricht* (Ithaca NY: Cornell University Press).

Pierson, P. (1996), 'The Path to European Integration: A Historical Institutionalist Analysis', *Comparative Political Analysis*, 29/2 (Apr.): 123–63.

Ruin, Olof (2000), 'The Europeanization of Swedish Politics', in Lee Miles (ed.), *Sweden and the European Union Evaluated* (London: Continuum), 51–65.

Schön, D., and Rein, M. (1994), *Frame Reflection: Towards the Resolution of Intractable Policy Controversies* (New York: Basic Books).

SOU (1996), *The Views and Experiences of Swedish Civil Servants regarding the Structure and Working Methods of the EU* (Stockholm: Government Printing Office).

Spence, D. (1993), 'The Role of the National Civil Service in European Lobbying: The British Case', in S. Mazey and J. Richardson (eds.), *Lobbying in the European Community* (Oxford: Oxford University Press), 47–73.

Sundelius, B. (1994), 'When Sweden Chose to Join the EC', in Walter Carlsnaes and Steve Smith (eds.), *European Foreign Policy: The EC and Changing Perspectives in Europe* (London: Sage), 177–201.

Swedish Institute (1996), 'Sweden in the European Union', *Fact Sheets on Sweden* (Mar.).

Westlake, M. (ed.) (1995), *The Council of the European Union* (London: Cartermill).

11

National Co-ordination in Brussels: The Role of Ireland's Permanent Representation

Brigid Laffan

Introduction

Ireland's permanent representation was established as a separate accreditation in 1967, following a government decision in July 1966. Prior to this time, the Irish ambassador in Brussels was accredited to Belgium, Luxembourg, and the three European Communities. The decision by the Irish government to set up a dedicated representation was part of its long-term strategy of ensuring that Ireland would be successful in its application for membership of the Union. Ireland's first application was stalled in January 1963 when President de Gaulle refused to continue accession negotiations with the United Kingdom. By July 1966, following a resolution of the 'empty chair' crisis, the Irish government wanted to be prepared for the eventual reopening of the enlargement process and the commencement of accession negotiations. Preparations included the creation of a separate EU mission in Brussels, the publication of a White Paper on membership in 1967, and an extensive programme of ministerial meetings with the Commission. The representation was a signal to the EU that Ireland wished to pursue its application with vigour.

The role of the EU mission in the period before eventual membership on the first of January 1973 involved a pre-negotiation phase, which lasted until June 1970, and the negotiating phase, which established the formal terms of Ireland's accession to the Union. Between 1967 and June 1970, the EU mission played a critical role in monitoring developments in the Commission and in the six member states on their attitude towards the first enlargement of the Union. The 1963 veto made enlargement a sensitive and complex issue for the member states and the EU institutions. The importance of British membership to Ireland and the desire for concurrent negotiations with the Union meant that the EU mission had the task of tracking with particular care developments in relation to the British application. The Irish government was always fearful that it might be left in a queue and not be in a position to join at the same time as the UK.

During this preparatory period, there was a continuing cycle of high-level contacts between the Irish government and the Commission, as part of the government's enlargement strategy. At the request of the Irish government, meetings were held between the Commission and the Irish Ministers for Agriculture and Fisheries, Industry and Commerce, Finance, and Labour. The Taoiseach (Prime Minister) conducted a series of bilateral meetings with the Commission and the member states, accompanied by the minister for finance in 1967. The pattern of Ireland's relations with the Union in this period was characterized by the pivotal role of the Prime Minister and the domestic economic ministries in the unfolding relations between Brussels and Dublin. A striking feature of the pre-negotiations was the limited role played by the long-standing Irish foreign minister, Mr Frank Aiken. Mr Aiken had little to do with the formalization of Ireland's evolving policies towards the EU, which was regarded as a decision about Ireland's economic development. That said, Ireland's EU mission was the responsibility of the Ministry of Foreign Affairs from the outset. Its liaison role in relation to the developing contacts between the Irish government and Brussels was a precursor of the blurring of the foreign/domestic divide characteristic of all permanent representations. By the time accession negotiations opened in July 1970, a new foreign minister, Dr Paddy Hillary, who later became Ireland's first Commissioner, asserted his role in this field and led the Irish delegation that conducted the negotiations. The head of Ireland's EU mission was a full member of the negotiating team for the duration of the accession talks. A government decision in 1973 gave the Foreign Ministry responsibility for the overall co-ordination of EU policy.[1]

Size and Development

Ireland's EU mission was not based on any particular model other than it conformed to the normal pattern found in these missions. Between 1967 and 1970 when accession negotiations began, the representation had five staff, consist-

[1] This chapter on the Irish permanent representation is part of a wider study of the 'Europeanisation of Public Policy in Ireland' that was part financed by the Social Science Research Council of the Royal Irish Academy. Over forty interviews were conducted with officials involved in the management of EU business and a survey was undertaken of all EU co-ordination units in the national administration. The author would like to express her appreciation of the financial assistance from the Royal Irish Academy and the generosity of those interviewed.

ing of one ambassador, three counsellors, and one third secretary. It increased to seven in 1971 when negotiations intensified and reached fifteen in 1973, when the focus shifted from accession to full membership of the EU. Thereafter, the permanent representation became an integral part of Ireland's management of EU membership.

The Irish representation received its 'baptism of fire' in 1975 when Ireland took over the Presidency for six months. This involved a new and small state organizing, in conjunction with the Council secretariat, the agenda and the schedule of meetings, in addition to chairing all meetings under the auspices of the Council. This term of office in the chair could be regarded as the end of Ireland's apprenticeship in the system. The Irish system of public administration was exposed to the full range of EU policy-making and was capable of managing the burden of the Presidency. EU business became part and parcel of public policy-making in Ireland. The Presidency had an immediate impact on the size of the representation, in that the number of diplomatic officers increased from fifteen in 1973 to twenty-four in 1975. The effects of the 1979 Presidency can also be seen in an increased complement of staff. The number of staff in the representation remained relatively stable during the remainder of the 1970s and 1980s when the overall number with diplomatic rank ranged between twenty-two and twenty-five, with an average of twenty-four. The next significant increase in staffing levels came in the 1990s when a number of domestic ministries felt the need for representation. The addition of staff from the Justice Ministry and the Attorney General's Office brought the staffing level to thirty-five with diplomatic rank by 1999. The expansion of staff from the mid-1990s onwards points to the growth of EU competence in the post-TEU/Amsterdam environment and to the Europeanization of a number of domestic ministries.

The size of the Irish representation is, in comparative terms, very small. It is the smallest representation apart from Luxembourg with increases associated with the Presidency and the addition of representation from new ministries. Within the representation, the ratio of senior staff (ambassadorial/counsellor/adviser) to more junior staff is about 30:70, with 30 per cent of the staff having the status of counsellor/adviser or above. This means that the representation has a far higher ratio of senior staff than would be the norm in an overseas embassy. (See Table 11.1.)

TABLE 11.1. *Staffing of the Irish representation, 1999 (officers of diplomatic rank)*

Ambassador	Counsellor	Advisers	First secretary	Third secretary	TOTAL
2	6	5	17	5	35

Source: europa.eu.int/idea.

The representation of domestic ministries in Brussels has gone through a process of evolution. In 1973, six ministries had staff in the representation, Foreign Affairs, Finance, Industry and Commerce, Agriculture and Fisheries, Labour, and the Office of the Revenue Commissioners. By 1978 these were joined by Transport and Power and Health and Social Welfare. In the 1982, the Ministry of Trade, Commerce, and Tourism seconded a member of staff to the representation. In the 1990s, the Ministries of the Marine (1991), Justice (1995), and Health (1996), and the Attorney General's Office all sent officials to Brussels. Changes in the names of the ministries and the separation of some ministries since membership alters somewhat the designation of the home ministry. By 1999, ten ministries, the Attorney General's Office, and the Revenue Commissioners had staff seconded to the representation. (See Table 11.2.) Apart from the Foreign Ministry, the department of Enterprise, Trade, and Employment had five staff in the representation and a further three ministries (Finance, Public Enterprise, and Justice) had three staff including a senior member of staff at counsellor level. No domestic ministry has more

TABLE 11.2. *Ministries with representation in Brussels, September 1999*

Department	Ambassador	Counsellor/ adviser	First secretary	Third secretary
Foreign Affairs	2	3	5	2
Finance	—	1	2	—
Revenue	—	—	1	1
Public Enterprise	—	1	1	1
Agriculture and Food	—	1	1	—
Environment	—	—	1	—
Marine	—	—	1	—
Enterprise, Trade and Employment	—	2	2	1
Justice, Equality and Law Reform	—	1	2	—
Social Community and Family Affairs	—	—	1	—
Health	—	1	—	—
Attorney General's Office	—	1	—	—

Source: europa.eu.int/idea.

than five staff in the representation. The Ministries of Agriculture, and the Revenue have two members of staff in Brussels with one each from the Marine, Environment, and Health. The number of officials from Agriculture has not increased since the original allocation of two in 1973. This partly reflects the fact that the Special Agricultural Committee is serviced from Dublin. A number of domestic ministries, notably, Defence, Arts, Culture, and the Gaeltacht, and Education, are not in the representation, although the Defence Ministry seconded someone in 1996 to Ireland's mission to Belgium and the Western European Union.

The Irish representation is organized along functional lines, with the permanent representative at the apex of the hierarchy followed by the deputy permanent representative, both career diplomats from the Foreign Ministry. There has never been any demand in the Irish system for the senior members of the representation to come from any other ministry. The next level in the hierarchy consists of the attachés at counsellor level who are responsible for their functional areas and may have a line responsibility *vis-è-vis* the more junior staff (first secretary and third secretary). There are nine counsellors in the Irish representation.

The division of responsibility follows the work of the Council, with its fragmentation into different policy areas and Council formations. Each person in the representation is responsible for a discrete area of work. They attend working party meetings and report on their areas of responsibility to their home departments and the senior members of the representation. For example, the three Finance Ministry officials have responsibility for structural funds and financial regulations (counsellor level), the budget (first secretary), and taxation (first secretary) respectively. The senior Finance official attends all working parties on the structural funds and anything to do with the regulation of financial services. The two more junior colleagues act as budget attaché and the attaché responsible for all working parties dealing with fiscal questions. The Foreign Ministry officials are divided into two groups with responsibility for a range of tasks such as institutional affairs and administration, press and information, in addition to the Council working groups normally serviced by this ministry.

It is important to distinguish between areas where Foreign Affairs takes the lead role and those areas where its task is to keep a watching brief and to coordinate the domestic ministries. Traditionally, it has tended to play a major role in the development of new policy areas, such as the development of cohesion policy, that are then passed on to the relevant domestic ministry. Two Foreign Affairs officials are responsible for acting as the members of the Antici and Merton Groups, which prepare an annotated agenda for the meetings of COREPER II and I. Foreign Affairs, since the implementation of the TEU, also has a CFSP attaché, and someone responsible for links with the European Parliament. A diplomat acts as the press officer for the representation. The main task of the Environment attaché is to attend meetings of the environmental working party. Until 1991, the Ministry of the Marine did not have a full-time official in the representation, with the result that Foreign Affairs allocated one of their staff to fisheries, and maintained that post even after the arrival of an official from the Ministry of the Marine for a number of years. This suggests that Foreign Affairs felt the need carefully to track the common fisheries policy so that they could judge the domestic policy position. One official interviewed suggested that the Marine was the ministry that had adapted with greatest difficulty to EU membership, in that its reflex response to proposals was 'a veto, walk out or take the Commission to Court'. The Foreign Ministry did not play as significant a role in any other substantive area of domestic policy. This can be partly explained by the fact that there were sensitive issues involving the states' territorial waters and the law of the sea involved, areas that the Ministry of the Marine was not competent to deal with. That said, Foreign Affairs was also deeply involved in the nitty gritty of fish quotas.

Although the staff of the representation is drawn from across the civil service, the Foreign Ministry has a powerful structural position in the system. The permanent representative and his deputy have always been senior diplomats, and this is unlikely ever to change. In addition, Foreign Affairs have three further senior staff, five first secretaries, and two third secretaries. A third of the staff in the representation and close to half of the senior staff are career diplomats. There has been erosion of the weight of Foreign Affairs with the addition of new domestic ministries, but it remains pivotal in the system.

The staff of the representation are formally part of the foreign service when in Brussels, and are paid by the Foreign Ministry and benefit from the usual diplomatic conditions of service. However, the domestic departments are responsible for deciding who should go to Brussels to represent them. Foreign Affairs has never attempted formally to direct the process of recruitment of staff to the representation beyond its own complement of staff, although it engages in informal contact on staffing matters with the home departments. The post of permanent representative to the EU is regarded in the Irish Diplomatic Service as one of the most senior postings, akin to a posting to Washington, London, or the UN. Since 1973, Ireland has had only six permanent representatives (see Table 11.3). The first incumbent, Sean Kennan served for the first eight months of Ireland's membership and was then replaced by Brendan Dillon, who served in Brussels from 1973 to 1981—a very long term in the representation. This was perhaps because the Irish system was finding its feet in the system and needed stability and continuity. He was followed by Andrew O'Rourke (five years), John Cambell (five years), Padraig Mackernan (three years), and Denis O'Leary (four years by 2000). Apart from Brendan Dillon, who spent eight years in Brussels, the average stay for the most senior Irish diplomat is five years. Two of the permanent representatives, Andrew

TABLE 11.3. *Ireland's permanent representatives*

Ambassador Kennan	1973 (8 months)
Ambassador Dillon	1973–81
Ambassador O'Rourke	1981–86
Ambassador Cambell	1986–92
Ambassador MacKearnan	1992–95
Ambassador O'Leary	1995–

O'Rourke and Denis O'Leary spent four years each as the deputy permanent representative, which gave them a solid period of preparation for the role of permanent representative. They came to the responsibilities of the permanent representative with in-depth knowledge of the Council system, and the role of COREPER in EU negotiations. Two of the representatives returned to Dublin to take up the position of secretary general of the Foreign Ministry, the most senior position in the foreign service.

The deputy representatives (COREPER II) spend between three and four years in Brussels, the length of a normal diplomatic posting. The position is the same for the other Foreign Ministry staff, for whom the representation is one posting among many in the evolution of their diplomatic careers. This is clearly not the case for the officials from the home civil service, who are unlikely to be posted abroad again. For them, the period in Brussels takes them outside their home department and exposes them to their colleagues from other ministries and other states. The average assignment to Brussels is for three to four years, although some officials have spent longer there. Some ministries such the Environment and Public Enterprise tend to have longer periods of secondment (five years). In general, domestic ministry officials spend a longer period in Brussels than their diplomatic colleagues. Attitudes towards time in Brussels vary across the service. In the early years, there was a tendency to regard time in the representation as time spent away from the home department on the cocktail circuit. It was not necessarily useful for future career prospects, although a number of former attachés rose to highest rank in their ministry. Attitudes towards time in Brussels are changing, given the salience of the EU level of policy-making and wider processes of Europeanization. Within all of the domestic ministries and the Foreign Ministry, officials with experience in the representation are regarded as having specialized and useful skills in dealing with Brussels. These skills range from experience at negotiations to in-depth knowledge about EU policy and process in a particular domain. Back home, these officials become part of a cadre of EU specialists in the Irish service. Their expertise may or may not be used immediately on return to Dublin.

There appears to be little formal planning of the staffing of the representation. Although departments know well in advance when they will need to replace their people in Brussels, they do not tend to give too much advanced notice, nor is there any formal training programme for those going to Brussels. That said, most officials sent to the representation have considerable experience in representing Ireland at working-party level. In interviews, a number of officials who had served time in the representation felt that they would have benefited from a more systematic preparatory phase including shadowing the area of work for six months so that they would have been *au fait* with the dossiers when they arrived in Brussels. There was also concern that some officials went to Brussels without adequate French-language skills. Following their time in Brussels, some of the officials find themselves assigned to EU work in their home departments, but this does not necessarily follow immediately. The cult of the generalist in the Irish system is strong, with the result that over-specialization can be a barrier to promotion. That said, EU-related work is developing as an identifiable and highly regarded specialization in the Irish system for a nucleus of officials. Officials with experience in the representation may find themselves assigned to EU-related work in a later phase of their career in their home department. For example, a key member of Ireland's 'Agenda 2000' team had served four years at the representation. In the Foreign Ministry, numerous diplomats with experience in the representation are assigned to the economic division (EU co-ordination) at some stage in their careers. A period in the representation brings with it the additional benefit of contacts in other government departments.

Working Methods

The working methods of the Irish representation are determined by the structure of the Council system, the number of staff, and Irish administrative culture. Its style also reflects the underlying values that govern Ireland's membership of the EU. The national representations are a microcosm of the national administrative culture and resources. A key factor in understanding the relationship between Ireland and the EU is that successive governments and the administration do not have to participate in EU policy-making in a hostile political and parliamentary environment. There is a deeply rooted political consensus on EU membership in the Irish Parliament, a Parliament that has weak mechanisms of control. Irish representatives do not have to control, disguise, or contain the impact of EU policy at national level. Rather, successive governments and senior civil servants were largely free to chart Ireland's course in the Union.

Ireland's approach is based on the primacy of the 'lead department' for each area of EU policy, with considerable autonomy given to each department and officials within departments in determining the broad lines of policy. 'Internalization' of EU business rather than containment characterizes the Irish system. Issues of high salience, cross-cutting issues, and issues that engender interdepartmental conflict require interdepartmental co-ordination and political intervention. Ireland's system of co-ordination at national level is less formalized and characterized by fewer committees than any other member state apart from Luxembourg. The system of interdepartmental committees has been very unstable, with different formations established at different times depending on the agenda. At present, national co-ordination is achieved by a group of ministers and secretaries (GMS) which acts as an interface between the political and administrative systems and is chaired by the Prime Minister. Its work is prepared by a group of senior officials (GSG). This committee only addresses the major dossiers such as a Presidency, the intergovernmental conference, and Agenda 2000. The cycle of meetings is not regular; rather it is agenda-driven and meets on a needs basis. The GMS met sixteen times in 1996 as a consequence of the Presidency, six times in 1997, seven in 1998, and has not met at all in 1999. Its work was superseded by the establishment of an expert technical group which met seven times in the lead-up to the Berlin European Council in March 1999. There are a number of interdepartmental committees on specific sectors but these tend to wax and wane depending on the Union's work programme. The domestic system of co-ordination is relatively light and much less bureaucratic than the systems in other member states. The style is consensual, collegial, and pragmatic, with a marked emphasis on those areas of Union policy that are of importance to Ireland: agriculture, the budget, structural funds, taxation, and EU regulations that affect Ireland's competitive position. Ireland's policy style owes much to the intimacy of the senior echelons of the Irish civil service and the ease of personal contact. The Irish representation works within and also reflects the underlying norms of the Irish system.

Size is an important factor in explaining Ireland's approach to the management of EU business. Irish policy-makers are clearly conscious of Ireland's relative size and presence at the negotiating table. There is considerable emphasis placed on getting the tactics of the negotiations right, rather than the tabling of position papers and negotiating on the totality of the proposal. There is a norm that EU policies represent 'value added' in most but not all fields. The task of the Irish negotiators is thus to ensure that the agreement emerging in Brussels can be lived with at home and that the balance of advantage lies with Irish preferences. Ireland has a smaller diplomatic and central government administration than its counterparts, with the result that it has fewer people to devote to any one area of EU policy than most of the other member states. Individual negotiators in the representation must, therefore, develop strategies for dealing with their relative lack of resources. Interviews with civil servants suggest that they learn to prioritize, scan a large amount of documentation, identify the five or six key issues for Ireland in any one dossier, and listen carefully to what is being said by other delegations. This ensures that they can benefit from the insights of other better resourced administrations and plan how to find acceptable solutions to the five or six key issues for Ireland. Briefing papers tend to concentrate on the key points of interest to Ireland rather than substantive discussion of the policy rationale underlying Commission thinking. The imperative is to arrive at an outcome that can be lived with at home. As a consequence of limited resources and because of a sense of where Ireland comes in the EU pecking order, the Irish approach is to address issues of immediate interest to Ireland rather than adopting a proactive approach to the building of the system. Irish representatives will not intervene unless they have to and tend not to have much to say in the general discussions that inevitably take place from time to time.

The Irish representation has an important hierarchical dimension in that the two senior officials are responsible for COREPER I and II, through which work flows upwards to the Council. The two senior members of the representation as 'plenipotentiaries' carry the authority of their position at the apex of the office. Within the representation there is a clear line of command. The permanent representative and his deputy must be briefed on all agenda items on the weekly agendas of COREPER and will have established in-house guidelines on how and when they want this material presented to them. Thus the permanent representative will work most closely with those officials responsible for areas of work that fall within his domain, and likewise for the deputy who tends to have responsibility for more technical areas. Their requirements are determined by the up-coming agenda and their attention is on the thirty to forty agenda items that they must respond to at the next COREPER meeting. The COREPER agenda is usually circulated on a Friday for the following Wednesday. The agenda is circulated in the representation, and in the home departments. The permanent representative will need briefing from the official with functional responsibility for a particular area of work in the representation. In turn, the seconded official will contact the home department for briefing material, if necessary, or may rely on his own judgement.

The senior diplomats in the representation want concise and targeted briefings that highlight for them the particular Irish angle or interest in relation to each agenda item. They do not want to be overwhelmed with technical detail or long briefings that are not to the point. The two senior officers in the representation must be capable of mastering a complex brief in any area of EU policy in a short space of time. The ambassadors tend to challenge everything, according to one interviewee, because they do not want to find themselves exposed at COREPER attempting to defend a position that was weakened through bad preparation or inattention to the evolution of the dossiers.

The cycle of COREPER business together with the work of the Merton and Antici Groups imposes co-ordination on the system. COREPER acts as a filtering node in the system; issues are pushed to the limit here and may proceed to the ministerial level or go back down to the working-group level again. COREPER meetings decide what needs to go to the political level, but there is an effort to sort out the technical issues before involving ministers. Within COREPER II and I, national positions/difficulties are highlighted and the representatives come under pressure from their counterparts. They have got to judge just how reasonable the national position is, as they do not want to cause negotiating problems on small issues. The members of COREPER II and I are members of an élite club operating at the coal-face between the national and the European and between the political and the technical. They see each other all of the time—at the interminable COREPER meetings, in the Council chamber, and at the social occasions that form part and parcel of this world. The aim of the ambassadors is to solve problems and to push the negotiations along. In some sense they engage in a collective conspiracy *vis-è-vis* their political masters and the member states. By the time a dossier has reached the COREPER level, the ambassadors have a keen sense of the limits at which compromise must be reached and they work collectively to ensure that the political level can solve the outstanding issues. They are very sensitive to each other's problems and will work to help the state in the most exposed position. Given the technical nature of much of the business in COREPER I, the deputy representative has to develop considerable knowledge of the nitty gritty of proposals so that he is not co-opted by the technical ministries. Inevitably, the size of the Irish administration and the relatively informality of its operating codes means that there may be a need for fire-fighting when a dossier gets to COREPER.

The working methods of the Irish representation are both collegial and fragmented. They are collegial in so far as the Irish representation is small and intimate, with heavy demands on all officials working there. Relatively junior staff may have responsibility for an important area of work and will be regarded as the key official in that area. The nature of the Council and the diverse background of the staff in the representation mean that it is also fragmented by functional area, with considerable autonomy within each policy domain. Each functional specialist will have to service the relevant committees, monitor developments in the Commission and in the other member states, and keep in touch with the home base. Individual officials are left to get on with their work and will only have to report upwards when COREPER and Council get involved.

The size of the Irish representation imposes its own imperatives on the working methods of the representation. Irish officials are likely to service more committees and thus have to attend more meetings than their counterparts from larger missions. This gives them less time for preparation, consultation, and for writing reports when meetings are over. Each individual official has to develop a strategy for managing overload.

Officials in the representation carry two affiliations: their affiliation to the representation and thus what might be defined as Ireland's collective interest, and their affiliation to their home department. The national lens remains very powerful within the representation as the staff are delegated officials working with their compatriots. One official, who was seconded to the representation and then to the Commission as an expert, said that he only felt that he had left Ireland when he moved to the Commission. This is because each member of the representation is in daily contact with the home department, feeding material back to Dublin for consideration, discussing problem issues, and taking briefings for upcoming meetings. A survey of EU co-ordination units in the domestic ministries underlined the importance of vertical links between the departmental representatives in Brussels and the home department. For all departments, apart from the Attorney General's Office, the departmental attaché in Brussels was the main source of documentation and information on EU developments in the different policy fields. Departments do not feel the need to go via the Foreign Ministry in Dublin.

The management of a Presidency is a major task for the permanent representation because so much of the Council's work is based in Brussels. In the run-up to a Presidency and during the period in office, the representation will be organized as a task force to plan and carry out the responsibilities of the chair. In 1996, Ireland conducted its fifth Presidency of the Council. Ireland has always taken the business of the Presidency very seriously, as it is seen as an opportunity to contribute to the workings of the EU and thus gain in presence and credibility. The Government White Paper on Foreign Policy in 1996 stated that 'The successful conduct of the presidency in the interests of the Union as a whole represents a significant challenge and a major priority for the government' (Foreign Affairs 1996: 60). Planning for the Irish Presidency began in early 1994 with the establishment of an Interdepartmental Co-ordinating Committee and Presidency co-ordinators in all departments. The interdepartmental committee fed into the work of the ministers and secretaries group (GMS), of which the permanent representative was a member. As the main conduit of information/reports from the Council secretariat to the Irish system, the permanent representation formed a key node in the management structure of the Irish Presidency. It was centrally involved in planning the schedule of meetings that would be held under the Presidency in Brussels and in Ireland. Furthermore, it played a very significant role in monitoring EU developments and in feeding these into the Irish system in the run-up to the Presidency. One analysis concluded that:

Participation by the Permanent Representation to the EU at these meetings in Dublin proved to be extremely important for inputting the latest Brussels intelligence to the thinking and planning of departments, as well as feeding into Brussels the concerns and needs of Dublin. The discussions held both at the centre and with individual departments indicated how critical the early warning systems and intelligence gathering role undertaken by the Permanent Representation in Brussels proved to be. (Humphreys 1997: 19)

During the Presidency, a decision was taken to run the Brussels end of the Presidency from the representation and not from Dublin. Hence, the Irish permanent representative was the key person in the management of the Council business conducted in Brussels during Ireland's six months in the chair. Ludlow's judgement of the 1996 Presidency was that:

Ireland passed the test with flying colours because they observed the two golden rules of any successful presidency. Firstly, the presidency is an office of the Union rather than a vehicle for the gratification of national ambitions. Secondly, efficiency is more highly esteemed than proud posturing amongst those most immediately affected . . . The Irish were remarkably efficient and they did not try to impose their own agenda. (Ludlow 1997: 2)

The Irish permanent representative was widely regarded as having done a masterful job in managing COREPER during this period.

Role: Arena or Actor

The staff of the Irish representation interact with the EU system in a number of different ways. Although links are maintained with the Commission in the pre-negotiating phase, the main focus of the representation is on the work of the Council. Officials at the representation regard servicing the Council system as their core business. They must attend and report on the meetings in their area of responsibility. Thus links with the Commission cabinets and services differ from one area to another and from one official to another. Some officials regarded good working relations with the Commission as a vital part of the job whereas others did not see the need for this or consider that they had the time for it. That said, many of them regarded the cabinet as a source of information on sensitive dossiers and as an early warning system on upcoming business. The relationship with the Commission was regarded as complex, requiring a clear understanding of where the other was coming from. Apart from negotiations, the representation is the Commission's first port of call, with formal communications between its services and Ireland.

The relationship with the Council is organic, as the representation is part of the Council system. Staff in the representation attend the Council's working parties on their own or as part of an Irish delegation. The CFSP counsellor attends meetings of the political committee with the political director. In some cases the staff of the representation lead the Irish delegation and in others they provide back-up to the home civil servants. They must also brief the permanent representative or deputy permanent representative on any item within their area on an upcoming COREPER agenda. The work programmes in any particular area of work dictate the work of the representation. In some policy sectors, the agenda of work is relatively predictable, whereas in others it is less so. That said, the intensity of meetings is well signposted, with detailed schedules for each Presidency issued seven months in advance. The Presidency Programme and the Commission's Work Programme set out by sector the anticipated flow of business. Most areas of EU business follow a predetermined cycle of meetings with a stable number of European Councils and Councils, both formal and informal, each year. These high-level ministerial meetings establish the rhythm of work in each sector. Each Presidency wants to be in a position to note a number of achievements in each sector. Experienced officials in the representation have considerable skill in judging when a dossier is ripe for consideration at the upper end of the EU hierarchy.

Relations with the European Parliament have developed as an important responsibility for the representation since the extension of EP powers in the Single Act. The representation has one official whose main task is to maintain contact with the EP, attend sessions in Strasbourg and Brussels, and brief Irish MEPs of the national position on issues emerging in parliamentary committees or in plenary. Because of limited staff resources, those responsible for functional policy areas do not track EP committees as attentively as might be warranted by co-decision. While Ireland would not have been to the fore in promoting the role of the EP, it identified the enhanced role of the Parliament as an important structural change in the EU system relatively quickly. A key feature of successive Irish Presidencies was attention to the EP. During the 1996 Presidency, the representation engaged in a deliberate strategy to familiarize Irish ministers and their staff with key MEPs and their staff.

The relationship between the representation and Dublin is multi-layered. Working from the lower echelons of the hierarchy upwards, each individual member of the representation is responsible for the negotiations in their discrete area of work. In this role, they are a linchpin of communication from the EU to the national and the national to the EU. As a dossier develops, they will seek to identify the key issues for Ireland in each proposal and will work out a response to these issues by consulting their home departments. Irish officials in working parties are not tightly instructed delegates with a negotiating mandate that they must adhere to. They may or may not get written briefings before meetings. They may or may not, in fact, consult with the home department. They operate on a 'need to consult' basis and have all developed a

checklist of the things they must watch out for. Irish officials have more negotiating latitude than many of their counterparts from other member states. The
Irish system operates on the basis that a member of the representation works
within the parameters of departmental and governmental policy, an overall
framework, and does not need highly structured and narrow instructions.
Inevitably there are tensions in the relationship between the representation and
Dublin, as the Brussels-based official is under pressure to aid or facilitate agreement and the home-based desk official may be more wedded to the national
status quo. Working out just when concessions must be made and reservations
lifted is the source of debate and dialogue between the two levels. The relationship between the Foreign Affairs staff in the representation and the Foreign
Ministry is less unusual as Foreign Affairs is used to dealing with overseas missions. The permanent representative and his deputy maintain contact with the
home departments and report on the outcome of all COREPER meetings to
the co-ordination division in Foreign Affairs.

There are differences between the role of the representation in different
policy sectors. Whereas the representation services COREPER I and II, the
other major committees, notably the Special Agricultural Committee, the
Monetary and Economic Committee, and the Article 113 Committee, are
serviced by home-based officials with attendance by an official from the representation as part of the delegation. The mix between representation responsibility and domestic management depends on custom and practice, on the
one hand, and the intensity of meetings, on the other. The Department of Agriculture, which has a central interest in the Union's policy process, maintains
only two staff in the representation. Home-based officials service the SCA and
most of the commodity groups, although the agricultural attachés based in the
representation also service a number of committees in this domain. Because
of the salience of the CAP, there is considerable involvement by Dublin officials in this area. The intensity of meetings is such that a significant number
of home-based officials are involved in Brussels networks.

Justice and Home Affairs (JHA) is an evolving area of EU concern, which has
placed considerable demands on national Justice ministries in the 1990s. The
Irish Ministry of Justice did not maintain an official presence in the representation until 1995 during the preparatory phase for the Irish Presidency. The
weight of JHA work during the Presidency led to the secondment of additional
officials in this area. By 1999, the ministry had three staff, one at counsellor
level, in the representation. These officials are responsible for the third pillar
and those areas that have moved from the third to the first pillar under the
Amsterdam Treaty. Their relationship with the home department is evolving,
given changes in the structures in this field. The core work is still serviced from
Dublin but a growing role for the representation can be anticipated.

Foreign policy is another distinctive area, given the relationship between
the second pillar, the common foreign and security policy, and the external

relations competencies in the first pillar. Following the TEU, an attempt has been made to establish better co-ordination mechanisms between the pillars so that the Union's international role is more effective. This has led to the practice of holding most of the meetings of the political committee and CFSP working parties in Brussels rather than in the capitals holding the Presidency. Because CFSP matters are now filtered through COREPER II to the Council, Ireland has a CFSP counsellor in the representation. This diplomat has responsibility for maintaining links between the political director based in Dublin and the permanent representative. A practice has also developed of holding joint working-party meetings between those responsible for pillars one and two in relation to Latin America, for example. The Irish delegates to such a meeting would be drawn from the political division in Dublin and the representation. Thus a feature of the 1990s was the growing linkage between the political aspects of the Union's foreign policy and traditional external relations.

The analysis of the working methods of the Irish representation and its relationship with Dublin points to a system based on functional autonomy with considerable latitude accorded to individual officials in the conduct of their duties. The representation operates on the basis of a model of trust between Dublin and Brussels, within which negotiating latitude is used. The system is less paper-driven than other systems, with much work done over the telephone. This standard operating style prevails in relation to all routine negotiations but becomes highly formalized on the major dossiers.

The negotiation of the Agenda 2000 package, for example, was managed in Dublin by a tightly co-ordinated group of officials operating across the main government departments, and serviced by the economic division in Foreign Affairs. Managing Agenda 2000 involved very close relations between the key Dublin-based officials and the relevant officials in the representation. Within the Council, Agenda 2000 spawned a number of high-level committees that fed into COREPER and Council such as 'Friends of the Presidency', the Structural Actions Working Group (SAWG), a high-level group of agricultural officials, in addition to the usual committee structure. The Structural Actions Working Group and the Friends of the Presidency were attended by the Finance attaché from the representation who received written briefing from Foreign Affairs in consultation with Agriculture and Finance and reported back to Dublin on the evolution of the negotiations. The output from both these committees was fed into COREPER and Council.

Effectiveness and Capacity to Implement Ambitions

The effectiveness of the Irish representation was greatly enhanced in the 1990s by two rather mundane developments. First, the current permanent representative upgraded the mission's IT and computer facilities which were very weak up to the end of the 1980s, when some reports were still being typed on electronic typewriters and not every member of the representation had a PC. Irish officials, unlike their UK counterparts, cannot draw on secretarial assistance to write up reports late in the evenings. The second very important change was the move in 1995 to the Rue Froissart just opposite the Council building and within range of the Commission and the Parliament. Prior to this time, the representation was located in downtown Brussels, with much time lost in travelling to and from meetings. The physical location of the representation imposed an additional burden on hard-pressed officials.

As regards its ability to implement ambitions, it is not clear that the Irish representation has ambitions beyond promoting within Council deliberations the preferences that emerge from the domestic policy process, and attempting to ensure that such preferences are negotiable in Brussels. In some negotiations, this will be relatively simple, given the match between Irish preferences and the emerging consensus, whereas at other times it may mean defending impossible positions, regardless of the personal views of the negotiator. At times, the permanent representative will work to rein in national demands so that they are more likely to succeed. This can be done by filtering information back to Dublin and by letting Dublin know that 'it was a bad day in COREPER today' or that Ireland was in a minority of one. However, the Irish permanent representative, like his counterparts from the other member states, will bow to the authority of the Irish government while at times letting his EU colleagues know that there is little he can do about the national position. For example, between December 1992 and October 1993, the Irish fought a lengthy battle with the Commission over Ireland's take from the structural funds. In Edinburgh (December 1992) the Irish Prime Minister announced that Ireland would get £8 billion from the Delors 11 package. This represented the same proportion (13 per cent approx) that was received from Delors 1. During the first half of 1993, the Irish representation was telling Dublin that the £8 billion was not likely to be delivered on as the regional affairs directorate had worked out a formula for distributing the aid based on socio-economic indicators. The Prime Minister would clearly lose face if the take from the structural fund was under £8 billion, with the result that the Irish launched what the government press secretary called the 'Irish "we want our £8 billion" Euro offensive' (Duignan 1995: 109). The negotiations were spearheaded by the head of the economics division in Foreign Affairs and Ireland's permanent representative. Both senior diplomats knew from the outset that Irish demands were unrealistic. As part of the campaign, Ireland threatened to veto the whole structural fund package at the June 1993 Foreign Affairs Council unless they got what had been anticipated. Bilateral negotiations in July 1993 left the Irish negotiating team with the impression that Ireland would get £7.8 billion, a figure sufficiently close to the eight billion for the Prime Minister to accept. Although there was nothing on paper, the Irish foreign minister shook hands on the deal with Jacques Delors, witnessed by the Irish permanent representative (Finley 1998: 174–9). By October, it became clear that Ireland would receive substantially less than £7.8 billion, notwithstanding the diplomatic offensive, an offensive that was launched because a Prime Minister could not lose face.

The Irish representation is run on the basis of a small cohesive unit with clearly delineated functional competencies. Although its staff are drawn from many government departments, there is a strong sense that they are there to promote the best interests of 'Ireland Inc.', however defined. Fighting turf battles in Brussels is not characteristic of the administrative culture. Rather, there is a tendency to ensure that there is a clear Irish line on a dossier as it develops. Individual officials differ in their capacity to network and establish key linkages in the other institutions and with other delegations. Those many officials who are comfortable and at ease in the multinational environment in Brussels become 'Brussels insiders', highly skilled at EU negotiations and multi-level politics. All officials maintain close relationships with their home departments, as they will eventually go back to base and will serve out their careers in Dublin. The size of the representation militates against extensive and systematic networking at the pre-negotiating phase, although some officials, notably those from Foreign Affairs, maintain close links with high-ranking Commission officials and the Irish Cabinet. These linkages are used to scout for information about upcoming Commission proposals and to ease the path to agreement on difficult dossiers. The permanent representative and the deputy permanent representative exercise a pivotal role in the hierarchy because of their status and their role in COREPER I and II, through which EU business is filtered to the Council and European Council levels. Ireland's five representatives were all experienced diplomats, who were highly regarded by senior officials in the domestic ministries and by ministers. Their work in COREPER and at Council level brings them into contact with government ministers and senior officials on a continuing basis. The importance of the role of permanent representative can be seen from his membership of GMS, which exercises a central role in managing Ireland's relations with the EU system. The ambassador has an overview of developments in the Union and the attitudes of the other member states. By definition, his counterparts in Dublin are more concerned with the domestic context.

While there are no systematic survey data on the perceived capacity of the Irish representation, Irish officials tend to be cited as good networkers by the officials from other member states. This helps militate against the small size of the representation. Irish officials have also developed effective strategies for dealing with thinly spread human resources. These strategies include careful assessment of the key difficulties for Ireland in any dossier, interventions at meetings on specific details rather than engaging in substantive discussion of the entire proposal, listening carefully to other delegations, and assessing where the final agreement is likely to rest. Irish officials are highly targeted and pragmatic in their approach. Evidence of voting suggests that Irish officials and ministers tend not to vote 'no' or to 'abstain', on the grounds that you get more if you are part of a winning coalition. There is a preference for steering a middle course in negotiations rather than being an outlier. Irish negotiators seek to get the tactics of the negotiations right by tacking to the Commission and like-minded states rather than devoting energy and resources to fighting battles that cannot be won. In comparative terms, the Irish representation is smaller than most and the pattern of instructions is less formal than is the norm in many other member states. That said, unlike the Italian representation, for example, the Irish do not make it up as they go along. All officials in the representation, because of their intensive contact with the home departments, are operating within broad policy principles.

The informal and personal nature of the Irish administration means that the working style of the Irish representation is less bureaucratic than the systems in many of the other member states. The predominant mode is to allow those responsible get on with the job without embedding them in an elaborate system of instructions and committees at national level. This approach is probably well suited to the shifting sands of EU negotiations and provides a measure of flexibility that is an advantage in negotiations. The effectiveness of this is seen in the perception that Ireland 'has an almost legendary status as a country, which consistently succeeds in winning favourable outcomes from EU programmes' (Kelly 1995: 5). The explanation offered for this is that 'it is almost always clear what the Irish demands are, and what scope exists for negotiation', because the 'Irish negotiating position is almost always clearly established in advance, and the Irish delegations are confident in accepting or rejecting compromises' (Kelly 1995). This congratulatory view of the Irish performance has been questioned by one of Ireland's leading historians, who concluded that 'The agile negotiator will appear the more effective performer.' And the 'political skills of Irish representatives in negotiating situations are widely acknowledged. But there seems to be no comparable criterion for assessing the calibre of conceptualization of the Irish case before negotiations begin at all. The Irish fight their ground well. Whether they choose the right ground on which to fight remains more conjectural' (Lee 1985: 5). The thinness of human resources, a pragmatic culture, and a focus on the short term militate against the kind of strategic thinking identified by Lee. Ireland's policy style may have served it well in the past but may be less suitable as Ireland is transformed from a poor and peripheral state into a net contributor of the Union budget. Senior policy-makers have not yet engaged in the process of repositioning Ireland in the EU system.

References

Duignan, S. (1995), *One Spin on the Merry-Go-Round* (Dublin: Blackwater Press).

Finley, F. (1998), *Snakes and Ladders* (Dublin: New Island Books).

Foreign Affairs (1996), *Challenges and Opportunities Abroad: White Paper on Foreign Policy* (Dublin: Government Publications; Pn. 2133).

Humphreys, P. C. (1997) *The Fifth Irish Presidency of the EU: Some Management Lessons* (Dublin: IPA).

Kelly, M. (1995), 'The Irish Performance in the EU', *Searbhis Pubhli*, 15/1: 5–14.

Lee, J. (1985), *Reflections on Ireland in the EEC* (Dublin: ICEM).

Ludlow, P. (1997), *A View from Brussels: A Quarterly Commentary on the EU*, iv (Brussels: CEPS).

Conclusion

Co-ordinating National Action in Brussels—a Comparative Perspective

Hussein Kassim and B. Guy Peters

The purpose of this volume has been to examine how member states attempt to co-ordinate national action at the European level. The preceding chapters have investigated the efforts of eleven governments in this direction, examined the institutions, structures, and processes that they have put in place in Brussels, and assessed their effectiveness. Mapping national co-ordination systems is a necessary first step towards understanding why some countries appear to be better than others at defending their national interests, but is also of more general relevance. At the national level, the way in which national EU policy is made, how national interests are articulated, and the extent to which—indeed, whether—ministers and officials negotiating in Brussels can be held to account at home, are important concerns. This is particularly true in the post-Maastricht era, when 'Europe' has become a salient political issue across the Union, and Brussels a major policy arena in a broad range of sectors, including areas of 'high politics', such as foreign policy, security, monetary policy, and home affairs. At the European level, national co-ordination has systemic implications. Member state strategies and arrangements necessarily affect EU institutions and the EU policy process. The speed at which Council business is transacted, and the effectiveness of co-ordination across policy sectors, for example, depend to a considerable extent on the performance and capacities of the national machinery put in place by the member states—a fact long recognized at the highest levels of the Union but one that has become increasingly urgent with the prospect of further enlargement (European Council 1999). However, the impact of national arrangements is not restricted only to the Council, where the involvement of the member states is 'organic' (Laffan, this volume); it extends also to the Commission, which, it has long been suspected, is 'shot through with national interests' (Wright 1996), and, more recently—if to a significantly lesser extent—the European Parliament.

How member states co-ordinate their European policies in Brussels is, moreover, relevant to the debate between competing conceptualizations of the Union (see Introduction above). According to the intergovernmentalist perspective, state executives bring to the Council table policy preferences that have been decided at home, independently of external influences (Moravscik 1993, 1998). Consultation with domestic societal interests determines the position to be pursued by national governments, which then engage in 'hard bargaining' at the European level to secure their objectives. From this perspective, national co-ordination is a process whereby the national interest is defined domestically and instructions are formulated, which are then transmitted to officials in the permanent representation in Brussels, whose task it is to follow them slavishly. An alternative image draws upon early neofunctionalism (Haas 1958; Lindberg 1970), sociological approaches (Kerremans 1996; Lewis 1998, 1999) and 'fusion' theory (Wessels 1997). It contests the view that preference formation takes place in splendid domestic isolation. The positions adopted by member states on legislative proposals before the EU are not the result of spontaneous domestic invention, nor are they the outcome of purely endogenous processes. Rather, they are influenced by, among other things, agenda-setting on the part of the Commission or the Council Presidency that compels governments to respond to initiatives and formulate their positions in the context of what is negotiable in the Council. The role of the permanent representation, under this conception, is not to push for whatever position has been decided in the national capital, but to inform and advise domestic ministries of what stances are realistic in the light of the aims and strategies of the other players, and to make relevant adjustments to the position defended in Brussels. Officials at the permanent representation are able to play this 'dual role', because they have learnt the written rules and unwritten codes of EU decision-making, and take a long-term view, appreciating that they are involved in an iterative game, and not just a one-off negotiation (Derlien 2000).

This concluding chapter addresses the main issues raised in the Introduction and presents the general findings that emerge from the country studies. It has three main aims. First, it puts forward three arguments on the basis of the national investigations. The first is that that all the member states have responded to the co-ordination need that arises from EU policy-making and most aspire to a careful crafting of policy, but that the nature of their response varies according to the prevailing national attitude to European integration, features of the national political and administrative opportunity structures, policy style, and available resources. The second is that, although there are some similarities between national arrangements with respect to some aspects of organization and core functions, there are also several very substantial differences. Neither the 'convergence hypothesis' nor the 'continuing divergence hypothesis' outlined in the Introduction is confirmed by the case-studies, but there is evidence that many of the factors identified by each are at work. The similarities, which tend to be limited to certain core characteristics, can be explained in terms of the impact of coercion and mimicry, while the differences reflect the influence of domestic structures and national policy ambitions. The third argument is related to effectiveness. Each set of national arrangements has its own particular strengths and weaknesses, but one common factor affecting performance is the efficiency of domestic co-ordination procedures.

The second aim is to consider the wider implications of the findings both for the functioning of the European Union as a system and for theorising about the EU. With respect to the former, national arrangements in Brussels do little to overcome the problem of segmentation that characterizes the Union. Concerning the latter, the case-studies suggest that the intergovernmentalist image is at odds with how national policy preferences are actually formed and the nature of the role played by the permanent representation. The alternative image approach outlined above, and described in the Introduction, offers a better guide on both counts. The third—and final—aim is to compare national co-ordination practices at the domestic level with those found at the European level. The contention put forward in this chapter is that the domestic co-ordination of EU policy is more effective than processes at the European level.

Comparing National Co-ordination at the European Level

The permanent representation is the centrepiece around which all member states attempt to co-ordinate national action in Brussels. It occupies a curious and ambivalent position remarked upon by commentators on the Council and all the contributors to this volume: it is not only a key body in the national administration, but an organic part of the EU system. As Maurer and Wessels observe in their chapter, the permanent representation operates: 'not only *between* "Brussels" and their country, but also *within* a set of EU institutions (Council Secretariat, Council substructures, other permanent representations, Commission cabinets, DGs, European Parliament, parliamentary committees, political groups, Committee of the Regions, ECOSOC), as well as third countries and organizations'. It serves two 'masters' and is 'Janus-faced'. Although confronting similar pressures as a result of its apparently contradictory location, and despite certain common elements, significant differences emerge with respect to the organization, function, and effectiveness of the Brussels-based missions of the member states.

Permanent Representations: Organization

Four organizational aspects of the permanent representation were examined by the contributors: size, composition, personnel policy, and internal co-ordination. Size was investigated, because it may be an important indicator of a member state's desire to co-ordinate national action in Brussels or reflect differing conceptions about how the task should be performed (Introduction, above), and may affect the capacity of the permanent representation to carry out certain activities (see below). Size may also be correlated with age. It is likely that new members favour large missions, since they undergo a proba-tionary period during which they become familiar with the workings of the EU and cultivate European expertise among national officials. With respect to this first feature, country studies showed considerable variation (see Table 12.1). The smallest in the sample were Ireland's—with thirty-five officials—and Belgium—thirty-eight—with only Luxembourg smaller at thirteen. Germany has the largest with eighty-one, while France (seventy-four) and Greece (sixty-eight) come second and third. Finland, Italy, Portugal, Spain, Sweden, and the UK all have complements of more than fifty.

These differences are explained by several factors. Geographical distance is, perhaps, the most important, accounting for the small size of the Belgian permanent representation and the Dutch, the moderate size of the French and British representations, and the large size of the missions of Greece, Italy, and Portugal. Length of membership is also important. New members, such

TABLE 12.1. *Size of permanent representations, June 2000*

Country	No. of officials
Austria	43
Belgium	40
Denmark	41
Finland	54
France	75
Germany	81
Greece	60
Ireland	35
Italy	51
Luxembourg	13
Netherlands	47
Portugal	56
Spain	58
Sweden	54
UK	54

Source: Vachers (2000).

as Portugal in the late 1980s and early 1990s (Magone, this volume), and Austria (Müller, this volume) and Sweden since their accession in 1995 (Mazey, this volume), have relatively large staffs, allowing national officials the opportunity to gain experience of working in Brussels and encouraging the development of a cadre of European specialists that can be deployed in the national administration. It also explains why the permanent representations of new member states have high rates of staff turnover in the years following accession. The experiences of Austria, Portugal, and Sweden show that new members find it necessary to circulate staff through Brussels. The transition from delegation to permanent representation involves a fundamental reorganization and transformation of activities, even where a mission has been long-standing or played a central part in accessions negotiations. Unlike a mission, the permanent representation has to manage participation in the Council in its manifold complexity.

Population size is a further factor (Hayes-Renshaw and Wallace 1997: 222). Luxembourg and Ireland, with the two smallest missions, are the Union's two smallest states (populations 0.4 and 2.6 million respectively), while Germany (81.7), the UK (58.6), France (58.1), and Italy (57.7), at the upper end of the scale, the most populous. The breadth of national interests is also relevant. Hayes-Renshaw and Wallace note that: 'Luxembourg has a fairly limited range of issues in which it is keenly interested, and frequently depends on its Benelux partners to represent it at certain meetings' (1997: 222). Ireland is also selective about the policy areas in which it is active (Laffan, this volume). France, Germany, and the UK, by contrast, have extremely broad interests, and require a large complement of officials to monitor developments and manage business on the spot in Brussels.

As suggested in the Introduction, size is also related to the broader features or purposes of national co-ordination. Spanou, in her chapter, for example, argues that distance alone does not explain the large size of the Greek permanent representation. The need to compensate for deficiencies in domestic co-ordination has been a motivation in posting and sustaining a sizeable complement of officials in Brussels. Kerremans and Beyers, by contrast, note that, although the Belgium's permanent representation is small in comparative terms, it is large given the fact that is located in the national capital alongside domestic ministries.

Size is further affected where a member state is due to hold, or holds, the Council Presidency. All governments draft in extra staff for this purpose (Hayes-Renshaw and Wallace 1997: 222). Portugal added an extra ten officials in advance of assuming the Presidency in the first semester of 2000. France's permanent representation (FRANREP) expanded from a complement of fifty plus to over seventy in preparation for assuming the presidency in the second half of 2000, and Sweden by twenty-two in advance of taking the council chair on 1 January 2001.

Composition was a second feature of the permanent representations examined in the country studies. The provenance of staff is important for several reasons. First, it determines what expertise the government can call on in Brussels. In addition, it has an impact on co-ordination. Where officials come from, who recruits and pays them, and where their primary loyalty rests—member state, ambassador, or home department—affects how easy they are to manage, influences the internal operation of the mission, and shapes its external lines of communication. The permanent representative is invariably a diplomat, and tends to spend a relatively long time in the job, compared to other diplomatic postings.[1] The post is extremely prestigious, very demanding (see Introduction), and 'considered without exception to be one of the most senior and important appointments in each national diplomatic service' (Hayes-Renshaw and Wallace 1997: 219).[2] Incumbents are typically high-fliers with distinguished records of service, able to draw on past European experience—Greece, apparently, is an exception—or exceptional negotiating skills. Belgium's ambassador, Van Daele, who was appointed in 1997, began his career in the Belgian permanent representation, for example, then served at the Belgian embassy in Athens during the accession negotiations with Greece, before returning to the Brussels mission as Antici Group member. After a spell as the spokesman for the foreign minister, he moved to Rome, then to the UN during the Gulf War. He became deputy political director in the Foreign Ministry in 1993, political director in 1994, and a member of Belgium's negotiating team in the 1996 IGC, before replacing Baron de Schoutheete on his retirement. Most member states consider such a background to be essential. As Kerremans and Beyers (this volume) observe:

Experience is important not just because of the jargon and the complexity of the EU, its institutions, its procedures, and its policies but also because the diplomatic network in Brussels is highly competitive. It is a network consisting of experienced diplomats and experts from the different member states and of experienced officials from institutions such as the Commission, the Council, and the European Parliament (the latter is important given the increasing importance of the co-decision procedure). It is equally a network where negotiating skills are tested, almost on a daily basis.

Experience is not the only consideration taken into account when appointing a permanent representative. In some member states, the appointment has a political dimension. In his study of France (this volume), Menon notes that President Mitterrand was keen during the first 'cohabitation' in 1986–8 that

---

[1]   An exception is 'one of the longest serving, Belgium's Joseph van der Meulen (1959–79) [who] was a senior official from the Ministry of Economic Affairs' (Hayes-Renshaw and Wallace 1997: 219).

[2]   As Soetendorp and Andeweg (this volume) observe in the case of the Netherlands that: 'it is the most coveted post for senior Dutch diplomats. It is now considered even more prestigious than the post in Washington.'

FRANREP should be headed by a socialist sympathizer (Lequesne 1993: 194). In Belgium, Kerremans and Beyers note that appointments at this elevated level are subject to the 'Belgian disease'. An overall balance in senior positions must be struck to ensure not only a balance between parties, but that the country's linguistic communities are appropriately represented.

There is greater variation in the appointment of the deputy permanent representative. In most countries—for example, France, Ireland, Portugal, and Sweden—he or she is like the ambassador also a diplomat. However, different conventions apply elsewhere. In the German permanent representation, the position is occupied by an official from the Ministry of Finance—previously the Ministry of the Economy—reflecting the division of responsibilities between foreign and finance ministries in domestic co-ordination (Maurer and Wessels, this volume). Similarly, there is no Foreign Office monopoly at the UK permanent representation, where the deputy ambassador comes either from HM Treasury (e.g. David Bostock 1995–2000) or from the Department of Trade and Industry (e.g. Bill Stow, appointed in 2000). After its accession, Austria appointed two deputies to ensure a balanced ticket between the SPÖ and the ÖVP (Müller, this volume) and to reflect the domestic separation of responsibility for co-ordination between the Socialist-held Chancellery and the Conservative-run Foreign Ministry (Müller 2000).[3] Greece, meanwhile, appoints an economic adviser at the same rank as the deputy ambassador, and entrusts the incumbent with the task of co-ordinating economic affairs inside the permanent representation. This arrangement, as in Germany, reflects the domestic division of labour in EU policy co-ordination.[4]

Junior members of staff in the permanent representations have long ceased to be drawn exclusively from the diplomatic service, but the case-studies show significant variation in the ratio between foreign office officials and those from technical ministries. Hayes-Renshaw and Wallace (1997: 220) argued that, on average, the ratio was approximately 40:60 in favour of technical officials, though they did highlight several exceptions: 'Belgium, because the technicians follow Community business from their ministries in Brussels; Luxembourg, because they have such limited numbers of personnel that they cannot afford to release technicians permanently to Brussels; and Italy, because of the preponderant weight of the Ministry of Foreign Affairs in . . . [European matters].' According to the case-studies conducted by Kerremans and Beyers (Belgium), and della Cananea (Italy) respectively, these observations still hold true, though the star of the Ministry of Foreign Affairs in Italy

---

[3] Since the formation of a new government in Austria in 2000, however, there has been only one deputy.

[4] In the Greek system, the Ministry for Foreign Affairs is responsible for the outward co-ordination of EU policy, while the Ministry of the Economy manages European affairs at home.

has been waning since the 1970s (della Cananea, this volume). Diplomats account for a relatively high proportion of officials in Greece's permanent representation (Spanou, this volume) and a low proportion in Austria's (Müller, this volume). Germany's permanent representation, meanwhile, is dominated by the Ministry of Foreign Affairs and the Economics Ministry.

The proportion of staff drawn from the diplomatic service is not the only indicator of the influence of the foreign ministry within or over the permanent representation. Most missions have a close relationship with the foreign ministry, since the latter controls the communications infrastructure linking the national capital with Brussels and the other European capitals. Often, the representation is formally accountable to the foreign ministry and in most cases—France is an exception—receives its instructions from it. More importantly, however, diplomats occupy influential positions or positions of 'structural power' (Laffan, Menon, this volume) inside the mission. Foreign office officials are typically responsible for political and institutional affairs, administration, and media relations. The Antici Group member invariably, and often the Mertens Group member, is a diplomat. Moreover, it is not unusual for foreign ministry officials to be entrusted with sectoral responsibilities (see below). In Ireland's permanent representation, for example, Laffan notes that the Irish Foreign Ministry has 'tended to play a major role in the development of new policy areas, such as the development of cohesion policy, that are then passed on to the relevant domestic ministry' (this volume).

The range of departments represented in the Brussels mission has continued to grow, reflecting the expanding competencies of the EU. Hayes-Renshaw and Wallace (1997: 221) separated permanent representations into four groups according to the ministries represented: Group I (all member states, 15/15): Foreign Affairs and Economic and Financial Affairs; Group II (14/15): Agriculture and Fisheries and Justice and Home Affairs; Group III (9–13/15): Transport and Communications, Health and Social Affairs, Employment and Labour, Education and Research, Industry and Trade, Energy and Environment; Group IV (in only a few): Regions, Taxation, and Customs questions, National Bank, Cultural Affairs and Merchant Navy. Even since 1997, there has been a significant shift from Group III to Group IV, as the number of departments present in the permanent representation has increased. Most contributors cite the Ministry of Defence, and sometimes Education, as the only departments with no presence in the mission, but even this has begun to change following the implementation of the CFSP provisions of the Amsterdam Treaty and the commitment undertaken by the heads of state and government at the Helsinki European Convention in December 1999 (Forster and Wallace 2000). In December 2000, several representations included officials from the ministry of defence, as well as military officers, in their staffs (Vachers 2000). More relevant, perhaps, is the distinction between those missions which are relatively homogeneous—for example, those of Portugal and the UK, where officials tend to come from the central administration—and those that also include representatives of subnational governments or authorities (Austria, Belgium, Germany, Spain), the national bank (Austria, Italy), and major interest groups (Austria).

Personnel policy—recruitment, career development, and staff development—was a third organizational aspect examined by contributors. As with composition, the method of recruitment has implications for internal co-ordination, the integration of the work of the mission as a whole, and the capacity and willingness of officers to co-ordinate across areas of functional responsibility. If officials are selected by their home ministries and continue to be paid by them, their commitment to the work of the permanent representation as a whole may be weak, and horizontal co-ordination problematic. However, where officials are personally responsible to the permanent representative, the latter must approve their selection or if they are seconded to the permanent representation, loyalty and a general attachment to the Brussels mission may be stronger. A further interest concerns the stage in their career at which officials are posted in Brussels—a preponderance of mid-ranking or senior officials may give the permanent representation enhanced authority in dealing with the national capital—and whether there is a well-established career path for officials wanting to develop EU expertise. The latter is likely to affect the ease with which recruits can be found. It also determines whether officials can be confident not only about seeking a position at the permanent representation, but also in moving to a posting on their return where their European experience will be appreciated.

In a few member states—the UK, for example—domestic departments have a limited role in the recruitment process, and appointments are made by the ambassador. Almost everywhere else, however, line ministries play an active part. In some countries—Austria, Belgium, and Sweden, for example—home departments enjoy virtual autonomy over the selection of personnel in their respective field. In others, including Ireland, Italy, and the Netherlands, ministries take staffing decisions, but the ambassador has a veto that is, in practice, difficult to impose. In France, Greece, and the UK appointments are made directly to the permanent representation and officials are responsible to the ambassador. This is true also of Ireland, though home departments continue to pay the salaries of their officials. In the Netherlands, officials are seconded to the Ministry of Foreign Affairs. This is also the case with Austria. However, Müller notes that the formal authority of the permanent representative is only theoretical, since 'the Ministry for Foreign Affairs has no influence on recruitment of staff members, the length of their service in Brussels, and much of their actual work' (this volume).

In terms of career trajectories, there are strong similarities in the experiences of nationals both at the top and in the more junior ranks of the permanent representation. In all the cases studied, the two top posts tend to be stepping stones towards even more elevated positions. Four examples illustrate the point. A former German permanent representative, Jürgen Trumpf, subsequently became state secretary—the most senior position—in the Foreign Affairs Ministry, and later secretary general of the Council of the European Union. Sir David Hannay UK permanent representative between 1985 and 1990, moved to the UK's permanent representation to the UN in New York, and remains a senior diplomatic figure. His successor, Sir John Kerr, left Brussels in 1995 for the US embassy in Washington and returned to London to head the Foreign and Commonwealth Office. Jan De Bock, a former Belgian deputy permanent representative, was appointed secretary general in Belgium's Foreign Ministry at the end of his term of office.

At more junior levels, with the exception of states that have recently acceded to the Union, there are no administration-wide programmes or schemes designed to promote or develop European expertise, or to support an EU-focused career path. This is somewhat surprising, given both the importance of the EU and recognition in all national capitals that EU work is extremely demanding and requires, in the words of a senior official at UKREP, 'people with higher than the usual self-starting abilities' (interview by the author, 1998).[5] Where it is present, the concern to develop cadres of European expertise exists at the level of individual ministries—see, for example, Soetendorp and Andeweg's discussion of arrangements in the Netherlands (above)—but there are often pronounced differences in departmental attitudes.[6] In the UK, the Ministry of Agriculture, Food, and Fisheries and, to a lesser extent, the Department of Trade and Industry, encourage officials to embark on an EU career track, including a spell at UKREP. MAFF in particular is keen to rotate officials between London and Brussels (Kassim 2000). However, the Home Office still has few officials with European experience—hence, the senior official handling JHA affairs in Brussels comes from the FCO—and civil servants from other ministries where work has only recently developed an EU dimension recount with disbelief the negative reaction of bosses at their home ministry on being notified that they would be taking up a posting at UKREP (Kassim, this volume).

Cross-national, rather than interdepartmental, differences are evident in the treatment of officials returning to the home administration from a stint at the permanent representation. In Ireland, expertise in EU matters is valued, but at the same time the generalist tradition remains strong. Officials who have worked at Ireland's permanent representation are likely eventually to be

---

[5] This has not always been the case. For example, Laffan (this volume) notes that, for a long time, officials in ministries in Dublin regarded Brussels as a cocktail circuit where little work was done and where seconded officials could take time out from 'real work'.

[6] Spanou notes, for example, that envy on the part of home-based bureaucrats of officials who have served at Greece's permanent representation affects the latters' prospects when they return to Athens.

appointed to posts where their European experience will be called upon, but not necessarily immediately upon their return (Laffan, this volume). In Greece, by contrast, as Spanou notes (this volume), officials who have worked at the permanent representation are regarded with distrust or envy, even in departments where European matters are a part of routine business. As a consequence, officials coming to the end of their stint in Brussels often prefer to enter the Commission rather than returning to Greece.

The length of time that officials serve at the permanent representation is of interest for several reasons. Not only is time necessary to master the complexities and intricacies of EU policy-making, but the accumulation of experience by officials in the mission also enhances the value of the representation as an instrument for defending and advancing national interests in Brussels. Respect for the permanent representation in the eyes of civil servants in the ministries at home and its authority within the national system reflect the level of expertise that it commands. A possible problem, however, is that the domestic administration will suspect Brussels-based officials of developing divided loyalties or 'going native'. In addition, there is the danger that the permanent representation as an 'agent' may exploit the asymmetry of information and experience that privileges its officials in relation to their domestic 'principals'.

The country studies show that, at the top, permanent representatives tend to spend a long time in post—though there are some exceptions, for example, Portugal—and longer than they would in 'normal' diplomatic postings. The average tenure is 4.8 years.[7] The reason, noted by several contributors (for example, Kerremans and Beyers, Magone, and Menon), is that COREPER is a small and intimate grouping, where personal reputation plays a crucial part. Its intricate codes must be learnt, credibility needs to be built, and an understanding of how the other members of the club operate must be developed in order for the permanent representative to become an effective operator in this most idiosyncratic milieu. Rapid turnover would not benefit individual members (and would be detrimental to COREPER as an institution)—a fact long appreciated by the member states. The exception made by the Belgian Foreign Service for the permanent representative, who typically serves a six-year term—two years longer than the normal diplomatic turn—and the long tenure of German ambassadors are indicative (Kerremans and Beyers, Maurer and Wessels, this volume). At lower levels, the length of service varies between missions, though in most, a period of high turnover follows after the member state has held the Presidency. In Ireland, officials tend to spend between three and four years in Brussels. Officials at Portugal's permanent representation tend to be there for significantly longer (Magone, this volume).

[7] Author's calculations from figures in de Zwann (1995), Westlake (1995), and Council data.

Most are there for five to six years, but a third have been in Brussels for more than nine.

The organization of work within the permanent representation and particularly the efforts at internal co-ordination are a fourth area of interest. The structures and mechanisms in the mission largely dictate whether meaningful national co-ordination occurs in Brussels at all. Three similarities emerge very strongly from the country studies. The first is that, so far as vertical relations are concerned—with the single exception of Italy (della Cananea, this volume)—the internal structure of the missions is flat. Mazey (this volume) remarks on the 'flat hierarchy' of the Swedish permanent representation and Menon (this volume) the 'short broad pyramid' that characterizes FRANREP. Germany is perhaps an exception, since officials from political and economic affairs are appointed to senior, supervisory positions, while technical experts from the line ministries occupy more junior roles. The 'dual track' (Derlien 2000) that separates officials into two streams is also a common feature even if it is more strongly accentuated in the German permanent representation than elsewhere (Maurer and Wessels, this volume). In all eleven missions, officials fall broadly into two groups. Members of one group work to the ambassador and COREPER II, and of the other to the deputy ambassador and COREPER I.

A second similarity is that junior officials in the missions enjoy considerable autonomy in their day-to-day work. Nearly all contributors highlight the high level of responsibility, independence, and authority that individual attachés enjoy. The volume of business transacted in Council working groups make it impossible for the permanent representative and the deputy to 'see everything or know everything' (Kerremans and Beyers, this volume). Most representations operate a 'need to know' rule, leaving troubleshooting to other actors in the system. In the UK, for example, the European secretariat of the Cabinet Office and, to a lesser extent, the Foreign and Commonwealth Office, sound the alarm if something goes awry in negotiations at official level. Otherwise, ambassadors and deputies are briefed by specialist desk officers on COREPER agenda items in advance of their weekly meeting. In addition, as national representatives on the spot in Brussels, officials at the permanent representation enjoy far greater access to senior officials, ministerial cabinets, or the private office, and even ministers, than would civil servants of the equivalent rank at home—further highlighting their high status.

A third common feature is the strong segmentation that marks horizontal relations within permanent representations. Whether separated into units that reflect the formations of the Council (as in the case, for example, the UK permanent representation) or domestic jurisdictions (as, for example, is the case in the missions of Austria, the Netherlands and Sweden), work in the mission is highly compartmentalized. Desk officers operate within narrow confines, their contacts and interactions bounded by their area of responsibility. In addition, the workload is extremely heavy. This leaves little time for contact with colleagues in other parts of the mission, whose work is dictated by the rhythms and routines of their own Council working groups. The compartmentalization of work is, in many permanent representations, reinforced by the segmented pattern of recruitment described above.

Permanent representations differ in the extent to which they attempt to overcome or mitigate the effects of sectoralization. Some have introduced formal mechanisms to promote the circulation of information. The Dutch permanent representation, for example, holds a daily meeting of its entire body of personnel. The purpose of these 'morning prayers' (Soetendorp and Andeweg, this volume; Wallace 1973: 63)—or, in the secular version, 'thought for the day' (de Zwann 1995: 23)—is to provide:

a forum for an informal exchange of information and views . . . [G]eneral policy lines and goals are discussed, as well as the strategies and tactics to achieve those goals. While the current dossiers that are dealt with by Dutch officials are not discussed in detail, officials do inform each other on these dossiers so that all of them gain a broader view of what is going on in Brussels at that moment. During these meetings, officials also seek advice from each other on how to handle a specific problem they might face. The problem may be with counterparts from other countries, but also with superiors at the ministerial department. As the meeting is confidential and no minutes are taken, officials burdened with what they regard as an impossible instruction from the Hague . . . may seek advice from their colleagues on how to get more leeway. (Andeweg and Soetendorp, this volume)

In other missions, including those of Germany, Ireland, Sweden, and the UK, weekly meetings of all staff members are convened for similar reasons, although their effectiveness is difficult to gauge. Other mechanisms include weekly meetings of the head of sections, as in UKREP, and the appointment of foreign office officials as desk officers in technical areas to break open the 'vertical brotherhoods' (Derlien 2000) that link specialists at the mission with officials in their home ministry. In the case of FRANREP, regional policies, fisheries and environmental policy were all handled by diplomats in 1992 (Lequesne 1993: 197)—a situation that still obtained in the latter two sectors in 2000 (Menon, this volume)—The same is true in Ireland's permanent representation (Laffan, this volume). Informal contacts across sectoral or subsectoral boundaries provide a further means to facilitate horizontal co-ordination. They are a feature of many missions, but are especially important in the permanent representations of Ireland (Laffan, this volume) and the UK (Kassim, this volume). For other member states, the compartmentalization of work is not a cause for anxiety. In the Belgian case, horizontal co-ordination is the responsibility not of the permanent representation, but of domestic ministries or sectoral subsystems at the technical level or the Friday P.11 co-ordination meeting when an issue reaches COREPER (Kerremans and Beyers, this volume; Kerremans 2000).

A further common feature of the way that permanent representations function—and one that is not limited only to vertical, horizontal, or indeed internal, co-ordination—is the role played by the Antici and Mertens group
members. Both are important figures in all missions, as well as playing a vital
role in preparing the work of the Council and assisting the Council Presidency
which is their primary task. Antici and Mertens Group members attend the
briefings organised by the Council Presidency on the eve of COREPER, where
the Presidency runs through the agenda of the forthcoming meeting, discussing each item of business, and highlighting any potential problems.
Member states may signal their particular concerns or reservations at this
point. After the meeting, the Antici or Mertens Group member returns to the
permanent representation, where he or she informs the ambassador or deputy
of any last-minute changes to the agenda and warns of potential problems.
It may be necessary for the group member to liaise with technical officials in
the mission who specialize in the area concerned, or to contact the line ministry or minister, or central co-ordinators in the national capital. In preparing
the ambassador and deputy for meetings of COREPER, the Antici and
Mertens Group members play an important co-ordinating role, collecting
information from technical expects in the sections, troubleshooting, and
bringing domestic ministries into the European level co-ordination process.
Although they perform broadly similar functions, some minor differences in
the status and role of Antici and Mertens Group members are apparent. In
France's permanent representation, for example, the Antici Group member is
responsible for co-ordinating foreign policy more broadly (see Menon, this
volume).

Functions

The activities and responsibilities of the permanent representations are clearly
a central concern in investigating national co-ordination at the European
level. Much of the existing literature, though extremely informative, tends to
treat the roles played by missions as generic.[8] The 'upstream' functions
ascribed to the permanent representation—and discussed in the Introduction—usually include the following:

• A postbox (Spence 1995)
• Providing an official point of contact between government and EU insti-
  tutions and other member states (Wallace 1973: 57)
• Providing a base for national negotiators (Spence 1995; Wright 1996)
• Providing the main negotiators at working-group level (Spence 1995)

---

[8] See e.g. Hayes-Renshaw *et al.* (1989), Hayes-Renshaw and Wallace (1997), Wright
(1996), and Spence (1997).

- A source of information and an antenna (Wright 1996; Wallace 1973)
- A mechanism for sensitizing EU institutions to national policy stances (Wright 1996)
- A point of contact for nationals in the EU institutions
- Interacting directly with representations of other member states (Spence 1995)
- Conducting negotiations in Council working groups and COREPER (Wright 1996: 160)
- Maintaining contact with private interests
- Maintaining links with the press (Spence 1995)

'Downstream' functions include:

- Reporting back to the appropriate national bodies (Wright 1996)
- Advising the national capital
- Participating in domestic co-ordination (Wallace 1973: 57)

The approach taken in the current volume departs from traditional accounts in two ways. First, it problematizes the list of functions typically ascribed to permanent representations. It sets aside the assumption that all tasks are carried out by all permanent representations and suggests the possibility either that not all tasks are performed by all permanent representations or that not all permanent representations perform all of the tasks identified. Second, it regards the functions that they carry out as dimensions rather than attributes. It treats them as characteristics that admit of degree, not as attributes that are either present or absent. This permits a more sensitive appraisal. It allows for the possibility that representations may prioritize some tasks, devote more resources to certain activities, or may perform some functions more or less well.

The findings that emerge support this approach. They suggest that only core 'upstream' functions—postbox, communicating with the Commission and Council, and providing a base for national negotiators—are performed similarly by all permanent representations. Of the remainder, some, such as providing the main negotiators for Council negotiations and interacting directly with representatives of other member states, show significant variation, while others, including maintaining contact with nationals in the EU institutions, the wider sensitizing of EU institutions to national policy stances, attempting to influence the policy agenda, maintaining contact with private interests, maintaining links with the press, and contributing to the running of the Presidency, reveal considerable differences. With respect to 'downstream' functions, there are some similarities in the information-providing and advising function, but very significant differences in the involvement and influence of the permanent representation in domestic co-ordination.

Upstream functions

There is broad similarity between the permanent representations in terms of
the first three 'upstream' functions identified. All the permanent representations studied perform the postbox function. They receive official documentation from the Commission and the Council, which they then distribute to the
relevant bodies at home. The representations are the official point of contact
for communication between the national government and EU institutions and
other member states in Brussels. In practice, however, as indicated in several
of the country studies, the formal channel of communication via the permanent representation has been increasingly circumvented by direct contact on
the part of domestic ministries with interlocutors in the Commission services
or technical experts in the missions of other member states. Moreover, with
few exceptions—Sweden is one (Mazey, this volume) and Italy another (della
Cananea, this volume)—the permanent representation provides a base for
national negotiators. Ministers attending the Council or senior officials participating in the political committee, the monetary and economic committee,
and the Article 133 (formerly, 113) committee, fly out from the national
capital and meet officials from the permanent representation for a briefing on
the topic to be discussed in advance of their Council session. Ministers are
accompanied at the Council by the permanent representative, and officials
from the permanent representation form part of the national delegation
alongside colleagues from the domestic administration at other meetings
within the Council.

Differences in national practice are evident in the performance of other
functions, however. The assumption that the permanent representation provides the main negotiators in meetings in Brussels—the third function—is
confirmed by the case-studies, but the way in which this task is carried out is
subject to three important qualifications. The first is that the technical nature
of some policy areas or some dossiers demands greater expertise than desk
offic-ers at the permanent representation can provide. In these instances,
national experts from the domestic ministries are flown out from the national
capital to attend the relevant meeting, usually to accompany a Brussels-based
colleague. Indeed, some sectoral formations of the Council, notably agriculture, are effectively run from the national capitals (Grant 1997: 147–82; Westlake 1995: 191–210; Hayes-Renshaw and Wallace 1997: 84–6). In other areas,
environmental policy and transport, experts are frequently summoned from
home to head the national delegation or to sit alongside officials from the permanent representation.

The size of the permanent representation is a second qualification. As noted
above, several missions are small, and command insufficient resources to
ensure coverage of all meetings. This is true, for example, of Austria and
Ireland. The consequence is that the fifteen member states are not always rep-

resented at the Council table—a somewhat surprising discovery. Size is not the only organizational feature that affects the capacity of a permanent representation to ensure that meetings are attended. A third factor is composition. Spanou (this volume) argues, for example, that the lack of technical expertise in some areas among its mission staff, combined with lack of support from the national capital, leads to situations where Greece is unrepresented at the Council table.

A further point is that the composition of delegations is often subject to national rules or conventions. Federal states often require that representatives of the subnational authorities are included whenever an issue that falls within their competence is discussed. Thus, the Austrian delegation in COREPER or the Council is likely to include joint representatives of the Länder (Müller, this volume). Similarly, Belgian delegations are likely to include an attaché, whose role is to co-ordinate between Belgium's six governments, when it looks likely that its negotiating brief may have to be revised. German delegations too regularly include a Länder representative where a dossier engages the responsibility of the subnational authorities. In the first half of 1999, Maurer and Wessels report that the Länder were represented at 184 Commission and 118 Council working groups. After devolution, moreover, the UK delegation, may include an official from the Scottish Executive when the dossier under discussion falls within the competence of the Scottish Parliament (e.g. agriculture, fisheries, regional although it was not unusual for Scottish Office officials to attend agriculture or fisheries Councils before 1999 when there was a special Scottish interest). A rather different rule governs the composition of Sweden's delegations. The division of labour between ministries, responsible for the initiation of legislation, and agencies, responsible for regulation and implementation, is reflected in the teams sent to meetings of the Council and the Commission respectively, though this separation has caused problems (Mazey, this volume).

Staff at all permanent representations examined in this volume emphasize the importance of the information-gathering and network-building roles entrusted to them. Collecting intelligence and cultivating contacts are regarded as priorities and justify the presence of the mission on the front line in Brussels. However, the extent of their ambitions, the methods employed, and the resources available for mobilization vary significantly between missions. The UK pursues a maximalist strategy, for example, in relation to both the Commission and the European Parliament. Particular effort is focused on the Commission. UKREP officials maintain an extensive infrastructure of contacts with Commission staff so that legislative activity can be monitored across a broad policy front. At the level of services, desk officers are encouraged to develop relationships with the officials responsible for policy in their area. UK officials are aware that initiatives are formulated by relatively junior officers in the directorates general, and use their contacts to detect where policy initiatives are likely to be launched. Relations are also cultivated at the political level. A good relationship with the UK Commissioners and their cabinets is useful for alerting UKREP officials to possible dangers or providing information that might be valuable in constructing alliances or directing lobbying efforts. With regard to the European Parliament, officials in the institutions section of UKREP are responsible for following the legislation as it passes through the various stages of the parliamentary process, and for monitoring 'what the EP is doing in its committees, in plenary and in its corridors' (interview). Efforts are made to cultivate relations with MEPs in influential positions, such as committee chairs or *rapporteurs*.

UKREP is not alone in recognizing the importance of good relations with EU institutions. The permanent representations of other member states—France (Menon, this volume), Germany (Maurer and Wessels, this volume), and the Netherlands (Andeweg and Soetendorp, this volume)—are also well aware of the value of network-building and cultivate links within the Commission and the Parliament. What distinguishes UKREP, however, is the comprehensive ambition and the scale of the resources committed to information gathering. For other missions—Greece's, for example—developing contacts is a personal matter, dependent on the energies of particular individuals (Spanou, this volume). For others, with fewer material resources, such as Ireland's and Portugal's, other priorities prevail and efforts are directed elsewhere (Laffan and Magone, this volume).

Closely related to establishing and maintaining channels of communication is the function of sensitizing EU institutions to national policy stances (Wright 1996). Again, all permanent representations recognize the importance of ensuring that its interests are effectively represented, but there are significant differences in the scope and energies invested in lobbying EU institutions. In this area too, UKREP has the most ambitious strategy. Recognizing that the best way to influence the content of policy is to intervene at the earliest possible moment, preferably even before a draft text has been composed, UKREP officials are encouraged to use their contacts with Commission officials to detect where policy initiatives are likely to emerge, so that the relevant domestic ministry can be alerted (Hull 1993). Ideally, the early production of a text in treaty language can be used to steer the proposal in a direction favourable to UK interests. Among other member states, only France also has the ambition of influencing the EU policy agenda (Menon, this volume).[9] Other member states attempt to sensitize the Commission to their preferred policy

---

[9] This marks a change of approach that was made only recently. Until the 1990s, France made little attempt to intervene in the earlier technical stages of decision-making and tended to leave it late and aim high (see Schmidt 1996; Menon, this volume). This often proved a successful strategy when Jacques Delors, a close associate of the then French President, François Mitterrand, was Commission President.

at a later stage in process. Ireland, for example, concentrates its efforts at the pre-negotiation phase and 'getting the negotiations right' in the Council (Laffan, this volume) rather than tabling proposals or suggesting action to Commission officials at the pre-drafting phase. Moreover, contact with the Commission is restricted to a limited number of policy sectors—agriculture, fisheries, structural funds—that are salient domestically. Greece, similarly, tends to mobilize later in the process (Spanou, this volume).

Permanent representations are similarly divided in their preparedness to use 'their' member(s) of the Commission to shape policy outcomes favourably. UKREP is prepared to move its lobbying activities up the line from services to cabinet and Commissioner, and to make its case at whichever level is necessary (Kassim, this volume). Whether its efforts are fruitful or not, however, depends on the personalities of the individuals concerned, their relationship with the governing party, and whether an issue is national (e.g. agriculture) or partisan (e.g. social policy). Other permanent representations are more reluctant to lobby the Commission. In the Belgium system, the job of lobbying Commission services is a responsibility of the domestic ministries, not the permanent representation. In addition, the independence of Commissioners is taken extremely seriously. Attempts to influence the Belgian member are considered taboo (Kerremans and Beyers, this volume).[10] In some member states, such as the Netherlands, such inhibitions have disappeared in recent years, and the Dutch permanent representation regards lobbying the Dutch Commissioner as an important means to ensure its interests are advanced (Soetendorp and Andeweg, this volume).

Differences between permanent representations in levels of contact with the European Parliament arise less because of scruples and more due to strategy or the availability of resources. The European Parliament has attracted increasing attention from national governments, particularly in the policy areas where the co-decision procedure applies. Some missions, including France, the UK, Ireland, and the Netherlands, have designated liaison officers, who maintain contact with MEPs, ensure that government concerns are communicated, and monitor the progress of dossiers, while other officials remain free to establish their own links. In the UK case, contacts made by UKREP are supplemented by briefings from Whitehall that are sent to MEPs on all legislative proposals before the EP, the detail of which depends upon the importance of the issue to the UK, as well as by specific briefs sent to members on particular committees. The Dutch permanent representation also has a designated official responsible for liaising with MEPs (Soetendorp and Andeweg, this volume). The German permanent representation is similarly concerned

---

[10] Though as Kerremans and Beyers (this volume) point out, efforts to sway Karel Van Miert were not likely to have been successful. The former Commissioner for Competition, and before that, Transport, was a strongly independent personality.

to ensure that its stance is well known within the Parliament, but requires that all desk officers liaise with MEPs rather than delegating the task to dedicated officers (Maurer and Wessels, this volume). Whichever approach is taken, officials at the permanent representation are likely to make contact with their own nationals in the first instance, whether they are MEPs from the governing party or coalition, or officials holding positions in the Parliament's administration. Nationals in influential positions—committee chairs or *rapporteurs*— are especially likely to be targeted. Some member states—the UK and the Netherlands among them—spread their net more widely than these 'natural assets', and appeal to like-minded MEPs from other states. A few states show little interest in the EP. According to Mazey (this volume), Sweden has few links with MEPs, while Greece's permanent representation lacks the resources to expend on cultivating relations with the Parliament.

Providing a point of contact for nationals working in EU institutions is a commitment undertaken by some, but by no means all, permanent representations, and is pursued with varying degrees of vigour by the former. Some member states take a very active role, first, in trying to establish contact with their nationals, particularly in the Commission. UKREP, for example, has a special unit that offers career support and advice to UK nationals (Kassim, this volume). FRANREP, meanwhile, has since the mid-1990s employed an official to maintain contact with French nationals, monitor their careers, and prompt intervention by the government to ensure that they are promoted at the appropriate stages (Menon, this volume). UKREP organizes regular social events for UK nationals, while FRANREP sends a newsletter to its nationals. As well as providing career support services, both permanent representations are also keen to use their contacts with nationals to ensure that the views of the governments are known inside the Commission. However, officials in both missions are insistent that, while they want to make sure that the government's position on an issue is understood, the intention is not to create or mobilize national networks or *filières nationales* within the institution (Kassim and Menon, this volume). Other missions, such as the Greece's permanent representation, take a more *ad hoc* approach or, as in the case of Belgium, make no particular effort in this direction at all. Ensuring that they are represented at various levels in the Commission in proportion to their share of the EU population is a second concern of some member states. The UK and France are particularly exercised on this point. The UK is under-represented in the middle echelons of the Commission, and UKREP, in close liaison with the Cabinet Office, is active in efforts to improve recruitment through, for example, the European fast stream programme, designed to prepare young high-fliers for the *concours*. France has, in the recent past, become much more concerned about its presence in the Commission bureaucracy. FRANREP is charged with responsibility for tracking upcoming vacancies in senior administrative positions—at A1, A2, and A3 level—in order to alert Paris in good time. It also plays an active role in the recruitment of detached national experts. It identifies areas where secondment opportunities are likely to arise, provides assistance to French detached national experts (DNEs) when they arrive, and helps them find a posting in the national administration at the end of their stay in Brussels (Menon, this volume).

Interacting directly with the representatives of other member states is a function where close convergence between national practices might have been anticipated. Formal interaction takes place routinely between desk officers in Council working groups. Informal communication occurs before, after, and between meetings, most usually over the telephone, and personal contact in the Council building, where all permanent representations have rooms. Differences are evident, however, in the extent to which informal networking is systematically undertaken by national officials at the permanent representation with their opposite numbers from other member states (see Beyers and Dierickx 1998). First, there are differences in the level of institutional support—and money—that is provided for this purpose. Officials at UKREP are given a modest entertainments budget to be used for socializing with their counterparts from other member states. For officials in Greece's permanent representation, there is no such allowance. Second, the nature of the job varies between member states. It is made clear to UKREP officials, for example, that good relations with their opposite numbers is an indispensable prerequisite for doing the job effectively. The practice of leaving a list of contacts for one's successor is not uncommon. Third, attitudes to coalition-building with other member states vary significantly (see Beyers and Dierickx 1998). In UKREP, the view taken by officials is that alliances are to be built with whomsoever is necessary to construct a qualified majority or blocking minority. Where efforts are made to find allies by Greek officials, they are most likely to be sought among other south European states. For other member states, strategic action of this sort is not a priority.

Conducting negotiations in Council working groups and COREPER is a function performed by all permanent representations, subject to the qualifications noted above. In all the cases studied, officials in Brussels influence to some degree the content of the negotiating instructions that they receive (see below). There is also broad similarity between national practices concerning COREPER and ministerial Council meetings. Ambassadors or deputy ambassadors, for example, make last-minute calls to co-ordinating bodies or ministers at home to confirm their instructions or to seek clarification, where necessary. Once in the meeting, delegations may make use of various conventions or understandings to postpone decisions on dossiers where problems have arisen, allowing them to seek authorization from the capital before returning to the subject under discussion.

Differences emerge between member states, however, in terms of the detail or flexibility of instructions, and the amount of latitude allowed to the ambassador or the deputy ambassador or ministers in interpreting or following instructions. UK instructions, for example, generally identify fall-back positions and allow some latitude to the UK permanent representative. Belgium's ambassador, by contrast, is accompanied by officials, whose job it is to make the necessary calls if the agreed position has to be adjusted (Kerremans and Beyers, this volume). Greece's representatives, meanwhile, in COREPER or ministerial meetings, may not receive instructions from the capital at all, particularly in areas that are not regarded as 'high politics', and may decide at the last minute in Brussels what position to pursue (Spanou, this volume). Similarly, it is not unusual, for Ireland's delegation not to receive formal instructions. In the Irish case, however, the close relationship between officials in the permanent representation and the relevant line ministries, and membership of a small élite, assures that Ireland's delegation is well aware of what is acceptable at home (Laffan, this volume). In COREPER, personality can be an important factor that allows some individuals greater latitude in interpreting their instructions. Ambassadors with exceptional diplomatic abilities, long experience of European affairs, and close personal contacts at the highest political level may enjoy a wider margin of manœuvre than their peers. Sir John Kerr and Pierre de Boissieu, former permanent representatives of the UK and France respectively, are two figures that famously enjoyed more discretion than most.

A second difference concerns the autonomy of national delegations in working groups. In member states where line ministries take the lead in defining the stance to be struck in Brussels and where interdepartmental co-ordination is weak, including Austria, Belgium (to some extent), Germany, and Greece, officials in working groups enjoy considerable autonomy. In these countries, EU policy-making is a segmented process. The position defended in Council working groups is decided by the closed vertical networks of officials hailing from the same ministry in the permanent representation and at domestic level. Central co-ordinating structures—committees such as the weekly Tuesday meetings between concerned parties in Austria and Europe delegates in Germany, and the P.11 co-ordination meeting that takes place on Friday in Belgium—either do not effectively come into operation until a dossier has reached COREPER or the preferences of the lead ministry usually carry the day. In other member states, such as France, Ireland, and the UK, the approach to EU policy-making is intergovernmental (Wallace 1973), and strong horizontal co-ordination is necessary to produce a position that is national, rather than departmental. Although lead departments play a key role in defining European policy and in domestic consultation, formal (France and the UK) or informal (Ireland) mechanisms operate to ensure that all concerned parties are consulted and that the resultant position is interdepartmentally agreed. In these cases, national delegations at working-group level must abide by guidelines authorized by central co-ordination.

Contact with private interests is another function of permanent representations that many authors have regarded as generic. The country studies in this volume show in fact that national missions have very different attitudes towards private interests. Three groups can be distinguished. Missions from the first group have structured relations with interest groups or social partners, and where private interests are granted an insider status. Austria takes this approach. An interest-group representative is posted at Austria's permanent representation and is responsible for forwarding information to colleagues involved in domestic co-ordination in Vienna and liaising with the officials in the permanent representation (Müller, this volume). A second group regards good relations with private interests as valuable and sees listening to those interests as part of the permanent representation's vocation, but does not have structured relationship with interest-group representatives. The Dutch and the UK permanent representations fall into this category. Both have special units whose purpose is to offer advice, information, and assistance in applying for EU funding (see Soetendorp and Andeweg, Kassim, this volume). Andeweg and Soetendorp observe that:

The Dutch permanent representation does serve as a centre of expertise for Dutch lobbyists coming to Brussels. They are informed about the current stage of decision-making on the dossier, about the line-up of actors, and an official from the permanent representation may even help them on their way by accompanying them to their first contacts. The permanent representative is a guest at the regular 'Egmont lunch', convened by twenty of the most important . . . 2000 Dutch lobbyists stationed in Brussels.

The German mission is also concerned to maintain contact with private interests (see Maurer and Wessels, this volume), while FRANREP has increasingly moved away from the somewhat dismissive approach to non-public actors that characterized it in the past (see Schmidt 1996) and has adopted a far more active role in relation to private interests (see Menon, this volume). The Belgium permanent representation stays in close touch with interest groups, particularly trade unions, employer organizations, and agricultural representatives (Kerremans and Beyers, this volume). Members of the third group have limited relations with interest groups. Greece's permanent representation is an example. Spanou notes that 'interest promotion is not seen as an integral part of the permanent representation's mission' and suggests that this attitude reflects 'an official mistrust on the part of Greek administrative culture' (this volume). Similar observations are made by Magone (this volume) about Portugal. Sweden's permanent representation also has poor links with private interests in Brussels, a situation which Mazey (this volume) attributes to the existence of formalized consultation at the national level which renders such contacts redundant.

National differences also emerge with respect to the role played by the permanent representation during the Council Presidency. Member states recognize, of course, that the permanent representation has a key role to play during the Presidency. Co-ordination with the Council secretariat and with the Commission, monitoring the European Parliament, and listening to national concerns, are responsibilities that need to be carried out in Brussels. Moreover, assessing whether an issue is ripe for decision and reading national concerns cannot be done effectively at a distance from the Belgian capital. However, member states organize the division of labour between permanent representation and domestic administration very differently. A UK Presidency is essentially run from Whitehall, for example (Kassim, this volume). The Foreign Secretary leads a ministerial group, supported by an official committee that is chaired by the head of the European secretariat. Day-to-day management is carried out from a dedicated unit in the Foreign and Commonwealth Office. When Ireland holds the Presidency, by contrast, its permanent representation is entrusted with far greater responsibility (Laffan, this volume).

Downstream functions

Of the downstream functions identified above, the strongest similarity emerges with respect to the first two: reporting back to the appropriate national bodies and advising the capital on action to be taken. All the permanent representations studied considered relaying intelligence gathered in Brussels to the national capital one of their principal responsibilities. They report back on meetings that take place in Brussels, interpret developments, and comment on the implications for domestic policy and interests (Hayes-Renshaw *et al.* 1989: 179). They also advise domestic actors about what positions are realistic or 'negotiable' in view of the stances taken, or likely to be taken, by the other member states. Moreover, whatever the formal arrangements for relaying information—the requirement in many countries is that reports should be communicated to the ministry of foreign affairs in the capital, whence they are forwarded to the ministries concerned—Brussels-based officials tend to make direct contact with their counterparts in the domestic ministries by mail, fax, or telephone, even where this is explicitly prohibited by national rules governing EU procedures.[11] However, the range of the information that officials in the permanent representations aim to collect varies. Some missions take a maximal approach to gathering information. Officials at UKREP, for example, not only scrutinize the Commission services and the Parliament, and keep in close contact with their counterparts in other missions, but monitor the policy process across the full range of EU action. Others limit their coverage of EU institutions (Greece, Portugal),

---

[11] This is the case in Greece, as Spanou notes in her chapter.

observe only salient sectors (Ireland), or focus principally on later phases of the policy process (Ireland). Belgium's permanent representation limits itself further by offering information only on the political-strategic aspects of dossier, not its content (Kerremans and Beyers, this volume). Variation in the extent to which network-building with officials from other member states is considered the responsibility of a permanent representation—also illustrative of this difference—was noted above.

The content of information conveyed to the capital, and the purposes it is intended to serve, also varies. Reports sent to the capital from FRANREP and UKREP are used to alert the central co-ordinators at home to breaches of interministerial discipline, departures from the agreed national line, or, in the case of the UK, situations where action is necessary to prevent the UK delegation from becoming isolated. Differences are apparent, in addition, in the way that the reporting function is performed even between permanent representations for which it is a priority. UKREP, for example, operates a same-day rule. A report on a meeting in Brussels must be sent to the FCO within twenty-four hours. Officials at FRANREP, however, may take up to three days to forward a *compte rendu*. Menon notes the remarks of one official based in Paris: 'on est souvent mieux informé en lisant *Agence Europe* qu'en attendant le télégram'.

The role of the permanent representation in domestic co-ordination processes—the third downstream function—is where greatest variation is apparent. The differences do not concern personal contact between officials based in Brussels and their counterparts or correspondents at home. Officials at all levels of seniority from a majority of the member states travel back to their home capital on a regular basis.[12] Ambassadors, for example, typically, meet with the Prime Minister and the foreign minister in advance of the European Council or the General Affairs Council. Desk officers too return regularly to discuss issues with technical officials face-to-face. Differences emerge with respect to the pattern of relations with the domestic administration, the role played by the permanent representation within domestic processes, its participation in co-ordinating structures, and the way in which permanent representations influence the definition of the instructions that they are sent. In all four respects, the differences between national practices correlate with a distinction that can broadly be drawn between member states with centralized co-ordination systems and those where EU policy-making is lead department-led. In a small number of member states, central co-ordinators play a role in the national process that extends beyond relaying documents to and from Brussels, and between ministries, to brokering agreements between ministries and, occasionally, imposing solutions. In lead department-led systems, the central co-ordinating machinery—the foreign ministry, the

---

[12] Although, according to Spanou (this volume), Greece may be an exception.

economics or finance ministry, or the Prime Minister's Office—plays a formal role in operating the communications infrastructure or forwarding documents to the relevant departments, but does not contribute towards defining the substance of policy. These organizational differences reflect contrasting understandings of the nature of EU policy-making and national interests. States with centralized systems of co-ordination view the Union as an intergovernmental forum, where the duty of government is to defend a national position that reconciles the perspectives of concerned departments. Others take the view that the principle of departmental sovereignty or autonomy that prevails domestically ought similarly to apply in EU policy-making.

Returning to the first of the differences outlined above—the pattern of relations with the domestic administration—the existence of strong sectoral ties has already been noted. Interaction between desk officers in the permanent representation and their correspondents in the line ministries is a general feature in all national systems of co-ordination. However, in centralized systems, desk officers are also in regular contact with the central co-ordinators. Thus, in France and the UK, officials in Brussels are in constant communication with technical experts in the line ministries, but they also keep the SGCI and the European secretariat, as well as the foreign ministry, informed about developments at the European level. In lead department-led systems, the central co-ordinating machinery is not an important interlocutor for the desk officers at the permanent representation.

Differences between centralized systems and those in which technical ministries take the lead are evident too in the role ascribed to the permanent representation. In member states where technical ministries take the lead, the principal function of the permanent representation is to service the needs of the lead department. Work is oriented around the objectives of the lead department and how they can best be achieved. This orientation is underpinned by recruitment policies and working practices that reinforce sectoral segmentation. In centralized systems, however, the permanent representation is expected to safeguard national interests and to advance the position agreed in interdepartmental forums. Desk officers are, of course, responsible for supplying information and offering advice to technical experts in the ministries. The difference is that they have additional duties. In the UK, for example, UKREP is one of three co-ordinating bodies, alongside the FCO and the European secretariat—the latter being the senior partner of the *troika* (Bender 1991, 1996). Officials in UKREP and FRANREP play a troubleshooting role, according to which they inform the central co-ordinators at home if representatives in Brussels stray from the agreed line or seem to be isolated, raising the threat that the national delegation may be sidelined.

A third area of difference concerns the participation of the permanent representation in the formal structures of domestic co-ordination. In all member states, interdepartmental committees are a feature of the formal process, even though their role and the authority that they exercise varies considerably (see Kassim 2000). They differ in regard to function (venue for information exchange, bargaining, problem-solving, conflict resolution), structure (number of tiers), location in the EU policy cycle (pre-proposal, pre-negotiation, Council working-group level, COREPER), and importance (one and only forum or one of many?). The permanent representation may or may not be a member of these formal interdepartmental structures. In the UK, officials from the permanent representation attend cabinet committee formations at all levels. In the Netherlands, however, the permanent representation is a member of the more senior interministerial formations, REIA (Raad voor Europese en Internale Aagelegenheden) and 'Co-Co' (the Co-ordination Commiteee for European Integration and Association Issues), which act as courts of appeal if departments cannot reach agreement. In Austria, meanwhile, the permanent representation does not attend the weekly co-ordination meeting. As suggested below, it does not, of course, follow that the mission does not have an input into policy. These arrangements do, however, reflect a particular conception of co-ordination.

The role and influence of the permanent representation in deciding instructions is a fourth area of difference in relation to domestic processes. The variation reflects, and is directly related to, the system of domestic co-ordination. Four groups can broadly be distinguished. The first consists of centralized systems. In these systems, the permanent representation is a participant in formal co-ordination processes, making a direct input into decision-making, and contributing to arbitration between conflicting viewpoints. In the UK, officials from the permanent representation attend meetings convened by the European secretariat as a matter of routine. In addition, the UK permanent representative participates in a Friday meeting in the Cabinet Office—either personally or by video-conference—to discuss the agenda of the coming week's COREPER. In these systems, the permanent representation receives from the central co-ordinating body binding instructions that embody a decision reached by all interested departments, and to which it has contributed both along sectoral channels and in the central co-ordinating process. Sweden also belongs to this group. Policy is made in Stockholm and conveyed to the permanent representation, but officials in Brussels play an influential role in shaping their instructions (Mazey, this volume).

In the second type of system, interdepartmental committees bring together interested parties, which may or may not include the permanent representation, but do not normally have the power to impose solutions where agreement cannot be reached. Power lies largely in the hands of the lead department, which, with the input of its 'placemen' in the permanent representation, decides the content of instructions. The permanent representation is an important actor, but has no arbitrating role and exercises its influence within closed departmental loops. Consequently, desk officers 'will not be surprised by the instructions its receives', as Müller notes with respect to Austria. The same observation applies to Belgium (Kerremans and Beyers, this volume).[13]

The third type is a variant of the second. Systems falling in this category share with the preceding type lead department-led processes, where the preferences of the responsible line ministry cannot usually be overridden in routine co-ordination. They differ, however, in having in place more senior interministerial committees that take charge of political issues, have the authority to resolve conflicts between departments, and act as courts of appeal. Germany, Ireland, and the Netherlands are members of this third group. In Germany—and the Netherlands, as noted above—the permanent representation is a member of the more senior committee. In Germany this is the state secretaries committee, established in 1963, which resolves conflicts in relation to dossiers falling within the ambit of COREPER II. In both systems, the permanent representation has a central co-ordinating responsibility in high politics, but at the technical level it ministers to the needs of the line departments.

Systems where the permanent representation takes the lead role in EU decision-making form the fourth group. This is the case in Portugal and Greece. In the former, the permanent representation occupies a commanding position in the system, because national actors defer to its expertise and on the grounds that its proximity to the EU's decision-making centre gives it privileged knowledge of the state of play in Brussels (Magone, this volume). In the latter, the failures of domestic co-ordination frequently leave Greece's permanent representation with the responsibility for determining the country's stance on EU issues.

The above discussion shows that, although there are some similarities in the roles played by permanent representations, there are often considerable differences in terms of the responsibilities with which they are entrusted, the tasks that they perform, and the scope and range of their activities. It thereby vindicates the alternative approach taken by this volume.

Comparing Permanent Representations: Explaining the Findings

Discovering the extent to which national arrangements have converged is an important concern of this volume. As the introductory chapter showed,

---

[13] At the technical level, desk officers in the Austrian permanent representation co-ordinate the line to be taken in the working group. Policy issues, however, may need to be cleared by senior officials or even the minister's cabinet.

there are good reasons for expecting both strong similarities and striking differences. What emerges from the country studies, however, is neither convergence around a common model nor extreme diversity, but a mixed pattern of similarity and difference. Broad similarities are apparent in the way that permanent representations are organized, staff composition, and performance of certain functions, upstream (postbox, point of official contact in Brussels between government and the EU institutions and other member states, base for national negotiators, providing the main negotiators at working-group level, source of information and antenna) and downstream (reporting back to appropriate national bodies, advising the capital on action to be taken).[14] However, there are important differences, particularly with respect to the internal operation of missions and the functions carried out by them. Upstream, these include the following: sensitizing EU institutions to national policy stances, a point of contact for nationals in the EU institutions, interacting directly with representations of other member states, conducting negotiations in working groups and COREPER, and maintaining contact with private interests. Differences are also evident with respect to the level of participation in domestic co-ordination.

The coexistence of common features and differences between Brussels-based missions can be explained in terms of the institutionalist reasoning—summarized as opposing hypotheses of 'convergence' and 'continuing divergence'—discussed in the Introduction. The similarities relate principally to the basic organization and core responsibilities of the permanent representations—features that are to a large extent imposed by the structure of the EU—and are best explained in terms of the sociological, rather than the rational choice, version. The sociological version anticipates convergence on the grounds that 'institutions that frequently interact or are exposed to each other over time develop similarities in organizational structures, processes, recruitment patterns, structures of meaning, principles of resource allocation, and reform patterns' (Olsen 1997: 161).[15] The mechanisms that bring this about include coercion, in an EU context, the obligations and pressures that flow from rules and regulations (DiMaggio and Powell 1991), and mimicry—the copying by some organizations of the mechanisms or features of other organizations without necessarily improving efficiency (March and Olsen 1989). In addition, frequent contact and interaction between national representatives may lead to the development of common norms, as officials are 'gradually socialized into the shared values and practices of the EU system' (Harmsen 1999: 84).[16] The result may be a 'gradual diffusion of those shared values

---

[14] However, even in these areas, there may be non-negligible differences.

[15] Olsen cites the work of Meyer and Rowan (1977), Thomas *et al.* (1987), DiMaggio and Powell (1991), Brunsson and Olsen (1993), and Scott and Meyer (1994).

[16] See also Haas (1958), Derlien (2000), Kerremans (1996), and Lewis (1998).

within national administrative systems', producing a culture over time that leads eventually to the 'emergence of increasingly similar national structures and processes' (Harmsen 1999: 84).

All three mechanisms identified by the sociological version—coercion, mimicry, and socialization—are in evidence. With respect to the first, member states are compelled to comply with the requirements of the EU system in order to participate in decision-making. The basic structures and institutions of the Union are clearly defined and well entrenched. The roles of national governments within the system, the points in the policy process at which they can intervene, and the form that their input takes are shaped by established rules, conventions, and norms. If a member state is to participate in the EU system, it must have a permanent representation that fulfils certain key obligations and complies with the required institutional form. Although it lies within their collective power to change these routines, member states cannot alter them individually. Individual governments confront the structures of the EU as institution-takers rather than institution-makers. In this sense, within a common environment, the member states are compelled—or 'coerced' (DiMaggio and Powell 1991)—to comply with the rules and adopt similar structures.

In addition to meeting the requirements imposed by the Union, similarities between national arrangements can also be explained by the process of mimicry, the second mechanism, that occurs between organizations that interact in the same institutional field. In such environments, organizations 'learn' from the way in which others confront similar challenges. In the case of national arrangements at the European level, new member states in particular typically borrow from existing members. Both Portugal (Magone, this volume) and Sweden (Mazey, this volume) used the British and French systems as models when they put their own arrangements in place. However, there is no evidence of a general process of 'optimization' (Harmsen 1999: 84)—the rational choice version—by means of which permanent representations copy from their counterparts the structures or procedures that have proved successful. Similarities cannot be explained, therefore, in terms of a gradual convergence around a technical superior model.

Socialization, the third mechanism, is in evidence as a general influence on national officials operating in Brussels, but it is not clear that it has produced institutional or structural change. Its impact is limited to behavioural norms. There is insufficient evidence to suggest that socialization generates a pressure towards convergence in the organization and responsibilities of permanent representations.

The differences relate to features of permanent representations that affect the way that they perform, but which are not crucial to their basic operation in terms of their EU obligations. They can be explained in terms of the 'continuing divergence hypothesis'. From this perspective, variation between national arrangements at the European level is to be expected. The differences that this approach anticipates are likely to be rooted in domestic structures and national idiosyncrasies (Wallace and Hayes-Renshaw 1997; Edwards 1996; Harmsen 1999).[17] Applying the insights of March and Olsen (1989), to national co-ordination systems, Harmsen (1999) argues that the responses of the member states to the demands of EU membership are likely to be interpreted in terms of pre-existing institutional structures and values. It can be expected that the differences that exist between domestic polities will be reproduced in structures in Brussels. Sophisticating this view, cross-national differences in co-ordination in Brussels might be anticipated on the grounds that there are significant differences between the member states in terms of European policy, the domestic political opportunity structure, the administrative opportunity structures, and national policy style.

This approach provides a convincing explanation of the differences found between national institutions, procedures, and processes at the European level. Taking European policy first, the general orientation of government towards Europe is reflected in several features of national arrangements in Brussels. It influences the scope of the permanent representation's activities in Brussels, in particular, the functions of information-gathering and reporting, network-building with institutions, scrutiny of Commission action, and its role in domestic co-ordination. Eurocautious member states, such as France and the UK, have large staffs that closely monitor developments at the European level, develop extensive networks in Brussels, report home frequently, and are closely integrated in the domestic system of European policy formation. This seems to confirm Derlien's suspicion that 'marvellous EU policy co-ordination may be an artefact produced or nurtured by politicians wishing to demonstrate their concern for the national interest to an anxious electorate' (2000: 75). Countries that are more enthusiastic about the European project and where there is a political consensus about the benefits of 'Europe', such as Belgium, and Germany, tend to take a more relaxed approach.

The political opportunity structure (territorial distribution of power, nature of executive, executive–legislative relations, party system) is a second factor. Two aspects are particularly important: the structure of the executive (prime ministerial, collegial, or ministerial) and the territorial organization of the state (unitary or federal). The first affects personnel policy, the internal organization of the permanent representation, and domestic participation. Where the principle of ministerial autonomy is in operation, lead department-led EU policy-making, as in Austria, Belgium, Germany, Greece, and the Netherlands, is the consequence. Decisions about recruitment are made by

---

[17] See Hayes-Renshaw *et al.* (1989: 135): 'It cannot be denied that national traditions and idiosyncrasies have repercussions on both the formal attributes and the behaviour of these missions'.

individual departments, the primary loyalty of desk officers in Brussels is to the home ministry, and horizontal co-ordination inside the mission is weak. This is the case, for example, in Austria, Belgium, and Germany. Where executive power is concentrated, as in Portugal, Sweden, and the UK, EU policy co-ordination can be centralized. Territorial organization has an impact on the composition of permanent representations, since subnational author-ities demand, and on negotiations, which are monitored by subnational authorities to ensure that their interests are safeguarded. Austria, Belgium, and Germany have all developed systems that incorporate subnational govern-ments in national EU policy-making processes. However, the involvement of an additional tier of state actors makes co-ordination extremely difficult. Maurer and Wessels (this volume) note that:

The German European policymaking system suffers from horizontal and vertical fragmentation, old-fashioned and cumbersome procedures, institutional pluralism, and 'negative co-ordination' . . . features [that] are associated with strategic timidity, late preference building and position-taking and, as a result, minority positions in the Council of Ministers. . . . In addition, the constitutionalized (vertical) division of power between the federal level and that of the Länder leads to a complex system involving not only a negotiating structure relating equivalent actors to each other, but also relationship across the hierarchies of governance which prevail at each level.

The challenge of co-ordination in unitary states, such as Portugal and Sweden, is far less daunting, by contrast (see Magone, Mazey, this volume).

The administrative opportunity structure is a third factor, of which domes-tic structures and rivalries, patterns of work, and culture are the relevant aspects. Their impact can most clearly be seen in the internal functioning of the permanent representation, notably, in internal co-ordination, and the interaction between the mission in Brussels and the domestic administration. The instinctive cross-departmental consultation that characterizes UKREP, for example, reflects the UK civil service tradition of information-sharing and positive co-ordination, whereas the segmented character of the Greek mission represents a projection of domestic practices. By contrast, '[t]he Greek admin-istrative system is characterized by . . . sectorization and fragmentation, low coordination, centralization and hierarchical structure, importance of infor-mal networks and personal strategies, as well as weak institutionalization of horizontal and staff functions' (Spanou, this volume)—features that are reproduced at the European level.

The fourth factor is policy style, which is most evident in the disposition of the permanent representation towards interest groups in Brussels. The influence of official attitudes towards private interests leads in four directions. Member states with corporatist structures at home (Austria) host represen-tatives of the social partners in their Brussels mission. Governments (the Netherlands, the UK) that consider that interest groups have a legitimate role, and that it is the duty of the state to represent their interests, tend to offer support and advice to private interests in Brussels. The permanent representations of countries, such as Greece and Portugal, where private interests are generally weak, there is little or no lobbying tradition, and the state is not considered to have an obligation to assist interest groups, do not generally invest time in receiving lobbyists or securing the support of domestic constituencies in Brussels. France and Sweden are anomalies, however. France has a strong statist tradition, but now increasingly offers support to domestic interests at the European level (compare, for example, Schmidt 1996; Menon, this volume). Sweden engages in extensive consultation domestically and therefore sees no point in repeating consultation in Brussels.

A final factor, not incorporated in the institutionalist approach outlined above, but which emerges strongly in the case-studies, is resources. Member states, especially small ones, do not have at their disposal the level of material support that they would like. Ireland is instructive in this connection. Not only is the mission necessarily small, but equipment in terms of secretarial and technical support has often been lacking. Laffan (this volume) notes, for example, that Ireland's permanent representation has simply not been able to provide the same level of reporting as larger missions for this reason.

Effectiveness

No analysis of national co-ordination would be complete without confronting the question of effectiveness, although the problems encountered in attempting to make such an assessment are well known. First, the information necessary to carry out a detailed audit is simply not available. The data that reveal, for example, the respective influence of the member states at each stage of the EU policy process and across a wide range of policy areas, on which an evaluation would need to be based, does not exist. Second, Vincent Wright's dictum about the need to relativize any such appraisal according to specific issues, policy types, requirements, and objectives, is validated by the country studies. A single measure of effectiveness would not to be appropriate in the light of such divergent ambitions. Some member states (e.g. France and the UK) have globalizing interests, some prioritize polity over policy issues (e.g. Germany, Italy), and others concentrate only on those sectors that are salient domestically (e.g. Ireland). Moreover, those that take an instrumentalist approach to membership of the Union are interested in immediate, tangible benefits, while those that regard European integration as intrinsically valuable may be less worried about parading the spoils and more concerned with 'staying in the game' (Peters, cited in Derlien 2000).

It does not follow from these considerations, however, that no observations about the effectiveness of national arrangements at the European level are possible. The discussion above has already drawn attention to the differences in the resources that member states command in Brussels, and it does not seem unreasonable to suppose that their effectiveness in advancing their interests is at least partly dependent on this capacity. The number of staff at the permanent representation is one dimension, but also relevant is the spread and depth of expertise that is available. The networks that can be mobilized by Brussels-based officials to collect information, persuade negotiating partners of the merits of a national position, or build coalitions, also form an important resource. In addition, the amount of institutional support provided by the national capital can strengthen the permanent representation.

Further general observations about effectiveness can be made in relation to the type of strategy that member states pursue at the European level. A broad distinction can be drawn between those that take a centralized approach—the UK, France, Portugal—and those where the lead department plays the key role in co-ordination—Austria, Belgium, the Netherlands. Their relative merits have been discussed in detail elsewhere (see especially Wright 1996), but are worth summarizing here briefly. Centralized systems are effective in that they ensure the production of a policy that is binding on all representatives, that it is coherently presented and consistent with wider policy objectives, and that it is communicated effectively in Brussels. Centralization also makes strategic action across several sectors a possibility. Co-ordinators collect information centrally and have a synoptic view of the state of negotiations across Council formations. However, centralization *per se* provides no guarantee of quality, nor that the positions produced are 'negotiable'. It also requires a comprehensive institutional infrastructure and makes extremely exacting demands on officials. Moreover, difficulties are likely to arise when the centre is 'divided', 'paralysed', or 'inept' (Wright 1996: 161), and centralized systems tend to be more prone to dogmatism and inflexibility. Furthermore, a centralized approach that stresses *ex ante* co-ordination may be counter-productive in the EU setting, 'for it leaves little room for the recurrent, multi-issue bargaining process at the European level and the informal norm of reciprocity' (Derlien, cited in Kassim 2000: 255).

Decentralized systems, by contrast, are more flexible. They do not require a vast administrative apparatus, or strict discipline. They can be more responsive as negotiations develop, and their officials more attuned to the coalition-building and bargaining that characterizes the EU. Moreover, within a sectoralized decision-making environment, a decentralized approach may offer a greater change of securing national interests, since 'hundreds of arrows may be more effective than one shot with Big Berta' (Derlien, cited in Kassim 2000: 255). However, there are also disadvantages. First, the possibility of playing a grand strategic game—making concessions at one table in exchange for gains at another—is distant in the absence of a central authority (see Müller, this volume). Second, striking contradictory positions in different

Council forums may result in a loss of credibility. Third, the stances struck by officials may be regarded by negotiating partners as provisional, pending final resolution at home.

More concretely, whichever of the above strategies is pursued, two gener-alizations concerning effectiveness at the European level emerge from the case-studies. The first is that the quality of national co-ordination in Brussels depends to a very large degree on domestic co-ordination processes and wider features of the political system at home. The performance of Italy's perma-nent representation, for example, has been adversely affected by time-consuming domestic procedures and competition between competing author-ities (della Cananea, this volume). Greece's mission, similarly, is inhibited *inter alia* by the uneven engagement on European matters of ministries in Athens, a fragmented administration, and the lack of political leadership (Spanou, this volume). A lack of understanding on the part of domestic officials about the speed at which Council business moves and the urgency with which information needs to be communicated between the national capital and the mission in Brussels has also been a problem for Austria (Müller, this volume) and Sweden (Mazey, this volume). As an experienced official has noted, delays at home can prevent active participation in Brussels (González-Sánchez 1992: 393).

Second, it should not be presumed that co-ordination is more effective in unitary than in federal states. Although co-ordination is relatively straight-forward in some countries that have unitary systems, for example, Ireland and Portugal, the same is not true of Greece. Also, although the co-ordination of European policy is not rated efficient in either Germany or Italy, Belgium with a more complex structure of governance has developed relatively effective mechanisms. Similarly, it should not be assumed that ministerial autonomy, as opposed to prime ministerial authority, produces ineffective co-ordination. The Dutch case demonstrates that effective co-ordination and collegial government can coexist.

A third observation is that administrative efficiency—effective co-ordination—is, of itself, no guarantee of influence. As Vincent Wright has observed (1996: 165): '[m]erely, to examine the machinery of co-ordination is to confuse the means and the outcomes'. The UK provides a particularly good example of this distinction. Its co-ordination system has attracted admiration from all quarters for its efficiency, but it has not followed that the UK has been able to shape EU policy favourably. Its reputation as 'an awkward partner' (George 1992) notwithstanding, the lack of policy congru-ence between the UK and its European partners in many policy domains—the internal market is a very significant exception—combined with its preference for intergovernmental over supranational solutions are far more important in this respect. No matter how skilled the messenger, the message is what counts.

TABLE 12.2. *The growth of Permanent Representations, 1958–2000*

	1958	1968	1978	1988	1998	2000
Belgium	6	17	24	27	35	53
France	5	19	26	28	—	89
Germany	5	28	41	42	—	87
Ireland	—	—	22	24	32	35
Italy	5	23	27	36	47	62
Luxembourg	1	3	2	2	12	13
The Netherlands	5	19	20	24	46	50
Denmark	—	—	26	32	—	47
United Kingdom	—	—	—	40	57	56
Greece	—	—	—	59	55	62
Portugal	—	—	—	37	48	49
Spain	—	—	—	32	61	63
Austria	—	—	—	—	53	41
Finland	—	—	—	—	—	51
Sweden	—	—	—	—	50	66

Source: 1958, 1968 Salmon (1971: 583–9); 1978, 1988, 1998, 2000 *Vacher's European Companion* (various).

Another way to approach the question of effectiveness is to consider the strengths and weaknesses of national systems. Table 12.2 summarizes some of the main features highlighted by the contributors in their country studies.

The National Co-ordination of EU Policy: The Wider Implications

The way in which member states co-ordinate action at the European level not only has consequences for their respective abilities to ensure that national interests are effectively represented and defended in Brussels. It also influences the functioning of EU institutions, especially—but not only—the Council, and, thereby, the Union as a system. In what they reveal about the role perceptions of officials in the permanent presentations and the functions performed by the Brussels-based missions, moreover, the country studies are extremely relevant to theoretical debates about the nature of the Union. Finally, a comparison of national co-ordination at the domestic and the European levels yields an interesting paradox in terms of the adjustment of organizations to their respective environments.

Systemic Implications

Two implications of the country studies are especially noteworthy. The first concerns the strong sectoral segmentation that marks national action in Brussels and the general weakness of horizontal co-ordination. As the preceding chapters have emphasized, a desk officer's routine, working relationships, and cognitive world are shaped by the working group that he or she covers. Contact between officials across, or even within, sections is rare. A few missions have horizontal mechanisms that are intended to exchange information between policy areas, but these are not designed to bring about co-ordination between officials. Though all dossiers are channelled through the ambassador and deputy ambassador, moreover, this 'dual track' is not a substitute for comprehensive intersectoral co-ordination, since attention is concentrated at this level on 'B' items which constitute a quarter of all business decided by the Council. If national co-ordination structures provide the 'backbone' of the Council (European Council 1999: 6), it is not at the European level that the member states co-ordinate what the Council fails so to do.

The second implication relates to the criticism that the EU is a 'mandarin's paradise' (Benn, cited in Young and Sloman 1982: 75; see also Van Schendlen 1996; Leonard 1998). According to this view, three-quarters of decisions taken by Council are made by unelected officials, whose actions are not scrutinized and who cannot be held accountable. However, though it is true that systems of parliamentary scrutiny vary considerably in relation to EU business[18]—compare, for example, Denmark (Pedersen 2000) and Portugal (Magone, this volume)—what emerges from the country studies in this volume is that the position adopted by national officials in Council negotiations is not decided by them alone. Officials routinely seek clearance from ministers or their representatives, and significant concessions must be authorized—and member states have put in place the mechanisms to achieve this. Moreover, in centralized systems, the stance taken by the national delegation has been agreed by the central co-ordinating body. In addition, a number of well-known cases show that ultimate authority lies in the national capital. The UK's boycott of EU business undertaken by the Major government in response to the EU's ban on the export of British beef, the ill-fated federalist blueprint brought forward by the Dutch government at Maastricht (Andeweg and Soetendorp, this volume), and the Irish PM's call for changes in the structural funds (Laffan, this volume), were undertaken despite contrary advice from officials in the respective permanent representations.

---

[18] As one former foreign secretary noted, what was most on his mind while negotiation in European forums was not what Margaret Thatcher's response was likely to be, but how Parliament would react (interview conducted by the author, London, 1999).

TABLE 12.3. *Main features, strengths, and weaknesses of national co-ordination in Brussels*

Member State	Observations
Austria	Ministerial autonomy reflected in domestic EU policy-making arrangements and internal organisation of Permanent Representation. Weakness of intersectoral co-operation leads to inability to act strategically across Council formations. Permanent Representation limited role in domestic system, and constrained by slowness of inter-departmental co-ordination of EU policy in Vienna. Weak networking in Brussels. Presence of Lander representatives and social partners in Permanent Representation.
Belgium	Complex system of co-ordination involving co-equal federal governments and sub-national governments. Effective mechanisms at domestic level (P. 11 meetings in advance of COREPER) and at European level (delegation includes attaché responsible for securing clearance from relevant authorities for departures from collectively agreed instructions if necessary). Permanent Representation plays limited role on account of lead role played by departments and location, and does not have authority to arbitrate between ministries. Contact on part of Permanent Representation with nationals in Commission services and College taboo.
France	Aspiration to speak with single voice. Co-ordination centred in SGCI in Paris. Permanent Representation has important input into domestic co-ordination processes and information-providing function, though reporting system is not as effective as that of the UK. Attempt to cultivate relations with nationals in Commission services and College. Efforts to improve recruitment of French administrators by Commission. Recent opening to private interests. Foreign Ministry occupies positions of key importance in the mission.
Germany	Domestic dual track co-ordination—Finance Ministry and Foreign Ministry—against background of autonomous line ministries, reflected in Permanent Representation. Horizontal and vertical fragmentation, and institutional pluralism leads to late preference building and position taking, and weakens Permanent Representation. Lander have well-developed foreign relations systems with major presence in Permanent Representation, as well as own independent missions in Brussels. Permanent Representation is important influence in formulation of European policy.

TABLE 12.3. (*Cont.*)

Member State	Observations
Greece	Large Permanent Representation undermined by lack of institutional and financial support from Athens, and poor domestic co-ordination characterised by absence of political leadership and fragmented national administration. Permanent Representation cannot provide expert negotiators across the board, and does not attempt systematically to cultivate relations with nationals in EU institutions. Inter-ministerial rivalries, particularly between Foreign Minsistry and Ministry for the National Economy, an internal feature of the Permanent Representation. Contact with private interests eschewed.
Ireland	Co-ordination restricted to areas of national interest and generally informal within small political and administrative elite, circulating between Dublin and Brussels. Small Permanent Representation with limited resources focuses on a few select issues. Reactive—definition of 'Irish angle—as policy discussion develops—rather than entrepreneurial in EU policy process. Limited ability to establish relations with Irish nationals in EU institutions.
Italy	Ability to mobilise in matters of 'high politics' not matched in routine co-ordination. Effectiveness of Permanent Representation weakened by inter-ministerial rivalries and cross-cutting competencies in Rome, especially between Prime Minister's Office and Foreign Ministry, and weak, cumbersome domestic co-ordination procedures. Conflicting relations reflected within Italian mission. Permanent Representation unusually hierarchical, and reactive.
Netherlands	Effective, if complex, domestic co-ordination mechanisms provide framework for co-operation between autonomous ministries in EU policy making, and supports work of Permanent Representation. Small Permanent Representation has developed strong *esprit de* corps that mitigates departmentism. Close relations with nationals in Commission services and, more recently, the College. Also directs efforts towards European Parliament, and not only Dutch MEPs. Its involvement in the EU policy process tend, however, to be reactive. The Permanent Representation has very open relationship with private interests.

Table 12.3. (*Cont.*)

Member State	Observations
Portugal	Centralised, sectorally-selective, co-ordination ambition met largely through effective domestic arrangements centred in the Foreign Ministry and Permanent Representation, respected on account of its specialist knowledge, expertise, and proximity to EU decision-making centre. Unitary state structure and low levels of associationalism limit complexity of European policy formulation. Networking in Brussels very restricted.
Sweden	Early post-accession strategy—attempt to handle EU matters within existing system of domestic co-ordination, and slow processing of information—proved problematic. Reform led to streamlining and introduction of more centralised arrangements. No networks in Brussels, and no special effort at openness to social partners or private interests in Brussels level on grounds that consultation takes place in Stockholm.
United Kingdom	Comprehensive co-ordination ambition. Aim as soon as possible to reach inter-departmentally agreed position, consistent with domestic policy, that defended coherently by UK representatives in Brussels. Permanent Representation important role in central co-ordinating triad with European Secretariat and Foreign and Commonwealth Office, as well as close relationship with Whitehall departments. Information provision subject to 24-hour reporting rule. UKREP officials network extensively with EU institutions with particular focus on the Commission, as part of strategy to influence policy intiation. Emphases on early reaction and coherence can produce 'trigger happy' tendency and inflexibility. Centrality of Whitehall and UKREP preserved after devolution.

Source: above chapters.

National Co-ordination and Competing Images of the EU

Two competing conceptualizations of the European Union—the intergovern-mentalist and an alternative approach—were described in the Introduction and outlined briefly at the beginning of the chapter. As noted, they offer very different understandings of two issues relevant to the current volume: first, the role of national officials; and second, the process of preference formation. In both cases, the country studies support the alternative view. With respect to the first, the preceding chapters emphasize that, while officials at the permanent representation owe their primary loyalty to their member state, they do not see themselves narrowly as national servants. Rather, they become socialized into EU norms and are committed to the success of the overall project rather than seeking only to advance national goals. They operate in two assumptive or cognitive worlds, promoting the interests of their member state, but also observing EU codes and values. National officials do not only represent national views to the European Union, but represent EU perspectives to their governments.

Concerning the second, the intergovernmentalist view that national preferences are fixed in a first domestic game, then defended in 'hard bargaining' by national officials in Council negotiations in a second game at the European level (Putnam 1988; Moravscik 1993, 1998), is strongly contested by the findings of the country studies. Setting aside the problematic intergovernmentalist assumption that national preferences are the result of spontaneous domestic processes and are not developed in reaction to EU initiatives, the idea that the position advanced by national delegations in Brussels is the product of a processes that are strictly domestic is hard to sustain in the light of evidence provided in the preceding chapters. One of the principal responsibilities of officials in the permanent representation is to inform the national capital of what positions are, and are not, negotiable in the light of the aims and objectives of other actors. The knowledge of what stance is realistic in European terms is used by national governments not only to determine their negotiating strategies, but to adjust and adopt the content of policy. Of course, the precise influence exercised by Brussels-based officials varies across time, from country to country, sector to sector, and dossier to dossier. However, all the country studies report that member states not only sensitize EU institutions to national concerns, but relay European-level considerations to domestic policy-makers and participate in the shaping of national preferences. To cite one of many examples, Menon (this volume) quotes an official at FRANREP who declared that: 'I have been surprised, since my arrival [in Brussels], by the degree to which our work involves formulating policy with Paris as opposed to simply executing policies formulated in Paris.'[19] National preferences do not emerge as the result of an introspective domestic process, but are forged within a specifically European context (Sandholtz 1996). The nature of the EU makes permanent two-way communication between national capital and Brussels essential. The European policy cycle is long and generates its own dynamics. Officials based in Brussels make a vital contribution to shaping national policy by providing up-to-date information on the prospects of achieving national

---

[19] Mazey (this volume) in the same vein quotes a Swedish official at the permanent representation: 'the work of the committee is so specalized that the Ministry relies upon me to decide what we should do'.

objectives in the light of changing moods and shifting alliances. Andeweg and Soetendorp report that 'officials in the Dutch permanent representation . . . emphasize that they do not serve as robotic messengers, as their national masters' voice in Brussels' (this volume) can be generalized.

National Co-ordination at Domestic and European Levels

Comparison between the findings of the current book and the companion volume, which investigated the national co-ordination of EU policy at the domestic level, reveals an interesting paradox—namely, that that co-ordination tends to be more successful at home than in Brussels—or at least apparent paradox, about this aspect of European policy-making. On the one hand, governments in most countries appear to have been very successful in creating co-ordination in some form at the national level. Most have been able to create institutions and procedures that are generally effective in co-ordinating the range of policy views coming from within government. Although certainly variable, this capacity tended to be present even in countries that were not particularly committed to imposing a central conception over European policy. On the other hand, the findings presented in this volume were that the co-ordination created at home tended to fall apart rather quickly once the arena was moved to Brussels. The basic agreement reached at home may not vanish entirely, but at least the ministries from the home governments were able to restore a substantial level of control over policy that they might have lost in the national co-ordination process.

This well-developed capacity to co-ordinate effectively at home was perhaps less anticipated than the failures of co-ordination at Brussels. The finding of relatively high levels of success was all the more surprising given that there were several different ways of organizing, all of which seemed to produce some benefits. Further, this co-ordination is occurring in the context of more conventional national politics in which the ministerial 'stove pipes' tend to be well institutionalized and generally successful in protecting their own interests against central agencies and other attempts to impose control over then. On the other hand, once moved to Brussels the issues have been moved more into the realm of foreign affairs where it would be more expected for ministries to stick together to preserve the national interest in the face of the 'foreigners'. The actual findings were, as pointed out, exactly the opposite of those expectations.

The conventional argument in organizational sociology is that institutions are isomorphic and tend to replicate the structures with which they interact (Dimaggio and Powell 1991). The interesting finding here is that in these cases the institutions or organizations in question appear to replicate the institutions that are further away rather than those that are more proximate.

That is, the institutions in the national capital tend to replicate the more centralizing needs of Brussels, while those located in Brussels tend to replicate very closely the ministerial structures of the national government. From these findings we can draw two conclusions. The first is that the choice of institutional structures is not as automatic as some of the sociological literature assumes, and the actors involved are choosing how to structure themselves to achieve their own political purposes. In particular, at the domestic level co-ordination structures are making clear choices to overcome, rather than replicate, the ministerial structure that they encounter there. Likewise, the permanent representations may need to build stronger political links with ministries given that they lack the political 'clout' of central agencies such as finance.

The second conclusion is to emphasize the importance of the lead ministry in the permanent representations. This conclusion, in turn, emphasizes another dimension of the literature of organizational theory, namely, the importance of organizational routines. The co-ordination efforts at the national capitals level are driven largely by central agencies whose principal purposes are co-ordination and control of other organizations in the public sector. On the other hand, the leadership of foreign affairs personnel in the Brussels representations is leadership coming from a ministry that typically is not a central agency and whose style of action is more that of a functional, line ministry. Therefore, the routines of these organizations are very different and their natural inclinations with respect to co-ordination are very different.

Conclusion

This volume has attempted to contribute towards remedying the neglect of an aspect of the EU system that has considerable significance for the individual member states, the European Union, and theorizing about European integration. Although it has revealed some similarities between national arrangements at the European level, very significant differences between the member states remain. Since these are deeply rooted in enduring national characteristics, the predominant pattern of differentation looks likely to persist.

References

Bender, B. (1991), 'Whitehall, Central Government and 1992', *Public Policy and Administration*, 6/1: 13–20.

Bender, B. (1996), 'Co-ordination of European Union Policy in Whitehall', text of a lecture given by Brian Bender, Head of the European Secretariat, at St Antony's College on 5 February 1996.

Beyers, Jan, and Dierickx, Guido (1998), 'The Working Groups of the Council of the European Union: Supranational or Intergovernmental Negotiations?', *Journal of Common Market Studies*, 36/3: 289–318.

Brunsson, N., and Olsen, J. P. (1993), *The Reforming Organization* (London: Routledge).

Derlien, Hans-Ulrich (2000), 'Germany: Failing Successfully?', in H. Kassim, B. G. Peters, and V. Wright (eds.), *The National Co-ordination of EU Policy: The Domestic Level* (Oxford: Oxford University Press), 54–78.

de Zwann (1995), *The Permanent Representatives Committee: Its Role in European Union Decision-Making* (Amsterdam: Elsevier).

DiMaggio, Paul J., and Powell, Walter W. (1991), 'The Iron Cage Revisited: Institutional Isomorphism and Collective Rationality', in W. W. Walter and P. J. DiMaggio (eds.), *The New Institutionalism in Organizational Analysis* (Chicago: University of Chicago Press), 63–82.

Edwards, Geoffrey (1996), 'National Sovereignty vs. Integration? The Council of Ministers', in J. Richardson (ed.), *The European Union: Power and Policy Making* (London: Routledge), 127–47.

European Council (1999), *Presidency Conclusions: Helsinki European Council, 10 and 11 December 1999*, Council of the European Union website, http.//europa.eu.int/council/off/conclu/index.htm

European Voice (2000), 'Berlin's Record Run of Defeats' (5–11 Oct.), 2.

George, S. (ed.) (1992), *Britain and the European Community: The Politics of Semi-Detachment* (Oxford: Oxford University Press).

González-Sánchez, Enrique (1992), 'La négociation des décisions communautaires par les fonctionnaires nationaux: Les Groupes de travail du Conseil', *Revue française d'administration publique*, 63: 391–400.

Grant, Wyn (1997), *The Common Agricultural Policy* (Basingstoke: Macmillan).

Haas, E. B. (1958), *The Uniting of Europe* (Stanford, Calif.: Stanford University Press).

Harmsen, R. (1999), 'The Europeanization of National Administrations: A Comparative Study of France and the Netherlands', *Governance*, 12/1: 81–113.

Hayes-Renshaw, Fiona, and Wallace, Helen (1997), *The Council of Ministers* (Basingstoke: Macmillan).

Hayes-Renshaw, Fiona, Lequesne, Christian, and Mayor Lopez, Pedro (1989), 'The Permanent Representations of the Member States to the European Communities', *Journal of Common Market Studies*, 28/2: 119–37.

Hull, Robert (1993), 'Lobbying Brussels: A View from Within', in S. Mazey and J. Richardson (eds.), *Lobbying in the European Community* (Oxford: Oxford University Press), 82–92.

Kassim, Hussein (2000a), 'The United Kingdom', in H. Kassim, B. Guy, and V. Wright (eds.), *The National Co-ordination of EU Policy: The Domestic Level* (Oxford: Oxford University Press), 22–53.

—— (2000b), 'Conclusion: The National Co-ordination of EU Policy: Confronting the Challenge', in H. Kassim, B. Guy, and V. Wright (eds.), *The National Co-ordination of EU Policy: The Domestic Level* (Oxford: Oxford University Press), 235–64.

Kerremans, Bart (1996), 'Do Institutions Make a Difference? Non-Institutionalism, Neo-Institutionalism and the Logic of Common Decision Making in the EU', *Governance*, 9/2: 216–40.

——(2000), 'Belgium', in H. Kassim, B. Guy, and V. Wright (eds.), *The National Co-ordination of EU Policy: The Domestic Level* (Oxford: Oxford University Press), 82–200.

Leonard, Mark (1998), *Rediscovering Europe* (London: Demos and Interbrand Newell and Sorrell).

Lequesne, Christian (1993), *Paris-Bruxelles: Comment se-fait la politique européenne de la France* (Paris: Presses de la Fondation Nationale des Sciences Politiques).

Lewis, J. (1998), 'Is the "Hard Bargaining" Image of the Council Misleading? The Committee of Permanent Representatives and the Local Elections Directive', *Journal of Common Market Studies*, 36/4: 457–77.

——(1999), 'Administrative Rivalry in the Council's Infrastructure: Diagnosing the Methods of Community in EU Decision-Making', paper delivered at the Sixth Biennial ECSA International Conference, 2–5 June.

Lindberg, Leon (1970), *The Political Dynamics of European Economic Integration* (Stanford, Calif.: Stanford University Press).

March, J., and Olsen, J. (1984), 'The New Institutionalism: Organizational Facts in Political Life', *American Political Science Review*, 78: 734–49.

————(1989), *Rediscovering Institutions: The Organizational Basis of Politics* (New York: Free Press).

Meyer, J., and Rowan, B. (1977), 'Institutionalized Organizations: Formal Structure as Myth and Ceremony', *International Review of Administrative Sciences*, 60: 271–90.

Moravcsik, Andrew (1993), 'Preferences and Power in the European Community: A Liberal Intergovernmentalist Approach', *Journal of Common Market Studies*, 31/4: 473–524.

——(1998), *The Choice for Europe* (Ithaca, NY: Cornell University Press).

Müller, W. C. (2000), 'Austria', in H. Kassim, B. G. Peters, and V. Wright (eds.), *The National Co-ordination of EU Policy: The Domestic Level* (Oxford: Oxford University Press).

Olsen, Johan P. (1997), 'European Challenges to the Nation State', in B. Steunenberg and F. van Vught (eds.), *Political Institutions and Public Policy* (Amsterdam: Kluwer Academic Publishers), 157–88.

Pedersen, Thomas (2000), 'Denmark', in H. Kassim, B. Guy, and V. Wright (eds.), *The National Co-ordination of EU Policy: The Domestic Level* (Oxford: Oxford University Press), 219–34.

Putnam, Robert D. (1988), 'Diplomacy and Domestic Politics: The Logic of Two-Level Games', *International Organization*, 43/2: 427–60.

Sandholtz, W. (1996), 'Membership Matters: Limits of the Functional Approach to European Institutions', *Journal of Common Market Studies*, 34/3: 403–29.

Schmidt, Vivien A. (1996), *From State to Market? The Transformation of French Business and Government* (Cambridge: Cambridge University Press).

Scott, W. R., and Meyer, J. W., *et al.* (1994), *Institutional Environments and Organizations* (Thousand Oaks, Calif.: Sage).

Spence, David (1995), 'The Co-ordination of European Policy by the Member

States', in Martin Westlake (ed.), *The Council of the European Union* (London: Cartermill).

Thomas, G. M. *et al.* (1987), *Institutional Structure* (Newbury Park, Calif.: Sage).

Vachers (2000) *Vacher's European Companion* (London: Vacher Dod Publishing Limited) 112, June.

Van Schendelen, M. P. C. M. (1996), ' "The Council Decides": Does the Council Decide?', *Journal of Common Market Studies*, 34/4: 531–48.

Wallace, Helen (1973), *National Governments and the European Communities* (London: Chatham House and PEP).

Wessels, Wolfgang (1997), 'An Ever Closer Fusion? A Dynamics Macropolitical View on Integration Processes', *Journal of Common Market Studies*, 35/2: 267–99.

Westlake, Martin (1995), *The Council of the European Union* (London: Cartermill).

Wright, Vincent (1996), 'The National Co-ordination of European Policy-Making Negotiating the Quagmire', in J. Richardson (ed.), *European Union. Policy and Policy-Making* (London: Routledge), 148–69.

Young, Hugo, and Sloman, Anne (1982), *No, Minister: An Inquiry into the Civil Service* (London: BBC).

INDEX